D0061329

LEARNING AND TEACHING IN DISTANCE EDUCATION

Open and Distance Learning Series

Series Editor: Fred Lockwood

LEARNING AND TEACHING IN DISTANCE EDUCATION

Pedagogical Analyses and Interpretations in an International Perspective

Otto Peters

KOGAN PAGE

Published in association with the
IET, OU

This book on the theory of learning and teaching in distance education
is dedicated to
Charles A Wedemeyer – the great visionary and to
Lord Perry of Walton – the great pragmatist
in the field of distance education

First published in German as 'Didaktik des Fernstudiums', by Luchterhand Verlag in 1997
English language edition first published by Kogan Page in 1998

Reprinted 2000

First published in paperback 2001

Kogan Page Limited
120 Pentonville Road
London N1 9JN
UK

Stylus Publishing Inc.
22883 Quicksilver Drive
Sterling VA 20166-2012
USA

© Otto Peters, 1998, 2001

British Library Cataloguing in Publication Data

A CIP record for this book is available from the British Library.

ISBN 0 7494 3594 1

Typeset by Kogan Page
Printed and bound in Great Britain by Biddles Ltd, Guildford and King's Lynn

Contents

Series editor's foreword

There is no dispute that open and distance learning methods have had a major impact on teaching and learning in the last 25 years. Furthermore, the spectacular growth in the use of the new media in schools, colleges, offices, factories, and homes, coupled with increasing emphasis on 'lifelong learning', will fuel this growth. It is in this context that the book *Learning and Teaching in Distance Education* by Otto Peters is so timely.

Many are still wary – even sceptical – of distance-education practices and how the apparently insurmountable effect of distance can be overcome. Others readily embrace the idea and generate materials that they believe are self-instructional. Unfortunately, however, examination of many materials and systems purporting to foster distance learning, within a particular cultural or national perspective, reveals them to be an obscene parody. Further, comparison of materials and systems from different cultures and countries often evokes criticisms that reveal no acknowledgement of the factors influencing a particular approach to the pedagogics. The problem is that few fully consider the fundamental issues that should inform practice and the creation of materials and systems . This book offers a close analysis of teaching and learning, and the network of issues and concerns, that underpin distance education; it offers a framework for the discussion and implementation of distance education pedagogics.

With deceptive skill, Otto reviews several existing models that permeate current practice, and that will influence future practice, and relates these to pedagogics. His careful analysis of the concepts of *dialogue, structure* and *autonomy* will challenge the cosy attitudes, beliefs, and practices, which have become all too familiar. His unpacking of the issues and teasing out of significant points not only mark him as a world scholar but one who is fully aware of current thinking and future directions of distance education in the digital learning environment.

The scope and depth of this book are impressive. It provides not only an overview of historical developments but explains the thinking that is influencing current practice and that which is likely to influence future practice around the world. His comments on the effect of different cultures and academic traditions on distance-education pedagogics, and on our understanding of teaching and learning in the digital learning environment, are insightful and provocative.

Professor Peters brings to the subject a wealth of experience, a breadth of knowledge, a quality of communication, and an enthusiasm that few in the world can match. This, coupled with his concrete examples, extensive list of references to published material, discussion of the contribution of key individuals, of fundamental ideas and of influential institutions around the world identifies this book as a major contribution to our thinking of open and distance-education. I am sure you, your colleagues and your learners will benefit from your study of it.

Fred Lockwood

Introduction

It may be that every sensible idea has already been conceived seven times. But if it is reflected on again, at another time and under different circumstances, it is no longer the same idea. (Ernst Bloch)

The subtitle of this book will on the one hand surprise some readers because they think that traditional pedagogical thought has long since been absorbed by *curriculum development* and *educational technology*. Others will be aware of pedagogics as a long tradition of the practice and theory of learning and teaching. Pedagogics describes and reflects not only methods of learning and teaching and their efficiency, but also their social preconditions, psychological implications and societal consequences. It is strictly practice-oriented, derives its theories from this practice, interprets learning and teaching as a historical phenomenon, and is always aware of the complexity of each teaching–learning situation. This book aims to provide that type of comprehensive approach to distance education.

Many readers will ask themselves whether such an approach is (still) possible. Protagonists and advocates of educational technology and curriculum development may even consider it to be a provocative idea. And students of practical and theoretical distance education will be sceptical – experience teaches them that they do not proceed in accordance with a concept that provides unity, let alone are able to refer to a theory that is harmonious in itself. What they in fact have to deal with in reality is a variety of relevant practical methods and theoretical approaches that are in part very far from each other but that, depending on the situation, form connections of a unique nature.

In this situation, the obvious thing would be to satisfy ourselves about these types of practical methods and theoretical approaches, because a 'theory of learning and teaching in distance education', however it is shaped, may not disregard any experience gained in the field. The question arises as to whether we could understand the total effect from various aspects of the topic and thereby classify distance education theoretically and temporarily as a type of 'pedagogics of distance education' – at least as a working hypothesis. If that were the case, the pedagogics of distance education would have to be based on the following practical methods and theoretical approaches, or at least refer to them: the tradition of academic teaching, pedagogics for higher education, the pedagogics of adult and continuing education, empirical research into learning and teaching, educational technology, electronic telecommunications, specific social-science findings, and general pedagogics.

The *tradition of academic teaching*, which has an effect on distance education and which is undoubtedly specific to different countries, is still underestimated in its importance for practical purposes. This is certainly the wrong thing to do, because this tradition is based on implicit theories on the significance of the respective scientific disciplines, of course contents selected and offered, of studying itself, and possibly even of the academic approach itself without this being of conscious or even incidental influence. It would be erroneous to neglect this tradition in a more technological understanding of academic teaching, to deny it, or even to fight against it.

University pedagogics, as it developed in Germany in the course of the nineteenth century (Schmidkunz, 1898; Rosenbrock, 1979), and many people have forgotten this, later achieved a broad effect never seen before, in particular since the 1970s (Huber, 1983/1995a), and also has references to distance education. It is above all important in so far as the pedagogics of distance education may not be reduced to the totality of those technological tricks and measures that merely enable learning and teaching at a distance. This new form of academic teaching has certainly found new groups of students whose special learning situation must be analysed and taken into account. The 'pedagogics of producing and imparting scientific knowledge' (von Hentig, 1970) can still contribute scientifically theoretical justifications of the acceptance and integration of university pedagogics even today.

In addition, because students taking part in distance education are usually mature students, and may even be middle-aged or older, and because distance education is implicitly or explicitly continuing education, theories of *adult and continuing education* (Siebert, 1996; Raapke, 1985; Siebert, 1984; Tiedgens, 1981) should at least – because of its very nature – be a factor in a pedagogics of distance education. From this aspect there have always been traditional reservations with regard to distance education. In spite of this, Pöggeler (1975, V), for example, counted self-study including distance teaching among 'the five methodological basic forms of adult education'. And according to Siebert (1984: 172) pedagogic activity in adult education takes place in 'distance education' as well.

However, in any exposition of this system of pedagogics, we are confronted with a particular set of problems as adult education pursues specific goals. In most disciplines, it will be very difficult to imagine that teaching can be oriented towards the students' *Lebenswelt*, their everyday knowledge and action (or their 'biographies' for example (Siebert, 1993: 60)), chiefly because of their different targets and their factual stringency. In the case of learning and teaching in distance education, even the concept of teaching by having regard to the 'interpretative patterns of learners', which has been propagated so much recently, is probably only able to play a theoretical role and would find it difficult to play a practical one.

The distance-teaching universities founded in the 1970s had to cope with tasks for which there were no examples in academic tradition, and to cope with them with practically no preparation, in order to enable themselves to bridge the distances between university and students and to enable guided self-study for tens of thousands of students. Courses of studies had to be worked out in great detail, arranged, produced and distributed, and not simply named or described in a few meagre words as in examination and study regulations. The problem was not just to stimulate learning processes from a distance, but to support, promote and evaluate them.

Empirical research into learning and teaching had in fact at that time developed planning, design, intervention, control and evaluation procedures that it was possible to use as *educational technology* and subsequently as *instructional design* in a pragmatic sense for the development of large-scale distance-education systems. Pedagogically oriented critics, who shudder in horror at the mere mention of expressions such as 'educational technology' (or even 'pedagogical technology'), overlook the advantages that these methods offered to those who wanted to develop large-scale, supra-regional learning and teaching projects with the help of modern communications media. After all, academic teaching was to be provided and evaluated with the help of television, radio and in part with computers. Educational technology enabled distance-teaching universities throughout the world to handle these innovations theoretically and practically. Since then, educational technology has changed several times and is interpreted today as 'instructional design'. The concept of 'pedagogic design' (Flechsig, 1987) shows how far this process has come even when post-modern trends are taken into account.

In the correlation shown here, a connection must also be made with the theoretical and practical field of *electronic telecommunications*. The problem in this case is to integrate the enormous range of experience gathered (above all in the USA) in industry and also in many institutes of higher education in imparting knowledge through the medium of television, and more recently with *teleconferencing* – but without any connection with or reference to the theory and practice of distance education (Duning, 1993). American universities have a tradition going back over 50 years of using film and television to teach. Large consortia have formed to bundle the courses offered by many universities and to make them accessible to all their members via satellite and cable television, whereby regional structures are created that change the overall university system. In the US electrical industry, the operation of its own institute of higher education, the *National Technological University*, should give pause for thought, for the university works with a *one-way video* and *two-way audio system* and concentrates on postgraduate studies, awarding master's degrees. Behind these trends is a powerful multinational scientific–technical–industrial complex with considerable influence. For this reason, the subject cannot simply be discussed under media pedagogics: distance-teaching pedagogics must also include a good deal of its socio-political relevance and potential dominance.

Distance-teaching pedagogics will also have to refer to the relevant findings of *distance-education research*, which has come into being in the last 20 years and has already reached an amazing extent – from an international point of view. The research concerns itself with problems of learning and teaching in distance education. The following areas are important here:

- *Empirical learning and teaching research.* This includes above all findings on the special motivational situation of distance students; on the vastly different preconditions applying; on the contexts for learning; on imparting and training effective strategies for self-controlled learning; on differentiating important learning types and styles; on digital learning and teaching; and on the function and significance of interpersonal communications. Recently Holmberg and Schuemer

(1997) have given a succinct summary of empirical findings relevant to learning in distance education. Distance-education experts must take note of these findings, let themselves be stimulated by them, and, where possible, take them into consideration in their analyses and constructions.

- *Development and evaluation research*. These research fields are of particular importance for the pedagogics of distance education because in many cases they have become an integral part of learning and teaching from the very start, a phenomenon that is not to be found in face-to-face teaching. Research here becomes an instrument of pedagogic action. If we follow the development of this particular type of research, we can recognize the following trends: firstly, the number of relevant projects is growing all the time; secondly, this type of research is spreading internationally; thirdly, its thematic focus is being displaced towards the field of digital information and communication; and, fourthly, there is increasing interest in the question of how the quality of distance education can be improved. The experience gained in this field has been documented and published, primarily by the Institute of Educational Technology of the Open University in Great Britain, the Zentrum für Fernstudienentwicklung and the Zentrales Institut für Fernstudienforschung in the German FernUniversität, and by the Deutsches Institut für Fernstudienforschung in the University of Tübingen.

- *Studies in social sciences*. No distance-education expert can work today with a clear conscience without taking account of (amongst other things) the pertinent socio-psychological and sociological findings on the social environment of distance students, which in many ways are greatly different from those of students in traditional universities and have a considerable influence on the pedagogic structure of distance education. The question here is also to explore the sensitivities of persons who take part in a full course of studies as adults, and work at the same time. I would like to refer, as examples, to Rudolf Miller (1991), with his study 'Erwachsene im Studium', and the research programme from Thomas Heinze (1984) entitled 'Lebenswelt von Fernstudierenden'.

There is already a detailed international overview of the fields of research relevant to distance education (Peters 1997). Earlier findings are documented in Börje Holmberg's documentation *Recent Research into Distance Education I* and *II* (1982a/b) and also in his *Bibliography of Writings on Distance Education* (1990).

Behind all this, and denied more than it is fully accepted, stands general pedagogics. This may appear strange to many people for the simple reason that, as far as they are concerned, pedagogics is concerned with teaching in schools and for this reason is not regarded by university teachers as being relevant to them. Their rejection increases to a real sense of aversion if they fear that university teaching could be developed into school-like teaching. However, we must not forget that all university teachers attended school for 12 or 13 years and were marked by the schools' traditions, and this experience has a lasting effect – unconsciously perhaps, but most definitely – on their own teaching behaviour. On the other hand, there are well known educationalists who quite definitely do *not* regard pedagogics in the context of school, but define it (properly) as the 'theory of learning and teaching *in all possible situations and contexts*' (Böhm, 1994: 169), and for some time have understood it as a science that 'has to do with learning *in all forms and teaching of all types and at all stages*' (Dolch, 1952: 40; Hausmann, 1959: 16). This means that the special type of academic learning and teaching represented by distance studies is without any doubt one of their objectives.

Important reasons for referring to general pedagogics are the epistemological and empirical findings of a centuries-old tradition that have a conscious or unconscious effect still, and the corresponding discussion of new models of learning and teaching. Today, for example, we are finding that people are falling back on the old perception of pedagogics as the 'art of teaching' (Comenius, Ratke), and are viewing the teaching session as a special form of theatrical acting (Hausmann, 1959), in so far as aesthetic considerations also apply.

The same might be said about the concept of 'pedagogic design' (Flechsig, 1994: 2; 1987: 4), nowadays influenced by post-modernism, in that 'designing' is without doubt an artistic process. Those who look in addition at the models of the individualization of the learning process in the US schools-reform movement (the Dalton Plan, the Winetka Plan), Montessori's ingenious pedagogic representation of 'materials' to stimulate and develop individual pupils' own activity with simultaneous withdrawal by the teacher into the background, the principles of 'self-activity' and 'free intellectual activity' inherent within Hugo Gaudig's term *'Arbeitsschule'*, the corresponding structures of learning to a great extent independently from the teacher, and also to approaches such as the theory of self-education (Henz, 1971: 342), to name just some of the other approaches, will see clearly the structural proximity – and even affinity – of these pedagogical designs to distance teaching.

It is difficult to understand why learning and teaching processes in distance teaching cannot be analysed profitably on the basis of the *levels of pedagogic action* according to Flechsig and Haller (1975) or with the help of Peterssen's *structure model* (1973). The model of *genetic structuralism* (Lenzen, 1973) could also be of advantage in the construction of learning processes in distance teaching. In the same way, newer pedagogic models could help – for example, to take much greater account than in the past of the central factors of communication, interaction, action and critical analysis in the development of distance-teaching courses and the organization of tutorials, study circles and workshops.

In addition, use of the idea of pedagogics has four other advantages: the *historical perspective* is regained, the *socio-cultural environment* is taken more into account, the category of *responsibility* plays a part once again, and – above all – learning and teaching and pedagogic processes are related structurally to one another. These are aspects that, as a consequence of the domination of technological ways of thinking and quasi-engineered proceedings in this field, have been neglected and to a great extent lost.

Now it must be admitted that learning and teaching at universities in present-day conditions can only be interpreted as a *pedagogical process* in a greatly reduced and altered form (Huber, 1991: 163). 'Education through science' (Humboldt) and education as a 'way of finding identity in a rational culture' (Mittelstrass, 1986: 74) still remain aspects that must also apply to distance studies, which can in the end also be defined as a medium for personality development.

If we take all these factors together, the result is a series of aspects and approaches that today play a part in the development of a theory of learning and teaching in distance education. Anyone wanting to develop a system of pedagogics for distance education would have to take them into account, and this would correspond to the front-line nature of pedagogics. Until this happens, the working areas I have referred to and their stocks of theories will continue to be combined and interplay with one another in the consciousness of those who analyse and develop distance education.

In a pluralistic society, we cannot expect anything else, particularly under the influence of post-modern thinking, which the 'radical plurality' of orientations and conceptions of knowledge has hoisted as its standard (Welsch, 1988: 23). According to this view, it would be wrong to continue to search for a stringently well-composed unity theory. We should rather examine a variety of theoretical aspects, clarification models and evaluation criteria. This is the sense in which we are to understand 'pedagogics of distance education' here. And this is the sense in which in the following pages I will present an overview of the present status of relevant experiences and discussions in a number of countries. If this road proves passable, a future distance-education pedagogics might be restricted to clarifying the specific contributions of participating disciplines and their relationships with one another, and making use in doing this not only of historical, hermeneutical and critical factors but also of empirical–technological methods and findings. This will be to describe, explain, establish, and justify processes of learning and teaching in distance education, and to give them in a general meaning a target and a direction.

This type of integration of different scientific–theoretical positions may be criticized by many as pedagogic eclecticism and basically not be regarded as feasible. But striving for this is nothing new and not at all unnatural within pedagogics and pedagogic thought. It was supported more than 20 years ago by Günther Dohmen (1972: 19) in his essay 'Teaching research and the formation of pedagogic theory in modern educational science' (1962: 191) with reference to Heinrich Roth and Wolfgang Brezinka. Roth believed (1962) that the study of educational reality can only succeed with the help of a 'methodological diversity orbiting around the object'. And Brezinka thought that the important thing was 'to use all possible aspects and methods, empirical and philosophical, instead of regarding them as mutually exclusive alternatives' (Peterssen, 1973: 53). Finally, Wolfgang Klafki (1971) also based his concept of a constructively critical science of education on a combination of hermeneutics, empiricism and ideological and sociological critiques. The project of developing an integrated pedagogics of distance education will therefore not be setting foot on unexplored methodological territory.

The knowledge gained here can be integrated in the pedagogic self-reflection of distance-educational practitioners. In this way, distance teaching pedagogics might come into existence as a *syncretic* discipline, which would stand out against the theoretical set pieces at present under discussion in the current literature. Once it had been created, it would be naturally dynamic and subject to the effects of future pedagogic 'fashions' and fluctuations of the *zeitgeist*, ie it would continue to change in exactly the same way we have experienced so fulminantly in the interpretation of learning and teaching in the last 30 years. This would without doubt also refer to the respective relationships of the constitutive disciplines to one another.

This type of integrated distance-teaching pedagogics would be required today, because distance education, seen from an international point of view, is at present partly in a period of upheaval never before experienced, and partly in a period of unprecedented development. It could accompany distance education on its difficult road into the information and communications era and simplify many processes of rethinking. It could dampen the fever for novelty and put into perspective the dominance of technological thought in support of distance education, and alleviate the abrupt change from consultative education to a much more individualized and media-supported distance education in Eastern Europe. It could also help the many distance-education institutes that have sprung up in developing countries in the last 15 years in order to pass on orientation, structural transparency and train people in reflective action. And, finally, this type of integrated distance-teaching pedagogics might also serve as meta-science for the many specialists working in distance-teaching universities.

The objective of this book is to make readers familiar with this particular *integrative* and *analytical* approach to learning and teaching in distance education. This is important in so far as in the present era of globalization the conceptual developments I have introduced here can no longer be evolved in national frameworks alone. On the contrary, they must be discussed *internationally*, because the unprecedented growth of distance education during the last 25 years and of Net-based learning during the last 5 years. Everywhere we can observe the merging of approaches, strategies and methods of distance education with those of Net-based learning now. The quest of educationists and policy makers for *virtual schools* and *virtual universities* has become a universal one. At many respective international conferences the call for developing open and flexible learning becomes stronger. The emergence of mass education is one of the consequences of this development. Unquestionably, this development is a truly international, if not global, phenomenon. Distance education will play an important role in dealing with all these issues everywhere in the years to come, especially in the sector of higher education, corporate training and continuing education. The *University of the Future* can no longer be designed without applying pedagogical principles of distance education and distributed learning.

The likelihood of the creation of an internationally discussed and agreed system of distance-teaching pedagogics is encouragingly good, and publication of this book may even be at just the right time to assist the process.

Chapter 1

Taking stock

In this chapter, some essential elements of the pedagogics of distance education will be outlined and integrated into the discussion, and to do this five specific factors of distance education will be stressed that make it stand out against other forms of university teaching. These five factors are: the special *combination of some conventional forms of learning and teaching*; the special use of *technical media*; one special *structural handicap*; the special *type of student* encountered in distance learning; and, finally, the special *forms of structuralization*. The reader will be introduced to fundamental teaching problems that are found only in distance education. The purpose of this chapter is to show clearly the relevant consequences of the special factors described.

1.1 Traditional access

If we look at the process of learning and teaching in distance education from the point of view of pedagogics, in its traditional form it is a matter of a more or less integrated combination of the forms of learning that were developed in traditional universities. These include:

- learning by reading printed material (textbooks, manuals, lexicons, scientific literature, lecture notes);
- learning by means of guided self-teaching (counselling at the start of studies, counselling by tutors, reading lists, working in accordance with the Keller plan);
- learning by means of independent scientific work (preparation for written examinations, preparing papers, final examinations);
- learning by means of personal communications (consultation hours of university teaching staff, course counselling, discussions with other students, practical casework, seminars);
- learning with the help of tapes and audiovisual media (enrichment of university

teaching by means of film, radio and television, internal television networks in universities, audiovisual networks of several seminar locations in different places); and

● learning by participating in traditional academic teaching (lectures, seminars, classes, laboratory work).

We can see from this that distance education is on the one hand neither new nor alien. It has its roots in, and makes use of, the teaching forms used in traditional universities. On the other hand, it is exactly these forms of teaching that demonstrate the special pedagogic structure of distance education, because it is in fact combined and integrated with other focal points, above all through the much greater (and almost over-) emphasis laid on *learning by reading* and the considerable restrictions on *learning by attending lectures, seminars and classes*.

It becomes clear here just how far and how much pedagogics for higher education is able to play the role of godfather in the development of the science of distance teaching. With such help it is possible to carry out a structural analysis of the six fundamental forms of learning listed above in order to describe their respective advantages, to establish and check hypotheses regarding their optimisation, and above all to develop effective models for their use in combination. We must get to know the *pedagogic core* of distance education much more exactly than before, be alive to its unique qualities for distance education, and maintain it, above all in the face of recent technological challenges. Up to now, the special interplay of these six traditional methods of learning and teaching has taken place largely in the dark; illuminating and interpreting this interplay may indeed be one of the first tasks facing us as we develop the science of distance teaching.

Just how important this kind of pedagogic foundation is for future developments is made quite clear, for example, when computer-based learning programs are demonstrated at congresses and are seen to ignore even the most elementary aspects of knowledge and experience on the subject. Their creators are more concerned with technical processes and performance than even the slightest regard for pedagogics, and regretfully they often even do this consciously and out of conviction. There is an anti-sociological feeling behind this, and even an anti-educational attitude.

This pedagogic core becomes even more important in the face of the intensive efforts being made by the relevant industry, led by hardware manufacturers, governments at national and European levels, and communications science. These efforts are aimed at creating a tightly knit information network for which distance education is simply nothing more than a new market. It appears to the representatives of such organizations that pedagogics is standing in the path of commercial or political success, or academic prestige, and considerations are therefore left by the wayside – if they get thought about at all.

1.2 The concept of the 'three generations'

Of course, it is no longer sufficient simply to refer to the pedagogic core of distance education as described here, because trends are always developing still further, especially in the theory but to a considerable extent in practice as well. D Randy Garrison (1993a, 1989, 1985), the Canadian distance-education expert, therefore differentiates between three generations of distance education. The traditional core referred to above is Garrison's *first* generation, which is not replaced by the second and third generations but continues to have an effect alongside, or in correlation with, these.

The second generation is based above all on the possibilities provided by the different versions of *teleconferencing*. According to Garrison, they have such a great effect on distance education that we should really refer to a new paradigm for it, which itself might be a reason for rethinking and redefining the concept of distance education. At first glance this proposal may appear attractive, because it would mean that more personal communication and academic discourse – something that traditional distance education is lacking – might be combined with second-generation distance education.

However, we must ask ourselves what type this second-generation distance education should be. Here we come up against a fundamental problem of distance-teaching pedagogics, something that we shall be returning to again and again in the following chapters. At this stage, we can restrict ourselves in preparation to a few consequences, for the concept says goodbye to looking after very large groups of students, in other words to the principle of *mass higher education*, and instead brings together a manageable number of students in a virtual room and makes use of the opportunities of technologically imparted, simultaneous and dynamic dialogues between lecturers and students and amongst the students themselves. Can this be reconciled with the *raison d'être* of distance education?

The third generation of distance education goes on to integrate the opportunities provided by learning with the help of *personal computers*, which are able to intensify trends in both the first and the second generation. Firstly, by providing suitable software they can give direction and, through interaction, added value to the self-teaching of the student who is learning in isolation; and they also make databases (including bibliographical databases, in a possible scientific or academic intranet) easily available to help students gain knowledge independently of their teachers. In addition, they can supplement second-generation distance education by means of *computer-mediated communication (CMC)*. From the point of view of the concepts shown here for the first and second generation, the third generation is neutral in terms of pedagogics, which permits distance education even greater flexibility and an enormous potential for change.

Without doubt, because of these trends distance education will considerably alter its pedagogic structure. There is enormous scope for creative pedagogic design opening up in front of us in immeasurable ways. How will this development of design be used? Where will its focal points be? Should further development depend on the contingencies of the 'trial-and-error' method? Or will it be defined by corresponding industrial standards? On the basis of previous experience, educational policy necessities, and educational objectives, would it not be much better if we grew into the phases of the second and third generations with clear pedagogic concepts? Detailed technological knowledge, which many acquire instead of this, is absolutely essential, but does not help us any further in this matter. For this reason, we will have to reclaim the primacy of pedagogics in the further development of distance education.

The concepts of the second and third generation have already had a serious effect on theoreticians and practitioners of distance education and altered their views. For many of them, first-generation distance education already appears antiquated.

1.3 A dilemma

D Randy Garrison (1993b), who was mentioned above because of his 'three generations' concept, has also highlighted two conspicuous features of distance education and related them to one another: the particularly high degree of *accessibility*, and the *quality* of each interactive learning and teaching process. In this way he has got to the nub of a major distance-learning/teaching problem.

In practice it is true that the greater the accessibility of students to their subject matter (for example, through the use of mass media such as print, radio and television), the greater the number of students and the more sporadic, fragmentary and thinner the direct and indirect interaction between teachers and students. This trend, which can be seen in larger distance-teaching universities, is criticized by several distance-education experts. Their attitude is that it is not sufficient simply to enable students to study in isolation with the help of distance-learning materials: students must be enabled in the first place to *discuss* with their teachers and other students, because this is the real foundation of academic teaching. This is why their rule of thumb is that the greater the accessibility, the poorer the quality of the studies. This brings educational policy and priorities into conflict with one another; it is characteristic for distance education on the whole and is the source of many disputes.

Garrison himself uses the rule of thumb. For him, a person's own grasp of the acquired and assimilated knowledge can only develop in discussion, whereby additional cognitive processes take place – often spontaneously and therefore not foreseeably, and certainly not empirically comprehensible, which he regards as being imperative for successful learning. He even regards this as the ideal of university teaching.

Consciously, or in part unconsciously, attempts have always been made, when distance-education institutes are being planned, to set up a balance between the degree of accessibility and the type and quality of the teaching-related dialogues being constructed. Distance universities that focus on guided self-study maintain study centres in which optional or obligatory seminars, tutorials, individual and group counselling can take place, and they also arrange study weeks at another university (eg the UK's Open University summer schools, or the weekend conferences held by the FernUniversität Hagen at the University of Oldenburg). Distance-education institutes that focus on face-to-face events make efforts to maintain carefully (and expensively) prepared study documents, and often make use of the help of experts in appropriate centres. In this way, different combinations are created, which group themselves around two ideal models.

One grouping is formed around the model that uses most funds and most effort for the professional development and production of qualitatively excellent teaching materials for the purposes of self-study, which are then distributed by post or other methods. No particular value is placed on attendance phases, although they are not dispensed with completely. The distance-teaching university of South Africa may serve as an example here: in the 1970s this university sent out a quarter of a million printed lectures each year but did not establish a single study centre.

The contrary model is exemplified by the distance teaching at the Radio and Television University in China, which provides for compulsory attendance for 24 hours each month in group lessons in a 'television class' in which the students discuss lectures broadcast by radio and television with a leader and several tutors. In fact, we should definitely refer to consultation studies in the countries of the former Eastern European communist bloc, in which the proportion of attendance events was relatively high, and in the former GDR amounted to as much as one-fifth of the courses to be taken at traditional universities, while printed course materials played a relatively subordinate role. Consultation studies can also be found in Vietnam. The proportion of a course requiring student attendance is therefore the cornerstone of this model. Many supporters of the first model in fact ask rather pointedly whether the second approach is distance education at all.

An interesting task for distance-teaching pedagogics might be to make clear through theoretical and experimental work whether – and if so where – the *pedagogic optimum* can be found between these two extremes. However, the local environment would have to be taken into account because the optimum articulation in teaching is naturally influenced by the dominant culture of learning found in traditional universities in each country. Universities that regard students as individuals to whom they grant the greatest freedom in the choice of and attendance at lectures, and which have not developed special additional counselling measures, have absolutely nothing against favouring the first model described above. In contrast, universities will favour the second model if their teaching takes place mainly in *classes* in which, it is claimed, the central point of teaching for both teachers and students is the class discussion, and in which the tradition of *tutoring* still has an effect. Similarly, universities in countries in which, for ideological reasons, the collective takes precedence before the individual are also likely to operate according to the second model.

A combination of increased accessibility and improved quality through greater stress on face-to-face phases can be achieved if a university decides not only to offer traditional studies and distance studies simultaneously (a 'dual mode'), but also to integrate the two types, which has taken place in several Australian universities.

1.4 The student

As we have already seen, those taking part in distance education are a special group. They differ from students in traditional universities because they are usually *older* adults. On average they are in their thirties, but it must be said that there is hardly ever an upper age limit – for example, a 68 year-old former teacher recently received her doctorate at the FernUniversität. The higher average age alters the pedagogic starting position as against traditional universities primarily in the following ways:

- Students will usually have a much greater experience of life. This means that they approach their studies quite differently, have a different attitude and assess it differently.
- Most of them bring considerable experience of working life to academic courses, and this also has an effect on the ways in which they study, in particular when the studies and the professional experience cover the same field. A serious consequence of this special feature affects the organisation of distance teaching. Most distance-learning students in fact have to study while they are working; in other words, they are part-time students.
- Many of them come from backgrounds in which academic studies were not offered when they were younger, and they use distance education as a second chance. The UK's Open University sees itself to a great extent as responsible for this type of student in Britain. Most students therefore differ greatly from younger students who are able to make full use of their first chance to study.
- There are distance students who want to reach a higher socio-economic status as a result of their experiences at work. These are the upwardly mobile students.
- Distance-learning students have more qualifications than students in traditional universities. Many achieved considerable success at school (even where they finished their education in evening classes, for example), and at university, and above all in their professions. This naturally has an effect on their motivation and their attitude to their studies.
- Studying at a relatively late age has in general a completely different function than with 19–25 year-old students because it fits into plans for life and life-cycles in a different way.

All these together show that we are dealing with a type of student for distance education who differs in several ways from the norm of those attending a campus-based university. In fact, the differences are so great that it is unreasonable validly to compare distance students with students at traditional universities.

We are therefore faced with a primary learning and teaching problem. Should we offer these students *the same* teaching as in traditional universities? Or should we take into account their age, their greater experience of life and employment, their different motivational situation, and even their double or triple load of studies, job and family? Put bluntly, should we develop a learning and teaching programme tailored to their special needs? Is it essential to plan and establish *adult studies*? Every educationalist will answer these questions with a 'yes'. It is quite natural that teaching is developed with regard to students in their special situations. But how this is done is then a complicated problem that also has pedagogic aspects.

The demand for the adaptation of studies to the special requirements of adults in employment has an unusual explosive effect in a distance-teaching university, because most university teachers reject it from the start. Why? Their attitude is connected to their academic socialization in traditional universities. As Schulmeister

(1983: 350) makes clear, traditional university education has primarily laid claim to a scientific approach to teaching, assuming that students are capable of learning, and has undervalued (or even ignored) the educational aspects. Expository teaching processes were the most suitable for this method.

The primacy of this 'scientific' approach to teaching was internalized by university teachers and created an attitude among them that there was only *one* form of teaching, which arises from the relevant research. This form of teaching must in principle be the same for all students. And in their opinion the reception of teaching and the acquisition of the corresponding knowledge is a matter for the students. This means that preparatory instruction has a low value, learning aids are not provided, and no concessions are made. Because in addition these university teachers deliberately teach in a *science-oriented* and *teacher-oriented* manner, they hold this viewpoint out of conviction. For this reason, adapting teaching to the different starting situation of older students and where necessary providing help for them to overcome learning difficulties specific to distance education does not usually enter their minds. For example, they find it difficult to plan greater *occupational* or *practical* references for distance students, to name just two dimensions of necessary adjustment.

This attitude can be seen in the FernUniversität as well. Help for students to overcome learning difficulties specific to distance education has therefore been developed to a slight extent only, or for some courses is not even available. The expository teaching process that dominates in traditional universities remains in place, in compliance with the wishes of the university's teachers. With great commitment they concentrate on developing printed distance-teaching units, but reject improved counselling and active support for students learning under particularly stressful or limiting local conditions; and if they do provide support, they do so half-heartedly. *How* students acquire knowledge is on the whole left to them, and this applies in the FernUniversität as well as other traditional universities. In the face of this startling situation, we can hardly expect student-oriented teaching at the FernUniversität. Most of the university's teachers would regard this as an undesirable school-like structuring of university teaching and would be greatly concerned about their academic dignity.

In this extremely difficult situation, the pedagogics of distance teaching has the task of making clear how learning and teaching can be *adult-oriented* and *distance education-oriented*, at the same time without losing any of its scientific character.

1.4.1 Adult-oriented teaching

Distance education can be adult-oriented if some of the principles of adult education pedagogics are taken into account that place the participants in the foreground from the very start. They can show the degree of activation, application and empathy on the part of teachers that is regarded as desirable, and the important part played by the subjectivity, identity and autonomy of adult students – who, after all, are the crucial element in the process. If we succeeded in transferring just a hint of this attitude to distance education, we would have achieved something.

A look at the pedagogics of vocational training can also be stimulating, in particular as distance students are also found in this area as jobholders. The problem of adult-oriented learning (see Lipsmeier, 1991: 131) is familiar here as well and students' psycho-social situation is taken into account, identity-supporting forms of learning are preferred, and teaching contents are derived from existing vocational experience. And not only this: for some time, experts have referred to a 'changed learning culture' in which students in employment receive not only knowledge but also 'methodological and social competence' (Arnold, 1995: 303). In addition, a great deal of value is placed on the development of the students' *personalities*. These aims cannot be achieved solely through the method of the presentation and reception of neutral knowledge.

1.4.2 Distance education-oriented teaching

Learning and teaching is distance education-oriented if it takes account of the special conditions of the world in which distance students live and of the special conditions appertaining to distance teaching.

There are some interesting examples of this at the FernUniversität. Where topics for degree theses in the faculties of electrical engineering, computer science and economics are selected from the students' own working areas, students can capitalize on their own working experience. The vocational orientation of courses cannot be any more intensive. And where additional teaching software is developed in the computer technology department and supplied on disks containing training programs that help students when they have difficulties working through the teaching texts, this support is certainly distance education-oriented.

With distance education-oriented teaching, students must be continuously motivated, guided during studies they have planned and organized themselves, stimulated to communicate and cooperate formally and informally with fellow students, and, with the help of a differentiating counselling system, must be observed, addressed individually, and taken seriously. This is not possible without work in the study centres. And it is not only necessary to make learning more effective but also to intensify the degree of academic socialization, which is considerably less than in traditional universities, because it has to maintain its ground alongside vocational socialization (Miller, 1991: 50).

The special sociographical preconditions for students studying by distance learning are important for academic teaching and should not be neglected when planning, developing and evaluating this teaching method.

1.5 Three types of operating mode within institutions

Whether a university is planned and developed from the very start exclusively for distance education (*single mode*), whether a traditional university also provides distance teaching (*dual mode*), or whether a university provides several forms of studying parallel to one another and leaves it up to students to use these forms in accordance with their own needs and opportunities (*mixed mode*), these are all operating modes that are in general decided upon through the criteria being set in educational policies and planning, higher educational or institutional and professional policies, and organizations and logistics. The pedagogical advantages or disadvantages are treated as secondary factors. Nevertheless, the pedagogical structure of distance education is different in each of these three institutional types, and this quite naturally has an effect on the processes of learning and teaching.

In fact, specific questions relating to distance-teaching pedagogics result from the different forms of the institutionalization, and these must be borne in mind. Put simply, three very different attitudes towards distance education and towards the expected learning and teaching behaviour may be combined here.

Many students take part in single-mode distance education, as practised in the larger distance and open universities. In fact, some of these universities have hundreds of thousands of students. Students are more or less left to their own devices because the counselling systems are insufficient. The type of distance students who work through their courses at home, separated from the university and isolated from teachers and fellow students, is the norm here. *Guided self-study* is characteristic of this type of learning and teaching.

The learning and teaching behaviour at a dual-mode university (such as those that have been developed in Australia, for example) is totally different. Here, only as many students are admitted to courses as can be taught in the respective *classes*. This means that the number of students is low. Their contact with the teachers who are responsible for them and with the university is closer and less likely to be broken off because they have to attend teaching events at the university on a regular basis. According to this concept, external students also 'attend' classes at the university, but at arm's length by making use of lecture notes, tapes and other teaching materials. The decisive pattern here is *indirect attendance at teaching events in a traditional university*. From the point of view of pedagogics, this is a fundamentally different concept.

Another form of distance education will be created in universities of the future, which will provide both face-to-face and distance teaching and make greater use of networked electronic information and communications media (mixed-mode universities). Such universities will be able to react extremely flexibly to the requirements of students, including adult students of any age. The dominant pedagogic pattern here will be *autonomous, self-guided learning*, in which students will decide whether they wish to make use of teaching offers available through various media and will use the considerable latitude on the basis of their own strategies – from intensive social contact in a small tutorial through to self-guided studies in a digital learning environment and the exchange of experience with other students using CMC and a network.

The task of distance-teaching pedagogics would be to examine these structurally extremely different types of distance education to discover their advantages and disadvantages, to describe the pedagogic guiding principles, traditions, conventions and ideologies behind them, and to analyse and compare the respective dominant learning and teaching strategies. However, they should certainly not be presented in an abstract form and with a purely theoretical intention; on the contrary, it will be necessary to interpret them in their respective historico-cultural context. The results to be achieved here could act as a catalyst in the expected process of the integration of methods of traditional university teaching and distance teaching.

1.6 Summary

Most authors who attempt to explain the phenomenon of distance education see the main characteristic as being the spatial separation of teachers and students and derive their fundamental concepts from this factor. This makes an infrastructural, and therefore fundamentally external, factor the starting point for efforts to determine the nature of distance education. Here I have attempted to describe distance education using the categories of pedagogics. The results show the following decisive peculiarities which distinguish distance education from traditional university teaching:

- 'Written' teaching dominates in contrast to 'spoken' teaching. 'Reading' learning is stressed as against 'listening' learning.
- As a result of the use of technical and electronic media, three distinct pedagogic structures have been formed which characterize learning and teaching.
- The sociographical status of distance students is quite different, in decisive ways, from that of students at traditional universities.
- Specific institutional and organizational preconditions are required for the development, control, and evaluation of learning and teaching.

Those who maintain in the face of the above that there are no essential differences between distance education and traditional university teaching are not thinking pedagogically but following different agenda. As the examples used and explained in this chapter show, distance-teaching pedagogics must be concerned with solving problems of its own nature which are not found in other combinations of teaching and studying. From the point of view of pedagogics, distance education is in fact a form of learning and teaching *sui generis*. For this reason, solving outstanding problems of distance-teaching pedagogics will have to be carried out with special theoretical approaches, interpretations, concepts and experience.

Chapter 2

Distance and proximity

Anyone who intends to put learning processes into operation in distance education in order to control, observe and evaluate them is confronted with special types of difficulties. Teachers and students are, of course, not near to each other but are at a distance. It might appear quite trivial to mention something as obvious as this, particularly as it is made quite clear in various languages – *distance* education, *Fern*studium, *tele*enseignement, educacion a *distancia*. However, we must still examine the problem here because important pedagogic processes are derived from it. For the better comprehension of recent concepts, some historical (and fundamental) ideas need first of all to be addressed because they are still having an effect today.

For thousands of years, learning and teaching always took place in close proximity, and this has become firmly anchored in human consciousness. Learning and teaching at a distance is therefore regarded from the very start as something extraordinary, not the equal of face-to-face teaching, and often regarded as being very difficult as well. It is characteristic of the phenomenon, for example, that in Australia the 'tyranny of distance' is referred to (Northcott, 1984: 39). Because the distance to students was regarded as a deficit, and proximity as desirable and necessary, the first pedagogic approaches specific to distance education aimed immediately at finding ways by which the spatial distance could be bridged, reduced or even eliminated. The question was asked: what must be done to make distance equivalent to proximity in distance education? Or, more precisely, what tricks might bring this about?

The pedagogics of distance education is derived basically from the efforts to find answers to these questions. These efforts can still be seen today, and will certainly occupy distance-education experts in the future as well. Up to the present, the efforts have been compressed into five models, namely the correspondence, conversation, teacher, tutor and technological-extension models. Pedagogically it is extremely productive to take a closer look at these models. Some of them still mark the present practice of distance education, even though both teachers and students are usually unaware of this.

2.1 The correspondence model

One approach that has survived from the era of 'lessons by mail' is the attempt to reduce the distance between teacher and student by means of written communications. At first, written communications, which were to replace the oral
communication in 'normal' lessons, were used as a foil for lessons (see Appendix).

The culture of letter writing has a long history. Plato passed on his ideas in this
way, and Paul wrote his epistles to groups of Middle Eastern and European
churches to spread Christian teachings; communications between the scholars of
Europe took place for centuries. The spread of scientific knowledge through the exchange of letters was *a priori* by this means, and became a matter of course. After the
introduction of compulsory schooling, the circle of those using correspondence
was extended. In the mid-nineteenth century, at first at a lower level, correspondence became a bridge between many teachers and their students and served at the
same time as the first basic pedagogic pattern for distance education.

The pedagogically relevant elements that were taken over from correspondence
are: first of all, reciprocal answering behaviour, through which a *written dialogue* is
created; secondly, the personal address; and, thirdly, the *personal tone* that is commonly found in letters. An internationally famous Australian distance-education
expert gave reasons for the last two elements as follows: 'By directly and informally
addressing the student, the writer presents himself as a person with an understanding of the learner's needs and interests…' And: 'The establishment of this personal
tone…wins the confidence of students…' (Erdos, 1967: 18). The personal address,
the rather informal style and kindness, it was thought, might help at the very least to
compensate for the lack of proximity in distance education.

This attitude was maintained even after there was a transition from handwritten
letters to printed documents or study material. The pattern of the teacher writing
the letters and then the student reading them and replying persisted in the heads of
the participants. People spoke of *correspondence courses* and *correspondence schools*. Even
today, units of distance-education courses are sometimes referred to as 'study letters', even at universities.

2.1.1 Commentary

The correspondence model has certainly proved its value in practice. Above all, in the
nineteenth century it contributed to the success of commercial distance-teaching
schools and colleges. It was quite obvious that after the establishment of a reliable
postal system on the basis of the railways, correspondence was able to become the
most important and therefore the most obvious communication medium, and it was
able to bridge the gap between teachers and students. The taking over of elements of
letter writing and using them in presenting teaching content was, nevertheless, a pedagogic invention that was certainly not obvious from the start. For the first time, a
method specific to distance education was developed, whose aim was to take away the
students' feeling of isolation by at least bringing the teacher into their imaginations.

However, if we look at the correspondence model from the point of view of its suitability for distance teaching, we must ask ourselves if the simulated proximity and intimacy are suitable. How is a person helped who is experienced in his or her profession and practised at his or her studies if a personal tone is used in subject presentation, and if he or she is addressed again and again in teaching texts in a deliberately informal style? How, for example, does an experienced adult-education teacher taking an additional course of studies react to attempts by lecturers to show themselves as persons who understand the teacher's learning needs and who are attempting to gain the teacher's confidence? And what is the effect of learning texts if such forms of address become intrusive through being used unthinkingly? It seems obvious that these efforts at overcoming distance stem from a different learning culture and do not conform to teaching in universities, in which traditionally the matter is in the foreground.

2.2 The conversation model

A further step towards reducing the distance between teachers and students was taken when people started to interpret distance education as the *simulation of a conversation* between teacher and student. The teaching text was deemed no longer to impart systematically arranged factual knowledge, like a specialized technical book, but to act like an instructive conversation between a teacher and a student or students. In extreme cases, the contents are even displayed in the form of a written dialogue.

This method of learning and teaching makes particular demands on those taking part. When writing teaching texts, teachers must imagine that they are speaking to someone, and this is supposed to make them use a *spoken language* wherever possible. From the other perspective, the way in which the contents are shown must enable students to imagine the teacher in person while they are reading and to carry on quiet dialogues. In an advanced form, students acquire the ability to develop this dialogue still further by not only asking questions themselves but also formulating possible answers as if they were the teacher. Reading teaching texts and assimilating their contents is thus transformed into an *internal* or *virtual dialogue*.

What are the pedagogic advantages of this simulation of an instructive discussion? They become clear if we analyse the concept of '*guided pedagogic conversation*' that was introduced by Börje Holmberg (1985: 26), who has been the most important advocate of this model and has even made it into the object of an empirical study (1982a/b). According to Holmberg, a teacher, as the author of a distance-education course, must create the atmosphere of a friendly lesson and observe its conventions, inspire the feeling of a personal connection between teacher and students, and in this way increase pleasure and motivation amongst the students. Taking part in the courses must provide students with intellectual pleasure because this favours them achieving the objectives of the studies. And he also provides authors of teaching texts with recommendations for achieving this: they should use a 'clear, somewhat colloquial language', write in a personal style and appeal to students' emotions as well as their intellect, avoid a great density of information, address students with tips and recommendations, draw their attention to important points, and encourage them to ask questions, express their own opinions and make judgements. In this way, a 'constant conversation' will be enabled between the author and the students, and this conversation will be stimulated by the interaction of the students with the prepared study material.

According to Holmberg, furthermore, teachers' empathy must be particularly great in distance education because, in spite of their indirect-only contact with their students, they must put themselves in the place of their students and assess their re-actions in advance. As a result of his examination Holmberg stated (1989a: 51): 'Em-pathy and personal approaches are thus considered guidelines for the presentation of learning matter in distance education.' Accordingly, he criticized the FernUniversität's printed material for not making sufficient use of simulated con-versations (1979: 18).

This model has its supporters in the Open University (OU) as well, and it influ-ences teaching methods of distance education in a similar manner. Barbara Hodgson (1993: 115) from the Institute of Educational Technology (part of the OU) recommends to authors of study letters: 'Probably the best style to develop is a conversational one...' And she adds that in her opinion 'a relatively informal, per-sonal and supportive atmosphere' should be generated. This can also be achieved by means of the style in which each distance education unit is written: 'It should sound as if it is addressed personally to one reader, it should be conversational in tone and should relate to the sort of experience that you would expect the typical reader to have. It should aim at readability, keeping to short words and short sentences as far as possible. Address the reader as "you" and do not be afraid of being present in your writing and call yourself "I". There are also times when it is useful to use "we" as a kind of compliment to imply that you and the learner are members of the same spe-cial group.'

It would be difficult to find another passage in literature on distance education in which the proximity between teachers and students is as strongly urged and striven for through the simulation of a conversation.

2.2.1 Commentary

As with the correspondence model, the conversation model can be viewed posi-tively. Where this model is used, printed study materials are given their own struc-ture specific to distance education. In this way they differ greatly from the printed materials used in traditional methods, namely those articles in scientific manuals or encyclopaedias that tend to keep the reader at a distance with their impersonal nature, strict objectivity, and density of information and system. If the conversa-tion in a study letter is managed well, it can certainly create a closeness between teachers and students and also reduce the distance to the areas of knowledge it wants to represent.

However, if we analyse its application in practice, once again we find doubts and reservations. It is understandable to want to reduce the distance between teachers and students in the way shown. And we can certainly appreciate with understanding and appreciation the efforts made to shape the relationship between teachers and students within the meaning of humanistic pedagogics. But it is questionable whether the conversation model is generally suitable for the presentation of scientific contents in the context of university teaching. In this context the need is to impart presentational forms, methods, ways of thinking and results specific to a subject that are not in practice compatible with the rather incidental form of a conversation. What should be aimed at is an introduction to methodological – and, above all, critical – observation and evaluation of phenomena, which demands a strict train of thought. Students should be introduced to scientific thinking through the way in which terms are defined, problems are illustrated and compartmentalized, hypotheses are formed, methods are tested for validity and apparent solutions are tested sceptically. Scientific thinking is targeted, logical, systematic and conscious of its methods and cannot be brought about with the help of a 'constant conversation'. The conversation model is only occasionally and only partly suitable in this context, therefore. Its origins in the traditions of correspondence education, which has completely different objectives and a completely different clientele, can be noticed again and again.

In the light of this interpretation, some of the recommendations of supporters of this model can only be followed with reservation, if at all. How can academic contents be imparted in a 'clear, somewhat colloquial language' and, where possible, with 'short words and sentences', when one of the main aims of a university education is to impart an academic language which contains words of many syllables in nearly all disciplines and which is so complex and differentiated that it demands long sentences? How can authors of academic texts be advised to write in a personal style, not to exceed a defined density of information and to address students emotionally as well? Is it not the case that with most contents a strict objectivity of the analysis and exposition is required? Is it not so that efforts made step by step to open up and understand a dense and initially inaccessible text provide more intellectual pleasure than the feeling of taking part in a simulated conversation? Can we really ask scientists and academics to act in a user-friendly manner if their subject matter is not, in fact, user-friendly?

Even if they put up with the demand and act as if they were, does it not feel as if it were artificial and contrived, whereas in the scientific community only authenticity convinces – even, and especially, when it is imparted through the media? We know and can experience every day that with the help of communications media people can be addressed emotionally. But the idea that empathy can be reproduced at will technically to support learning is still certainly alien to most people. It would seem that this model is more suitable for students who are still comparatively young or still relatively inexperienced as regards learning.

Finally in this commentary, it should be borne in mind that it may be wrong to assume that a transition from speaking to writing and from listening to reading means a change of medium only. Rather, we must realize that literacy and freedom of expression have caused different ways of thinking, expressing oneself, studying, remembering etc, all with far-reaching consequences (Ong, 1987). Chirographical and typographical methods have opened up entirely new and specific possibilities for the art of teaching and learning – possibilities that were unthinkable in oral teaching. They create new teaching and learning behaviours. Hence, it is the task of teachers to discern and to exploit the *technology of writing*. If they merely imitate oral teaching in written form they are certainly on the wrong track. A similar phenomenon can be observed today when distance educators endeavour to imitate face-to-face teaching with the new technology of digital learning environments.

2.3 The teacher model

An additional form of reducing the distance between teacher and student was developed when people started to compensate for the physical absence of the teacher by means of the special way in which course content was offered. In this model, teachers transfer their skill and their art to the teaching text so that this can exercise all important teaching functions in their place. In this way they are, so to speak, contained in the teaching text and therefore always present when students start to interact with the teaching text.

What are these teacher functions exactly? In a typical learning-and-teaching situation – for example, in classes in a school or college – we may see the following. Teachers

- stimulate and steer students' attention;
- motivate students;
- state and give reasons for *learning aims*;
- bring existing knowledge into students' consciousness that can be related to the object of the lesson;
- offer the lesson contents in portions and in a sequence that make absorption and comprehension easier;
- show difficult circumstances in greater clarity and with repetition;
- provide tips on how best to learn the contents, use *feedback* to make sure that learning and teaching is successful;
- train with the students, and
- help them to apply what they have learnt.

Can these functions be transferred at all to the written word? Certainly. A special art for doing this has even been developed. Good texts make efforts to arouse, captivate, steer and retain attention – for example, with eye-catching titles, striking graphical designs or impressive wording. In introductions it is usually shown how important the subject to be learnt may be in certain contexts, and also what advantages may arise if a person learns what is being presented. This can arouse, strengthen and steer the students' interest and activate (or reactivate) their motivation. To make it easier to absorb and assimilate course content, existing knowledge of the area being dealt with is put together.

Usually, *teaching objectives* are not only expressly named but are also described and discussed. Frequently, the structure of what is presented has a pedagogic nature, and not merely a scientific–systematic one, such as in the corresponding articles in textbooks and specialized literature. For example, an advance organizer at the beginning of the text can make it easier to process the subject matter being presented because it contains in a nutshell what the main text wishes to impart. In addition, access to that menu may lead directly to the core of the problem to be presented, whereby the preconditions for its comprehension are presented.

As in oral lessons, some content may be summarized, and other may be introduced in passing (but for good reason). A term introduced in a text may be explained in great detail in an accompanying *glossary* – recently, disk-based information (within teaching software) has also been offered for the clarification of particularly complicated sets of facts. Or a method is selected that seems helpful for practical reasons: clarity comes through the *practical work* and *self-test problems* woven into the text, which are introduced to encourage students to think about the subject, and through *assignments* they send in, which are used to test the *success of learning*.

As we can see, distance students do not have to do without teachers because they are present in the text. The efforts made to achieve learning success are even more conscious, systematic, differentiated and longer-lasting than in the traditional forms of university teaching. They make the assistance normally provided by the teachers constantly perceptible to the distance student and to reduce the distance involved.

2.3.1 Commentary

In comparison with the models previously described, the teacher model is definitely an advance. It is above all supported by genuinely pedagogical patterns, while the first two models, correspondence and conversation, are based on sequences of actions that in fact have little to do with teaching. In the teacher model, the teacher adapts to a much greater extent to the students; there is a great arsenal of measures that are intended to support and guarantee their learning. If we want to make a correct evaluation of this special feature, all we have to do is to take a close look at traditional methods of presenting scientific/academic material through expository forms such as lectures, papers, textbooks, newspapers or notes. In contrast, the pedagogical assistance provided by the teacher model breaks through traditional receptive learning behaviour by making students constantly conscious that they are in a learning process and which phases of this process they are passing through at a particular moment. The students are stimulated and made to develop their own activities, eg by thinking about questions and answering them, recognising and seeing through problems, solving problems, training and repeating what they have learnt. This model finds its culmination in the ambition of many university teachers to integrate all the necessary teaching functions in a calculated and effective manner into their teaching text in such a way that the text itself becomes self-instructive.

The influence of this model on distance education as it is currently practised is considerable, which is surprising as most university teachers reject this type of 'teaching' completely because it reminds them too much of school. It may once again be the special situation of distance students and the aim of overcoming the distance between them that leads them to make concessions to compensate for the perceived deficit caused by distance, and to do this even though the development of these pedagogically structured teaching texts demands considerable expense and above-average commitment.

Educational technology of the 1970s did not replace this model, but favoured, supported and reinforced it, because it made careful planning and an empirical method acceptable for preparing teaching. The *zeitgeist* was just right for this objectivization of teaching functions. Without the support of educational technology, the teacher model may well have been rejected as turning university education into an unacceptable school-like structure. As it was, wherever value was placed on the careful development of teaching texts or appropriate media, the spatial distance was reduced by means of indirect interactivity between teachers and students.

2.4 The tutor model

Distance is reduced here by the teaching text simulating a tutorial. This 'tutorial in print' (Rowntree, 1992: 82) is understood as the equivalent of an actual tutorial. Interestingly, this model comes from England, the mother country of the tutorial tradition.

So as to make the difference to the conversation and teacher models quite clear, we will have to refer to the original function of the tutor. A *tutor* was typically not someone who was responsible for teaching but a *fellow* attached to a university who advised students on general questions concerning their studies, integrated them into college life and provided other support. Quite often there was a personal relationship between student and tutor. Tutors were therefore not teachers but advisers, and in the most favourable cases something like an older friend. One of the original meanings of the word in Latin is in fact 'protector'.

Nowadays, the term tutor is also used to define a person who provides help with learning in the narrow sense, but in contrast to the teacher model, in which the student is kept on a reasonably tight rein, this model presupposes basically that the amounts to be learnt will be learnt independently. The 'tutorial in print' simply assumes the counselling function where difficulties may be expected. Rowntree (1992: 119) recommends that it should make the student acquainted with the objective of the study units and introduce them to the subject matter, discuss preconditions for successful learning, provide tips with regard to the time required for working through individual sections and help students to summarize and reflect on what they have learnt. Above all, it should make students not only read and reproduce ideas and concepts but also apply them, which is why they should always be asked to develop appropriate activities.

In this type of procedure, monological and expository teaching is completely abandoned. The aim of the teaching text is not to present contents but to give the impression of a conversation with an imaginary tutor. Questions are put, advice is given, opinions are expressed and correlations explained. And students are also helped not to fall into the trap of thinking that they are working in isolation from the university and in the final analysis of thinking that they are alone. Proximity is simulated in this strange way as well.

2.4.1 Commentary

This model is remarkable because of the attitude to students that can be found behind it. It reflects not only consideration and helpfulness but also tactful reservation. We can actually feel the respect for students learning independently and on their own responsibility. There is none of the obtrusive importunity of the correspondence and conversation models, or of the regularly overattentive commitment of the teacher model that attempts to assume responsibility for each learning step. This tutor model appears, therefore, to be suitable for adult students with an inclination towards autonomous learning.

2.5 The technological-extension model

Another way of bridging the distance between teachers and students in distance education is quite simply to let distance students, with the help of technical information and communications media, attend teaching events taking place at traditional universities. This saves the trouble and expense of developing teaching methods tailored to distance education for these students, and even of establishing distance-education universities, because what distance education is in this case is merely traditional studies carried out at a distance. In this case, then, distance students are provided with access to things they would normally have to do without, namely to oral, and therefore in a certain sense authentic, presentations at the university itself. An example of this model is the distance studies with audio tapes run by Waterloo University in Ontario, Canada.

The technological-extension model as used at Waterloo, which is certainly an extreme example, restricts itself basically to recording the spoken word at certain teaching events and to sending the tapes to registered external students. At present, the university produces and copies about 90,000 of these tapes every year. The university also has a stock of around 200,000 additional teaching tapes. Production and mailing are relatively simple and cheap. Where necessary, the university also sends with the tapes the same notes and textbooks that students use in traditional universities for studying by themselves. The university does *not* usually develop special distance-education courses, and it even strictly refuses to adapt existing printed material for traditional courses to the needs of distance students.

In this way, the circle of students can be expanded at practically no cost, and at the same time the amounts earned through course fees increases, because the university charges CAN$276 for each course for which a student registers. Considering the fact that there are around 18,000 registered distance students, this makes a considerable impression on the university accounts (University of Waterloo, 1996/1997).

2.5.1 Commentary

The originators of this model were following a plan to reduce the distance between teachers and students in distance education by assuming that they could enable attendance at teaching events at a traditional university with the help of a technological medium, even if it was asynchronous. Without any doubt they have succeeded in doing this. There is still only an impression of proximity, but it is undoubtedly more evident than in the other models we have discussed. This leads it to do without all pedagogical simulations of closeness that have been discussed previously, and therefore without any form of presentation specific to distance education. In principle, what this model does is to reduce not only the spatial distance but also the distance between distance education and traditional forms of university education. To that extent, it creates a special form of proximity that has never before been seen.

From the point of view of pedagogics, this transmission of the traditional university into the distance student's living-room may be regarded as the exact opposite of the teacher model, because in this case those running the courses deliberately and out of a sense of conviction do not develop course material tailored to distance education that would enable self-teaching, and refuse to take any account of the special needs of adult and working students. However, a mere copy of the learning and teaching activities in the classes of a college cannot do justice to these needs.

Protagonists of the technological-extension model may justify its adoption by claiming that distance students become indirect members of the learning groups at teaching events in the university. If we take a closer look, however, they take part from a keyhole perspective only, because the tapes record the spoken word only and all non-verbal stimuli are ignored, so that body language cannot have any effect. They do not take part in what is happening in classes; they are merely onlookers. In addition, there is the erroneous supposition here that the learning behaviour of adult and (mainly) employed and experienced students can be brought into accord with that of college students who are still in adolescence – who are, in other words, in a period of radical psychosocial change in which they have to learn to assume adult roles and where in their colleges they are in a sort of social reservation.

Seen from the point of view of distance-education pedagogics, what we have here is practically a zero model. What we see here has fundamentally nothing at all to do with distance education but merely with extending the range of traditional university education. However, special – if not critical – attention should be paid to it because at present it is being increasingly practised with the help of electronic media, because virtual classrooms, virtual colleges, the virtual university, and all variations on the theme of teleconferencing work basically on the same principle, but on a more advanced technological and communications level. This model is also used where several learning groups separated geographically are connected to one another via cable or satellite television and follow lectures by a university teacher.

2.6 Transactional distance

Michael Moore (1993: 22), from Penn State University, deserves the credit for explaining on a different theoretical level everything that has been attempted with the help of the correspondence, conversation, teacher, tutor and technological-extension models, namely the reduction of the distance between teachers and students by means of simulations, and introducing a term for it. He differentiates in distance education between spatial and communicative or mental distance and has introduced the term '*transactional distance*' for the latter.

Transactional distance depends on whether students are left alone with their distance education materials or whether they can communicate with their teachers. The transactional function is determined by the extent to which teachers and students can interact ('*dialogue*'). At the same time, it is influenced by the extent to which the learning path is determined by pre-planned teaching programmes ('*structure*'). Accordingly, the transactional distance is greatest when teachers and students do not communicate with one another at all and the teaching programme is pre-planned and prescribed down to the last detail, so that individual learning needs cannot be taken into account. And it is therefore shortest where the teaching programme is open, ie not determined and with frequent dialogues in which the prior knowledge, interests and desires of individual students have an effect and are able to influence the path of learning and teaching. The following overview makes this clear:

Table 2.1 *Examples of transactional distance*

Transactional distance	Type	Example	Abbrev
Greatest	Teaching programme without dialogue or structure	Independent learning on the basis of own reading	-D-S
	Teaching programme without dialogue but with structure	Teaching programmes on radio or television	-D+S
	Teaching programme with dialogue and structure	Typical distance-education course	+D+S
Smallest	Teaching programme with dialogue but without structure	Tutorial care in accordance with Carl Rogers' theories	+D-S

Source: Moore 1977: 39

According to Moore, a reduction of the transactional distance is most certainly not an objective to be aimed at in all cases. In each learning and teaching situation, everything depends on the correct *dosage* of dialogue and structure. In many cases, a great or even an extremely great transactional distance may be desirable because it is an important precondition for independent learning, which is highly valued in distance education. For this reason a third variable enters Moore's concept of transactional distance, namely the extent to which students may determine their own learning (*autonomy*). According to this variable, distance education is also to be evaluated on the basis of how much room it offers for independent learning. Students' autonomy is at its greatest where they determine their own learning aims and learning paths, they control the success of their own learning, and where they are not restricted when learning either by dialogue or a prescribed structure (such as private self-studies). Their autonomy is at its lowest level where all learning aims are prescribed, learning paths are determined by structures and dialogues, and control of learning is carried out by others, for instance as occurs in examination-oriented studies at a traditional university. Transactional distance that is too great prevents this form of learning altogether.

Thus, transactional distance is a function of *three* variables, which change from situation to situation and in some cases work against each other or even exclude each other. Depending on the characteristics of the persons taking part, the content of the teaching and what it aims to achieve, the necessary methods and the traditional teaching culture, a certain optimum ratio of these three variables has to be found and from that a transactional distance determined that matches the situation. Distance-education pedagogics therefore consist of those strategies and techniques with the help of which it is possible to balance the transactional distance with the requirements of the respective learning and teaching situation.

2.6.1 Commentary

The concept of transactional distance is a significant contribution to distance-education pedagogics. It characterizes the special structure of distance education exactly, with little effort and in an illuminative manner. Its particular attributes become clear here. It describes not only the opportunities already existing in distance education for reducing mental and communicative distances, but also interprets their pedagogical relevance.

By showing the transactional distance not as a fixed quantity but as a variable, which results from the changing interplay amongst dialogue, the structured nature of the teaching programme being presented, and the autonomy of the students, a convincing explanation is provided of the enormous flexibility of this form of academic teaching. The concept also provides an insight into the pedagogical complexity of distance education, which becomes even more clear when it is compared with the traditional forms of academic teaching, which are methodologically more restricted and one-sided in their articulation (see Schulmeister, 1983, 1995: 343).

Moore is not dogmatic and does not speak out in favour of one or other of the teaching forms referred to, each of which, however, could be used to optimize customary distance education. However, his sober analysis makes it clear how distance education can develop in light of the tensions between these in-part contradictory methodological concepts. It seems clear that the royal road to reform of distance education, which must be regarded as a permanent task, lies in the respective combination of the three distinct forms of teaching.

2.6.2 Empirical confirmation

Farhad Saba (1990: 344) has applied the theory of transactional distance to learning situations in which work is done with an *integrated telecommunications technology*. His experience shows that the structure and dialogue in this type of learning situation is easier to change and bring into balance than is otherwise the case. A balance between both can be achieved that corresponds to the interests and intentions of both teachers and autonomous students. Moore's theory of the dynamics of these two variables is confirmed here.

To give an indication of the additional leeway granted to the dialogue, for example, by an integrated telecommunications system during learning and teaching, let us remind ourselves of its special achievements: it not only transmits data but also the voice and image of both teachers and students, both synchronously and interactively. In ideal cases, teachers and distance students can, simultaneously and jointly: work through the same teaching programme; immediately discuss any problems that arise; discuss and correct written work; use the same database simultaneously and jointly; make a sketch or a graph appear; discuss and solve a problem; and record results in writing. And in this way a high degree of proximity is simulated that is not possible with the models discussed above.

This *virtual proximity* offers the possibility of immediate access with the same system to an immeasurable amount of stored files that contain teaching texts and modules of certain learning programmes with different degrees of difficulty. Saba (1990: 350) therefore established the following hypothesis: With learning and teaching in distance education, virtual proximity optimizes not only the dialogue but also the structure. The reason he gave for this hypothesis was the reduction in the time between the acts of learning and teaching. During the dialogue phase, teachers can recognize a student's special learning preconditions and needs, discuss them with the student with regard to the learning aims, and then decide immediately with the student which modules of which learning programme at which level are to be worked through in this situation. These modules are then immediately available. Integrated telecommunications systems therefore not only enable the proportion devoted to dialogue to be increased and thus to reduce the structure, but also increase the proportion devoted to structure and in this way restrict the dialogue to a desirable and acceptable extent. Saba sees a *cybernetic relationship* between the two variables, which he illustrates by means of a control loop.

Saba's considerations are interesting not only because of his pointer to the cybernetic relationship of the duration of dialogue and structure, but also because of the possibility he indicates of using integrated digital telecommunications to improve the pedagogical quality of both the dialogue and the structure. However, the virtual proximity (*virtual contiguity*) he describes is also of considerable theoretical importance, which was hinted at in the distance-education system that uses tapes. In principle, this contiguity makes redundant all previously described efforts at reducing the apparent spatial distance for distance students. Strictly speaking, distance education pedagogics in the true sense of the phrase stops at this point, because methods taken from face-to-face teaching or traditional courses can be applied. In that regard we have arrived once again at a particularly critical point in our considerations of pedagogics.

It must be said, however, that Saba's experiments and hypotheses have up to now had only theoretical relevance. The general application of his concept has in fact been faced with opposition in the form of practical hurdles. Not only will it take a considerable length of time until the majority of distance students have access to a fully equipped integrated PC, but the software would have to be improved as well. In addition, the optical fibre cable network under the ISDN standard will have to be made available to all, and this will not be possible in the USA, for example, until the year 2000. While these hurdles can probably be overcome in time, the hurdle still remains of the costs of additional teaching staff required by this type of system. The dialogue examined here between one teacher and one student must continue to remain an exception with distance-teaching universities in which tens or even hundreds of thousand of students are enrolled. An increase in teaching staff at present – and indeed in the future – is not to be expected.

2.7 Summary

The five models shown in this chapter that have arisen from the development of distance education provide an indication of how complex their pedagogical structure is. With the exception of the guided conversation, they have not yet been precisely described and not yet absorbed into the theory of learning and teaching in distance education. At the same time, they play an important role because they are contained implicitly in distance-educational practice. One task of pedagogics in relation to distance education would be to interpret its fine structure and make scholars aware of the complexities of its theoretical basis.

It will hardly be possible to give preference to one of these five models because components of each are found in each type of distance education, and in addition because, in the digital era that we are now entering, completely new models will be formed on this foundation. Michael Moore's concept of the transactional distance can be instrumental in this process. However, to keep solid ground under our feet initially and to demonstrate the structural differences of distance education, it is advantageous to bear in mind the traditional pedagogical core of distance education described above. If we want to know where the journey is going to take us during the further development of distance education, we first have to recognize where this form of learning and teaching comes from. This has been shown in this second chapter.

Chapter 3

Three constitutive concepts

Because of the importance to the further theoretical and practical development of distance education that Moore's interpretation of the interplay of *dialogue*, *structure*, and *autonomy* can have, in this chapter we shall analyse perceptions that may be found behind these three concepts. Using them, academic learning and teaching in distance education is able to articulate itself in various characteristic ways.

Discussion of the three concepts is important in this context because pedagogical dialogues, technologically structured learning, and autonomous learning are scarcely to be found in everyday university teaching, or at least only in rudimentary form, and in addition are quite controversial. In the mainly expository teaching carried out in traditional universities, pedagogical dialogues and academic discourses do not have the position that we might wish them to have in the interests of students. Teaching programmes developed in accordance with educational technology play an absolutely minimal role, apart from *computer-based instruction* in some areas of mathematics and computer science. And in the framework of traditional types of teaching, institutional degree courses and examination regulations, autonomous learning is only able to develop in a basic way in more advanced teaching schemes. While we can say that carefully planned teaching programmes prepared down to the last detail dominate in distance-teaching universities as we know them in Europe, it is still true that dialogue learning and self-determined, self-controlled learning are still considerably restricted.

Because university teachers have internalized traditional forms of teaching and unconsciously measure innovative concepts against these forms, it is easy to find criticism of the proposals for reform that arise from the three concepts we have referred to, and this criticism is found in traditional and distance-teaching universities. The following is an extreme simplification of the main objections:

1. long discussions are a waste of time;
2. study materials developed in accordance with educational technology reduce learning and teaching to a mere means–ends rationality; and

3. average students do not possess the preconditions required for autonomous learning – they are completely unable to plan something as demanding and complicated as a university degree course themselves and to conclude it without guidance.

If distance education, as we have shown and demanded, consists fundamentally of the integration of instructive dialogues, structured learning and teaching programmes and activities covered by autonomous learning, we cannot expect that these concepts will be accepted everywhere from the start with everyone involved being committed to their realization. On the contrary, we will meet with scepticism, doubts and rejection, and attempts will be made to adhere to the customary traditional practices. For this reason the three constitutive concepts will be established in greater detail and their application for learning and teaching in distance education will be justified.

3.1 Dialogue

The concept of 'dialogue' does not mean the written presentation of contents in simulated letters or conversations in the way we described and discussed under the correspondence and conversation models, but rather means direct and indirect oral interaction between teachers and students, in other words, an *actual* dialogue.

Moore (1993: 24) characterizes the dialogue by contrasting it with other interactions in learning and teaching:

> A dialogue is targeted, constructive and appreciated by participants. Each party listens respectfully and with interest to the other. Each party contributes something to its progress and refers to contributions made by the other parties. There may be negative and neutral interactions. However, the term 'dialogue' always refers to positive interactions. Value is placed on the joint solution of the problem under discussion and the idea is to arrive at a deeper understanding on the part of the students.

This concept, he continues, is committed to humanistic pedagogics for which the dialogue from person to person is of central importance in so far as it is unstructured and open-ended – it was developed, above all, for counselling situations. In the terms used by Reinhard and Anne-Marie Tausch (1977), dialogical learning demands from participants 'partnership, respect, warmth, consideration, elementary understanding, honesty and sincerity'.

In his list of the constitutive concepts of distance education, Moore put the dialogue in first place. This will have surprised many university teachers, including those with experience of distance education. Does this function actually play such an important role in the pedagogic structure of distance education? Doubts arise because (and in particular in Europe) the dominant idea is that distance students typically and mainly undergo a self-teaching process and work through their study materials at home alone. The sense of doubt may well be also caused by the lasting effects of Schelsky's legendary book *Einsamkeit und Freiheit* (1963), which was once said to have been characteristic of studies at traditional universities.

The partnership dialogue between teachers and students in the sense described presents great difficulties in teaching in practice, in spite of the tradition of seminars and colloquia, because both schools and universities neglect it in favour of monological presentational teaching methods. In universities, the necessity in many faculties to provide for extremely large groups of students restricts opportunities for dialogue still further. In today's 'mass' universities, dialogical learning and teaching situations have become more the exception than the rule, if we disregard the more 'exotic' subjects. In some cases, dialogues in small groups were even evaluated negatively, and the disparaging judgements of university teachers are an indication of this (for reports, see Wolf Rieck and Ulrich Peter Ritter, 1983/1985: 386).

In spite of the reform movement in the 1970s, the dialogue has not been able to establish itself as an important and regular form of academic learning and teaching; in fact, a trend towards the isolation of students can even be seen. In the case of distance education, the use of the dialogical principle meets with this rather aloof attitude as well, although the attitude is usually unconscious or not admitted to. The most crass expression of rejection comes from those professors who have been pleading for years for the study centres to be abolished on the grounds that they are superfluous because the printed course materials are *self-instructive*.

More exact data on professors' attitudes to this concept have been recorded at the FernUniversität. Of the 62 persons who were questioned, it was significant that just half were prepared to reply. The reasons for this may be indifference and rejection. Nevertheless, of those who took part in the poll, about half regarded dialogical learning in distance education as 'essential' and another third as 'necessary'. This is a good foundation and starting position for appropriate reforms.

Along with the rather neutral and even defensive attitudes of university professors referred to above, there are also operational difficulties in distance education because direct and indirect oral interaction is really only possible in tutorials and counselling sessions in study centres, and via the telephone, written correspondence or with the help of other technical media. In addition, for most students activities in study centres contribute little to the acquisition of competence because few students actually attend regularly. As the dialogues in this context are also labour-intensive and therefore expensive, distance-teaching universities are unable to finance this type of dialogical instruction for all students.

If a demand is made in this situation for the dialogical principle to come more intensively into play in distance education, and if it is thought possible that it could be used now and even more in the future, this results in problems which it is extremely difficult to solve. At the same time, they will have to be addressed, because if this is not done, the future of this form of academic study is uncertain. However, these operational difficulties may be reduced in distance education of the second and third generation, for in these cases oral interactivity for the learning and teaching process can be intensified dramatically through the use of audio- and video-conferencing. It seems, therefore, that a more intensive, more personal, more individual and more dynamic dialogue may indeed be possible for certain phases of distance education –

although it would, of course, be *virtual*. We will be taking a closer look at this later on in Chapter 6.

To outline the importance of dialogue in learning and teaching in distance education, its pedagogic function should be indicated. Where there is a dialogue between teachers and students in distance education, the sole question is most certainly not merely to help the students overcome difficulties that may occur when they work through their study materials, which would be of only superficial help. Dialogue not only has help functions but is also an *independent* form of learning and teaching with special pedagogical tasks. To make this clear, and to establish just how important these tasks are, we shall be looking at the dialogue below from the aspect of several disciplines: scientific pedagogics, pedagogics for higher education, distance-education pedagogics, pedagogics as a whole, philosophy, anthropology and sociology are all important. Those who pay sufficient attention to dialogical learning in distance education with regard to these aspects, and do not disregard it by reducing learning and teaching to a mere working-through of prepared study materials, make distance education not only more effective in the sense of achieving its demanding goals but also provide it with additional pedagogical substance and relevance.

3.1.1 Aspects of scientific pedagogics

Here we should turn to Hartmut von Hentig's theory (1970: 25), with which he made the close correlation between knowledge and communication clearer than anyone else. Among the reasons he gave for this were the following: if the inter-subjective verifiability of scientific knowledge is deemed to be a *conditio sine qua non* for academic work, communication becomes a constitutive and integral component of knowledge and science. Those who merely store knowledge in their memories do not therefore take part in the scientific process. The necessary connection between knowledge and communication (von Hentig,1971: 871) is therefore deemed to be a pedagogical principle. Applied to distance education this means that those who wish to limit studies to the reception of printed materials damage the substance of these studies, and even their scientific nature.

Ludwig Huber, an educational scientist, drew the following consequence for traditional universities from this realization. Learning and teaching must be dissociated from the start from 'merely handing down knowledge that has become academic knowledge' by binding teaching to the process of knowledge. This, on the other hand, can only be done through 'the informal participation in the scientific process (of communication among academics) and productive (new or reinventive) thinking' (Huber, 1983/1995b: 497–8). Oral dialogues may be used in the first place here.

Those who suspect that the opinion of these two authors is a product of the reform movements of the 1970s is mistaken. The particular nexus between knowledge and communication was underlined by Friedrich Daniel Ernst Schleiermacher (1956: 224) at the beginning of the nineteenth century. What 'some scientifically-minded person has worked out for himself in seclusion' was for

Schleiermacher merely an 'empty shell', and he accordingly claimed that 'the first law of all efforts aimed at knowledge must be: communication.'

If we acquire knowledge in distance education in isolation from others and store it in our memories, we are not really taking part in the process of knowledge even if this knowledge is extremely extensive and differentiated. For this reason, communicating knowledge is not a mere addition or supplement but a *fundamental precondition* for academic instruction. The 'necessary connection between knowledge and communication' (von Hentig, 1971: 871) must therefore be regarded as a pedagogical principle for distance education as well. For this reason, distance education cannot do without the dialogue, in particular because the danger of giving academic instruction in school-like structures through formulated and therefore fully determined degree courses is greater in this type of educational system than in traditional universities. If distance students are restricted to the written communication of knowledge – in written examinations, written work, and degree examinations – the structure of academic studies is seriously reduced.

3.1.2 Aspects of pedagogics for higher education

Insistence on the dialogical principle is not a present-day reformist fashion; on the contrary, we can follow it back to classical times. In archaic periods, the ceremonial monologue of the priest-teacher characterized the learning and teaching process, and we can still experience traces of this today, but 'throughout the ancient world... the dialogue was the preferred tool of philosophic discussion' because it made the presentation of philosophical problems 'vivid', and it 'vitalized' them by means of statement and rejoinder (Schischkoff, 1991: 140). The famous *Socratic dialogues* have had an effect right up to the present day. The dialogical form of imparting knowledge played an important role around the year AD400 in the school of the famous Indian Buddhist monastery at Nalanda, because teachers spent the whole day discussing with their adepts (Keay, 1980: 96). Another approach is found in Europe in the teaching methods in mediaeval and modern universities. Here, the dialogical method of discussion was found alongside the acroamatic (monological) presentation and founded the tradition of *disputation*. In more modern times, the traditional *colloquium* and the *seminar* were used in the cause of dialogical learning.

At present, reflecting on scientific problems is activated and intensified by participation in dialogue. By exchanging different opinions, opposing opinions, taking sides, always doubting results and exercising criticism, students discover a different relationship to the matter under discussion from the one they arrive at if they merely read, mark and inwardly digest. Interest in the subject is increased, students are highly involved, and this involvement can turn into commitment.

With greater reference to scientific discussion, students can learn the following skills by means of active participation in a dialogue. They learn:

- to argue purposefully and in the language of their discipline;
- to take up, give reasons for, maintain, modify or abandon their own theoretical points of view in the course of a discussion;
- to enquire into and evaluate critically knowledge presented by other students;

- to absorb from a discussion any impetus to the discussion affecting their own reflections, and on the other hand to provide impetus themselves for the advancement of the discussion;
- to reflect critically and self-confidently (at a meta-level) together with other students on the knowledge they have gained and on the methods used;
- to experience collective advances in knowledge; and
- where possible, to proceed rationally, systematically and methodically in the oral presentation of their own ideas.

These skills and talents, which are just some examples, cannot be acquired merely by means of receptive learning. They cannot be imparted by printed distance-education units, no matter how ingenious and well-contrived. And even the most thorough reading of the best authors cannot help. That is why dialogue in distance education is absolutely essential.

Those who are convinced by the limited success of mainly *expository* teaching and a mainly *receptive* learning style and hold up the objectives of a traditional academic course of studies as an example to follow cannot fail to be upset by the resulting discrepancy. A *presenting–delivering* teaching method (Dolch, 1952) can at the very most bring about learning in the sense of *acquisition, maintenance* and the *reproduction* of knowledge and skills by rote. However, if we take up a recommendation of the *Wissenschaftsrat* (1966: 14), what is wanted is the 'ability to think independently and critically', but also the ability to 'apply' this critical thought, to try out the resulting 'rational characteristics' and to prove oneself. This cannot be achieved in a system that makes use of mainly expository–receptive learning, as exemplified by reading and working through prepared study materials. As we have seen, the dialogue offers opportunities that no other form of teaching possesses.

3.1.3 Aspects of distance-education pedagogics

According to Martin Buber (1954), in a dialogue the I–it relationship (ie the subject–object relationship) changes to an I–you relationship (ie a subject–subject relationship). Because of the large number of students, the great anonymity of the teachers, the objectivization of the teaching functions and their technical realization for students, there is usually only I–it relationships in distance education. A dialogue provides an opportunity to establish at the very least isolated or partial I–you relationships in which the individuality and personality of both teachers and students come into play and in fact become *educative* in the first place. This gives rise to what humanistic pedagogics refers to as the *pedagogic connection* (Weniger) or the *pedagogic relationship* (Klafki), and which can be transferred analogously to the relationship between teachers and 'their' students – but only in a dialogue.

3.1.4 Pedagogical aspects

Dialogues become significant for pedagogics because here speech, thought and action are closely connected to one another and bring about the individual and social development of the persons involved. 'The development of the individual and of society can only be explained and understood in a manner relevant to pedagogy in the interplay between thought, action and speech' (Kron, 1996: 270). In a dialogue, speech turns into a social act, whereas this is not the case with the isolated reading of printed material.

Franz Pöggeler, the adult educationalist (1974: 203), saw an 'existence form of modern man' in dialogue and described it as the *'definiens* and *constituens* of humanity'. With this in mind, it is difficult to imagine a successful degree course that neglects the dialogical principle.

3.1.5 Philosophical aspects

A dialogue forces people to contact each other directly and on the basis of their own decisions to listen to the partner, to take them seriously, and to discover, satisfy and confirm themselves. Contact between a person's own self and others, which cannot be planned and also includes the risk of failure, becomes possible and can lead to existential encounters. In a dialogue, people experience in an irreplaceable way a form of activity that is important for the existence of mankind.

3.1.6 Anthropological aspects

A dialogue is one of the basic facts of human existence because it is the medium for the creation of language, for becoming a person, and for all forms of living together. According to Franz Pöggeler again (1974: 203), humanity constitutes itself in the first place through dialogues with fellow beings:

> The dialogue is the sounding-board that tells us more about ourselves as individuals than we can discover from ourselves and for ourselves. The fellow-being as a partner in a dialogue is a mirror of our own self-knowledge... because a dialogue is not just the expression of a human need for contact but above all the longing for self-knowledge and self-certainty.

Accordingly, Pöggeler believes *'dico ergo sum'*.

Distance students who are unable to participate in dialogues between teachers and students because of unfavourable conditions, such as not having an opportunity to do so for financial or administrative reasons, or even because of insufficient pedagogical insight, miss an important dimension of academic study through holding to the motto *'lego ergo non sum'*.

3.1.7 Preliminary summary

Is it possible to do without this original form of gaining knowledge – not just of imparting knowledge – in the development of distance-education systems? Can we keep this existential experience of the self from distance students? And can we excuse its absence with the argument that face-to-face teaching in today's mass universities does not actually apply the dialogical principle, because seminars in those circumstances usually consist of a monologue in the form of someone reading a paper, and discussions in colloquia are usually dominated by professors? Can we restrict direct oral communication in distance education, or even do without it completely, with the argument that adult and employed distance students have sufficient real opportunities to develop their capacity for dialogue in their jobs and private lives? Certainly not. Dialogical learning and teaching, and participation in the process of knowledge, are unique and therefore incomparable procedures.

If we take distance education seriously and understand it to be something more than the mere distribution and reading of study materials, we must provide sufficient opportunities for dialogues. If, in addition, we understand academic studies as a process in which the aim is *education through knowledge*, we cannot do without a considerable proportion of dialogical learning and teaching in distance education. Furthermore, if we consider the great extent to which the development of scientific thinking depends on its genesis and practice in dialogues with teachers and other students, and how intensively speech, thought and action require each other, we are strengthened in this belief. If, on the other hand, learning in dialogues is neglected, or even done without completely, studies not only lack an important dimension for qualifications in academic professions, but also depth and, if we follow Pöggeler's argument, humanity as well.

3.1.8 Sociological aspects

There may be readers to whom some of these characterizations and interpretations appear too stilted, too exaggerated, perhaps even too extravagant. This impression may be caused by the fact that historical contemplation and interpretation of learning and teaching from a humanist viewpoint has already become alien to the means–aims outlook that is becoming steadily stronger. As we saw in the introduction, pedagogic reflection is supported as well by these findings, and this will be shown below in an example.

The critical objections that have been alluded to do not refute, or even question, the essentials of the arguments on the great importance of dialogue for distance education. All the same, it may be of use to readers to reinforce still further the claims made concerning the special significance of dialogue in distance education with sociological concepts in a correspondingly sober and value-free set of conceptual statements. What is meant by the term 'dialogue' plays a central part in important relationships in other contexts as *social interaction* and *communication*.

'Social interaction' as understood in sociology means the exchange of mutually related actions in a social situation. These actions are influenced by the values and attitudes of each of the orientation and action partners (the *significant other*) which are themselves derived from corresponding societal values. In the scope of these interactions the *socialization* of individuals is carried out by learning symbols and roles. In this way, individuals learn their identity as persons and become interactively competent, ie capable of social activities. To achieve this, they must acquire above all two skills: they must acquire *role distance* (Goffman, 1972) and be able to take roles (Mead, 1975). 'Role distance' empowers an individual to reflect on and interpret norms existing in a social group, which is necessary and important for the development of the individual's own identity. The importance of oral communication in this process must be stressed, because it is the *'central means of social interaction'* (Miller, 1978: 60).

'Communication' as understood by social psychology is above all oral interaction in which the important thing is the meaning and the significance of the message. It aims at mutual understanding and enables action in a manner that understands the meaning. Great value is placed on the *relationship level*, which is separated from the contents level, and on *meta-communication* and the *symmetry of communication*, which presupposes that the communication partners are equal and have equal rights.

With these theories in mind, learning and teaching is fundamentally defined as an interaction and communications process. To underline the significance of this way of thinking, especially for academic socialization, let us think back to the *theory of communicative competence* as developed by Jürgen Habermas (1971). Communicative competence is formed by carrying out symbolically imparted – in other words, communicative – actions. Only this communicative action is able to maintain and create meaning. It is oriented towards existing norms, which must be understood and accepted by the partners. Its epitome is the 'dialogical rationality of the discourse' (Langewand, 1983/1995: 430).

In this way, great importance is attached to language, gestures and communicative action, and this is seen in particular in learning and teaching in universities, because discourse in an academic dialogue starts where mutual understanding of a set of facts breaks down and agreement needs to be sought. Education in universities therefore has to train students' communicative competence and in this way to lead them to and qualify them for discursive action. A discourse, in other words communication not dominated by a single party with the aim of agreement, becomes the medium for academic work and education.

3.1.9 Summary

If we analyse distance education under these aspects, we find serious deficits. Where is the social situation in which distance students acquire communicative competence through interaction with significant others? Where can they take over the values and behavioural patterns of academic life? Where can they practise role distance? Where can they learn to project themselves into their partner's mind. Where do students encounter that atmosphere of sympathetic understanding and respect that can only be created in direct contact with others? How does symmetrical communication between teachers and students arise? All of this is missing.

As a result, distance students cannot acquire their identity as students and academics, and so corresponding academic conduct cannot be integrated into the process of *academic socialization*. 'The "one-dimensionality" of distance education with its practically exclusive communication through media' tends to prevent this (Miller, 1991: 50). Instead, it must be suspected, *professional* (rather than academic) socialization takes its place, particularly as this continues throughout their studies for most distance students. The meagre level of *academic* socialization through a distance-teaching university is unable to hold its ground against this.

In fact, we can even go so far as to say that the few approaches to academic socialization, where they exist, have probably been eroded. The 'lack of communication in distance education' permits 'feelings of insufficiency to be created in many students which probably reflect the climatic conditions of our society and force numerous students into isolation as students', suspects Rudolf Miller (1991: 50). The wide spatial gap between students and teachers and amongst students themselves, and the isolated working methods, play a part here.

The argument is hollow that important socialization processes take place for employed adults in *other* areas of life and are therefore not as important as for young students in traditional universities. There is a great difference between cases in which the *significant other* is a supervisor, for example the head of personnel, or a colleague in an electrical engineering company, or a professor, lecturer or fellow-student in the electrical engineering department of a university. And in each case there are different values to be internalized after distancing oneself from them, reflecting on them and interpreting them.

In this type of situation, who might be prepared to plead the case *against* intensifying the interactive and communication parts of distance education? And who is there who is still surprised that Moore regards dialogue not only as a fixed and natural element in the pedagogical structure of distance education but also grants it precedence there?

3.2 Structure

3.2.1 Definition of the term

In the term 'structure', Moore (1993: 26) defined a concept of learning and teaching that, from its approach and in important characteristics, differs from the concept of dialogical learning and in some parts is even in contrast to it. It is not open to spontaneous interventions and unforeseen developments but is 'closed' because it is consistently planned on a targeted basis and with small steps, its time is regimented and it is uniformly controlled and evaluated. The main instrument of this learning and teaching are printed courses or multimedia learning packages which contain carefully developed and optimized courses and set learning into motion and control it, vicariously, for university teachers.

Moore (1993: 26) chose the brief description of 'structure' for this concept, because he regarded the main characteristic as the structuring of the learning and teaching process – right down to the last detail. He used the example of a teaching film for television to show just how far this structuring could go: in the film 'literally every word, every action of the teacher, every minute of the available time and even the tiniest detail of the contents were laid down beforehand'. As a result, there was practically no opportunity for learners to deviate from the learning path or to vary it to take account of individual learning requirements or spontaneous contributions.

The structuring of learning and teaching is in fact nothing new and certainly not unique to distance education. *Presenting knowledge through books*, for example, has always been broken down by means of components such as a foreword, an introduction, chapters, a summary and a conclusion. And in the last two centuries, the *articulation of instruction* has been a central theme of pedagogics. What is meant here is the arrangement of learning and teaching by determining the time and place it occurs. We should also not forget the great part played since Herbart by the *pedagogics of formal stages*. What we mean here is the structuring of the learning and teaching process in stages and phases, with different learning and teaching activities in each stage and phase. Since the 1970s, models have been discussed of *structural communication* (Hodgson, 1974) and *structured writing* (or mapping) (Horn, 1973).

What is nevertheless new in Moore's suggested concept is therefore not structuring in itself but the extreme extent of its application. Its development cannot be understood without reference to educational technology. This provided the concept model and the methodological instruments and propagated it worldwide. This means that learning and teaching take place in accordance with a different learning and teaching model, namely the behaviourist model, which is based on other scientific (positivist) premises and is realized with the help of other (empirical) processes. Consequently, the task of teaching is approached in quite a different manner from usual; engineering-type thinking takes hold and dominates. *Efficiency* and objectivized *success controls* become important.

With regard to the structuring of learning and teaching in distance education, it takes place on the basis of criteria from educational technology. Strictly speaking, learning and teaching aims are analysed, selected and defined to achieve teaching objectives with their help, technical media are used to make this process more efficient, tests are constructed to see whether the declared objectives have in fact been achieved, and evaluations are carried out to optimize the established structure.

This structure is seen most clearly and most densely in *programmed instructions*. It was the representative of a theory of teaching in which each word, each learning step, each teaching strategy was planned and developed with the greatest care and in which the teaching contents that were to be presented were broken down into small portions of information in order to simplify learning and make teaching more successful. It was claimed that this was in concert with the findings and experience of learning psychology – in other words it was strictly in accordance with the scientific method, and oriented towards a systematic approach. This pattern had an effect on the development of distance education courses, above all when professional educational technologists took part.

3.2.2 Reservations on structure

From the point of view of pedagogics, there are reservations – some of which are motivated by criticism of educational technology in the behaviourist sense – to those distance-education courses that have been developed on the basis of educational technology and are therefore heavily structured. Here are some of these reservations:

● The courses are concentrated too much on learning and teaching functions and ignore other important functions, eg the participation of students in the process of knowledge. They tend to put learning into a 'school'-type format.

- The structure of the courses is largely determined by defined teaching objectives, because only with such objectives having been defined can the teaching itself be constructed and its results measured objectively. However, this completely ignores those items that cannot be categorized, subjected to operational definitions, or evaluated by standardized tests. This naturally changes the course structure.
- Usually the shortest path to an objective is taken, and diversions are avoided rather than permitted. In this way, learning attitudes and standpoints are neglected which also form a part of academic studies, eg repeated attempts to perceive a problem, repeated meditative observation of a phenomenon from various self-chosen points of view, the slowly growing conviction that the correct approach has been chosen, as well as (alternatively) the experience of coming to a dead end or failing in some other way in a train of thought.
- The courses reduce the originally complex learning and teaching process to a one-dimensional process, namely an exactly calculated interplay of defined learning and teaching functions. In this way, for example, the historical, social and political dimension is often missing.
- The courses lack any 'situational' content, as it constitutes learning and teaching in traditional universities, where things actually happen in front of the students' eyes.
- They neglect learning through participation, reflection and meta-communication.
- They are extremely teacher-centred, a peculiarity that is easily reinforced and cemented and that perpetuates a pedagogical paradigm that really belongs to the past.
- Finally, they flagrantly contradict the structuralist learning model, which is at present once again finding favour with learning researchers.

3.2.3 Advantages of structure

Why is the concept of structured learning extremely attractive in spite of the deficiencies and faults we have referred to and in the face of the reservations of distance-teaching universities? Why has it been successful in the latter and determined the focal point of learning and teaching for 25 years? One explanation for this has to do with a generalized (and cultural) way of thinking, and there are two pedagogical reasons as well.

Firstly, the acceptance of structured learning in distance education can be explained with the *zeitgeist* of the 1960s and 1970s in the Western world. In those years, people were more receptive than today towards a basic feeling of optimism, which embraced all those who believed that procedures that had been tried and tested in science and technology could now be used with similarly great success to solve pedagogical and learning and teaching problems. As a result, the idea was welcomed that university teaching, in the same way as an industrial product, could be rationally planned, systematically developed, subjected to airtight controls, improved using the results of experience, and its success measured for all to see.

Secondly, people looked at the possibility of manipulating objectivized learning behaviour. What was fascinating was the idea that through the interplay of renowned university teachers and experienced experts, who have specialized in certain specific areas of learning and teaching, courses could be developed with a particularly high quality which, ideally, would be better than anything that can be offered in traditional universities.

Thirdly, in every society there are those who are unable to gain access to educational opportunities for social, geographical or financial reasons, or because of their age. Anyone who is motivated by reasons of educational policy or pedagogics must be concerned about this situation and aim at offering more education for more people. They are attracted or even inspired by the possibility of reproducing and offering perfected teaching behaviour to a liberal extent. The prospect of being able to reach nearly all those interested and capable of academic work, and of enabling them to have a university education, has indeed inspired politicians and educationalists throughout the world and leads them to overlook the learning and teaching disadvantages of this procedure.

3.2.4 Structural communication

Since the 1970s, models have been discussed of the 'structured writing' (Horn, 1973) and 'structural communication' (Hodgson, 1974) that are mentioned earlier in this section. Structured writing is based on the idea that the preparation of written material may improve the functions of presentation, revision and reference. The pages are structured by 'maps' that shape the information. There are overview maps, structure maps, summary maps, individual concept maps, procedure maps, and compare/contrast tables. Lists, 'trees' and 'blocks' are also used. All of these graphic elements are usually cross-indexed and cross-referenced. The experts in this field believe that mapping helps 'to augment the ability of human beings to interact with their new information environment' and 'to make learning and reference work easier and quicker' (Romiszowski, 1986: 209).

Egan (1976) has described the techniques of structural communication, and John Bååth, in his excellent treatise 'Correspondence education in the light of a number of contemporary teaching models' (1979), has carefully analysed them in order to find out how far they can be applied to distance education. By quoting Egan (1976: 16), he points out that this kind of structural teaching is based on the theory that learning can take place at various levels of intellectual activity. The learners, however, need 'some kind of intellectual challenge, in order to be able to raise their thinking from the usual sensitive level (or the very lowest, the automatic level) to a more "conscious" – reflective – stage or to the very highest, the creative form'. Hence, teaching material should be structured in such a way that the learners are caused, by means of a 'guided dialogue', to identify the problems, to think them over, to be creative in finding solutions and to pass reflective judgements on other options.

In order to achieve this, the protagonists of structural communication subdivide their teaching texts into six distinct units – which nevertheless are interrelated. The six are:

1. Intention
2. Presentation
3. Investigation
4. Response Matrix
5. Discussion
6. Viewpoints

The third and fourth units in the list are critical. 'Investigation' means that the facts are structured in such a way that the *whole* field of knowledge to be analysed becomes visible and that the relationships between its elements become transparent. The roots of this technique in *Gestalt* thinking become clear here. And, prepared in such a way, the students start working with a 'response matrix', which contains between 10 and 30 items (facts, models, hypotheses, formulas etc) for consideration. The students are expected to investigate them and to select and combine some of them in order to find the solution to the problems posed in the Investigation unit. In the subsequent Discussion unit, the students can read pre-prepared reactions of the teacher to these results. If necessary, the learners are asked to go back to the second unit and do the subsequent units again.

Romiszowski (1986: 182) has identified the following specific pedagogical advantages of this particular way of designing auto-instructional material:

- Each learner is challenged to think for himself.
- Each has to face the real facts of the case.
- Each is making skilled inferences from the facts.
- Several interrelated perspectives are considered.
- Alternative solutions to each problem are raised.
- The positive imagination of each learner is brought into play.
- The coherence and consistency of the propositions of each learner are analysed.
- Exchanges are adapted to individual differences.
- An optimal consensus is reached with a commitment to act.
- No learner is left out of, or dominates over, the group.

Is this special method of structured writing applicable to distance education? John Bååth (1979: 56) thinks so, and refers to similarities 'between a study unit in a structural communication and a study unit in a correspondence course'. However, he advises readers to base only short courses on the structural communication model; long and comprehensive courses should merely use particular elements of this technique. The Investigation and Response Matrix units, for example, could be inserted in self-test exercises and, together with the Discussion unit, could be used for postal two-way communication.

Looking back on these remarkable theoretical approaches, which draw their principles mainly from the work of psychologists, we can state that both are cognitive approaches to self-instruction. We can summarize the pedagogical benefits from them as follows: they individualize the learning process, activate the students, stimulate interactivity between the students and the printed teaching material and – judged in the light of our latest experiences in the digital learning environment – introduce the students to the preliminary stages of hypertext learning as they navigate the response matrix as well. Clearly, the structured writing and the structural communication method has much untapped potential for learning and teaching at a distance, especially in digital learning environments.

3.2.5 Summary

This section has brought to the fore the importance of heavily structured distance-education courses as well as the necessity to develop them on an educational-technology basis. The creation of courses in the form of exactly planned, constructed, tested and evaluated teaching and learning systems – which is what distance-education courses are – is the precondition for their perfection and mass distribution. Spontaneous dialogues between people cannot be mass-produced and made available to any number of consumers because of the openness of the teaching and learning situation peculiar to them. In that regard, the contribution of heavily structured courses must be considered of high worth, for they offer the distance students a secure foundation, give them direction, and provide a consistency of approach. Mass higher education, in the manner in which it has been held to be necessary since the 1970s and 1980s in some large industrial countries, is probably impossible without these kinds of support.

Although the concept of dialogue has to be given preference for reasons of pedagogical desirability, the concept of structure is and remains something that distance teaching universities and open universities will be unable to abandon, chiefly because of the evidence of its practical value. Pragmatic considerations are decisive here.

In contrast, the models of structured writing and structural communication show that the closeness of heavily structured distance-teaching material can nevertheless be open in style to a certain degree so as to allow the students space for developing important elements of autonomous learning behaviour. Here, possibilities of reforming the traditional structured teaching texts becomes discernible.

3.3 Autonomy

3.3.1 Description of the term

The term 'autonomy' has played a great part in German pedagogics, because it traditionally referred to the relationship of pedagogics to other disciplines as it became emancipated. However, Moore restricted the term to 'the self-determination of students'. In his understanding of the term, students learning autonomously are able to decide on their learning themselves of their own accord.

Moore used this concept in the 1970s, when the behaviourist method dominated development work for distance education and ignored important dimensions of learning and teaching. In this way he took up a position against the hegemony of educational technologists when all the world was promising themselves so much from a technological change in pedagogics (Flechsig, 1969) and propagation of programmed instruction found hardly any resistance at all. As Moore went on to explain, the model for the autonomous student was found in adult education in the USA. According to Malcolm Knowles, one of its classical advocates, autonomy is natural behaviour for adults, and above all where they consider themselves self-directed according to their own conception of themselves (see Moore, 1993: 31).

In the Federal Republic of Germany the expressions 'autonomous learner' and 'autonomous learning' have only been in use in the last 30 years, namely in the context of experiments in the area of programmed learning and the introduction and spread of distance education. The expressions presented themselves as characterizations of the special situation of students in these new forms of learning and teaching. However, they have not found a home in our pedagogical language; they are not found in encyclopaedias or teaching manuals either. Even more suspicious is the fact that in those locations in which a corresponding entry might be found, there are usually entries about 'authoritarian' teaching and, in particular detail, 'authority'. This is a significant finding with regard to the subject of this section.

Nor is the term 'autonomous learning' found in pedagogics for higher education or in the pedagogics of adult education, nor can any equivalent be found. Furthermore, 'autopedagogics', 'self-study' and 'working alone' are all terms that were created and used in other contexts. For this reason there have been a series of literal translations from English that have been taken over into the specialized German: 'self-controlled learning', 'self-regulated learning',' self-organized learning' and 'self-determined learning'. This can be seen as a sign of the growing importance of autonomous learning, as well as for an increasing readiness to confront the term.

But what exactly is autonomous learning? It is important to go beyond Moore's definition because autonomous learning means more than 'self-controlled' learning. The descriptor comes from the area of constitutional law, where it means self-government, and it is also used in a philosophical and pedagogical sense. This disproves the hastily formed opinion that autonomous learning is merely a techno-organizational peculiarity of instruction design, in the same way as terms such as 'group', 'partner' or 'single instruction' have each been given a specific meaning in that context. The narrowness of the meaning of the increasingly commonly used term of 'self-controlled learning' may have led to this. But the term 'autonomy' is broad and has depth, because it is anchored in many ways in our philosophical traditions.

In relation to the philosophical dimension of the term, Immanuel Kant should first be mentioned here, for he wanted to liberate people from 'mental immaturity brought on by their own fault' by causing them to 'make use of their understanding without outside help'. For Kant, moralising was of primary importance in education. 'But this cannot prescribe and determine from outside, if it wishes to actuate the moral freedom of the autonomous pupil, but may only awaken and safeguard' (Kant quoted in Böhm, 1994: 365). One of Kant's maxims, which can be directly related to autonomous learning, is 'Those who educate use actions whose aim is to be no longer necessary. Those who are educated must learn to do for themselves what others have previously done for them' (Sommer, 1988: 29).

In relation to the pedagogical dimension, here 'autonomy' means a state of affairs in which a person is no longer the *object* of educational guidance, influences, effects and obligations, but the *subject* of his or her own education. This understanding is not new, and has nothing at all to do with anti-authoritarian education. Pestalozzi characterized it aptly with the aphorism 'Man is a self-created work'. Autonomous learners are therefore not objects but subjects of the learning and teaching process. This makes some traditional and still current conceptions of learning and teaching obsolete. These include, for example, the idea that teachers can achieve their teaching objectives with the students entrusted to them by giving, imparting or teaching them something which they then absorb and retain; or the conviction that on the whole they, the teachers, are the originators, initiators and masters of processes, a conviction that throughout the history of instruction, from its archaic beginnings right through to the present time, has been expressed through autocratic behaviour and even physical violence.

Put more exactly, and with the help of pedagogical categories, learners are always autonomous when they themselves take over and exercise the functions of teachers – in other words, when they themselves recognize their learning needs, formulate learning objectives, select contents, draw up learning strategies, procure teaching materials and media, identify additional human and physical resources and make use of them, and themselves organize, control, inspect and evaluate their learning.

This is certainly a demanding task. Some people may even be intimidated by it and others think that autonomous learning is quite simply an excessive demand. The whole thing is in fact much more difficult. Those who wish to plan and control their own learning must in principle be capable of '*meta-cognition*', because learners not only have to develop and transform cognitive structures, and change surface structures into depth structures (Lenzen, 1976: 15), but also simultaneously *reflect* on this process.

Here we can see the psychological dimension of autonomous learning. Educational psychologists define it differently from educators and pedagogicians. According to Zimmerman (1989: 1–26), learners cannot, for example, be called autonomous until they are 'meta-cognitively, motivationally and behaviorally' active participants in their own learning processes. The defining characteristic of meta-cognition presupposes special intellectual skills: learners must be able to stand back and keep their distance from their own actions, and to accompany them with 'critical contemplation' (Frey 1995: 29).

In this book the *pedagogical* definition of autonomous learning will be used. This makes clear what the term is about and at the same time indicates the direction to be taken by any efforts at reform. However, because it explains the process of autonomous learning from an extreme position, and therefore sets it up as an absolute, it will have to be relativized and interpreted beforehand.

Simply from the logical perspective, the autonomy of learners presupposes their heteronomy; there is a relationship between the two. From the point of view of development psychology, the process of the formation of personality is seen anyway as a dialectical process between self-organization and the influences of the physical and social environment, between emancipation and bonding. The process of autonomous learning that is embedded in this is in principle subjected to the same interplay. 'Unadulterated' autonomous learning is not possible anyway; the autonomous learner is in no way an 'intellectual Robinson Crusoe' (Moore, 1972: 81). Learning is, rather, a continual process of coming to terms with the circumstances of the environment, as current structuralist positions show us with new urgency. This dialectical process can without doubt lead to different degrees and shapes of autonomous learning.

It is true to say that autonomous learning in this sense does not yet play a determining role in distance education – so long as we disregard the pioneering role of the Empire State College in Saratoga Springs, New York State, USA, where, with the help of 'contract learning', a viable concept of autonomous learning has been practised for more than 20 years now. The after-effects of the traditional model of monological presentation and the reactive absorption of knowledge are generally still being felt in the traditional universities, and this model has a great effect on university teaching. This means that teachers are more prepared to develop printed distance-education courses with great commitment, and in this way to build up and diversify the range of teaching, than to stand up for autonomous learning. These media strengthen their habitual method of presentation; autonomous learning, on the other hand, forces them to a great extent to abandon their method, for it does not conform to their conception of academic teaching, and for many teachers it has the impression of being something strange, if not exotic. In addition, in their opinion students have not (yet) been sufficiently prepared for such a radically new approach, which is likely therefore to lead to the students' failure. People tend to keep their distance from this form of academic teaching and this is to be regretted, because if we analyse the corresponding findings of educational theoreticians and the relevant state of discussions at meetings and conferences, we quite soon arrive at results which place autonomous learning in a bright light.

In relation to performing further developmental work on the subject, it must be borne in mind that the concept of autonomous learning is not something that has been 'pulled out of a hat', nor is it an *idée fixe* of notorious reformers. On the contrary, it has been familiar for some time in both the theory and the practice of learning and teaching. In contrast, traditional expository teaching processes are in many ways already obsolete with regard to the new demands of educating students, relating as they do to an earlier stage in society and being nowadays extremely unsuitable. In traditional universities, this applies above all with regard to lectures, and in distance-teaching universities to the way in which distance-education courses are prepared down to the very last detail. Autonomous learning appears, in contrast, to conform to modern trends and to be oriented towards the future.

To justify the concept of autonomous learning more exactly and to prove its importance, we can point to the following situations: its origins in the tradition of Jewish learning; its importance at an early stage in German and American reform pedagogics; its theoretical incorporation in general pedagogics; its high rank in adult education; its growing importance in vocational training and further training; and the relevant findings of educational psychological research. If the concept of autonomous learning is in fact essential to the pedagogical structure of distance education, it will have to be explained, specified and justified still further in these pages.

3.3.2 First concepts in the Jewish tradition

Individual learning has always been regarded as extremely important by Jews, and Kurt Graff (1980) pointed this out in his book *Die jüdische Tradition und das Konzept des autonomen Lernen*: 'Reading books is the basic qualification for all traditional Jewish teachers'. The expression 'he can learn' means nothing more than 'he has learnt to manage and understand texts' (Graff, 1980: 153). As far back as the *Sayings of the Fathers*, indications of autonomous learning may be found, according to which there are four different types:

1. learning from books;
2. learning out loud (loud reading, repeating by rote);
3. learning with understanding; and
4. learning in the peace of the spirit.

This is probably the oldest approach to a pedagogic system for autonomous learning that exists. It should be noted here that learning is not shown from the perspective of the teacher but from that of the learner.

3.3.3 Impetus from reform pedagogics

What has been referred to as autonomous learning is nothing new in German and American pedagogics; on the contrary, it has been a central topic of reform pedagogics since the beginning of this century. Countless concepts for independent learning were developed and tested in this context. Their most influential protagonists in Germany were Hugo Gaudig and Otto Scheibner.

   Gaudig (1922: 33) strove for the 'independence' and 'automatic activity' of learners, stating: 'Free mental activity is action under one's own steam, with one's own power, in self-chosen paths, toward freely selected objectives.' And to make the radical change of focal points in the learning and teaching process even more clear, he wrote (1923: 1): 'The highest peak is not reached when the teacher's technique is that of a virtuoso, but when the student comes into the secure possession of a technique for intellectual work.'

   As an advocate of the 'activity school' movement, Scheibner (1962: 25 and 36) interpreted independent learning as a working process in the course of which the student has the following tasks:

1. Set a working objective or absorb and record a set task in his will.
2. Look for, provide, and check the usability of working material; select and organize it.
3. Draft the working path as a plan and draw up the work steps.
4. Carry out the work steps and work sections as independent but related steps and sections, and keep them connected to one another.
5. Record, inspect, test, judge, secure, arrange and evaluate the results.

This development to a form of learning that puts itself beyond the reach of the continual influence of the teacher and promotes the independence of learners can be found in the same period in both Italy and the USA. Names such as Maria Montessori, Frederic Burke, Carlton W Washburne and Clinton Morrison represent corresponding projects.

3.3.4 Impetus from the theory of pedagogics

The concept of autonomous learning conforms in many of its characteristics to tradition and the educational objectives currently under discussion. Thus it has a strong pedagogic component. In classical theories of education, education as empowerment to rational self-determination is an important deciding factor, which has had an effect up to the present day. Wolfgang Klafki (1986: 548) has described it with terms such as 'self-determination', 'liberty', 'emancipation', 'autonomy', 'adultness', 'reason' and 'self-action'. Here he sees self-action as the 'central form of performance in the educational process'.

3.3.5 Impetus from adult education

In German adult education and further training, *self-determination* is held to be the ultimate objective. To characterize the self-determination of a student's own learning, learning by adults is separated from learning in schools and universities. The voluntary nature of learning is always stressed as an important criterion. *Didactic self-selection* is a typical theme. According to Franz Pöggeler (1974: 36), the criterion of voluntariness should 'not be abandoned because of pressure for achievement from society'. In his catalogue of characteristics of adult education, characteristic number 9 states: 'Adults must have the opportunity of selecting the contents, forms and institutions for their further training independently and critically. Those taking part should be adequately advised and informed of the learning objectives of the courses they have selected. They should be given the opportunity to participate in decision-making concerning the choice of methods.' And under number 10 he states expressly: 'Responsible adults take part in their continuing education in full responsibility and bear the risk of the success of the relevant educational process.' Finally, autonomy and independence also play an important part with regard to learning one's own identity.

The origins of the concept of autonomous learning in US adult education have already been referred to. This concept has a firm place in educational thought in the USA, and its genesis is significant for distance education. Seemingly as a consequence of the greater emphasis put on the individual, the person who sets himself learning objectives of his own free will and pursues and achieves them in his own way plays a much more important role in the American psyche than in the German. This idea forms part of America's traditional cultural concept of the self: 'The concept of self-reliance is deeply embedded in our nation's history' claim the psychologists Berry J Zimmerman and Dale H Schunk (1989: XII), and they add with regard to the example of the USA's greatest autonomous learner, Benjamin Franklin:

'Self-regulation empowered individuals with limited formal educational and mea-gre material resources to succeed in America in a scale unattainable elsewhere.' Franklin did actually start as a poor printer's apprentice and developed through au-tonomous learning into a famous politician, author and scientist. The reference to his meagre resources lets us see the social-reform aspect of this concept. It is embed-ded in the myth of the *self-made man*, and that is why it has ideological overtones. The opportunities for autonomous, self-controlled learning were also shown by the well known adult educationalist Cyril O Houle (1984) in his study *Patterns of Learning* by means of impressive case studies from the history of the learning process for certain famous persons.

In passing, the extent should be noted to which the concept of autonomous learning affects even official US education policy. It can be seen from the following guideline issued by John W Gardner, a former US Secretary of Health, Education and Welfare: 'The ultimate goal of the educational system is to shift to the individual the burden of pursuing his own education' (Zimmerman and Schunk 1989, V). Seen from this attitude, it is understandable why the universities in that country place so much value on 'independent learning' (Wedemeyer 1981, XX). In the spe-cialist departments of continuing education in most universities, there are sections responsible for this special type of learning, which includes distance education.

3.3.6 Impetus from the field of vocational education

In recent years, the concept of autonomous learning has even appeared in the pedagogics of vocational learning. According to Rolf Arnold (1995: 295), consider-able changes have taken place in the pedagogics of *vocational learning*. According to him, there is a change taking place at present 'from the culture of teaching to the cul-ture of learning'. The phase in which professional knowledge was imparted almost exclusively orally (through lectures or training courses) is being replaced by a phase which is characterized by learning forms such as *self-controlled learning* and *pro-ject-orientation*. He quotes in this context Ch-K Friede (1988: 6), who understood learning as an action whose execution is 'consciously controlled, regulated and ac-companied by self-instruction and self-description' and is concluded by 'self-control and self-corroboration'.

3.3.7 Impetus from learning research

Empirical *learning research* has taken up autonomous learning for some time now un-der the nomenclature of 'self-controlled learning' (Friedrich and Mandel, 1995) and 'self-regulated learning' (Zimmerman and Schunk, 1989). In their work, au-tonomous learning has been seen as a component of a typical human characteristic, namely the desire to understand and control oneself (Zimmerman and Schunk 1989, IX), which has always fascinated mankind. This desire expresses itself in part in learning and the success of learning. Educational psychologists have examined (and are examining) how learners adapt cognitively, motivationally and behaviourally to autonomous learning, and they have developed highly differentiated educational psychology theories on this, discussing the individual preconditions for autonomous learning and describing how it can best be practised. Their research is even claimed to be especially urgent because traditional forms of learning and teaching – above all in vocational further training – are recognized to be no longer adequate. Helmut Felix Friedrich (1996: 42) has assessed the current situation as follows:

> Whereas the debates [on self-controlled learning] 10 to 15 years ago were to a great extent inter-disciplinary discussions in which educational scientists and psychologists announced: 'you may use self-controlled learning,' today they say: 'you *must* use self-controlled learning.'

3.3.8 Summary

As the examples given above confirm, the concept of autonomous learning is in no way a particularly original construction, inconsistent with traditional forms of academic teaching. In fact, the demand for it to be applied is pedagogically legitimate. A difficult situation arises for distance-teaching pedagogics from the positions referred to here and from current practice, because there is a great divide between theoretical claims and practical implementation. If those practising autonomous learning want merely to keep in step with theoretical developments, the question must be raised as to why autonomous learning is so little used in regular distance education, although it conforms as no other way of learning does to the declared educational objectives, it plays an important role in both American and German adult and continuing education, it is becoming increasingly important in vocational further training, it is even said to determine school lessons for children and teenagers, and it is regarded by educational psychological researchers as particularly relevant and – in the face of the challenges facing industry and society today – particularly important.

The distance-teaching universities and open universities founded in the 1970s and 1980s were, and still are today, under pressure from the traditions of conventional universities, where expository teaching (in both spoken and printed form) and receptive learning dominate, where course content is prescribed, and where enclosed learning situations are the norm. Some have since been taken over by distance-teaching universities where they have been supported and strengthened in a framework of the development of distance-education courses by more or less behaviourist positions. At the same time, humanistic psychology gained ground in the 1970s and introduced the concepts of 'self-realization' (E Fromm, K Horney) and 'self-actualization' (K Goldstein, A Maslow). Furthermore, Carl Rogers transferred the principles of client-related conversation therapy to learning. As a result of this thinking, teachers were no longer in the foreground, but learners; the passive receptivity of learners changed to positive activity; the enclosed teaching situation became an open one; and relationships between teachers and learners, which had tended to be authoritarian, became partnerships. Learning and teaching formats such as *autonomous group discussions, project work* and *learning-by-doing* were held to be suitable results of this change of approach.

Both directions are of course in a tense relationship with one another, and in these circumstances distance-teaching pedagogics must develop productively in its own right.

Chapter 4

The three concepts in practice

4.1 Dialogical learning

How is the concept of dialogical learning used in distance-teaching universities? It is in fact used everywhere in the same way with the standard methods, but there are remarkable differences with regard to the degree of application and the amount of time and effort spent. These differences can probably be explained primarily by the divergent cultures for academic learning and teaching, but also by the different conceptions of what constitutes good university teaching, and by the extent of available resources. On the whole, different effects arising from the following forms of dialogical learning can be found.

4.1.1 Dialogue during course counselling

Distance universities, for whom counselling for their distance students is important, make efforts to offer them a continuous dialogue with the university by assigning them to a *course counsellor* who is available to help them personally throughout their studies. The Open University in Great Britain, the Universidad Estatal a Distancia in Costa Rica, and the Universidad National Abierta in Venezuela, to name just three, all work on this principle. The dialogue between course counsellors and their distance students is made easier if a friendly or even confidential relationship is built up over the years. Dialogues take place at agreed locations, and by phone or in writing.

This type of study counselling provides students with the feeling that they have a contact partner at all times, and in particular in critical situations. The dialogue, which may continue over many years, is important for the integration of distance students into a university that does not actually exist in concrete form, ie that is not campus-based, because such a dialogue provides its students with continuity, stability, focus and reality. The *continuity of concern*, which David Sewart (1978) continually called for from distance-teaching universities as a natural attitude towards their students, finds its most convincing expression here.

But even without this 'ideal solution' it may be regarded as progress if there are any course counsellors at all available in worthwhile numbers, even if they change from meeting to meeting. The degree of importance that a distance-teaching university attaches to dialogue involving these course counsellors and the degree to which it actually takes place can also be seen by the numbers of these course counsellors employed on a full or part-time basis, and by how many students are assigned to each counsellor.

What are the usual subjects discussed in counselling? At the Netherlands Open Universiteit these are above all questions of vocational orientation, enrolment in distance-education courses and financial problems. At the UK's Open University, students are motivated for their studies: the contents of the student's course are discussed (including future employment opportunities), general study problems are analysed, students are encouraged to come to informal meetings or group discussions, strategies are drawn up for preparing for examinations, advice is given on the choice of a summer school, students in danger of dropping out are counselled, and personal and social needs are also discussed, including those concerning the family. In order to provide these discussions with a solid and reliable foundation, student counsellors are provided with a computer printout showing the student's achievements up to the meeting. With the help of the printout, counsellors can diagnose a student's strengths and weaknesses and the counselling session can be adapted accordingly. Counselling can be relatively intensive because each counsellor is assigned only 35 students.

The FernUniversität does not have any comparable system of course counselling through suitably trained specialists. The relevant tasks are carried out by mentors employed on a part-time basis, who mainly exercise tutorial functions with regard to teaching. This means that it is impossible to develop relevant competences and increasing experience of people specially prepared for their profession, who should of course really be trained for their job. In addition, counselling takes place only at the student's request. And, even when it does occur, it cannot be based on knowledge of a student's files because the strict provisions of Germany's Data Protection Act mean that they are not accessible.

The question of whether a dialogue with distance students on matters that do not relate directly to teaching is really necessary is answered in the negative by university teachers in some faculties because they are interested primarily in the presentation of course contents. Even teachers at the UK's *Open University* were originally of the same opinion (Perry, 1976: 113). However, pedagogically trained persons and adult-education experts advance reasons for bearing in mind the *complete life situation* of distance students, showing interest in it and taking account of it during teaching. Older students find themselves at a structurally different starting position from that of young adults in a 'regular' course at a traditional university. For this reason it might be expected that there is a considerably greater demand for counselling for a greater number of students. Distance-teaching pedagogics could in fact profit from it if it oriented itself towards some relevant principles of adult-education pedagogics (see Siebert, 1996) – for example, reference to the world in which the students are living, learner orientation, references to their patterns of interpretation, and their emotional state at various times. Because these principles hardly come into play at all in self-instructing study materials, it would certainly be advantageous to the students – and some form of compensation for lack of contact – if they were at least taken into consideration in counselling situations.

4.1.2 Dialogue in study centres

The next group of partners in spoken dialogues are the tutors, available to students for consultation in study centres although the extent of their availability varies greatly. In general there are 30 students for each tutor. Bernadette Robinson (1995: 224), who has many years of experience in distance education in countries all over the world, also reports on institutions in which the ratio between tutors and students varies between 1:3 and 1:300. These differences quite naturally have an effect on the frequency and quality of the dialogues that arise.

Dialogues between tutors and students refer to the contents of the courses that the students are working through and therefore differ greatly depending on the department, subject and course year. In most reports on distance-teaching universities, there is almost a stereotypical reason given, namely that talks with tutors are held to help 'to overcome study problems' (eg Reddy, 1988: 101). Of course, this is in fact an important aspect but, as we have said, it would be regrettable if the dialogue between tutors and students did not extend beyond this.

Dialogical learning should cover much more than extra instruction and learning training. It should really help students to strengthen the cognitive structures that have been developed with the help of the course materials, to differentiate them, to let them appear in a different light, and to change them. This can happen, for example, by discussing methodical and methodological questions, treating aspects of scientific theory, imparting difficult interpretation patterns, tracing the historical dimensions of what has been learnt, and opening up perspectives. The level of the discussion is raised through this, and the gains for students for their own studies are increased.

The *forms* of dialogue vary as well. Students may be tutored in groups or singly. Tutors often impart regular instruction, give brief lectures, chair seminars or moderate discussions. Often there are personal discussions by special arrangement, or informal talks can take place at special academic open days. If there are favourable conditions in the social environment, eg in Britain, meetings may also take place in private in the tutor's home. These dialogues may also be supplemented by occasional telephone calls, and telephone conference tutorials can take place for several students at the same time.

Another form of dialogue – one that students frequently do not perceive, but which is still important – is the exchange of ideas and experiences with other students in breaks, on buses, etc, or at informal meetings.

In the summer semester of 1992 at the FernUniversität, nearly 73 per cent of the active students took part in counselling with a mentor at least once, and the rate for women students was at least ten per cent higher. Around 80 per cent evaluated these talks as 'unreservedly positive' or 'on the whole positive'. However – and this is important in the context to be shown here – longer discussions tended to be seen as problematic because they were 'relatively frequently regarded as a waste of time' (von Prümmer and Rossié, 1994: 33). It can be seen here just how much students are used to expository teaching and receptive learning and how little they are aware of the importance of oral discussions for the success of learning, especially in distance education.

The insight into the necessity of direct personal communication appears to have grown in the last few years. Previously it was always denied by the proponents of 'pure' distance education, technology enthusiasts and from some management representatives for cost reasons, or its importance was at least played down. But in a national report on Japanese distance education, one of the main problems was given as the task of 'arranging face-to-face meetings' (Kato, 1992: 373); the University of South Africa sent delegations to the Open Universiteit in the Netherlands and the Open University in the United Kingdom and on the basis of the experience gathered it decided to introduce counsellors and tutors for the first time; and the Open University of Sri Lanka saw a major difficulty in the lack of a dialogue with its students and has made efforts to overcome this (Kato, 1992: 685). However, lack of funds means that this problem is, in general, practically insoluble.

4.1.3 Dialogue in student working groups

Some distance-teaching universities recommend their students to make efforts themselves to enable dialogues by inviting a small number of students in the same area in order to take part in joint discussions of learning and teaching problems, to exchange experiences, and to form fixed working groups or study circles ('*self-help groups*'). These dialogues are informal because students are among their peers – a quality that is often lacking in tutorials and seminars, or only found occasionally in more formal arrangements.

Those taking part are able to speak freely and have an opportunity to say exactly what they think. They can speak about their own difficulties, which often then appear in a completely different light or are even (to an extent at least) resolved. Dialogues of this nature often contribute to self-confirmation and self-knowledge. They motivate, because it is enjoyable to be able to prove oneself in a discussion or to make use of the help of a fellow student. They reduce self-doubt and feelings of inadequacy because participants become aware of the study problems of others and because they are made conscious for the first time in these dialogues of their own competence.

Unfortunately, this form of dialogue is rarely found, mainly because of a lack of time available for it, but also because distance-teaching universities fail to see the pedagogical potential of self-organized working groups. They certainly do not regard them as being as important as they in fact are. It must also be said that the students, who are often described as 'single combatants' and who are frequently single-minded and absorbed by a topic, are not always prepared to take part in such activities. They are not at all clear about the importance of these dialogues for their own academic education, socialization and for the further development of their own person.

In the 1992 summer semester at the FernUniversität, nearly 30 per cent of students took part at least once in a student working group, and 24 per cent of these had attended more than once. Slightly more than 41 per cent assessed their discussions in these groups as 'unreservedly good' (von Prümmer and Rossié, 1994, 91, 93).

The Internet provides new opportunities for these working groups. Students of the Open University in the UK are increasingly contacting each other in this way, and by this means regular 'electronic self-help groups' are being created. According to the experiences reported by Katy Jennison (1997: 85), a call for help seldom remains unanswered. Completely new social relationships are created in this way. Students 'meet' in virtual clubs, associations and bars. Universities should take note of this trend and take it into account in their pedagogic plans. They bring 'life' into the dialogue through stimulating arguments, mutual help and developing friendships.

4.1.4 Dialogue in seminars and practical courses

The most intensive form of dialogical learning takes place in seminars and practical courses that last for either a single day or are sometimes spread over several days. The similarity to corresponding teaching events in traditional universities is apparent here. Professors considerably restrict the reading of papers because they are more concerned with obtaining the impressions of individual participants. This is necessary for the subsequent award of suitable subjects for Masters or degree theses. For this reason, the academic discourse is in the foreground, in which a great number of students take part wherever possible.

Seminars and practical courses are popular in the FernUniversität and are increasingly in demand. It is significant that 65 per cent of active students took part more than once in a seminar or practical course running over several days, but only 19 per cent attended one-day events of this kind (von Prümmer and Rossié, 1994: 29). The number of teachers offering additional seminars of their own accord is on the increase, particularly in the humanities and social sciences.

4.1.5 Dialogue in residential schools

The concept of dialogical learning is at its most intense where students spend five to ten days on campus living and studying together – in other words taking part in obligatory holiday or compact seminars, *summer schools* (Great Britain) or *residential schools* (Australia). Here, crash courses in oral interaction can be made into vehicles of learning and teaching. Unfortunately they rarely form part of the learning and teaching system in distance-teaching universities. The University of New England in the USA, the British Open University and some Correspondence Directorates in India are interesting exceptions.

If distance students come together in this way and take part in academic events, this is, of course, profitable in any case in the context discussed here. But, in addition, the manner in which participants talk and discuss is of considerable pedagogical importance. Should these events take place in exactly the same way as in traditional universities? The tendency is to answer this question with a 'yes' if the respondent attended a traditional university, as this played a significant role in the person's biography and distance 'has lent enchantment to the view' after so many years. The idea is to give distance students what they miss by being students of distance-teaching universities, and what they normally cannot do, namely study at a 'proper' university.

Walter Perry (1976: 117) had this in mind when he suggested in the foundation of the Open University in the UK that summer schools should be introduced. He saw these simply as a 'necessary extra' to give distance students the opportunity to 'taste the flavour of an on-campus situation in contact with many other students'. The University of New England also regards this experience as being important because it makes all external students visit the campus so as 'to enjoy a brief period of traditional university life as a full student in residence' (Keegan, 1986: 203).

Evaluating on-campus academic teaching in this way is understandable. From the point of view of distance-teaching pedagogics, however, we can see that the view contains a negation of the task of developing a form of distance education that may be regarded as a fully equal alternative to traditional forms of studying. Compact seminars or summer schools would then exercise their function primarily as an integral component of the learning and teaching system in distance education and would develop their own pedagogical forms. Dialogues would have to refer to the problems and contexts of the subjects treated there. And one other thing must be remembered: this quality time must not be abused for the presentation of new, systematically arranged knowledge (for example through traditional lectures and papers), but wherever possible it should instead be used for intensive discussions, exchanges of ideas, joint problem-solving, illuminating what students have already learnt from other aspects of their study, critical questioning, reflecting on the value of research results, and applying acquired knowledge. Communication and debate are in the foreground; training in academic dialogue is what is required.

In addition, there is a variety of informal talks that provide a sense of reality for the rather abstract relationships between students and teachers and amongst students themselves in distance education. Seen in this way, in other words with a completely different pedagogic concept from that of teaching at traditional universities, compact seminars and summer schools on a university campus are given their own special meaning – and as such are absolutely essential.

4.1.6 Dialogue with departmental contacts

Dialogues with members of departments or faculties are important for students because these persons are solely and exclusively responsible for teaching and research. To a great extent they can also meet the authors of some study courses or people whose task it is to organise the corrections of assignments or even to mark them, to issue subjects for dissertations for examinations, to hold orals and to mark written examinations. Even if students meet department members from time to time only, this can still be important for them personally and for their studies. Here they can obtain information from the source. They get to know academics who were previously only names to them. Repeated and intensified face-to-face contacts of this nature can even generate the feeling of belonging and of having an 'academic home'. And of course it should not be forgotten that students can also get the feeling of the atmosphere in the departments where research and teaching takes place.

At the FernUniversität there are dialogues between active students and members of departments – mostly the staff members in charge of answering queries, whose names are listed in the handbooks. In special cases, professors and lecturers also take part. These contacts are always the result of initiatives by students, and the dialogues are mainly directed at teaching, tests or examinations. About one-third of students ask about additional book lists, discuss course contents, or put questions on how to work through tasks for sending in to the university. Almost seven out of ten students have taken part in this type of talk at least once a semester, and six from ten have had corresponding contact with the examinations office or the dean of studies. The departments are the most important contact locations for personal contacts (von Prümmer and Rossié, 1994: 16, 17).

These example show how disadvantageous it can be if distance-teaching universities do not set up departments because they are concerned with educational reforms, for example the Open Universiteit of the Netherlands. If this means that there are no dialogues of the type referred to here, an important structural characteristic is missing from the university.

4.1.7 Dialogue on the basis of technical contacts

The final portion of this section is reserved for dialogues between individual students and their tutors or markers that are generated by means of correspondence, telephone calls, fax or e-mail. They are of less importance than face-to-face dialogues. First of all, the pedagogical content of these dialogues is often minimal. For example, letters sent by markers to distance students often contain only the corrected assignment in which the right answers are ticked off and incorrect solutions marked. In many cases, sample answers are used. In addition, the students will be informed of their grade. Telephone calls usually refer to organizational questions and not to questions concerning course content, and the calls must be kept short because of the costs. E-mails are reserved mostly for corresponding with the administration staff and the library. At the same time, in distance education, all new communications media must play a part. They help to overcome students' isolation.

We have seen that written assignments are treated with brevity and the reason for this is probably the workloads of the markers and their lack of time, rather than any indolence or indifference. What is far more serious is the inadequate insight into the importance that the instructional written dialogue can have in distance education. In general, this special form of dialogue is underestimated. Now, if tutor-marked assignments were to be replaced by computer-marked assignments, the limited concept that people have of this task becomes clear. Not only teachers and students but also tutors themselves often have little idea of the intensive and successful effect on the learning process that can be brought about by a continuous dialogue on errors or successful assignments. It may be that this brings back too many memories of school and is therefore not rated very highly. Tutors and markers are often unable to appreciate how discouraging it is for students to have to wait weeks for a written reply. This is the reason why several researchers have dealt with problems of 'delayed and immediate feedback' (Diehl, 1982), the 'turn-around time of assignments' (Reckedahl, 1989), 'tutoring frequency' (Holmberg and Schuemer, 1989), and 'submission density' (Bååth, 1989). These reports were edited by Börje Holmberg (1989b), who in his introduction holds that mediated communication is a 'basic characteristic' of distance education.

Distance students are never more attentive and readier to listen and absorb than when their work is evaluated and commented upon. With their feedback, tutors reach students at the time when they need this information more than ever and can process it more easily than in other situations (Robinson, 1981: 155). This 'fruitful moment' (Copei, 1966) must be used for the written exchange of opinion. Not only can corrections be made and comments made on the work, but the right findings can be acknowledged and recognized, distortions criticized, diffuse arguments given shape, other methods proposed, and above all reasons given for the student's grading. With more academically demanding work, comments and suggestions may refer to the literature used, the scientific approach, the line of argument, and to the other academics who have worked in the field under discussion. But above all, suggestions for further study can be given. Tutors who work in this way are not teaching but promoting and simplifying students' own independent work. In doing this, they carry out demanding pedagogical tasks for which ability, skill, empathy and experience are required. However, the actual significance of these written dialogues lies in the interaction of an individual student with an individual teacher, in other words in the *individualization* of distance education.

Written dialogues of this type should not be mistaken for *anonymous* or *variable* tutoring, which is what happens when an army of markers deals with assignments in the sequence in which they are received. As with course counsellors, it can certainly be an advantage if students gradually get to know, through these written dialogues, the correspondence partners who mark their assignments and are thus better able to adapt themselves in time to their way of teaching through writing. This is why it is an advantage if the same tutors who participate in oral dialogues in the study centres also take over the task of written-study counselling and the marking of assignments, as, for example, in the Universidad National De Education a Distancia in Spain or the Open University in the UK. By visiting study centres, students can get to know the tutors personally and continue the written dialogue face to face. In the reverse case, it is also better for those marking assignments if they know their correspondence partners.

When distance-teaching universities were conceived, a mistake was made with regard to supplementary written dialogues because these were seen more as burdensome obligations in the context of marking assignments – something that is on the periphery of the learning and teaching process. More expense, more personnel, more professional attention to individual students, and above all systematic training for markers, would probably have an effect on study success and on the satisfaction of students. While it is possible to fight for and acquire millions for additional technical equipment for a distance-teaching university, it appears to be hopeless from the very start to obtain additional funds for strengthening the written dialogue. There is a lack of insight into its pedagogical value. The written dialogue carried on through the years can without doubt be regarded as the heart of learning and teaching in distance education.

Telephone dialogues between teachers and students often take place because the telephone is easily accessible and user-friendly. On the other hand, the problem here is the availability of people to talk to in the university. For this reason, several distance-teaching universities have established regular telephone 'surgeries'. However, longer and more detailed telephone calls are often prohibitive because of the cost, and for this reason the Athabasca University in Canada pays for surgery calls itself, which also shows the high value the university places on this form of dialogue.

The telephone is very popular at the FernUniversität. Just over 85 per cent would like to use it for communicating with the university, and in the summer semester of 1992 nine out ten students in fact did this at least once. It must be said that these figures included calls concerning organizational and administrative questions. University teachers themselves are usually called in urgent cases only, for example where the construction of a degree thesis remains unsatisfactory in spite of many changes that have been discussed, where an important book is unavailable, or where reservations arise with regard to an imminent oral examination, and these situations are often pedagogically significant. Calls to teachers only in such significant circumstances should prevent the teachers from keeping callers at bay by being laconic or showing a lack of courtesy, which can occur as a result of time pressures and/or work overloads but which is destructive because of its discouraging effect.

Individual telephone conversations between teachers and students are common in the UK's Open University as well. This form of dialogue is appreciated there because participants hear the *real voices of real people*, and the way can be paved for personal relationships. This is also seen as another way in which the mainly impersonal learning can be humanized (Robinson, 1993: 195). This is why students are given their tutor's home telephone number and encouraged to call if they need help. On the other hand, tutors themselves phone students if they do not come to the study centres or if their assignments need to be discussed. The university pays the telephone charges for disabled distance students.

Fax communication changes the dialogue in that the written word is transmitted. Because teachers are not always available and answering machines are for brief messages only, this new medium is becoming more and more popular. The written form forces users to be precise and brief and to consider what they want to say, which thereby creates a new form of dialogue on another communicative level. It can also have pedagogical advantages, especially as illustrations, drawings, photographs, graphs, tables, etc can also be faxed.

In the FernUniversität, fax was used considerably as early as 1992, when just over 30 per cent of those questioned said they had 'a lot' of experience with faxes, and a further 29 per cent had at least 'some' experience. Of those questioned who had had experience using faxes for communication, 48 per cent assessed them as 'highly effective' and a further 43 per cent as 'useful'. Faxes are increasingly being used, and are viewed by students more favourably than telephones with answering machines (von Prümmer and Rossié, 1994: 99).

The use of e-mail is also increasing considerably nowadays. In the early 1990s, of the active students with experience of this medium as many as 39 per cent described e-mail as 'highly effective' for distance education and 50 per cent as 'useful' (von Prümmer and Rossié, 1994: 99). Those percentages have probably increased by now.

In Chapter 6 we will be looking at dialogical learning through another mechanism, namely that of *teleconferencing*.

4.1.8 Interpretation

If we take another look at the ways shown here in which dialogues in distance education are facilitated, there is a temptation to be both pleasantly surprised at the extent to which the FernUniversität makes use of them. The high value placed by students on communication with departments, participation in tutorial counselling, and above all student working groups is completely unexpected. Such assessments provide a totally different image of distance education to the one shown in previous experience.

However, this positive image must be modified. The reason for it is that only *active* students were questioned. Active students are those who are duly enrolled, are aiming for a degree, take part in study counselling with their mentors, and send in their assignments on schedule. If the great number of students in further education were to be used as a basis, and the large number of more or less inactive enrolled students was included, the assessment values would naturally fall to considerably below these levels. But even the statistics shown here on active students are not proof that dialogical learning forms a large proportion of distance education at the FernUniversität. The usual case is that distance-teaching universities provide little opportunity for this type of learning because of a lack of personnel, tight monetary control and time constraints. Dialogical learning – *face to face* – makes up only a small part of the learning and teaching in the FernUniversität, and this is in fact characteristic of all the larger distance-teaching universities.

Uncritical proponents of the idea of distance education sometimes tend to gloss over these circumstances because they assume that distance students decide on this form of studying because they like working alone. Their mental structure, so the argument goes, makes them prefer working with books to working with teachers and fellow students. This claim has become something of a cliché in discussions in the past. It may be that it hides an unconscious justification of the real but unsatisfactory status quo of distance education.

In their extensive study *Kommunikation im Fernstudium*, Christine von Prümmer and Ute Rossié (1994: 4) discovered a completely different situation. According to their findings, the great majority (93.8 per cent) of distance students would like personal discussions. This conclusion should make those working on the evaluation and optimization of the learning and teaching system for distance education think seriously about their approach. If concepts were *participant-oriented*, as the pedagogics of adult education suggests, this desire for more personal discussions would have to be given more consideration. Von Prümmer (1995: 294) argues that students would be more motivated and more successful if a high degree of congruity could be achieved in learning and teaching between actual and preferred forms of communication.

In fact, there is a considerable difference. Only 12 per cent of those questioned had taken part in a personal discussion with the FernUniversität on at least five occasions, another 51 per cent between one and four times, and 31 per cent never. What is actually new in this study is not the proof of just how little opportunity there is in distance education for dialogical learning, or how little this is used, for that has been known for some time to be a structural characteristic of distance education. What is really surprising is the extent to which students *want* it, and women much more than men.

4.1.9 Summary

Realization of these insights and findings in most distance-teaching universities leaves a great deal to be desired, for the reasons given. In general, great efforts must be made to provide for dialogical teaching forms on a larger scale, for teaching organiszers to pay more attention to them, and for the work of tutors, mentors and counsellors to be intensified.

This means that both teachers and students will have to rethink. They will have to be convinced of the importance of the dialogue in academic teaching in general and in distance education in particular. They will have to abandon the idea of seeing learning and teaching as an almost insurmountable *quantitative* task, and to concentrate instead on the *qualitative* aspects of the learning and teaching process. Distance students will have to keep an eye on the development of their own cognitive structures, on the development and differentiation of their own academic way of thinking, on reflections on their thoughts, and at the same time make efforts to acquire appropriate social competence. The task of distance-teaching universities here is to supplement the mass dissemination of objectivized instruction with the help of self-instructing study materials through the cultivation of individual learning processes, and in this way to differentiate on a person-related basis.

All this will not be possible without increased allocation of funds for more full-time staff for student counselling. In any case, the increased importance of dialogue in distance education must be reflected in the distribution of existing financing in the budgets of distance-teaching universities.

In the face of past experience, the model of a *mixed-mode university* is gaining in interest as a concept of the university of the future because here the proportion of dialogical learning required for distance education and in digital studies can be best organized and secured in the long run.

4.2 Structured learning

In distance-teaching universities, courses are developed that lay down study paths more or less exactly. With the help of such courses, students can familiarize themselves step by step with the presented material by using the given method. This means that courses have to be planned, developed and, where possible, tested as well. They present not only the course contents but also a great number of pedagogical implications. Both of these together provide a structure for students to learn in.

Why is this done? Why aren't subjects simply indicated and general tips provided for working through them, especially as students would have much more freedom for independent learning with this type of method? US universities work mainly along these lines, whereas European distance-teaching universities structure learning more, the reason behind the latter probably being the desire to help students with the difficult business of 'self-teaching'. It may also be that teachers who teach at a distance are concerned with the success of their own work – perhaps they attach great importance to what they say being understood exactly as it is meant. Whatever the reason, most distance-teaching universities do in fact offer heavily structured courses. In this chapter it will be shown *why* this is and *how far* structuring goes. In explanation, the teaching methods from the early years of distance education and the development procedures from the foundation years of the great distance-teaching universities will be called upon.

4.2.1 Structural roots

A brief review shows how simple today's differentiated and increasingly complex structures of learning and teaching programmes were in the beginning. There were only two characteristic forms of these programmes, namely *self-teaching* and *correspondence courses*.

Self-teaching

This does not mean free learning by autodidacts but systematic self-instruction on the basis of prepared and printed materials. As an example we can look at the courses offered in Germany from 1856 onwards by Charles Toussaint and Gustav Langenscheidt. The aim of these courses was to enable written language instruction for self-teaching for adults in the languages taught in the *gymnasien*. In many ways they corresponded to the texts used in standard textbooks, above all in the parts dealing with grammar. The contents were at least divided up into modules. And students were, just as in standard textbooks, provided with self-checking exercises, where the solutions to the exercises were provided in the course material so that students could check their own work.

Correspondence courses

According to tradition, in the 1830s a shorthand teacher in England started to send brief lessons and exercises to students *on postcards* to provide instruction; and the students replied by letter or similarly by postcard. Structurally, this is a completely different model, because the basis of instruction here is the *written dialogue* between teacher and student.

In Germany, this form of instruction was found in its purest form in the distance teaching used by the National Association of Christian Trade Unions, which was distributed from Königswinter from 1930. 'Its special feature was that it was completely individual. It was in fact "individual correspondence instruction in the narrowest sense and without example". The "leader" of the distance teaching actually corresponded directly with each individual student, and this correspondence was the sole material basis of instruction' (Delling, 1985: 20). Furthermore, the leader was responsible for diagnosing the individual interests of students and for formulating corresponding assignments.

The integration of both forms of teaching

A precise example of the integration of both these forms of teaching is the Rustinsche Lerninstitut für brieflichen Unterricht, whose main task is instructing students taking the *abitur*, the higher secondary school-leaving certificate in Germany. Its teaching modules were all structured in accordance with the specially developed *Rustin method* that actually combined *self-teaching* and *correspondence instruction*, and in fact was patented because of its special features.

Students first of all had to deal with the teaching material themselves (study course), then read a dialogue, and reflect on it, that contained the teacher's questions and the pupil's answers. Thirdly, there was a summary of the material; fourthly the material was repeated through questions; and, fifthly, by means of questions and answers there was a lead-in to the material in the next module. Sixthly and finally, every module contained assignments the answers to which were sent in and marked by teachers.

These six forms of pedagogical presentation were characteristically used in a consistent and systematic fashion in all the teaching modules. All sections were broken down into subsections and printed in columns so that the paragraphs formed small blocks, and in addition each had a number in square brackets that simplified finding certain sections in the overall course and made cross-referencing easier. Stressed words were printed spaced out, and formulas for learning were offset as marginal notes.

Pedagogical structural features

If these three typical historical models are analysed, a number of important pedagogical structural features come to light immediately. The aim of the features is to facilitate, simplify and support learning without the presence of a teacher, as shown in Table 4.1.

Table 4.1 shows that in the beginnings of distance education a considerable number of pedagogically effective factors were already included in a text to make the presentation of the contents into a *teaching* text. Taken together, the pedagogically effective factors shown – and others could be included as well – already show a relatively complex structure.

Table 4.1 *Structural elements of early distance education*

Presentation medium:	Printed material
Distribution medium:	Post
Pedagogically effective factors:	Dosing
	Portioning
	Sequencing
	Scheduling
	Simulated dialogue
	Summarizing
	Questions for repetition
	Questions for training
	Self-tests
	Written individual instruction
	Correction of written assignments
	Serial numbering of all chapters to make access easier
	Cross-references
	Marginal notes
	Emphasizing by spaced printing
Pedagogical principles:	References to addressees
	Individualization

4.2.2 Present-day structuring of learning and teaching programmes

Structured learning and teaching programmes in printed form have now become the most prominent and characteristic feature of distance education at many distance-teaching universities. They have achieved central importance in such institutions because they replace the traditional teaching functions by initiating, controlling, accompanying and evaluating the corresponding learning processes in students. In this way they have become the heart of the learning and teaching system in university distance education.

If we look closer at the structure of these learning and teaching programmes, those 15 pedagogically effective factors immediately come to mind that were characteristic of early distance education. They were taken over and integrated by distance-teaching universities and their application has long become routine.

In fact, this is rather a surprising process. When the large distance-teaching universities were founded in the 1970s, techniques were taken over that stemmed from the field of learning and teaching in secondary education and were derived from school-based learning. Would it not have been better to have developed instead learning and teaching techniques that had an affinity to academic teaching forms? This was probably not done because distance teaching for European universities was virgin territory, whereas distance instruction in general had over 120 years of tradition behind it and the experience gained in those years was readily available for reuse.

Because those 15 structural elements were taken over for reuse, the question arises whether we can speak of the pedagogical continuity of distance education and distance studies. This can be answered in part in the affirmative, but to an even greater extent in the negative. The establishment of the distance-teaching universities meant the creation of a type of distance education that differed from all other previous types of distance instruction in important points. The structural change was based on the combination of *distance-education tradition* and *educational technology*. It went deep and initiated a new era of distance education, which has now been labelled '*first-generation distance education*'.

Because of this combination, the structure of the learning and teaching programmes looks quite different. They have been developed, worked out in detail, standardized, optimized and perfected with an effort never before experienced. In this way, the concentration of pedagogical strategies, and therefore the density of learning and teaching programmes in distance education, has without doubt reached a peak. It is instructive to remind ourselves how this happened.

When in the 1970s and 1980s the large distance-teaching universities, under the influence of then successful educational technology, began to teach by using that technology, something unheard-of happened. There had never before been a comparable event in the history of higher education, if we disregard the changes to teaching brought about by the invention of printing. With the development of structured learning and teaching programmes for distance education, the traditions of academic teaching were broken. This process is all the more remarkable as these traditions had been carefully maintained and had resisted many efforts at reform.

The distance-education courses referred to here have in contrast turned into the crystallization points of several innovations: the optimistic and confident use of *technical media*, the deliberate use of findings from *teaching research*, the routine use of *empirical processes of development and control*, and bundling the knowledge and skills of several *specialist experts*. Academic teaching was severely technicized, made more scientific in its communication forms, and turned into a product of cooperation based on the division of labour. Only when we bring to mind how much these innovations support and improve each other does it become clear just how radical the turning away from traditional forms of academic learning and teaching has become.

We have become witnesses of a great development and modernization thrust that has substantially changed the conception of university pedagogics, and this is something we should be aware of no matter how we assess the changes. The thrust of change should have created a great stir among the guardians of traditional academic teaching and led to protests, but there were only a few critics and they had no voice worthy of mention. This almost revolutionary change to teaching is pushed in the centre of our observations because self-contained prefabricated distance-education courses represent the most extreme form of structured learning and teaching that can be encountered in practical distance education.

Course development in the UK's Open University through course teams

Just how far the structured distance-education course could become a product of rational planning, systematic development, empirical testing and continuous assessment in the sense of educational technology can best be demonstrated through the example of the UK's Open University because the new development that was initiated in the 1970s proceeded to plan and in fact went furthest of all similar institutions.

Following the *zeitgeist* of the times, members of the Planning Committee of the Open University insisted that full-time educational technologists be employed. They argued that a number of problems had to be solved that were alien to traditional academic teaching and therefore could not be managed by university teachers alone: specialized course development, programmed learning, developing and using teaching programmes for television and radio, taking the special learning requirements and the special learning behaviour of adults into consideration, and assessing the learning performance of large groups of students (Perry, 1976: 77). In addition, continuous assessment of the *Open University system*, in other words institutional research, was demanded, which is a problem that has never even been considered at a university, let alone taken up or solved. None of these tasks could have been solved with pedagogically effective factors taken over from the nineteenth century.

The Open University then actually initiated educational technologies. To provide its work with the required institutional support, the Institute of Educational Technology was founded under the leadership of Professor David Hawkridge. The most important task of this institute is to advise and support university teachers in developing distance-teaching courses. The seriousness with which the Open University regarded this task when it was founded can be seen in how the solution of these problems was institutionally enabled and assured. Course teams were set up and given the status of senate committees. They are particularly important because they show a pragmatic way out of a dilemma. This dilemma is either to decide consistently between tradition and what is technologically possible, between communication and rational action, or (and this is without doubt much more difficult) to combine both. The concept of course teams at the Open University was to facilitate an integrated solution.

Because the course team stipulates the structure of the distance-teaching course that is to be completed beforehand, and is also responsible for a great number of elements and differentiations, we will take a brief look at its work here. At the Open University, distance-teaching courses are not, as in many other distance-education institutions, written by individual university teachers, but are developed *jointly* by a group of university teachers and other experts on a division-of-work basis. Each course team is led by a *chairperson* who is responsible, as a university teacher, for the scientific and pedagogic quality of that part of the course content. Otherwise this person has few formal competences regarding the development of the course, but makes his or her mark through the successful leadership of the team's work.

The course team also includes the *authors* of the individual course units. These may be members of the staff of the Open University or another university. They have contact with students by taking part in the Open University's summer schools. Some also have experience as part-time tutors in study centres. The task of these authors consists of making critical assessments of the respective teaching texts while they are being written, providing advice, and where possible guaranteeing the inter-disciplinary nature of the courses. In addition, *members of the Institute of Educational Technology* also take part, acting as experts for determining learning aims, developing self-learning material, applying specific teaching strategies, and for test and assessment procedures. The *staff tutor* also takes part, being the member of the respective department who is responsible for the work of the tutors in the study centres and for arranging the summer courses.

Representatives of the BBC also take part in course development in order to investigate the optimal conditions for suitable teaching programmes in radio and television and to bring in aspects of mass communications into course development. Editors discuss texts with the authors, calculate production costs and prepare the agreed texts for publication. Back-up for all of this is provided by a coordinator (Mason and Goodenough, 1981: 111).

We can see how a distance-education course is conceived, constructed, amended, tested and finally determined by this team, and how many different perspectives come into play. We can also see the different perspectives, attitudes and practical experiences that play a part in the work. Both have considerable influence on the pedagogical structure of learning and teaching programmes for development. While the author's own experiences in teaching and research, spontaneous ideas and even reactions to events (for example in examinations) can be absorbed into the structure of a learning and teaching programme written by a university teacher and provide it with a personal touch, the individual nature of teaching is lost with a course objectivised through discussions that is created on the basis of scientifically founded development work. While individual course authors have considerable leeway in content and personal terms, the team is restricted by a given *symmetrical structuring* of the learning and teaching process.

The decisions that the course team has to take within the given framework are various: the teaching aims have to be thoroughly discussed and exactly defined, not only for the overall course but also for the individual course units. The contents must be selected and coordinated carefully with regard to the aims and the preset learning time. Tests and examination questions must be set at the beginning, and not, as is the usual practice, at the end, because they have to be brought into a relationship with the learning aims. Self-test problems must be thought out and set, possibilities for action suggested, problems for discussions in study centres represented, and topics for assignments formulated. Also important are the intentional redundancies, which support the process of self-teaching. Tips on the type of required learning must be given in general and at suitable places. Topics for assignments must be set. Everything must be thought out and decided upon in advance because each course must be 'prefabricated' when the student sits down to start to study.

There is no other form of academic teaching in which students are supported with the help of a pedagogical structuring so intentionally, deliberately, carefully, considerately, and with the promise of success. (This type of learning and teaching programme may safely be described as promising success, because it must have already proved its worth during testing on another comparable population of students.) The pedagogical structure of the course is thus the product of the joint efforts of many experts, who on average take 12 to 18 months to plan, develop, test and assess a course.

What this actually means becomes clear if we imagine a student sitting alone and isolated at home and working through a course, while in the background are five, eight or even twelve experts each aiming to provide help individually and from many aspects. This effort is *specific to distance education* because it only 'pays its way' at large universities as a result of the large numbers of students usually found there.

The structuring of teaching programmes by course teams is an original idea of the British Open University, and according to its first vice-chancellor it is its 'most important contribution to teaching practice at the tertiary level' (Perry, 1976: 91). This idea has gained ground in other distance-teaching universities. For example, the Korean National Open University regards the establishment of a course team of this nature as an 'imperative' (Kim, 1993: 158). Other distance-teaching universities have even used the idea as a model by copying it: the Dutch Open Universiteit uses the idea, as do the Deakin University in Australia, the Allama Iqbal Open University in Pakistan, the Sukhothai Thammathirat Open University in Thailand, recently the University of South Africa, and to a certain extent the Open University in Israel as well. But the British ideal has never really been matched, perhaps for financial reasons, because of a lack of cooperation, insufficient familiarity with the procedures of committee work, or an unwillingness to accept and respect decisions arrived at democratically (Mason and Goodenough, 1981: 112). Cultural differences also have an effect on efforts of this nature. However, in the theoretical discussion of distance education the course team model has been successful. It is still discussed at meetings and conferences even now.

Other forms of development work

At several distance-teaching universities, the interplay of traditional teaching and educational-technology standards is regulated differently, and this naturally has an effect on the structure of the courses. What usually happens here is that the development of courses is left to the university teachers themselves. However, they are familiar with educational-technology requirements and those specific to distance education by means of guidelines for authors, as well as in talks with educational technologists. If these opportunities are ignored, presentation structures may develop that are similar to those of a lecture or a textbook or a academic paper, and that therefore neglect the element of self-instruction. These cases usually occur where external authors are entrusted with the drawing-up of distance-teaching courses. Even if they follow the written instructions, but do this en passant and with a complete lack of interest, the structure required for distance students cannot be achieved. But even distance-teaching universities themselves have university teachers who are either unwilling or unable to cope with and assimilate the principles and procedures of educational technology, as Walter Perry (1976: 81) found in the Open University itself.

In practical distance education, many courses can be identified with different teaching structures. By and large, however, over the years full-time university teachers have gained considerable competence in the development of structured learning and teaching programmes. Just how a learning and teaching programme can be structured to make it self-instructing appears to have become internalized to a great extent. Mason and Goodenough (1983: 110) have identified five types of course development on the basis of the number and weighting of the experts involved in each case, and these types, slightly amended, are shown below.

- *Type 1*: a single university teacher writes course material for a traditional university course (lecture notes, textbooks, etc) that are also used as a working foundation for distance students.
- *Type 2*: a university teacher is solely responsible as course author for the development of a course and works with an editor alone.
- *Type 3*: a university teacher cooperates as author in a loose combination with educational technologists and an editor.
- *Type 4*: An educational technologist or a group of educational technologists is responsible for developing a course. In order to cover and guarantee the contents, they have the topics that are to be dealt with worked out in the form of basis texts by (usually) external university teachers, and these basis texts are then reworked by the educational technologists into self-learning teaching texts. The educational technologists, and not the authors, then work together with the editor.
- *Type 5*: university teachers, educational technologists from various disciplines, media specialists, test experts, graphic artists and an editor work together in a course team and develop a course for which they are jointly responsible.

According to the above we could differentiate structured learning and teaching programmes for distance students according to the degree of their educational-technology basis and their self-learning potential. Type 1 is completely lacking in both. If lecture notes and textbooks that were originally developed for studies at a traditional university are handed to distance students instead of a specially developed course, this indicates a lack of interest in the special requirements of distance education (such as appears to be the case, for example, at the University of Waterloo in Canada), but also because of economic backwardness, as was observed (and in some cases may still be observed) in the former GDR, the countries of the former communist bloc, right through to Vietnam and the People's Republic of China. Courses of distance education that have to operate with working material with such a slight structure are regrettably not the exception, and are in fact widespread. Often, people have to be thankful at least to have printed material available for distance students, even if it originates in a format more suited to traditional universities, because even this is most certainly not always the case. Reports on distance education in many countries are full of complaints about this situation.

The structure of distance-education courses was developed most strongly on the basis of the principles of educational technology and self-instruction (type 4 above). However, educational technological exuberance, a lack of pedagogical sensitivity, and a false assessment of the role of academic teaching traditions have degraded university teachers practically to the level of 'subcontractors'. In this type of course development, they act merely as subject-matter specialists who are kept away from the work of designing a course pedagogically because it is assumed that they have no idea of educational technology and, in particular, no idea of the peculiarities of learning and teaching in distance education, such that they are unable to find their way round in this brave new world. They are therefore included simply on an ad hoc basis and asked to formulate drafts for the presentation of the relevant aspects of the course.

An instructive example is supplied by the Universidad Nacional Abierta in Venezuela, founded in 1977. The group of educational technologists gathered there carried out their development work particularly thoroughly in that they not only worked out the design for the university's courses but also the contents by carrying out curricular work. They analysed the circumstances and requirements of the employment that students were aiming for, and then derived broad and detailed teaching aims. Using the drafts for the presentation of the course contents submitted by the university teachers, they then developed the actual distance-education modules themselves with regard to the qualifications to be gained. In this way they turned themselves into the masters of the complete process, including, to an extent, control over questions of content.

The separation of university teachers and educational technologists that took place here proved to be a serious strategic error. The university teachers reacted in two ways. Some ignored the principles and processes of the educational technologists and submitted the courses they had themselves developed directly to the printers for publication and dissemination. Others followed all the suggestions and instructions coming from the educational technologists but were no longer able to identify with courses that were developed in this way. They lost interest and no longer wanted to work with the courses, and were also not prepared to commit themselves to the task (Rumble, 1982: 195).

This crisis led people to understand just how important it is on the one hand to instruct university teachers at the very least in the fundamentals of educational technology, and on the other to expect educational technologists to understand the position of the respective discipline and to acquaint themselves with it. It is only in this way that both parties will be put into a position that enables them to understand each other and work together. This was exactly the objective of the UK's Open University when it institutionalized the continuous dialogue between both sides in the form of a course team. The Universidad Nacional Abierta learned from its negative start and then set up 'integrated design units' that are also aimed at ensuring collaboration between university teachers and educational technologists. In this way, they are approaching the type 5 approach.

This example has been explained in detail because there are educational and financial politicians in many countries who prefer distance-teaching universities that employ as *few* full-time university teachers as possible, so that courses are usually written by external authors on a part-time basis. Production, distribution, and support for students is controlled, carried out and monitored by educational technologists. This attitude towards distance-teaching universities will naturally have an effect on the structure of learning and teaching programmes.

The following deficiencies in the approach can be seen from the start:

- teaching and research are unconnected;
- experience in the two fields of teaching and research cannot be gained continually and consistently without internal departments;
- course management suffers if committed academics cannot provide continuous support for the learning and teaching process;
- specific experience in writing structured learning and teaching programmes is not accumulated;
- it is impossible to form a profile unique to a particular distance-teaching university in either teaching or research; and
- the university's scientific and social reputation must necessarily suffer with this type of internal structure, and this will have an effect on the value of degrees and examination certificates.

These deficiencies lead to poorly structured learning and teaching programmes that cannot be justified pedagogically. A regular body of *full-time* professors is required working together in faculties, and the same selection criteria and working conditions must apply for them as in traditional universities. The development of learning and teaching programmes for distance education cannot be accomplished 'on the side', as if they were an essay or an article for a magazine; the work demands years of concentration and commitment in order to formulate well structured courses. Those who water this requirement down should not be surprised when distance education has to struggle desperately for parity of esteem – as is the case in many countries.

Course development at the FernUniversität

Learning and teaching programmes are not developed by a specially convened course team at the FernUniversität either, because this procedure was rejected out of hand by professors during the foundation phase. Their firm opinion was that *they themselves* should retain full responsibility for courses, and that the courses should contain their 'signatures' and not be watered down by the collaboration of insufficiently qualified team members. In addition, the argument continued, scientific facts and their practical presentation were not something that could be decided on by a majority, which is the practice in course teams. Finally – and this was the decisive point – they saw restrictions on the freedom of teaching, which in the Federal Republic of Germany is protected in the Basic Law (the constitution) in the same way as freedom of research.

Instead of the approach described in the previous subsection, the FernUniversität developed a model of relaxed and flexible collaboration between teaching staff and educational technologists. In their function as course authors, many professors are pleased to make use of the advice and help provided by subject specialists and by the educational, media and technical experts in the Zentrum für Fernstudienentwicklung, which now employs 35 experts. The collaboration of the subject specialists from this centre has proved particularly advantageous for working out learning and teaching structures for courses, because these experts can themselves direct their educational-technology recommendations from the very start to the specific nature of the pedagogical structure of the respective discipline. On the one hand they are themselves representatives of the respective discipline, and at the same time educational technologists, and because of this twin qualification they are able to come to an understanding much more easily with the university teachers in the discipline to which they have been assigned.

Above all, the specialists are in a position to see and process specific pedagogical and educational-technology problems in the context of the contents of their subject. In that respect they are go-betweens between traditional and technically imparted academic teaching. Because of their work, but also because of the assistance they provide for the development of audio-visual and digital media and for course evaluation, the university's teachers now have a considerable amount of experience that has been subjected to pedagogical reflection. They now routinely cope with the task of developing self-instructing distance-education courses with distance-teaching pedagogical proficiency.

Does it really have to be regarded as a pedagogical deficiency if structured distance-education courses are not drawn up through teamwork? Not at all. These courses reflect the personal way of thinking, the power of representation, and the originality of individual university teachers. Learning and teaching programmes drawn up in teamwork, on the other hand, often appear to be smooth and impersonal. Above all, these learning and teaching programmes are directly or indirectly connected to the research work of the respective author, who in turn links his or her personal reputation as a researcher and teacher to the course. To that degree, courses are constructed that are *different* from those created by teamwork.

As far as their pedagogical design is concerned, this method of working probably cannot achieve the level of quality that can be reached through long collaboration between several experts in a course team. On the other hand, Desmond Keegan, who has a great deal of expert knowledge in the field of distance education and whose international experience means that he is able to compare approaches in a way that nobody else can, is impressed by the *academic* quality of the courses developed by the FernUniversität in its own particular way. In his opinion, they are of a 'demanding and academically rigorous nature'. And, he adds, they have been tested in detail by other universities and their standards have proved to be as high, if not higher, than corresponding courses at traditional universities (Keegan,1982: 100).

This indication of the comparability of the teaching programme in a distance-teaching university with that of a traditional university is typical and is found in other countries as well. Conversely, it is foreign to university teachers in the FernUniversität – they would never think of comparing the quality of their structured learning and teaching programme with the teaching programmes in another university because they have been aware from the very start of their own standing in research and teaching and that of their colleagues elsewhere. In addition, the question is superfluous because students at the FernUniversität may change at any time to a traditional university, and the FernUniversität accepts students from traditional universities, and each type of university accepts the grades achieved in the other.

4.2.3 Examples at the FernUniversität

Just how heavily the learning and teaching programmes at the FernUniversität move from mere information through to self-instruction because of their structuring can be seen from the structure of a standard course that always has the following elements: an introduction, a bibliography, a glossary, assignments, and sample answers.

Each of these elements has pedagogic functions. In this context, the *introduction* is of particular importance because it can show the complete learning and teaching process – its macrostructure – and prepare, initiate and steer the learning process. Ideally, the introduction is influenced with many pedagogically effective factors that each perform specific pedagogic functions. The following overview can make this clear:

Table 4.2 *The pedagogical structure of the Introduction to a teaching text*

Structural elements	Pedagogical functions
Invitation and welcome	Motivation
Characterizing the course contents	Arousal and steering of attention, awakening of interest
Description of the required preliminary knowledge	Linking contents to be learnt with knowledge structures already in existence
Indications of correlations to other areas of knowledge and possibly to job practice	Integration of the contents to be learnt in more extensive contexts
Description of rough learning and teaching objectives	Directing attention to the knowledge and skills to be aimed for
Naming advantages obtained by reaching the learning goals	Motivation
Indicating tutorials and study days in the study centres	Characterizing social and communicative learning as desirable, and prompting relevant action
Encouraging the setting up of course-based study groups	Activating students to social and communicative learning
Counselling with regard to learning how to learn (ie study techniques)	Guiding, back-up, support
Introducing the author and other members of staff	Setting up virtual social relationships between teachers and students

If the structure of individual course modules is considered, their uniformity can once again be seen. An attempt is made to present the following elements in a course unit:

- contents;
- lists, explanations, legends;
- bibliography;
- teaching aims;
- teaching text;
- appendices;
- solutions to test questions; and
- assignments.

The sequence itself is a help because it simplifies orientation with the individual course elements during learning. Of course, the focus is on presentation of the course contents, but this does not simply mean the transmission of information because the way the presentation is carried out already has pedagogically effective factors. Some of these will be shown in the following table by way of example:

Table 4.3 *The implicit structure of a course unit*

Structural elements	Pedagogical functions
Learning and teaching aims	Arousal of attention and steering it towards defined knowledge and skills that are to be acquired
Preorientation	Providing a structure that links subjects to be learnt with prior knowledge and into which the subjects to be learnt can be embedded (subsumed)
Introduction	Introduction to the field, for example through confrontation with a central problem
Presentation of contents	Sequencing, stressing what is important, demarcating, showing perspectives for further study, etc. Imparting the ability to set practically arranged information in relationship. Summarizing to show what has been learnt in a concentrated form. Cross-references.

The other elements referred to also have very specific pedagogical functions in distance education. The bibliography, for example, which is just an appendix elsewhere, becomes important in a teaching text, in particular if comments are provided to accompany it. Even its positioning within a teaching text expresses the important role played by specialized literature in the presentation of scientific facts and, nowadays, in particular in academic teaching. In addition, it encourages the development of activities and helps students independently to discover and use other points of access to the contents.

A glossary enables students to recognize central terms and concepts outside the current text, to rethink them, to grasp and test definitions, and in this way to open up a second path to the contents represented. Assignments force students to apply what they have learnt, transfer it to other situations, and achieve meta-cognition.

These pedagogically effective factors are often expressed in the arrangement and design of the teaching texts. Students can orientate themselves using visual aids. Below is an example of the effects this can have in the scope of the microstructure of a teaching text:

Table 4.4 *The explicit structure of a course unit*

Orienting structural feature	Pedagogical functions
Indication of learning and teaching aims	Arousal of attention and steering it towards defined knowledge and skills that are to be acquired. Motivation, creation of purposefulness, making clear the difference between attitudes, knowledge and skills, showing why it is desirable to reach the learning aims
Headlines	Indicating the core of the facts being treated, or summarizing them
Abstracts	Making an understanding of the contents easier as an early descriptor of the piece of work
Graphics	A help to structure problems, gain overviews, make abstract facts more 'visible' by means of spatial relationships of the elements to one another. A help to develop and change individual knowledge structures if, for instance, diagrams, conceptual networks and structures are used
Arrangement in 'blocks' and characterization by marginal notes	Understanding a number of sentences in a logical context is made easier. The corresponding marginal notes make the student conscious of the function that the respective 'block' is intended to have in the learning and teaching process. For example, marginal notes can be used for the following: preorientation, preconditions, presenting teaching contents, definition, analogy, classification, terms, concept, theory, rule, facts, problem, problem solution, findings,

	criticism procedure, process, summary, exercise, repetition, application, transfer, and stressing what is important.
Frames and underlining, bold, italic print, decimal numbering	A help to find other text sources for integration
Branching	Individualization, where several learning paths are provided
Cross-references	Differentiation and strengthening of knowledge structures
Problems, questions, and assignments	A safeguard for the acquired cognitive structure, including attempts to develop meta-cognitive structures

Table 4.4 should be sufficient to show just how much a teaching text differs from an academic paper, for example. Its function consists not only in imparting scientific facts but also – and essentially – in the help that is provided to students so that they can evolve their own learning activities and change their own cognitive structures. According to Jan Elen (1996: 84), this help is provided through two types of intervention, namely by 'explanatory' and 'controlling' contributions. A teaching text is therefore interspersed with interventions of this nature.

The 'art of teaching' by the teachers in the distance-teaching universities is now based not on their rhetorical qualities, as in traditional universities, but on how they combine in their teaching texts the functions of imparting, explaining, and controlling, and how they structure them with regard to the cognitive requirements of their students. What is decisive here is the transition from mere presentation of teaching contents to enabling and initiating cognisant and learning processes.

To achieve this, the developed structure can be broad-meshed or narrow-meshed and in this way provide students with more or less freedom. This arrangement leads to a special set of problems that can be made clear by means of the following extreme example. If, for example, the structure is restricted to choosing a topic and there are no further explanations or controls, students will be left to their own devices. On the other hand, they are then free to achieve the learning aims through their own reading, for example, or by research or their own experiments. If, on the other hand, the learning and teaching programme is written down to the last detail in small steps, such as with programmed instruction, and if feedback is required for control purposes after each learning step to see whether the intended learning has in fact taken place, students may have the feeling that they are being supported during every learning step; but, equally, the structure means that students may feel too tightly controlled, and may find it difficult to evolve their own learning initiatives. Of course, there are naturally many shades of structure between these two extremes. It requires a good deal of thought, empathy and experience to find the 'right' degree when writing teaching texts.

4.2.4 Structural extensions

Printed material is still the medium that to the greatest extent determines the structure of distance education at most distance-teaching universities. Students spend most of their time dealing with printed material; their learning behaviour is determined by reading. This is typical for the larger autonomous distance-teaching universities, although the Central Radio and Television University in China and the University of the Air in Japan form exceptions (see Sections 7.4 and 7.5 respectively).

The structuring of learning by means of a printed distance-education course is strengthened, reinforced and further differentiated, in the sense of steering students through the use of other technical media. Teaching programmes on radio and television provide distance education (which is in itself independent of location and time) with a defined *time and location structure*, and therefore impose restraints to learning. Distance education on the 'tutored video instruction' model, on the other hand, is completely flexible in this regard because video presentations can be interrupted at any time to discuss what has been learnt – although learning steps are prescribed here as well, even if they are not programmed.

4.2.5 Commentary

The importance of structured learning programmes in distance education is difficult to estimate because a pedagogical conflict of aims arises immediately. On the one hand it is possible to reach large groups of people with this type of teaching and to pass on quality study contents; on the other hand, this takes place too much in an expository form, and is really obsolete, because it makes students dependent and non-self-sufficient. This is a very complex situation, which distance-teaching pedagogics should make transparent. It might be an advantage if the following questions were examined.

- What exactly are the advantages and disadvantages of thoroughly structured learning and teaching in distance education?
- What are the conditions and circumstances under which the further development of structured teaching programmes might be advocated and advised?
- What advantages do structured teaching programmes and learning packages provide in the context of digital learning and teaching?
- What are the differences in the development of structured learning and teaching programmes in individual academic disciplines? Can certain specific pedagogical experiences be discussed, generalized and, if possible, used in structuring the learning and teaching programmes?
- How should we regard the practice if developing heavily structured learning and teaching programmes above all for the first cycle of a degree programme and less structured learning and teaching programmes for the second cycle, while for even more advanced students introductions, guidance and controls are done away with completely and phases of autonomous learning begin?
- Should we start to let structured learning and teaching programmes, which have

been successfully introduced and proved their worth in distance education, now gradually run down, and should we move over to other possible forms of distance education? Should they not be replaced from the very start for reasons of fundamental learning theory by models of exploratory, discovering, and self-instructing learning that support attitudes and behaviour that are absolutely essential for independent academic work?

● What are the part tasks that structured teaching programmes could take over in the flexible and variable range of teaching available in a university of the future?

4.2.6 Necessary transformations

Whatever the answers to these questions, the structure of distance education will change rapidly in any case to the extent that the new, highly effective and easily accessible digital information and communications media are used more and more. Just how topical this process is could be seen at the 18th World Conference of the International Council for Distance Education at Penn State University in 1997. The subject was 'The New Learning Environment', whereby, of course, the new *technological* learning environment is meant. One thousand people from 80 countries concentrated on the problem of how learning and teaching in distance education should be structured in the digital era. Not a single voice was raised in warning against technicizing university education. The structure of distance education, we know already, will look *different*. Digital media do not simply add something new to traditional academic teaching; rather, they change its structure and essence. This abrupt change can lead to attractive pedagogical configurations that have up to now been impossible in distance education.

But what should happen to the structure I have described here in detail that has been typical for distance education up to now? There is no doubt that it will determine distance education for some time to come. At the same time it *must* be changed and adapted to the new situations. In this context, a model is gaining in importance that is being developed at present in the Universidad Nacional Abierta in Venezuela to encourage and initiate the process of transformation from the technology of printing to the technology of the Internet (de Romero, 1997: 441). Within this model, the distance education of the future should have the following characteristics:

● tutorial help is available quickly;
● there are usually several information media used in an integrated form;
● teaching contents are illuminated from various standpoints;
● students can interact with the teaching programmes presented to them;
● course contents contain interfaces and cross-references (links) to additional information, including from other sources; and
● with the help of an integrated mailbox, students can contact their professors at any time.

This type of model provides initial orientation points for the revision of old courses and the development of new ones. All distance-teaching universities that were founded in the 1970s and 1980s are faced with this problem of transition. A corresponding model, which is being developed at the Open Universiteit in the Netherlands, goes one step further, because here content, student and support models, together with the model of a learning path, are being developed for flexible autonomous learning where each has to be coordinated with the other in a digital learning environment (Martens et al, 1997: 238).

A manual issued by the Empire State College for course developers (Eastmond and Lawrence, 1997: 106) may also be helpful with the coming new structuring tasks. It shows how the previous pedagogical structure of course design, presentation and assessment must be changed in the digital environment. The structure of distance education in the future must orient towards three basic patterns, whereby the first medium in each case is the lead medium:

- *Pattern 1*: printed material (textbooks), study guides, exploratory learning on-line, and communication on-line;
- *Pattern 2*: printed material (textbooks), study guides, teleconferencing;
- *Pattern 3*: learning and teaching on-line, study guides on-line, problem presentation on-line, discussions on-line.

Handling these three structural patterns will certainly simplify the gradual changeover to learning and teaching in the digital teaching environment. We can imagine just how considerable parts of the teaching programmes at distance-teaching universities will gradually be transformed in this way.

To indicate how complex the structure of digital learning and teaching will be, we shall take a look at a typology (Paulsen, 1997: 120) that distinguishes between four distinct learning situations for learning in a digital environment, each of them demanding special forms of working that themselves have different pedagogical structures.

1. *Working alone (the WWW paradigm)*: on-line specialist magazines, databases, virtual books, a virtual library.
2. *One teacher and one student (the e-mail paradigm)*: learning contracts, support through mentoring, electronic correspondence.
3. *One teacher and many students (the bulletin board paradigm)*: lectures, papers, symposia, role plays.
4. *Many teachers and many students (the computer-conferencing paradigm)*: debates, simulations, role playing, discussion groups, brainstorming, project groups, and forums.

In the face of the abundance of these new opportunities for pedagogical design, there will be structuring that can be much more variable and flexible than has ever been the case before in distance education. In the future it will be possible to adapt teaching more easily to students' learning requirements, the technical peculiarities of individual disciplines, the world of employment and students' private lives, and above all to the rapidly changing requirements of industrial society. We will find structures that not only enable presentational and prescriptive teaching but also autonomous and self-directed learning. Pedagogical design will become a strategy with many variations.

4.2.7 Perspectives

If we take into account new models and typologies such as those shown here on work in the digital learning environment, the structuring of distance-education courses to achieve definitive learning effects can be taken too far. It is possible to relate the printed and spoken word to graphics (including animations) and to still and moving pictures, and this reinforces the presentation stimuli. The structuring of distance-education courses is probably most dense at these places. Of course – and this is what is fascinating about digital learning and teaching – there are at the same time many opportunities for spontaneous investigation, for obtaining information on one's own initiative, and for autonomous learning (for example, using simulations). In these cases, learning paths are *not* laid down beforehand by strict structuring. Heteronomous and autonomous learning lie close together in this type of structure and, in this regard, digital learning environments are ambivalent.

To relate multimedia learning and teaching effects to one another, teachers must link the structural elements of media to one another. Printed distance-education courses contain links to presentations contributed by the different media. Symbols are used to make more transparent and accessible the highly complex structure that is created. With *hypertext* and *hypermedia*, the complexity of the presentational structure is no longer transparent; students navigate the text as if they were in uncharted waters. In the future of distance education, when not only work with high-performance computers and advanced network technologies but also with new technologies for transmitting teaching sequences for distance education can be carried out, the degree of complexity of the pedagogical structure may even increase. This will move us all a long way from the simple structure of the traditional pedagogical triangle (teacher–content–student).

4.3 Autonomous learning

What role does autonomous learning play in practical distance education? Corresponding analyses provide a conflicting impression: on the one hand students work more autonomously here than in any other field of education; on the other, their learning in customary forms of distance education is much more tied down, structured, linked to terms of reference and regulated than in traditional universities – in other words their learning is to a great extent heteronomous.

The first impression referred to has become the one that characterizes the image of distance students. It is based on their independence from fixed locations, times and lecturers. This type of independence is unusual for the traditional educational system and is therefore the one thing that is noticed first. It not only provides students with the opportunity to develop initiative in the planning and organization of their learning and to take special action, but even *forces* them to do this. In fact, they can and must decide where, when, how long, how much, how intensively, in what sequence and in what rhythm they want to study. In this way they assume more responsibility for their own learning than other students.

Often, certain groups of students – and they are not exactly small groups – do not have anything to do with the support system in distance-teaching universities for years, and yet they still manage to achieve good results in their examinations. Another even larger group of students does not even sit the examinations. In this way a considerable measure of autonomy and self-direction occurs. It is true that this form of autonomy refers only to the *external* course of studying and only under heteronomous terms of reference, but the 'freedom' from locational, temporal and personal bonds is praised as a particular pedagogical advantage by most advocates of distance education – in a similar fashion, it should be pointed out, to the propagation of programmed instruction in the 1960s.

This formal–organizational independence is, however, curtailed and restricted with distance students, and this fact can easily be observed if a closer look is taken. For example, why cannot distance students start their studies whenever they want, and not only at the beginning of a semester or academic year? Why are they subjected to the strict phasing of learning laid down by the deadlines for sending in their assignments? Why do assignments have to be sent in by certain dates? Should not distance students be able to determine these deadlines themselves, especially as this is technically possible without any difficulties? Why are their studies limited anyway by rules and regulations, conditions and institutional sanctions? As we can see, even the often-praised autonomy of distance students with regard to their external learning behaviour is usually institutionally restricted.

Let me add a note here: the institutional restrictions referred to above show just how traditional rules and regulations from conventional universities have an unnecessary after-effect on the transition from conventional studies to distance education. A similar phenomenon can be observed currently in the transition from first-generation distance education to second- and third-generation forms, for instance when teaching texts that were originally printed are transferred in the old way to CD-ROM. In the early days of film, cinematographers continued to film traditional fairground shows and theatrical representations because the enormous potential of film had not yet been recognized and could therefore not be used for artistic purposes – it took years before the transition was made. The use of computers for learning and teaching in distance education is likely to be subject to similar constraints for some time to come.

What is more serious, however, is the restriction of students' autonomy with regard to *curricular* decisions. Study objectives, contents and focal points are usually standardized on a national basis by means of study and examination regulations. Structured teaching programmes are developed at great expense, as described in Section 4.2. This means that students hardly collaborate at all in decisions concerning learning objectives, contents and paths. And learning controls are also taken over by the institutions. There is certainly no better example of an extremely *heteronomously* determined instructional system, if we disregard programmed instruction (with or without computers). The curriculum is to a great extent *determined externally* and learning stipulated by this curriculum is heteronomous. There have been suggestions that student representatives should take part in the development of these learning materials, to reduce this defect somewhat, but where has this actually been done?

Both forms of restriction on autonomy meet with criticism, although this takes place in theoretical discussions on the situation rather than in practice. With regard to the formalism of study, it is believed that the restrictions are unreasonable because students are adults (of all ages), and critics even go so far as to say that this regimentation impairs their integrity. Börje Holmberg (1989a: 155) reported on the widely held opinion that with adult students, who have work, family and social commitments, no one other than the students themselves should stipulate the schedules for their studies. And with reference to Daniel and Marquies (1979: 34), Holmberg introduced the argument that a teaching system that respected the freedom and autonomy of students should not hamper them with external restraints.

Criticism becomes harsher when the restriction on the autonomy of students with regard to the curriculum is assessed. If this autonomy is placed in relationship to the general educational objectives that are frequently invoked, the following questions arise: what can a long course of study over many years contribute to the development of self-determination and self-responsibility if its objectives, contents and methods of presentation are all without exception determined externally? How can this type of course strengthen the ability to live life in freedom if learning is prescribed step by step for years and years? How can students be led to maturity if they are not put into a position where they can act independently during learning as well? How can they develop initiative, creativity and the willingness to accept risks if they are prevented from taking the initiative on their own responsibility in curricular questions? How can they arrive at self-knowledge – at Kant's 'independent use of reason' – if all they do during learning is absorb what others have thought? Closed curricula and expository learning are certainly not favourable for achieving these goals; in fact they are in opposition. For distance education the same thing applies as Rolf Schulmeister (1983: 332) remarked about education at universities: it is adult education, with a great deal of licence, in a few areas only; in other areas it is a 'continuation of school learning', on the tight reins of study and examination regulations. Seen from this aspect, there is little space for the development of autonomous learning; in fact, there is a temptation to ask whether autonomous learning can be achieved at all with the present system of distance education.

4.3.1 Current tasks for higher-education pedagogics

What can be done in this situation? According to the working methods of humanistic pedagogics, which stipulates that when a teaching system is constructed, work must start from the basis of the respective historical situation and actual practice (Klafki, 1970: 75), the elements of autonomous learning would first of all have to be described and assessed, in the way that they are already familiar to us from traditional and distance-teaching universities in spite of their heteronomous structure.

If we look at the situation in the traditional universities and see that books are read by students 'on their own initiative', or a mathematical problem is recognized and gone over in students' minds, or a passage from a book is discussed informally with other students, or students think about problems they have come across in their work, we can see that all these examples are the first tentative approaches to autonomous learning. These activities are often referred to as 'self-study' or 'own work' and regarded as legitimate learning situations in academic studies (Rieck and Ritter, 1983/1995: 394).

In addition, there are practices that have been developed still further, and some of these will be referred to with the help of four incisive examples.

1. A theology student makes an extensive database of all those passages in the Bible that are important to him personally. On his own initiative he not only develops individual knowledge structures for comprehending the Scriptures but can also register frequent occurrences of certain words, phrases or themes, and in this way gains personal access to topics that have been particularly intensively processed theologically.
2. During lectures by a certain professor, a history student registers with great assiduity all those passages he does *not* understand and makes regular efforts to work through them afterwards and to grasp their significance. In this way he is able to find his own personal 'scarlet thread' that is able to provide him with a sense of direction throughout the whole of his studies and guide him through the mass of knowledge that initially appears complex and impenetrable.
3. A student deepens and intensifies his readings of historical texts by first reading them 'humbly' over and over again and 'subjecting' himself to what the author wrote and meant, and he takes in knowledge from this position. Only then does he counter this with his own comprehension and point of view, and thereby changes from being the 'servant' of the text to the 'master'.
4. A student makes a catalogue of all passages in literary texts that touch her and cause her to be affected and involved existentially. This provides her with an overview of her individual reaction to literature and she makes it the object of constant reflection by keeping a diary.

Examples of this nature show how students can certainly take the initiative in autonomous activities even with expository teaching. What we see here are at the very least auxiliary strategies for coping with the extreme complexities of university studies that students have thought out for themselves and implemented in an original manner.

Independent procedures become even clearer when seminar topics or degree theses, together with all the necessary preliminary work of planning, structuring, demarcating, developing and presenting the results, are worked on independently. Dissertation projects are the high point of these efforts towards achieving autonomy and self-direction, because here students usually make do with a few hints and tips from their professors. In these approaches to independent academic work, all students have – consciously or unconsciously – the model of a competent and experienced scholar in mind, who produces autonomous knowledge and is possibly personified by a particular university teacher.

It is remarkable that hardly any attention has been paid by researchers to the autonomous-learning component of academic studies – certainly much less than to lectures and seminars – although a considerable amount of the overall time spent studying – one-half to two-thirds, according to surveys by Keil (1975: 149) – is devoted to it.

A second step would be an examination of how these approaches to autonomous learning appear in distance education. Here we can find most of the approaches that exist for traditional universities. In addition, there are forms of autonomous learning that are specific to distance education. For example, some students evaluate their acquired knowledge in the light of their work and private experience. Others relate critical knowledge that they acquire through their own reading to the content of study papers. Yet others extend and deepen the knowledge acquired through study papers by reading a textbook on the same subject on their own initiative. Or they solve problems that come spontaneously to mind by consulting manuals or encyclopaedias.

Another remarkable example relates to an electrical engineering student who worked through a distance-education course from the FernUniversität by using it as a foundation for drawing up his *own* course on the same subject that contained or placed in the foreground everything that was important to him *personally*, either theoretically or in his work. This autonomous approach to 'learning by research' demonstrates the individualization of learning and its potential relationship to work practices.

One step further and we find those university teachers who allow free space for relatively independent and autonomous learning in the distance-education courses they write. Even in the case of a distance-education course preplanned down to the very last detail, there are still occasions and opportunities for autonomous learning. One such example, again from the FernUniversität, relates to a study paper containing an introduction to 'Old European Writing'. It provides students with the choice of solving one of three problems independently. One consists of interpreting two or three selected scenes from the Bayeux Tapestry, including the inscriptions. The tapestry shows scenes of the events leading up to the Norman Conquest of Britain and the Battle of Hastings itself. Another assignment is the interpretation of a historical source from this period that the student selects himself. The third assignment enables students to choose and work on a subject that they are interested in, even if it has nothing at all to do with the subject of the study letter. In this way, autonomous learning is deliberately stimulated and enabled, because all three assignments contain approaches to 'discovery learning' and even to 'learning through research'.

An empirical study should be carried out of the extent to which, and the circumstances under which, these and similar approaches to independent learning are already practised in distance education and are possible even with time pressures or work overloads. Suitable approaches would then have to be assessed and developed further. Strategies for autonomous learning in distance education could as a result be identified, described, discussed and passed on. Learning would then no longer be autonomous in the strict meaning of the word, but this new form of learning could nevertheless be supported and promoted.

At the FernUniversität, the preconditions for a intensified development of these approaches are looking encouraging. Of the 31 professors who answered a questionnaire on the subject recently, half were of the opinion that autonomous learning must be supported.

In a third step, it would have to be shown how, in the presentation of course material, teachers themselves can stimulate and facilitate autonomous learning through greater organizational measures. For example, there is something to be gained if teaching is provided in the form of modules, instead of carefully prepared study materials that prescribe the learning path with great precision. With modules, students can select those they are interested in and that are important to them and can put together an individual course. This would certainly be a starting-point for curricular collaboration.

Other possibilities for promoting autonomous learning would be available if, instead of distance-education courses programmed from A to Z, purely *guideline programmes* were compiled containing general recommendations for independent reading and an encouragement to design an individually organized course. This is practically the standard case for units at US distance-teaching universities. Here, these syllabuses contain the learning objectives, breakdowns of the subjects, general introductions, abstracts, bibliographical references and sometimes working material.

Finally, course organizers could go over to having a particularly topic or problem compiled as autonomously as possible within the framework of a distance-education course. If this was successful, an attempt could be made to create special learning arrangements for some parts of the course in which autonomous learning is presupposed and provoked.

Distance-education courses presented with the help of computers could provide considerably extended leeway for autonomous learning. The digitalization of learning and teaching enables *simulations* in many disciplines that favour learning by discovery. Students of electrical engineering, for example, can change the parameters of particular circuits on the screen to find out for themselves what happens. Once they have acquired sufficient competence, they can think up and test their own circuits.

If the approaches to autonomous learning in distance education that are indicated here are successful, teachers and students must adopt a different attitude with regard to this type of plan. The approaches described must not be regarded, as up to now, as something incidental, but must be seen as important, worthwhile, significant and as central to the system of distance-teaching pedagogics. It is necessary to pay much closer attention to them, and wherever possible to support and develop them still further. Expository teaching and receptive learning usually run routinely, because they have become *a habit* through the many years spent in school, but autonomous learning has to be initiated and encouraged *deliberately* on the basis of own decisions. Both teachers and students must be fully aware of this.

However, simply focusing attention on autonomous learning in this manner is not enough. It must be actively promoted, and here we can orient the thinking towards some tried and tested models of autonomous learning, even though these go much further than what has been dealt with here so far.

4.3.2 Models of autonomous learning in distance education

In solving the problems referred to above, distance-teaching pedagogics can work with some models that have already been applied in practice in some countries. The pedagogical–psychological background is formed by the attitudes to learning and teaching in humanistic psychology. Nowadays, this covers project learning, contract learning, and private learning. However, these models – and this must be said from the outset – are usually based on unusual circumstances that do not obtain everywhere. For theoretical reasons, however, it is stimulating and useful to examine them because they can provide insights into autonomous learning in distance education as well with other opportunities. They may even inspire suitable experiments and trials.

The humanistic learning and teaching model

According to advocates of humanistic philosophy (Fromm, Horney, Goldstein, Maslow, Bühler), individuals strive for *self-realization, self-actualization*, and *self-fulfilment*. They have a great potential to comprehend themselves, to alter their self-awareness, and to display self-directed behaviour, provided that they are able to act in a social climate that is not contrary to this. Self-regulated learning can therefore only evolve if students are able to act in a supportive, favourable and understanding social environment.

For the initiation of autonomous learning, behaviour must be expected of the teacher that is in general contrary to traditional behaviour at universities. In particular, students must reinterpret their role in the learning and teaching process. Put more exactly, they must recognize and accept the change of roles that autonomous learning demands. During the learning process they are no longer the source and administrator, no longer the gatekeepers and imparters of knowledge, but now have to identify themselves with the role of counsellor, enabler and facilitator, whose tasks are still new and unfamiliar.

What is even more difficult, the very people who have up to now been solely competent and responsible for the development of teaching must learn to withdraw and 'let go' (Arnold, 1995: 303) in order to allow students to take on their new role. The new task for teachers consists in creating *learning environments*, making a learning climate advantageous to autonomous learning, treating students from the very start with respect in an atmosphere of warmth, empathy and understanding, not measuring the learning objectives and working schedules drawn up by students rigorously against their own fixed opinions, interpreting learning results with great openness, carrying on a dialogue with students on an equal footing, and making personal appearances only when students ask them for help and advice.

In this type of learning environment, a space is created in which students as well can change their learning behaviour. They free themselves from their accustomed receptive learning and evolve a persistent and insistent form of scientific curiosity that causes them to acquire information for their own satisfaction and on their own initiative. They are eager to become familiar with suitable sources of information and stores of knowledge and to use them skilfully. They train their ability to evaluate stocks of information and knowledge and to test whether they are useful, advantageous, essential or irrelevant for their intended learning. And they learn just how important it is to become more and more competent in doing this.

Further, in this model students aspire to ask questions on their own initiative, to recognize incongruities, to get to the bottom of problems, to describe problems exactly, and (at least initially) try to solve them themselves. They learn to have the courage to be spontaneous and creative during thinking and not to repress these feelings out of respect, timidity or requirements of conformity. They zealously pursue the aim of sharing and discussing with others the knowledge that they themselves have acquired, not regarding this as a waste of time. What is particularly difficult in all of this is to take a (critical) look at themselves, to gain confidence in their own ability to learn, and to display sufficient self-confidence as a student.

The changes in the behaviour of teachers and students shown here are, seen conceptually, the result of a Copernican turning point from a 'closed' to an 'open' learning and teaching system, from prescribed and externally developed course materials towards self-discovered, self-selected and self-tested learning experiences, from expository 'teaching pedagogy' to 'enabling pedagogy' (see Arnold, 1993: 51).

Carl Rogers' influence is clear here. The conceptual approach, according to which there is a close connection between autonomous learning and the development of the personality, is used here as a basis. This is the reason why, in Section 3.3 above, I referred to both the pedagogical *and* the didactical dimensions of the concept of autonomous learning and its context. Rogers assumes in general the value and the dignity of the individual and trusts in his or her ability to set goals and provide self-direction. However, he continuously stresses that the individual must be in a favourable environment in which he or she can integrate with honest, warm-hearted, sympathetic people. If this precondition is fulfilled, each individual can discover his or her self, gain self-respect and develop an ability for self-directed learning (Rogers and Freiberg, 1994: III).

These insights, based on many years of research, were not only used by Rogers himself in his now famous non-directive client-centred therapy, but also in counselling and instruction at all stages. It inspired him to a model of learner-centred and non-directive education that he described in his book *Freedom to Learn*. This book (Rogers and Freiberg, 1994) had an enormous influence throughout the world and is now in its third edition.

In traditional distance education, the application of this model encounters considerable difficulties because direct personal contact between teachers and students and amongst students themselves are usually greatly restricted. It becomes all the more important, it might be thought, in those cases where these contacts are in fact achieved. For example, efforts might be made in study centres to cast off the residues of an outdated hierarchical understanding of roles and to create a climate in which forces for self-regulation and self-determination can be released. As institutions that communicate with students with the help of a bureaucratic administration, distance-teaching universities could display open and student-friendly behaviour, or at least non-directive behaviour.

The model of project-oriented studying

This form of acquiring knowledge played an important role in reform pedagogics as 'project lessons' at the time it was promoted by John Dewey (1905) and W H Kilpatrick (1935). From a pragmatic point of view, both of these researchers linked learning with *'systematic action'* that was aimed at leading students to display more independence and more responsibility. In the 1960s and 1970s, interest in Europe in the project method increased (Frey, 1995: 47). Relatively independently of this, in the 1970s at many universities in Germany, student associations and the National Association of University Assistants demanded – and even practised – *project-oriented studying* as part of university reforms. This was directed against learning and teaching based mainly on the reception of information and was based instead on concepts of learning by research. This demanded that students work independently, plan their projects independently of their professors, and are solely responsible for their self-development; they are oriented to problems and not to the systematic order of their own specialist discipline; and they apply the scientific method and acquire appropriate proficiencies. It is assumed that participants collaborate on an equal footing (Wildt, 1983/1995: 672).

In distance education, an important step in the direction of autonomous learning would be taken if authors and course teams could decide to have at least part of the prescribed teaching content drawn up by the students themselves on the basis of the project method. Central topics and problems of a given area could be dealt with by individuals, groups of partners, or in small groups. The independence of the students would be guaranteed in that they themselves would be the ones who, in the framework of the given task, selected topics, drew up strategies for solving problems and for learning, bore the risk of getting lost down by-ways or even of becoming completely thwarted, and assessed and presented the results of the work.

There is certainly some leeway for the integration of this type of project-oriented work into degree courses, although this varies from department to department. A start could be made with small enquiry projects, such as the encouragement of exploration into the teaching texts, or setting tasks for solving problems that promote and trigger 'learning by discovery'. Later on, students could be encouraged in the framework of larger projects to work on the central problem of a thematic area. In certain circumstances, projects are conceivable that run parallel to the traditional studying of standardized teaching texts throughout the whole period of studies, and that supplement it methodologically through their special procedures. Studies would then be 'twin-track'.

The model of contract learning

If a search is made for a model of autonomous learning in distance education that is actually put into practice and in addition is successful, the Empire State College in the USA immediately comes to mind. In this college, circumstances are actually occurring that elsewhere are regarded as pedagogical ideals or even as Utopian. Here students actually determine not only the time, location and duration of their studies but also its contents and aims, the working methods, and the form of self-examination. Seen from the point of view of distance-teaching pedagogics, this institute is an ideal model, particularly in an era in which autonomous learning is being extensively and repeatedly discussed but so little practised.

At this college – and we will be taking a closer look at this below in Section 7.6 – autonomous learning is planned, discussed, controlled and evaluated with the help of special *'learning contracts'*, which are developed and drawn up by the students themselves. Each contract describes the learning objectives that the individual student wishes to achieve in a certain period, the literature they wish to use, how often they will probably contact the mentors assigned to them in order to discuss the results they have achieved to date and go through any problems that might have arisen, and which credits they hope to gain with regard to graduation. The draft agreement is then negotiated with a mentor and has to be ratified by a member of the appropriate faculty. Subsequently, students work at home away from the university completely independently so as to comply with the terms of the contract; but they may use local libraries and consult specialists.

There is no doubt that students are granted a great deal of autonomy in this model. They enjoy a great deal of curricular self-determination. Their studies are individualized to an extent that is hardly possible to achieve elsewhere. At the same time, the college's interests are also guaranteed, because in the final analysis it is the departments that have to determine whether the learning contracts conform to the academic standards of their college, whether the achieved results can be accepted, and whether credits can be granted. This model has the advantage of having been tested and used as a basis for the complete learning and teaching system for over 20 years in the Empire State College in New York.

The 'examination preparation' model

Private preparations for a university examination also enable students to acquire a great degree of autonomy. This can always happen where universities or state institutions examine and award degrees but do not teach. In these cases, students – who are essentially left to their own resources – orient themselves in accordance with the respective examination regulations and reading lists and attempt to find other resources for learning. In some cases the university will supply support if asked, but this is usually only with regard to the examinations.

This model is obviously not the result of pedagogical considerations that have student emancipation as their objective, but is simply the result of necessity. It is used where the social status and external circumstances of applicants, or the lack of a university, do not permit regular studies. In spite of this, in our context it serves as proof that it is possible for studies to be successful without academic teachers, mentors and counsellors, and as verification of the possibility of studies that are to a great extent self-planned and for which the student is responsible. This is an extreme model of non-directive autonomous distance education. It has the advantage that it can look back on 150 years of practice in the University of London, which used it to enable those people to study who were unable to do so at Oxford or Cambridge, or who lived in the Colonies and had no access to a university. At present, the New York State Educational Department is working with the same model. In 1971 it introduced the Regents' External Degree, which is recognized by the State of New York.

4.3.3 Perspectives

What is the future of autonomous learning in distance education? Any prognosis will have to differentiate between first-generation and third-generation distance education.

At traditional distance-teaching universities there will probably be no 'Copernican change' to autonomous learning, for the following six reasons:

1. They have developed, 'broken in' and tested learning and teaching systems on the basis of printed distance-education courses that are now structurally anchored. The forces of the traditional academic learning culture are as powerful here as in other universities and cannot be easily influenced, let alone diverted radically onto other paths, at least as far as prevalence of expository teaching and receptive learning is concerned.
2. The image of a sympathetic, understanding warm-hearted and helpful counsellor, who holds back unless asked and tends not to intervene, does not (yet) correspond to the image and concept that professors have of themselves, at least in Germany.
3. There is very little inclination to restrict or even abandon the tried and tested imparting of knowledge by expository methods in favour of untried, labour-intensive (think of the tutors and mentors required) and time-consuming autonomous learning.
4. Many distance students might object that they had insufficient time to provide curricular work and work out degree course for themselves, especially as at present they find it acceptable and agreeable to have this work carried out by a team of experts.
5. A distance-teaching university, like any other university, exercises a rigid process of selection for society that is unconsciously reflected and hierarchically graded in the behaviour of its teachers and students, where stopping this social mechanism must be regarded as completely infeasible.
6. A relaxed and supportive learning environment on a partnership basis, as is required for creative self-directed learning to evolve, can come into existence in a competitive society only with difficulty, because universities are preparing students for it. The universities tend to develop and internalize within the students an attitude of decisive self-assertion, tough competitive thinking, and 'survival tactics'.

The situation in first-generation distance education establishments is therefore paradoxical, and basically even tragic, for supporters of autonomous learning. All adult education experts and educationalists have known for some time that expository teaching and receptive learning are outmoded and that they have considerable disadvantages as methods of imparting knowledge. And all these experts also know that it is very important instead to prepare students for autonomous learning, to train them in it, and to make this method a habit – in particular because in our information and learning society it will have to be practised on a lifetime basis. Many of them even believe that distance education itself offers unusually favourable external conditions.

In spite of all this, distance education will not adopt autonomous learning as the basic form of academic studies. The circumstances are not ready. At most, the islands of autonomous learning in the broad stream of heteronomous learning will increase; and here and there heteronomous learning may be modified in the direction of autonomous learning. Some of the examples here show this. But neither will alter the fundamental structure of heteronomous learning in distance education.

The situation may be different in third-generation distance education because digitalization of the learning environment will open up new opportunities, including ones for autonomous learning. This new generation will on the one hand contain creative programming that evokes and supports independent thought and evaluation from students, enables independent problem-solving, provokes independent experimental activities, and initiates exploratory learning and learning through discovery. Strictly speaking, in all these cases it is the teachers and programmers who occasion these activities by looking ahead and preparing. Their approach to autonomous learning is therefore still imparted in a heteronomous manner.

Thus students who actively solve given training and application assignments within their digital learning environment on their own initiative and then check whether they have been successful, or who make use of a tutorial session provided in the teaching programme, or who take decisions in the scope of a simulated situation, are therefore *not* actually acting autonomously, even if this may on occasion appear to be the case. In fact, they are being controlled from outside, directly, indirectly, and sometimes very subtly, and to a much greater extent than in printed distance-education courses developed in accordance with the requirements of distance education. What we see here is heteronomous learning. Nevertheless, the digital learning environment does provide students who wish to learn completely autonomously with many opportunities, some of which have not yet been realized. We will return to these in Chapter 6.

As we saw in Section 3.3, there can be no autonomous learning in the strict sense of the term, because autonomous and heteronomous learning give rise to each other and, as a result, learning and teaching systems in distance education are conceivable that combine both forms of teaching, namely the presentational–instructional method and the acquiring–structuring method, whereby autonomous learning will be more or less in the foreground, depending on the discipline and the subject. The future may indeed belong to this type of pedagogical symbiosis.

The digital learning environment will certainly be equipped for the task. An example of this is the 'teaching software' for continuing education in Practical Computer Science at the FernUniversität. This is aimed at students who require guidance and provides them with a linear teaching programme in the behavioural sense. However, the same programme addresses autonomous learners as well, who pursue their own learning aims and strategies because they can use defined search-and-selection procedures (Heuel and Postel, 1993). What we have here, therefore, is a pedagogical hybrid, apparently a promising step on the road to the world of autonomous learning striven for by so many. This kind of hybrid programme could serve both the 'high' and 'low' learners in adult education between whom Patricia Cross (1981: 66) differentiates.

4.4 Summary

All told, the concepts of structure, dialogue and autonomy that Moore underlined are in fact important orientation aids in the development and interpretation of distance education. It all depends on their interplay, so that one-sidedness can be avoided. The degree to which these criteria can be taken into consideration depends naturally on the respective educational concepts, the structure of the teaching contents in the individual disciplines and the predominant academic learning culture.

Where learning and teaching in distance education has to be optimized, what must be done, among other things, is to check whether the relationship of these criteria to one another in a given situation is 'right', or must be changed. In fact, the Chinese Central Radio and Television University (see Section 7.4) and some Australian universities, for example, which have made group dialogue or classes the basis of distance education, are at present taking increasing account of the criterion 'structure'. And distance-teaching universities whose teaching programmes consist almost exclusively of complete distance-education courses are making efforts to intensify dialogical learning. All universities that have succeeded in arriving at an acceptable balance between structure and dialogue will have to make efforts beyond this to create more opportunities for development of, and freedom for, autonomous learning.

Chapter 5

Modifying concepts

5.1 Open learning

5.1.1 The current situation

In the English-language literature, distance education is often linked with the concept of 'open learning'. The impetus for this came from the UK's Open University, which was founded in 1969, and there were good reasons for calling this institution 'open'. The ground was well prepared for the rapid acceptance of this designation when the international discussion on open learning got under way, and the label had an intensive propaganda effect that helped a favourable image to be created for the new institution. By saying farewell in this way to traditional correspondence education, because of its enormous effect the Open University sent signals that were received throughout the world by governments and universities, and absorbed by them as well. There are now 14 universities that title themselves explicitly as 'Open University'. The 23 larger distance-teaching universities that are known to the specialist world (Holmberg, 1994) are also touched or affected by the new concept because the guiding principle of open learning has permeated discussions on distance education since the Open University was founded.

At present it can be seen how the terms 'distance education' and 'open learning' are starting to fuse. The two terms are already used as synonyms in many parts of the world, although strictly speaking they are distinct but overlapping. In 1985, the journal *Teaching at a Distance* was renamed *Open Learning*. Accordingly, in 1994 the Swiss government convened an international conference in Geneva on the subject of 'Open and Distance Learning'. And even the seventeenth world conference of the International Council for Distance Education (ICDE) in Birmingham took place under the motto 'Quality in Distance and Open Learning'. These terms are also used together regularly in the European Union and UNESCO, although usually only distance education is meant. However, Helmut Fritsch (1991: 16) opposes the synonymous use of these two terms by pointing out that in distance education and open learning responsibility is located in different places. And Desmond Keegan (1993: 290) rejects this equation of both terms with the sarcastic argument that 'open and flexible learning systems seldom work with distance education and distance education systems are often neither flexible nor open'.

In spite of this, express reference will be made here to the concept of open learning, because it demonstrates paradigmatically not only how learning and teaching behaviour in distance education has developed differently, but also which political, social, economic and pedagogic factors have to be taken into account. For this reason, all distance education theoreticians and practitioners should take part in a fundamental discussion of this concept.

5.1.2 Defining terms

If we look at 'open learning' at first separately from 'distance education', what we mean in general is the acquisition of knowledge, skills and attitudes that in principle are *open to all*, in other words, nobody is excluded (*the equality principle*). If learning is in fact to be possible in this manner, traditional educational barriers must be removed, including economic difficulties with those whose income is too low, gender-specific educational practices, unfavourable socio-cultural milieus, or membership of minority groups (*the principle of equality of opportunity*). Learning in this case is not bound to defined life-cycles, nor to defined locations and times. It must be possible to learn at any time and everywhere (*the principle of lifelong and ubiquitous learning*).

If we turn from the external to the internal conditions for open learning, teaching programmes should not be completely developed and determined beforehand in an empirical, scientific manner, but should be 'open' for unforeseen developments in the build-up of individual ability to act (*the principle of open curricula*). Accordingly, the course of learning should not be stipulated rigidly and independently of the students but should start from, and be shaped by, their individual value perspectives, interests and experiences (*the principle of learner-relatedness*). Students should not be the objects but the subjects of the teaching process.

For this reason, learning and teaching institutions should be created in which students can organize their learning themselves (*the principle of autonomous learning*). Learning itself is not initiated and steered by means of ritualized presentation and reception processes but by discussions and active management (*the principle of learning through communication and interaction*). Finally, this type of learning does not take place in relatively enclosed institutions that are defined (and often paralysed) by bureaucratic organization, but is opened up by keeping to the practices of everyday life (*the principle of relatedness to everyday life*).

These requirements are not, as might be thought, Utopian, because technological progress enables them to be fulfilled. This was the case in the 1960s and 1970s, and is most certainly the case today, because now much more effective media for communication and information can be used for learning and teaching.

5.1.3 Correlations

A succinct and extremely pragmatic explanation for the special correlation between distance education and open learning was provided by John Daniel (1988: 127), Vice-Chancellor of the UK's Open University. He derives this explanation from a definition of distance education. In his analysis, 'distance education' simply means those forms of learning and teaching that make a much greater use of other forms of communication than face-to-face teaching. These forms may be called 'open learning' because they make learning accessible to more people. *Extended accessibility* is therefore a first criterion.

In this context we should not forget a point of conflict. There are university teachers who do not wish to have anything to do with these innovative experiments, primarily for the sake of upholding tradition, and reject the principle of open learning. If they teach and research at a distance-teaching university, they strive to approximate and adapt their teaching system as far as possible to the teaching methods of the traditional universities. Basically, they regard distance education merely as a form of traditional university teaching provided through different media, and hold that open learning has nothing at all to do with them. However, Daniel's definition shows just how intensively the nature of study changes simply by means of extended accessibility. Although the university teachers who speak out against open learning would never admit this, they in fact work in a university that may not be 'open' but has certainly been 'opened'.

Additional criteria were referred to by Lord Crowther, the first Chancellor of the Open University, during its inauguration ceremony in 1969. He stated that it should be open in four ways, namely to people, places, methods and ideas (Tunstall, 1974: X). Along with the principle of extended accessibility referred to above, this alludes to the characteristic connection of distance education with a great number of learning locations throughout a country, whereby the distance from the university is no longer a barrier to learning. This *independence of the learning location* is therefore a second category of 'openness'.

Openness as to methods is a necessary precondition for the foundation of every distance-teaching university, because learning and teaching behaviour must be fundamentally different for the simple reason that knowledge is transmitted by means of technical information and communications media. In this way, an otherwise unknown and hardly attainable measure of *methodological flexibility* is achieved. This places a distance-teaching university in a position where it can make much better use of the methods of open learning than a traditional university.

Openness to new ideas would never be denied by any university teacher because this is part of their profession and of their conception of themselves. At the same time, teachers at a distance-teaching university must also cope with conceptions and ideas brought to them by students from the world of work, or by experts from radio and television stations, by representatives of other universities with which the distance-teaching university cooperates, by educational technologists, and possibly by adult-education specialists as well. If these groups do not summon up the required open-mindedness to conceptions and experiences from other academic and practical areas, a distance-teaching university will suffer much more than a traditional university.

If we use these four criteria as a basis, namely the opening-up of access to more students, the geographical independence of the institution's location, methodological flexibility, and an intensified exchange of ideas, then every distance-teaching university, including the FernUniversität in Hagen, might be described as an 'open university'. The reason for this is found in their uniqueness. Therefore, use of the double term 'open and distance learning', which is spreading at present, is certainly justified, even if it does sound a little intrusive that the ornamental epithet 'open' is so clearly and frequently linked with this form of learning and teaching. All distance-teaching universities may also describe themselves as 'open' because, in contrast to traditional universities, they expose their teaching programmes to outside view through published course material and teaching programmes on radio and television, so that professionals and public alike can acquire information on the programmes at any time. Tunstall (1974: IX) refers in this context to openness 'in the sense of a goldfish bowl': people stand around the aquarium admiring the beautiful swimming movements of the colourful fish but without being seen themselves.

5.1.4 Didactic activities

There may a number of university teachers who regard the concept of open learning as attractive but reject its application in university teaching. However, in the context of the efforts towards reforming universities in the 1970s and 1980s, there were in fact tendencies in Germany towards open learning in universities, and this is something we must keep in mind. The concept of open learning grew in part out of the critique of traditional university teaching which came into being in the struggles following 1968.

The aim, then, was to create *equality of opportunity*, to strengthen the autonomy and self-activity of students through *learning by research activities*, to abolish the hierarchical relationship between teachers and students and replace it by a partnership, to integrate the learning interests of students in university education, because these were ignored by university teachers as a result of their intensive orientation towards teaching contents and their systematic presentation, to relate studies more to life and work, and to aspire to communicative action as an effective method of disseminating knowledge. The reform ideas of the concept of open learning are therefore certainly feasible even for the area of traditional university teaching. In addition in Germany – and this is something that is particularly important in our context – in order to provide more opportunities for open learning, the *Sozialistischer Studentenbund* and the Conference of Non-professional Teachers demanded the introduction of distance education in universities in the Federal Republic of Germany.

If we look at distance education in respect of the reform aims referred to above, we can see clearly its particular affinity to open learning. It tends to be egalitarian, helps to realize equality of opportunity, is based largely on the self-activity of autonomous learners, has more intensive references to life and work, and, in the study centres, places great value on intensified interaction and communication. However (and this must be appreciated as well), the demands derived from this are not only not supported by most university teachers, including those in the FernUniversität, but are in fact very often rejected because they deviate too much from the traditional ideas of what constitutes university teaching.

5.1.5 Economic, social and political influences

It is not only didactical aspects, in the narrow sense, of open learning that foster the establishment of open universities. There are also deeper causes, namely motives and influences that have a societal background. The term 'open university' can be interpreted multidimensionally. Van den Boom and Schlusmans (1989: 6) showed these dimensions clearly in their study *Didactics of Open Education – Background, Analysis and Approaches*. They show us what protagonists of open learning understand by the term 'open university' above and beyond the criteria we have already mentioned: They combine this term with the following expectations and demands:

- university education is to be made less expensive;
- more people are to be enabled to take part in cultural life;
- the overcrowded traditional universities are to be relieved;
- new groups of students are to be formed;
- the further democratization of society is to be supported by enabling more people to study while working, thus making the world in which they live more transparent to them and empowering them to act autonomously;
- lifelong learning, which has been propagated for decades, is to receive better opportunities for realization; and
- additional chances and further impetus are to be provided for people to gain more qualifications, so as to enable them to survive in today's employment(/unemployment) world.

Another important motive is not contained in this list, although it played a significant part in the founding of open universities: *opening up access* to university education. This has been realized in the UK's Open University and the Open Universiteit in the Netherlands, but remains an explosive issue of educational and university policy in Germany, because the FernUniversität here is forced to fall back on those restrictive regulations that apply to all other universities as well.

Where distance education has been developed with the aims of *open learning,* the demands listed above provide considerable energy. If these expectations and requirements are taken into account in the development of an open university, and even if this is only done in part, the university may be described without fear of contradiction as a 'reform university'. This has pedagogical consequences as well, because student numbers are of a size never seen in traditional universities, and also because these students display learning behaviour that is alien to students at traditional universities.

From here it is easy to show the many points at which the pedagogical structure of distance education at distance-teaching universities and open universities differs from that at traditional universities. It is not merely the innovative system of course development and the distribution of teaching, or the bridging of distances and the necessity of self-study, as many observers think. The fact is – and this must be stressed – that this distance education is anchored in societal, social and economic processes in a way that is different from the traditional universities. This is another reason for avoiding superficial comparisons.

If we take these endeavours together and examine them in detail, we become aware of a strong educational policy and social reformist trend that gives meaning to the concept of open learning. This is particularly intensive in the UK, where the term 'open learning' played a considerable part in the discussions on the further development of the education system and therefore had an intensive political colouring. The Open University was founded in 1969 in an atmosphere generated by educational policy discussions. But the concept played a considerable role beyond this, as can be seen in Nigel Paine's monograph *Open Learning in Transition* (1988). The foundation of the National Extension College, and its intensive efforts to establish 'second-chance education' must be seen in this context, but also the efforts made at the time to establish an Open Tech and an Open College alongside the Open University. The National Extension College has also earned praise for passing on the concept of open learning in developing countries.

In the USA, the concepts of open learning manifested themselves through the foundation of alternative institutes of higher education that provided for non-traditional study. Their aim was to enable adults, including members of minority groups who were attending poorer schools, to attend university on a technological basis. I would like to refer here to the Empire State College, the 'University Without Walls' movement that grew strongly in the 1970s but has since been broken up, the Regents Degree Program in the state of New York, the University of Mid-America and the Independence University. These alternative forms of university education were supported at the time by foundations and governments. The importance attributed to this movement by academics can be see in two excellent books: Cyril O Houle's *The External Degree* (1974) and Patricia Cross's *Adults as Learners. Increasing Participation and Facilitating Learning* (1981). Patricia Cross has in addition discussed forms of open learning in other books, and with an intensity that is difficult to find in any other country.

With the realization of the concept of open learning in the tertiary sector, the two educational-policy and socio-politically motivated reform movements in the UK and the USA followed above all the aim of creating additional learning opportunities for *adults*, which means, pedagogically speaking, the development of a university education system tailored to the needs of adults that is not simply a copy of traditional university education.

Ross H Paul from the Laurentian University in Canada provides a revealing insight (1993) into the atmosphere in which this discussion is held at open universities. His arguments attract attention initially because of their particular adult-educational ethos and egalitarian *élan*. In his opinion, all open universities believe that most adult students can study with success at a university, independently of their age, gender, economic status, domicile, occupational status and prior education, if they are given the opportunity and provided with support. This extremely idealistic pedagogical assessment would be contradicted more or less violently by university teachers at the FernUniversität (for example). Once again it can be seen how great are the effects of different cultural and academic traditions and other factors in society on the pedagogical structure of distance education. We can also see how easily adult educational maxims and academic requirement levels in different learning cultures can clash in the pedagogical development of distance education.

It is also pedagogically interesting to see the form that support for adult students in open learning should take. This presupposes a considerable amount of administrative flexibility on the part of the university (matriculation at any time; no restrictions on sending in assignments; cooperation in setting examination dates; and the provision of a faculty-based information, counselling and tutor service). And students are granted greater curricular self-determination. They should be able to make their own decisions on the content and structure of what they learn. Put more precisely, as far as possible they should be able to choose how they learn, when they learn, where they learn and what they learn (Paine, 1988: XI).

In view of the learning and teaching culture in continental European universities, these demands appear to us to be Utopian. But we do not have to assume that open universities are far in advance of the FernUniversität in this aspect. According to Paul (1993), the ideal of this kind of open learning is not achieved at all in practice in open universities, for all that can be found are certain approximations. He diagnoses, in rather a sanguine fashion, an enormous gap between this pedagogical theory and its realization. Harris (1988) goes even further in his criticism. In the open universities he sees 'merely a modernisation of traditional practice that subjects students in addition to a rationalising and more individualising control'. The same could be claimed with regard to continental European distance-teaching universities.

There are several reasons why distance-education practice has not kept pace with its declared aims, apart from that fact that we are dealing with general human experience here. Two reasons are often overlooked, which is why Paul refers to them expressly. Among other things, open universities have to overcome barriers that are found in the *persons* taking part in the learning and teaching process. Professors who experienced their professional socialization at a traditional university are not prepared to become supporters of open learning. Secondly – and this is perhaps even more serious – students themselves bring extremely conventional expectations with them when they start studying, and these have a great effect on the newly conceived learning and teaching processes. Anthropogenous and socio-cultural factors have an intense effect on open learning in distance education, factors that can easily be neglected or even overlooked in a merely instructional technology approach.

The concept of open learning has not played any significant role in the FernUniversität. There was no commitment by it to such aims, even in the 1970s and 1980s. Although there were at least corresponding projects in adult education, a majority could not be found in this institution for (for example) consistently opening up access to the university and for more open forms of learning and teaching. On the contrary, there was firm resistance for ten years to efforts to enable open access to the university. And even the statutory task of commitment to continuing education has been realized only slowly and without much conviction. In comparison with the open universities in the UK and the Netherlands, the FernUniversität has gone down its own special conservative and reluctant road. There may be good reasons for this, but if we compare the UK's Open University with the German FernUniversität and use international standards from the viewpoint of education policy and distance-teaching pedagogics, the FernUniversität has not kept up because it has not let itself be sufficiently guided in its work by the concepts of open learning and the open university.

5.1.6 Commentary

Those two concepts of 'open learning' and 'the open university' provide perspectives for pedagogical reforms of distance education. They should be determining the work of theoreticians and practitioners even where their aims are long-range, demanding, and can therefore only be achieved in part initially. The social value-judgements linked with these concepts lend special weight and significance to distance education with regard to education policy.

5.2 Lifelong learning

5.2.1 The current situation

There are trends in pedagogics that appear rapidly and then gradually lose their relevance. We can see this in the example of some of the activities that were fiercely propagated in Germany in the 1970s. But now we no longer hear of efforts to counter the *educational catastrophe*, to reduce the educational disadvantages of *Catholic girls in rural districts*, to introduce *programmed instruction* or to make more use of *language laboratories* in language lessons. Other trends continue to arise, and can continue to be encountered even decades later. The propagation of the concept of 'lifelong learning' is one of these.

With this concept we can in fact see two stages of development towards its current relevance. The first stage was initiated in about 1970, when supranational educational organizations such as UNESCO, the OECD, the Council of Europe and the Standing Committee of European Education Ministers introduced the concept of lifelong learning into international discussions under different slogans and committed themselves to its realization – something that is without precedent in the history of pedagogics, it should be noted. The concept retained its relevance, even if it was reduced in the 1980s. The second stage started around the mid-1990s, and interest in the concept is now greater than ever before and is of a completely different quality. The economic, technical and social changes we have experienced and the new challenges set by the information society have made this necessary. The slogan 'lifelong learning' is once again on everybody's lips.

The new relevance found its expression in important meetings and conferences. The German Minister of Education, Science, Research and Technology supported a specialized conference entitled 'Lifelong learning' in 1985, and in 1996 organized a working conference on the subject entitled 'Self-determined lifelong learning'. In the same year, the National Conference in Germany for Lifelong Learning was held in Bonn on the subject 'Lifelong learning – the march into the future. A fashionable trend or an educational necessity?' In addition, the Ministry published educational policy guidelines on the subject (Dohmen, 1996). Furthermore, at the most recent German Adult Education Conference in Leipzig, lifelong learning was a central subject.

On a pan-European level, people are coming together who are continuing to pursue the aims of lifelong learning. There is now a European Lifelong Learning Initiative (ELLI) in the European Union. In Bonn there is a National Committee for Lifelong Learning in Germany, and there are similar activities in 18 other countries. In order to demonstrate just how important this topic is for us today, we should not forget the European Year of Lifelong Learning, which the European Commission proclaimed for 1996.

5.2.2 Explanation of the term

The difficulty in describing (and limiting) the term 'lifelong learning' arises from the history of its creation. Basically it describes a whole range of terms in which are found objectives in partial strategies that are supported by different international institutions. In 1970 the Council of Europe introduced the term 'permanent education' into the debate; in 1972 UNESCO followed with the demand for 'lifelong learning'; and in 1973 the OECD contributed the term 'recurrent education'. All three concepts aimed at no longer restricting learning to childhood and youth and to the prescribed institutions, but at putting a different emphasis on school education, vocational training and continuing education in the life-cycle. The aim was to spread learning over a person's lifetime.

However, this basic idea was interpreted and accentuated differently. Among other things, a series of characteristic features of this concept became clear, some of which refer to the new concept of *education* and others to the new kind of *learning*. The following show some examples from both groups.

A new understanding of education

Set out below are seven pointers to a new understanding of education. They are as follows:

1. *The educational process is viewed as a whole*. Education takes place in all phases of a person's life as well as in all situations and under all circumstances. All stages and forms of learning are included with the aim of unifying the educational process

2. *There is a change of pedagogical–didactical paradigms*. Education is no longer to be regarded as imparting and assimilating set contents but as a lifelong process that takes place within a person to aid personal development, to communicate with others, to question the world on the basis of personal experience and increasingly to bring self-realization (see Faure et al, 1973: 43).

3. *Several forms of education are integrated*. Formal education, non-formal education and informal education do not run alongside one another but must be related to one another. They complement and interpenetrate one another.
4. *Education and training are subject to a general functional change*. They no longer serve preparation for life and work but are themselves *an integral part of life and work* (see Skager and Dave, 1977: 6).
5. *Methods of experiencing and perceiving the educational process are mixed*. The previous unchangeable pattern of education and training, work, leisure time, and then retirement is broken down, and activities such as learning, working, recuperating and enjoying leisure interweave with one another (see OECD/CERI, 1973: 7–8)
6. *The role of traditional educational institutes is relativized*. Institutional and non-institutional education complement and embrace each other. This means that institutionalized education loses its monopoly position.
7. *The reform aim of egalitarian education is pursued*. In principle, everyone can take part in lifelong learning, and not just members of economically privileged or favoured classes. This contributes to the breakdown of educational privileges, the realignment of learning opportunities, and therefore to the democratization of education.

A new understanding of learning
For an analysis of the special pedagogical structure of distance education, it is an advantage if we are aware of the concepts that the supporters of lifelong learning have developed from learning itself. Below are nine of those most important features:

1. *Learning is regarded as a 'central basic function of human life'* (Dohmen, 1996: 23).
2. *Learning in adulthood is re-evaluated*. Learning in adulthood is no longer regarded as being contrary to tradition but as normal, desirable and necessary.
3. *High flexibility of the learning and teaching process is aimed for*. A quick change of content, methods, media and working methods enables better adjustment to changes to life and working relationships.
4. *Self-determined learning is demanded*. Lifelong learning is also seen as individually planned learning for which the student is responsible – in other words, autonomous learning.
5. *Great value is placed on learning how to learn*. This is above all necessary because traditional expository teaching and receptive learning do not impart any qualifications in this regard. But learning how to learn is essential for lifelong learning, especially in informal and self-initiated learning situations.
6. *Alternative structures and arrangements for learning are allowed*. Along with traditional and conventional forms of learning, new learning opportunities are likely to appear in unconventional forms as well.
7. *Great importance is attached to innovative and creative learning*. A receptiveness for new forms of learning and teaching and a readiness to try them out and take them over are presupposed.
8. *Social reform goals are aimed at*. The aim of more efficient learning for all throughout the whole of life is a 'better' life and a 'more attractive' future, not only for

the individual student but for society as well. Progress for humanity is the aim.

9. *Learning makes a specific contribution to the design and safeguarding of a humane future.* Lifelong learning is regarded as the sole way out of our society's crises resulting from war, violence, destruction of the environment, unemployment and social disenfranchisement.

Current aspects of lifelong learning

The concept of lifelong learning has been able to have such a great effect because it has been continuously and rigorously propagated by the three international institutions I have referred to as a guiding principle and instrument for a fundamental reform of educational systems throughout the world. Under the effect of the unstable developments of the recent past and the (probably) aggravated difficulties of the future, the concept of lifelong learning has been adapted to new requirements by UNESCO and the OECD. This has led to a changed understanding in some ways as to what lifelong learning actually is. Its aim is to help to meet the challenges of the future that are likely to result from (among other things) technological change, globalization of production and trade, growing financial problems for the state, increasing unemployment, ethnic conflicts, increasing crime, war and violence. According to Dohmen (1996: 23–8), great importance will therefore be placed on the following (among others):

- More importance than ever before will be placed on informal self-determined learning.
- In the realization of the concept of lifelong learning, a much more important role will be created for electronic information and communications media.
- All formal and informal learning will be integrated, with the help of the new media and communications technology, into an open-networked learning society.
- An open learning society will be created whose opportunities will be opened up through innovative information and counselling services.
- Realization of lifelong learning will be regarded as an important contribution to the overdue reform of the educational system.
- Lifelong learning must be made accessible in the same way for everyone.
- Open self-learning in the context of life and work will be regarded as an important component of lifelong learning.

5.2.3 Affinities

The campaign for lifelong learning, which has now lasted over two-and-a-half decades, has had a favourable effect in many ways on the development of distance education. By changing deep-rooted habits of thinking with regard to the functions of education and learning and by making the new attitudes and understanding known to politicians, specialists and an interested public, it has prepared the ground for a degree of acceptance of distance-teaching universities in the 1970s and 1980s that was not really expected – at least not to the extent encountered. A different climate of thinking was created, long-held taboos were weakened, and the willingness to experiment grew. Consequently, resistance to innovations as represented by distance education decreased.

The deeper reason for this can be seen in the following important structural correspondence of distance education with tendencies of lifelong learning:

1. The demand for a reappraisal of learning in adulthood has already been fulfilled in distance education. It is no longer a matter of visions, plans and intentions but it has actually been practised for 25 years and is institutionally safeguarded.
2. In many countries, distance-teaching universities extend the university landscape and have altered it in relation to the concept of lifelong learning.
3. Distance education conforms to the demand for the creation of additional alternative forms of learning. With regard to traditional university teaching, it can be seen as an alternative *par excellence* and be considered as a contribution to the innovation of the educational system.
4. The requirement that learning should be seen not only as preparation for life as an adult but also as an integral component of life and work has already been fulfilled by distance students. Learning usually takes place alongside students' private lives and alongside their working lives, but has an effect on both areas – and sometimes a significant effect. In many cases, learning is in fact integrated into life, work, leisure time and retirement.
5. Distance education enables participants, while they are learning, to realize who they are on the basis of their own experience.
6. In distance education, methods of experiencing and perceiving are mixed, whereas in traditional concepts of education they follow one another. Training and education, work and study, leisure time and study, and retirement and study do not exclude each other but complement each other. The different distribution of learning throughout life has already taken place here.
7. Distance education conforms to a great extent to the demand for greater attention to be paid to self-determined learning, as we have seen in Section 4.3. According to this concept, students have the opportunity themselves to determine where, when, how long, how much, how intensively, in what order and what rhythm they wish to learn, and to take responsibility for their selection. This self-determination can also be extended to cover the choice and sequence of contents, as in the model of contract learning and its successful application at the Empire State College.
8. Distance-teaching universities are dependent on 'learning how to learn' to a much greater extent than traditional universities. In fact, without an introduction to the strategies of self-study and training in special study techniques, distance education cannot take place at all.
9. Distance-teaching universities serve the aim of equalization of educational opportunities to a greater extent than other universities in that they introduce new groups of students to university education. These are people who would not normally be able to take part at that (tertiary) level of education because of their age, or where they live, or because of other special circumstances.
10. In many cases, distance students are motivated by the possibility of subsequent professional and social advancement.

11. Distance education must be seen as an essential contribution to the development of an open learning society, because practically everyone can take part at any time in university-level education, interrupt it or terminate it, and because teaching is so transparent as a result of the use of public media, much more so than in any traditional university. To use a slogan from American educational policy, distance teaching universities are literally 'universities without walls'.
12. As media-based universities, the experience of distance-teaching universities means that they have a much easier and quicker access to forms of disseminating knowledge used by the digital information and communications media. They are already on the road to the 'virtual university'.

If we take all these affinities together, we can see the great extent to which distance education is a model for the introduction and development of lifelong learning. In the future it will remain an asset in the transformation to the open learning society that we must aim for on the strength of this concept.

5.3 Industrialized learning and teaching

5.3.1 Relevance

The impetus for the interpretation of distance education as an '*industrialized*' form of learning and teaching, or as the *most* industrialized form of learning and teaching, came thirty years ago (Peters, 1967). Interest in this has never waned and, on the contrary, has increased. In recent years, the discussion on this attitude towards distance education has even been intensified (Peters, 1989; Campion, 1993; Farnes, 1993; Raggatt, 1993; Peters, 1994; Rumble, 1995a–c). The discussion is therefore of some importance because the aspect of industrialization is not found in pedagogical literature with regard to any other form of learning and teaching. The discussion underlines once again the special character of distance education.

5.3.2 Description of the concept

In the 1960s, when distance education was still being disregarded in pedagogics (in spite of the fact that even then it had a 70-year-long history to look back on) and was also still *terra incognita* for intensive and systematic research, it was difficult to review this form of learning and teaching, let alone to theorize about it. However, in the face of the increasing interest, it was high time that its pedagogical advantages and deficiencies were recognized and people made aware of its special features. Attempts were made to describe it using traditional pedagogical categories (Peters, 1967), but these remained unsatisfactory. For how could the description be complete if the restricted subject matter, the special role of the media and, in relation to demographic conditions, the advanced age and employment of students in distance learning were not properly dealt with? Or if distance education was characterized by the separation of students from teachers and fellow students, what about the indirect communication by means of correspondence that occurred and the predominant use of the medium of printed material? It was always seen merely as a special form of *traditional study* – although in reality it differs from this to a considerable extent.

To grasp what was special and 'essential' about distance education it was necessary to take a look at its *structural* differences. It is helpful here to examine the reasons for, and the circumstances of, its creation. For example, the question might be asked why distance teaching had developed in the mid-nineteenth century *outside* the institutions which a state had established for educating and training its citizens. Why was it able to gain in importance in the following decades, although it was neither intended nor desired, let alone planned, by those responsible for the nation's education? If we follow this line of questioning we come across the first indications of the different structural nature of distance education. In fact, we come up against a fundamental difference. In the case of distance education, funds were not to be applied, as is usual with state education, so that people could be educated and trained; people were supposed to learn so that the institute providing the instruction could *make* money, in other words make a profit. There were *commercial* reasons for the creation of distance education. Its pioneers were businessmen.

But there was yet another pointer: businessmen, the first operators of correspondence schools when the Industrial Age began to flourish, recognized the extraordinary opportunities available to those who no longer remained satisfied with the traditional methods of learning and teaching, as private schools wanted to, but who were prepared to use the new methods of industrial goods production in the learning and teaching process.

It is difficult to imagine how such a complete change in learning and teaching methods could have been any more radical. Beforehand, everything on the teaching side had been in a *single* hand, but now there was *division of labour* – for example, planning, developing and presenting the subject matter and correcting assignments was now done by different persons at different times and at different locations. The development of written courses *before* the start of teaching itself became more and more important, and corresponded to production planning in the industrialized production process, which was also carried out by specially qualified experts. Where teachers had previously literally used their physical presence to present the subject, this was now done on a *mechanized* (and later *automated*) basis and, where teaching had been individualized to a great extent by the personality of the teacher, it was now *standardized*, *normalized* and *formalized*. If teaching had previously been at all times a unique 'event' in the subjective experience of participants in interplay with a learning group, it was now *objectivized*, being offered to all participants of a defined course in the same way and with the possibility of repetition at will. The most important consequence of objectivization was that teaching became a product that could be altered and *optimized*, and above all sold – not just locally but anywhere, like an industrially manufactured product. In fact, people began to advertise the product 'teaching' and to open up cross-border markets to improve sales.

Because of these structural characteristics, distance teaching in the nineteenth century and distance education in the twentieth differ in decisive points from traditional face-to-face teaching with a group of learners. Its organizers rationalized teaching to a much greater extent than was usual in traditional teaching. To do this, they used machines – the printing press – to make use of the benefits of mass production, transport mechanisms for distribution of instruction, and they also aimed at acquiring as many students (ie paying customers) as possible, and in fact the number of students was regarded as a guide to success. All these special features make it obvious that distance teaching at this period is to be regarded as a structurally fundamentally different system of learning and teaching. This justifies seeing it in fact as the most (intensively) industrialized form of learning and teaching.

The concept of industrialized teaching was confirmed by the work of the distance-teaching universities founded since the 1970s, above all by the UK's Open University (see Section 7.2). What was so spectacular about the work of these new institutions? The application of the principle of *mass* production and *mass* consumption to academic teaching. It is no accident that distance-teaching universities are among the largest universities in their respective countries; in some cases, they have to cope with hundreds of thousands of students (see Daniel, 1997). In this way they cooperate in the worldwide transformation process that is making academic education not just accessible to society's élite but to as many people as possible who are willing and able to study.

Peter Raggatt (1993: 21) characterized the working methods of these distance-teaching universities using the example of the UK's Open University, which he knows well as he is a member of its School of Education. He regards the following features of industrialization as being characteristic: restriction to a limited number of standard products, the application of mass-production methods, automation, the division of labour to carry out specialized tasks, centralized control, and a hierarchically structured bureaucracy. In Raggatt's judgement, the learning and teaching process at the Open University has exactly these features. Here, the number of distance-education courses is restricted, as many as possible being published in a single printing run, which achieves the effect of mass production (ie high volume and low unit cost). Also for cost reasons, these courses are used for several years; in fact, they often have a working life of around eight years. Considerable cost savings through the increased production of longer, standardized courses for relatively large homogeneous groups of students make a significant difference. Raggatt described this development stage of industrialization as 'Fordism' (after the motor car mass-producer), and all distance-teaching universities work more or less in accordance with this form of industrialization.

5.3.3 A controversy

Some authors have attempted to relativize the validity of this characterization. David Sewart (1992: 229) pointed quite rightly to the application of principles of mass production in today's mass universities in which there are certain forms of division of labour, specialization and increasing alienation between teachers and students. And Nick Farnes (1993: 10) has even shown how the different phases of industrialization have had an effect on the overall educational system and enabled it to cope with the problems of mass production. This was the only possible way at the time to establish general primary school education on the basis of compulsory schooling, and from there to advance to the expansion of secondary education and tertiary education, a development that is culminating at present in efforts to establish mass higher education.

However, Greville Rumble (1995a: 19) is of the opinion that regarding industrialization as typical of distance education is incorrect, because proof can also be shown of the industrialization of learning and teaching in classrooms and group instruction. If trends towards industrialization can be verified in traditional universities, critics claim that the characterization of distance education as industrialized learning and teaching loses its force. In addition, characterising distance education as the most industrialized form of learning and teaching is regarded as an overstatement, and also nowadays something of an irrelevance because, for some time now, we outside the Third World have been in a post-industrialist era – the Information Age.

The effect of industrial methods at traditional universities cannot in fact be disputed. Why should it be? These developments merely confirm once again how industrialized methods of thinking and acting penetrate *all* areas of life and work, infiltrate them and alter them. But the concept of industrialized learning and teaching no longer refers to the application of one or even several principles of industrialization, but to the analogy between the learning and teaching process and the process of industrial production. In both cases, *all* their constitutive features are concentrated and linked to one another in a systematic sequence. Industrialized teaching therefore means – and this must be repeated here – careful prior planning on a division of labour basis, costly development, and objectivization through media, and this makes academic teaching into a product that can be mass-produced in the same way as an industrial product: it can be kept in store, distributed over a wide area, evaluated and optimized.

Where else in the academic world can a comparable form of teaching be found? Nowhere, even if professors responsible for a field demarcate their subjects from one another (specialization), solve accruing problems with members of the middle hierarchy (the division of labour), discuss with students on the telephone, transmit their lectures to other rooms via the university's own TV system if lecture halls are crowded, and drive to university by car (mechanization). However, these effects of industrialization remain external to learning and teaching at a traditional university. In principle they still take place in accordance with the same structural patterns that stem from the pre-industrial age. The objections therefore do not hold water.

In addition, as a reaction to these critical relativizations we can also point to the fundamental and far-reaching difference between teaching at a traditional university and at a distance teaching university. No matter how much technological and organizational effort is used to operate and maintain traditional universities, in particular mass universities, teaching itself is *oral* at such institutions, the same as occurred many thousands of years ago in India, Egypt and Greece. In distance-teaching universities, on the other hand, it takes place in an additional *coded* and *media-based* form and only on the basis of a bundle of industrialized processes. Is this statement banal? Not at all! All it does is bring out the peculiarity of the most industrialized teaching, which will be explained by means of a brief industrial–sociological observation with recourse to Habermas (see Peters, 1968: 62).

Traditional teaching is *communicative* action that grew out of traditional oral culture and is therefore elemental. Distance education, on the other hand, is only possible on the basis of *instrumentally rational and strategic* actions that have to be imparted technologically. To underline the difference still further with some of Habermas' categories, which he used to describe the industrialized society, the communicative structure of oral teaching can be described as follows: it is determined by reciprocal behavioural expectations and societal norms; it brings about the internalization of roles; and it uses an intersubjectively divided language of communication. In distance education, the communicative structure is completely different: the actions of teachers and students are determined mainly through technical rules; it is a question of skills and qualifications rather than roles; and a context-free language is used. This difference is decisive, and it is the result of an industrial process.

Let me stress once again that work processes at the periphery of learning and teaching *can* be industrialized to a great extent at traditional universities. In distance teaching universities they *must* be. Rumble refers above all to these work processes – printing, despatch, etc – because he is interested in the management of learning and teaching systems. As educational theoreticians, however, we must concentrate on the process of interaction between teachers and students If we do this, we can only classify oral teaching at traditional universities as 'pre-industrial' on the basis of the criteria of the concept presented here; and, with regard to distance education, we must regard the set formula of the most industrialized form of learning and teaching as illuminating.

5.3.4 New concepts of industrialization

It should be borne in mind that Peter Raggatt did not refer to these Fordist characteristics to eulogize the Open University but to criticize it. According to Raggatt, the Fordism of the Open University (and, of course, of other distance-teaching universities operating in a similar way) is an obsolete model. He is not alone in this opinion and finds support from authors such as Campion and Renner (1992), Farnes (1993), and Campion (1995). In their opinion, distance education must adjust itself to the fundamental changes that all industrial societies are experiencing at the moment. Today, work is often organized and carried out in a completely different way to that of 20 years ago. The new problems facing distance education cannot be solved with the obsolete methods of rationalization through mass production, and new concepts must therefore be developed for its future developments. Approaches are already being discussed, particularly *neo*-industrialized and *post*-industrialized forms of learning and teaching in distance education.

Neo-industrialization
Neo-industrialization (or neo-Fordism) has led to many changes in working life. The characteristic slogans here are 'high product innovation', 'high process variability', but at the same time, 'low employee responsibility' (Badham and Mathews,

1989, as quoted by Campion and Renner 1992: 12). The endeavour to achieve product innovation and process variability is a reaction to the development of the market and the changes in demand. It is at present both necessary and possible because, on the one hand, the demands of consumers with more spending power have become higher, more specific and more varied, and, on the other hand, the production and distribution of goods have been adapted to meet this need by having been to a large extent computerized. The aim is no longer to produce the same goods in the same quality at the lowest possible price for as many consumers as possible with the same needs. As we know, Ford sold more than 15 million copies of the same car model, and this method of production led to a great equalization of consumption. The problem now is to address many very *specific* consumer wishes. Goods are therefore produced in smaller volumes and constantly adapted to new requirements. In contrast, and this is typical for this concept, work is still being organized on the lines of the concept of industrialisation. This means: hierarchical graduations of responsibility and centralized control with the help of a bureaucratized administration.

If distance-teaching universities wished to meet the challenges of neo-Fordism, they would have to stop offering their courses, developed at great expense, standardized and produced in large numbers, which become more outdated from year to year in spite of all good intentions regarding course updating, and instead of this undertake targeted efforts to adapt them rapidly to the new requirements and to 'consumer wishes' – in this case the different requirements of their students. Accordingly, what is no longer needed are large-scale courses for as many students as possible, but a variety of courses with low numbers where the course content is constantly being updated (see Farnes, 1993).

Post-industrialization

With post-industrialization (or post-Fordism), the same aims can be found as with neo-industrialization, namely high product innovation and high process variability. But in addition – and this is decisive – there is a radically different direction in the organization of work sequences, because the aim now is 'high labour responsibility'.

Considerable changes have had to be made to achieve this. Goods are no longer mass-produced in the same form and kept in stock: with the help of computers they are now manufactured 'on demand' and 'just in time'. Even the special wishes of smaller consumer groups can be satisfied in this way. At the same time, the organization of work itself is changed in this phase. Division of labour is limited, and if possible done away with altogether. Instead, smaller working groups with more qualifications and greater responsibility are formed. Hierarchical forms of organization are replaced by horizontal networks of relationships. Instead of semi-skilled workers trained to operate machinery, there is a smaller number employees who are more highly qualified, more flexible and more versatile, and who can be complemented by a varying number of employees engaged on a temporary basis to carry out current tasks only. Cost savings are the first commandment for increasing productivity, which is why companies aim for lean design, lean production and lean supply.

Those who are following this development must ask themselves whether requirements in the world of academic education and continuing education have not increased as well, and become more varied, and whether they can be satisfied with the previous methods of (industrialized) distance education. If the answer to this question is 'no', then we must consider whether distance-teaching universities should not also attempt to recognize rapidly changing demands for education and continuing education and satisfy them by means of courses that can be drawn up and amended easily (equivalent to rapid product innovation).

This itself would force distance-teaching universities to alter their working processes. Instead of a centrally controlled system of development and production on the basis of a division of labour, many smaller decentralized working groups would be formed, who would each be responsible for the development of their own teaching programmes and would therefore be more autonomous – both internally to the institution and externally to the world at large. But what is even more important is that the classical forms of learning and teaching in distance education (standardized courses, standardized counselling) would have to be replaced or complemented by forms that were much more flexible with regard to curricula, time, and location (ie an allowance for variability of processes). Phrases such as 'autonomous learning', 'independent learning in the digital learning environment', 'teleconferencing', 'intensive personal counselling', 'contract learning' and the combination with, and integration of, forms of traditional university teaching indicate the direction that the development might take. It would be a revolution.

5.3.5 Pedagogical consequences

In the context of this book the importance of the concepts of industrialized and post-industrialized learning and teaching sketched out here depends on whether and how far they are helpful for the planning, development, control and interpretation of distance education. This point is often put by sceptics, who are unable to see how concepts that work with terms from industrial sociology, or, even worse, from the field of industrial production itself, can be valid in pedagogical circumstances and reproduce them. To them, what happens in factories and lecture halls seems utterly different.

In fact, it does appear to be difficult to derive starting points from these concepts, for example for the selection and evaluation of learning aims and contents, which is a main concern of humanistic pedagogics. The clarification of genuine pedagogical or adult-education questions using these concepts also appears to be difficult, if not downright impossible. The horizon of values does not become visible in the theories of industrial production, if we disregard those of instrumental nature such as productivity or efficiency. Nevertheless, deeper analysis leads to interesting insights.

First of all, a general assessment must be made. Many decisions that are taken in the planning, development, and revision of learning and teaching systems in distance education in compliance with, and taking account of, the criteria of industrialization may in the first place serve to control the overall process, but can at the same time have an effect on the ways and means by which university teachers teach and students learn, and whereby questions of pedagogics in the narrow sense therefore come into play. A systemic connection is found from the very start between learning and teaching systems interpreted or developed in accordance with concepts of industrialization and the general processes of learning and teaching, because the education and training of students is viewed as the 'product' in the process. All measures that enable students to learn, that make it easier for them to learn, or that improve learning are pedagogical from this very intention, no matter what criteria of industrialization or post-industrialization are being used by those considering the matter pedagogically. The mixture of economic, technological, organizational, and pedagogical influences, which can of course be verified in every event organized in traditional university teaching, is simply more obvious in distance education. Because the pedagogical consequences of the three concepts outlined here, which are derived from forms of production, are naturally different, we will be examining them separately.

The concept of industrialized learning and teaching
The following seven effects that are specifically pedagogical can be seen:

1. The concept of industrialized learning and teaching opens up a macro-pedagogical perspective to those taking part in the planning and development of distance education. While traditional pedagogics focused primarily during planning and preparation on the micro-pedagogical perspective, ie on the interaction between teachers and students, the view here is extended to cover the totality of all activities of the participants.
2. For students it provides deep impressions of the connection between *all* learning and teaching activities and their integration in the process. The learning and teaching process does not start at the beginning of a lecture or seminar, but much earlier. And it does not end when students leave the lecture hall or the seminar room, but much later. The division of labour leads to the following sequence: planning, developing, distributing, presentation, counselling and evaluation. These are all connected with and affect one another.
3. The greatest effect of industrialized teaching is, however, a far-reaching change in teaching behaviour, and perhaps even more so in learning behaviour. Where specialization based on the division of labour reduces university teachers to subject-matter specialists, requires the distribution of teaching matter with the help of technical media, and enables isolated initiated self-study that is only interrupted occasionally by face-to-face communication with others, these are considerable changes in the field of pedagogics.
4. The concept of industrialized learning and teaching makes it easier for participants to behave in conformity with the system when learning and teaching. Industrialized learning and teaching is constituted through the interplay of many system elements. Only if we prepare ourselves for this and see ourselves as part of a whole system can we be successful in avoiding dysfunctional pedagogical actions. Those who adhere to the attitudes and ideas of pre-industrial teaching methods will certainly come to grief with them in distance education. The concepts of industrialized learning and teaching help us to recognize and avoid mixing elements of systems that are structurally completely different.

5.   Seen from a macro-pedagogical point of view, the direct effects on learning and teaching are particularly serious and obvious. If industrialized working methods mean that tens or even hundreds of thousands of people are provided with an opportunity to continue their education by studying – although they would never have been able to do this in a conventional system – the effects on adult education and pedagogics cannot be overestimated, even if support for classes remote from the educational system through distance education is at present no longer *en vogue*.

6.   For learning and teaching itself, the development of courses on the basis of the division of labour and through the cooperation of specialists is extremely important, because high-quality material is created that is pedagogically suitable, reflects the latest levels of research, and is presented particularly effectively. To a certain extent this enables a considerable improvement of the learning and teaching situation. At the same time, however, this pedagogical advantage turns out to be a *disadvantage* if we look at it from the aspect of another way of understanding learning. It benefits, strengthens and entrenches the *modus* of expository teaching and receptive learning that it is in fact supposed to overcome. Autonomous learning is extremely difficult to put into place when learners are guided in short steps in courses worked out to the smallest detail.

7.   The development of closed curricula, and of the learning and teaching models and learning paths that provide for them, also gives benefit. This makes the development of *open* curricula more difficult because, basically, there cannot really be plans for proceeding down self-chosen learning paths, creating a flexible system of multifaceted learning programmes using different situations, media or institutions, and taking account of the life and work situation of students. Open learning, in the real sense of the word, cannot take place.

The concept of neo-industrial learning and teaching

If this alternative concept were realized, the range of courses offered by distance teaching universities would be changed structurally, because 'major' courses with long service lives would be replaced by short-term 'minor' courses that can be amended and renewed quickly and that are directed at many different learning interests (equivalent to rapid product innovation). This must, of course have an effect on the way in which students learn. Because students must at this stage make their study wishes known, so that they can be considered, it is necessary that they become clear about what they really want to do and about the study programmes that can be most useful to them in their particular situation. Students should thus be considerably active in their approach, and they will be forced to abandon receptive learning. By itself, this would appear to be pedagogical progress. Because multifaceted courses must be adapted to the special learning situations of students and their study objects, such courses must also be student-oriented.

Distance education courses would still be developed centrally on the basis of division of labour, but mass production would be considerably restricted. Organization of teaching would be local, and would be moved to study centres, for example, which would have more *face-to-face phases* than is possible in industrialized learning.

The task here is to develop different forms in teaching (process variability). To achieve this, the aim is to establish mixed-mode universities in which comparatively small groups of students work, because support for very large groups is no longer either planned or possible. The learning and teaching process finds support through more social contacts and more communication.

The concept of post-industrial learning and teaching

Decisive changes to learning and teaching behaviour would also take place under the influence of post-Fordism. The following scenario should make this clear.

Because an advanced division of labour is withdrawn and decentralization is aimed at, classical course development teams have the ground removed from under their feet. Instead, variable and short-term courses are developed on their own responsibility by small working groups in the faculties and departments. Professors and lecturers belong to these small working groups, which are responsible for everything to do with their courses – not just for planning and design, but also for production, distribution, evaluation and continuous course care. They would also have to familiarize themselves with production technologies in the field of printing and video, but this has been made much easier by modern technical media for DTP, electronic publishing and media publishing (Kaderali et al, 1994), which are all extremely user-friendly. Up to now, technical media have brought about a division of labour more in the field of teaching, but the concentration can now be on development work with the help of these new media.

The responsibility of the teachers is restricted, however, because chairmanship of the group revolves among group members, and representatives of students, tutors and other participants in learning and teaching, or those affected by it, are included as partners. It is no longer expected that participants in course development are specialized experts but that they are in possession of broad and multifaceted competence. With regard to curricular work, university teachers would no longer be expected to pass on the results of their research in the form of courses but to find out exactly the learning requirements of defined groups of students and make every effort to satisfy these requirements as quickly and effectively as possible.

This also has an effect on learning behaviour. The traditional relationship between teachers and students is altered in that learning is determined much more by the students themselves. The post-modern awareness of life makes a more continuous communication and interaction in the group into a focal point for distance education and allocates a rather attendant and supplementary role to learning in isolation with structured texts. In this way, the previous relationship of the two learning forms to one another, which is a consequence of the concept of independent learning, is turned on its head.

In order to be able to achieve this kind of distance education, supporters of post-industrialized learning are also aiming at the establishment of the organizational form of the dual or mixed-mode university. Mixed forms, consisting of a distance-teaching university and a traditional university working together, would lead to a considerable diversification of the teaching programmes for students of *both* groups and reduce the cost of studying (Campion and Renner, 1992:

11). In this kind of institution, learning in small groups would be favoured, which means that the aim of mass higher education would become less important. On the whole, according to Campion at least (1991), distance education would become 'more decentralized, more democratic, more oriented to co-determination, more open and more flexible', which means that the learning and teaching would be differentiated from that of industrialized distance education from a pedagogical point of view of as well, because it would also provide better conditions for socialization.

Two tasks for distance-teaching pedagogics

Firstly, the validity and binding nature of the concepts of neo-Fordism and post-Fordism have to be examined. The conclusion by analogy that has been indicated might be unfounded and may be incorrect. Along with Greville Rumble (1995b: 26), many observers will not believe in an automatic adaptation of the methods of distance education to the latest structural alterations to the methods of industrial production, particularly when they only become clear in some sectors and are exemplified above all in just a few branches – for example, motor vehicle production. Yet if there continue to be correlations between the methods of the industrial production of goods and those of industrialized learning and teaching, they are certainly not as unsupported as has been claimed. Some of the analogies presented are astonishing, if they are in fact correct, but so were those that led in the first place to the development of the concept of industrialized learning and teaching itself.

Secondly, post-industrial models should be worked out, and experiments carried out with them in practice, if the feasibility of the post-industrial concept is to be verified. These models would have to correspond to the theoretical premises referred to, as well as absorbing the concepts of open, autonomous and communicative learning. Above all, however, they would have to make use of the new opportunities made available by digitally based learning and teaching. We may then be able to see the outlines and structures of a 'university of the future' (see Section 8.2).

5.3.6 Doubts and misgivings

During discussions of the two post-industrial concepts of distance education, some critical points are encountered that up to now have not been included sufficiently in the calculations. These are:

- Universities have survived many reforms unchanged at heart. Distance-teaching universities are still universities. In particular, where we are dealing with autonomous, self-governing institutions it is easy for the openly propagated or even concealed self-interest of professors or institutions themselves to resist the realization of the post-industrial concepts.
- Distance-teaching universities are involved in both higher education and in continuing education. While it is possible in the case of continuing education to imagine a variable system of 'smaller' courses tailored exactly to the requirements of students, this is more difficult in the case of more rigid, examina-

tion-related specialist degree courses. In any case, resistance to a fresh approach would be at its greatest here.

- Distance-teaching universities have fixed structures that were designed and developed with regard to industrialized learning and teaching, and by and large they have proved their value within the meaning of this system. Many university teachers would strenuously oppose replacing these structures for new ones that are either untried or have only been tested in experimental situations.
- The models of post- and neo-Fordist distance education abandon some constitutive advantages of industrialized learning and teaching: the relative independence of time and location is restricted, professional course development and scientific accompaniment is reduced, cost savings through large numbers of students are no longer possible.
- Some of the students at distance-teaching universities and open universities will be excluded because their employment cannot be reconciled with attendance at a mixed-mode university.
- Commercial organizers of distance education will not wish to do without the economic advantages of the mass production of standardized distance-education courses and will probably retain adherence to that approach.
- Distance education of the future could, in certain circumstances, be organized along the lines of *all three concepts*. This seems clear, because theoreticians of post-industrial production regard it as possible that the three different concepts can exist alongside each other in the economy of a country or region, and be in competition with one another (Campion and Renner, 1992: 12).
- The post-industrial concept is criticized by quite a few experts because its influence on social and industrial transformations is not proven. The optimism that more democratic methods of production will be established with its help does not appear to be justified. Campion and Renner (1992: 13) mention no less than six authors who have expressed doubts on this topic.
- The trend I have referred to, of employing only a hard core of highly qualified specialists at a distance-teaching university, who are then complemented as and when required by staff on short-term contracts (described as 'core and peripheral staffing'), recalls the practice of private distance schools and cannot be considered acceptable for reasons of academic quality and organizational requirements, but above all for social reasons.

Perhaps these misgivings will be found in due course to be without foundation when the digital revolution thoroughly mixes up the areas of distance education and traditional university education and forces both to new methods of working. But until then they will continue to play a part in relevant discussions.

5.3.7 Commentary

The concept of *industrialized* learning obviously provided many distance-education experts and practitioners in the 1960s and 1970s with an explanatory pattern that made clear to them just how their actions differed from those of their colleagues in traditional university education – not merely accidentally but structurally. It starts, as they could see, from other premises, follows other laws, and provides in part enormous opportunities that people were able to substantiate logically. Those among them who thought pedagogically were able not only to recognize the particular strengths inherent in distance education because of its industrialized structure, but also to substantiate them theoretically. At the same time, it was easier for them to accept its not inconsiderable deficits as inherent. Above all it could be seen just how unsuitable the widespread habit is of evaluating the conception, working methods and results of distance education with the help of criteria that were developed in conventional academic systems and correspond to pre-industrial criteria.

5.4 Post-modern learning

In the previously shown concepts of the industrialization of learning and teaching the effect of changes in work and society is assumed, but here we are dealing with a more general problem of cultural life: modern attitudes and ways of thinking are gradually being replaced and there is a hesitant turning to post-modern ones.

At this point many readers will throw up their hands in dismay and refuse to discuss this. Everything that they have heard or read under this topic, they might argue, is incoherent, heterogeneous and contradictory, and cannot be ordered or put into a systematic way of thinking. In addition, these developments often take place in more artistic fields. Many may also dislike the behaviour of supporters of post-modernism: their playful attitudes, their carefreeness, their eclecticism, their irony, because it is in direct contradiction to the 'seriousness of late modernism' (Kellner, 1990: 37). Or they are put off by the light-hearted slogan 'anything goes', which delivers our actions up to arbitrariness. However, those who do not recognize an intellectual movement of our times, which promises to become representative of a fundamental paradigmatic change in the complete culture of Europe and America, cannot help to shape the present and the future – and here we expressly include distance education.

5.4.1 Relevance

Post-modernism is a way of thinking and an attitude that has developed as a reaction to the modern age, and at present it is slowly, almost stealthily, creeping into our consciousness. In the past few years it has already brought about changes in areas such as art, architecture, literature, mathematics, philosophy, political theory, theology and science, and has reached education. For educational theoreticians, this altered consciousness must be of great interest from the very start because they are confronted with it to a greater extent than people in other professions. This is why the number of publications dealing with the effects of post-modernism on modern people in the areas of education and culture has increased in the last few years.

In England, Peter Jarvis (1993: 165) described a kind of preliminary stage of post-modernism and drew attention after Giddens (1990: 53) and others to important changes to consciousness early in the post-modern period. Examples of this are the characteristic importance in this epoch of increased reflectivity, which is a precondition for changes in society, and individualisation, which makes people look into their own identity, recognize their own goals, and pursue them in their own way. Just how important these two characteristics alone have become for the development of learning and teaching in distance education is described by Jarvis. As a result he refers to distance education as a 'symbol of the late modern'.

In Germany, Heinz-Hermann Krüger (1990) published a book under the title *Abschied von der Aufklärung – Perspektiven der Erziehungswissenschaft*, which contained three fundamental articles and ten others dealing with the topic from many aspects. Horst Siebert (1993: 134) dealt with this subject and showed just how post-modern thinking affects adult education.

In the USA, William E Doll (1993) developed a 'post-modern perspective on curriculum' in which he made clear the fundamental difference between closed and open systems in education. He objects strongly to the closed curricula of the modern period and pleads in favour of the open curricula of the post-modern era. Possible consequences with regard to distance education have also been discussed (Peters 1993).

5.4.2 New aspects

Up to now, post-modernism has not been described *per se* but has instead only been articulated in the form of a critique of modernity. Fundamental assumptions and insights, which have been regarded as obvious since the Age of the Enlightenment and supplied people in the Industrial Age with important reference points for understanding the world, are declared to be false, and not after careful consideration but with a love of decisive and committed contradiction. Radical criticism is reserved above all for unquestioning belief in science, any overemphasis on technology, the conviction that society can be rationally guided and controlled, a belief in the power of education to change people, and above all for the idea of emancipation and of self-determined autonomous subjects. On the whole, there is a denunciation of the optimistic idea of the general progress of humankind, which means, of course, that the hope for a better (ie more civilized and culturally developed) world also diminishes.

5.4.3 The relevance for distance education

This fundamental critique must by its very nature hit all educationalists hard because basic principles of their previous thought and actions are interpreted as being false and, accordingly, no longer legitimate. If we can no longer believe in the possibility of educating people, the question arises automatically whether there is any further foundation for education. If the general classical aim of education of producing an adult, autonomous, self-responsible, moral person no longer applies, what can take its place? Can arbitrariness actually take its place? If all efforts at educating people to 'self-determination, co-partnership and a capacity for solidarity' (Klafki, 1986: 474) were based on Utopian ideas and are therefore in the end fruitless, is this not the end of all education? Indeed, the number of educationalists driven by these ideas is increasing.

The post-modern critique must also have an effect on the mission, working methods and self-image of the universities. In Australia, Mick Campion and William Renner (1992: 22) drew attention to what this can mean. They noted:

> If the post-modern critique is accepted – no matter what the degree of validity – the aims of university education and the... strategies for achieving them must be questioned. Many assumptions that have gained practical importance in the modern era will have to be rethought in the context of the discussion on the actual role of science, the role of knowledge and therefore the role of the university as well.

In fact, the situation of teachers at universities may indeed become precarious if the value placed on science is in general reduced, technological progress is discredited, and the possibilities of political/social progress is denied all round. What should their teaching programmes look like if, as Lyotard (1977) claims, 'the end of the great meta-discourses and of metaphysics' has come and the great hopes that were placed in modern social theories have dissolved?

These new pedagogical and university education problems in the background serve to highlight the difficulties facing distance education. In past decades, the idea has fixed itself in public consciousness that distance education is typically a matter of adults who want to grasp a second opportunity of joining the ranks of higher earners through additional education and training. Put another way, distance students are ambitious and want to increase their occupational, professional and social status. People imagined persons who pursued this goal had enormous will-power, great perseverance, and untiring diligence.

This attitude and behaviour are nothing special in industrial meritocracies. They are not socially sanctioned, as 'swotting' is in school; on the contrary, they are acknowledged and even supported. In the end, of course, industrial societies survive through people with those qualities. The Protestant work ethic, which, according to Max Weber, had a determining effect on the 'spirit of capitalism', may have served here as a historical influence. It encouraged people to set longer-term life objectives, to endure extraordinary loads and stress, and not only to accept patiently the postponement of gratification required for their achievement but even to regard it as right. To that extent we could regard distance students as particularly marked prototypes of the Industrial Age, in which trends of the modern era have intensified.

These distance students must find things extremely difficult when they realize more and more just how little their attitudes and their ambitions correspond to the spirit of the new age. And how should distance-teaching universities react when they can no longer reckon with those highly motivated and success-oriented students who are prepared to make sacrifices of time and 'quality of life' in the present for rewards in the future? Will they not lose the largest and most important part of their clientele, the part that appeared in the first place to justify the establishment of distance teaching universities? Even worse, Käte Meyer-Drawe (1990: 87) dives deeper and considers whether:

... the end of the great fairy tale of education for all has not come, whether it does not harbour a humanly impossible conception of subjectivity and rationality that is doomed to fail because the *imago dei* is still seen in the 'lost man' (Heydorn) and not man as animal *rationale mortale*.

If this were true, it would damage and relativize an important pedagogical and educational policy axiom of distance education, which would then probably lose all its validity, as its traditional objective was to open the gate to a university education for as many people as possible.

In the face of the trends outlined briefly here, the following question arises for theoreticians and practitioners of distance education: does learning and teaching in distance education have to be adapted to the change in the awareness of life and consciousness that can already be felt? And is any adaptation particularly urgent because this new sensitivity is in many points diametrically opposed to the earlier outlook?

There are good reasons for these considerations in so far as the post-modern change of consciousness referred to here is not based at all on assumptions and speculations but has been verified empirically. Intensive analyses of the contents of diaries from the nineteenth and twentieth centuries have led to results that are extremely interesting with regard to distance education. There has in fact been a deep structural change in values that allows the modern self to be distinguished from the post-modern self. It might be better to refer to a *shift* of values, which took place in the following dimensions: from rationality to irrationality, from unemotional action to emotional expression, from institutional roles and standards to individual roles and standards, from duties to society to duties to oneself, and, finally, from satisfaction with a completed performance to orientation towards personal gratification (Wood and Zurcher, 1988: 126).

The consequence of this change is that the post-modern self is disposed to behaviour that no longer corresponds to distance education in its industrialized character. Here are just a few examples: the post-modern person rejects gratification postponed to the future for phases of strenuous work and sacrifice in the present; instead that person wants to have fun and to be able to be happy *now*. He avoids routine and occupies himself with 'something meaningful'. He does not want to exercise self-control but would prefer to 'express himself'. And he does not like to live in isolation but to have good social contacts. But the most important thing for our context is that he does not strive for economic improvement because he is more interested in the development of his own personality. All these findings are in flagrant contradiction to the attitudes and characteristics expected of traditional distance-education students.

It must be said here that there were clear signs of these changes in the learning and teaching practice of the FernUniversität at a very early stage. In his empirical examinations, Jörn Bartels found attitudes that did not fit in with the image of the occupational and social climber. When graduates of the Faculty of Economics were asked – in the mid-1980s – what the criteria were that they valued most in a description of their jobs, 91 per cent said 'job satisfaction' and 84 per cent stated 'independent working', while 'a good salary' was only in fifth place (Bartels, 1987: 180). Furthermore, 57 per cent regarded the aim of 'self-development' as having a high priority, as against only about 43 per cent who referred to aims of gaining professional qualifications in this category. These are unexpected results for economics graduates, because people traditionally expect these students to concentrate on their careers and high earnings. The findings are reinforced by the fact they are practically the same as the results of research at the UK's Open University, where the corresponding values were 56 per cent and 44 per cent (Bartels, 1987: 86).

The question must be asked in the context of these developments as to how the post-modern change in values will affect the pedagogical structure of distance education. Up to now, it has looked as if the post-industrialized scenario of distance education, with short courses tailored to students' requirements, with its mixture of isolated, autonomously planned self-study, with teaching and discussion groups face-to-face on campus, with virtual seminars and the exchange of ideas with fellow students electronically would correspond more to the changed post-modern awareness of life than distance education in the era of Fordism. Open, flexible, communicative and action-oriented learning will be more suitable for it than separately working through closed-curricular, thoroughly structured distance-education courses that are centrally planned and controlled. And so here we can see how post-industrial and post-modern trends complement each other; indeed, Campion and Renner (1992: 21) have already pointed to their internal correlation.

5.5 Summary

The concepts of open, lifelong, post-industrial and post-modern learning that have been shown in this chapter open up perspectives and dimensions for the reform of distance education. Whether this reform will actually take place remains to be seen. This will depend on whether the developers of new distance-education institutions and new distance-education projects possess creative pedagogical imagination and the will to shape things that will triumph over those forces that wish to adhere both to routines that make work easier and to obsolete patterns. But even if no changes actually take place, discussion of the concepts themselves is not something that can be done without. In the context of this presentation, it is in fact necessary and even essential.

How can we substantiate this? All learning and teaching is determined (among other things) by the persons taking part and the dominant ideas and attitudes of the respective society and epoch. This is why those anthropogenous and socio-cultural conditions must be analysed that are regarded as the categorically basic conditions for learning and teaching. According to this theory, the concepts described here, and the efforts to realize them, have an effect on those teaching and studying at university and influence their actions. Naturally, this is the same for all persons who create new institutional opportunities for distance education, organize it and develop suitable teaching programmes. Because they are children of their times, they have perforce to react to the concepts shown in this chapter. They may do this by rejecting them out of hand, passing over them in silence, accepting them wholeheartedly, or applying and testing them where possible in practical situations. Put another way, whatever the reaction, these four concepts are today part of the repertoire of opportunities for pedagogical action for all those involved in teaching in distance education.

In this chapter we have described a singular situation. Never in the history of pedagogics has there ever been such a constellation of concepts. If they merely characterized the special nature of the situation in which learning and teaching is taking place in distance education today, their contribution would be enormous. In fact, they help to recognize trends such as those being discussed at present in university pedagogics, in adult education pedagogics, in work and industry, and in the field of culture. Although these concepts stem from different theoretical and practical fields, we can foresee that in their realization they will complement and support each other and perhaps even permeate each other.

The concepts shown here have three things in common. Firstly, most teachers take notice of them hesitantly, where they do not reject them; secondly, their realization is needed for today, but is not taking place to the extent required; and because this is the case, thirdly, they are regarded as being more future-oriented.

The concept of 'open learning' offers interesting opportunities for the further development of distance education, which can only be exhausted if teachers and students work out a new conception of themselves, and if learning and teaching in distance education is structured, arranged and organized differently so that it can be adapted flexibly to the different learning requirements of a very heterogeneous clientele. The concept provides a favourable precondition for the system of autonomous and self-determined learning described in Chapter 3, which cannot be conceived of in a largely regimented learning and teaching system based on expository methods.

The concept of 'lifelong learning' will continue to have an effect on the further development of distance education and probably has the best chances of realization in practice in distance education. Accustoming the public to the idea of learning over a lifetime, which is provided for by this concept, is favourable to the assessment of distance education and its image.

The concepts of 'post-industrial learning' and 'post-modern learning' can also be seen in close correlation. Both have their origins in the reaction to the profound economic, technological, and social changes in the last decades. Both have developed dispositions for thought and action that will be important in the further development of distance education. These will probably not be realized in practice until new distance-education systems are established, because this promises to be extremely difficult in the fixed institutional and structural designs of existing distance-teaching universities. Both concepts have a completely different relationship to the institution and the administration of a distance-teaching university from those of the industrialized distance teaching university.

Section 5.4 on post-modern trends has the function of drawing attention to a second force that could prompt changes in the methods of distance education, make them obvious and bring them about. Post-industrial changes in the production of goods and in the services sector are therefore not the only factors that influence the theory and practice of distance education. A new intellectual movement in the cultural area also provides supports by having an effect on public consciousness in a certain way. How this will affect the practice of learning and teaching in distance education is something that educationalists will have to observe extremely carefully.

Chapter 6

Digital information and communication

With the adaptation to digital information and communications technologies that has now become necessary, distance-teaching pedagogics sees itself confronted by a development that is without example in its impact and puts all previous pedagogical innovations in the shade. This is not just a single technical innovation, but a whole series of developments that have come together at present and are thus intensified. The developments are:

1. the further development of the PC, with its facility to store information and present it on request in fractions of a second, and to provide interactive learning programmes by means of software;
2. the improvement in telecommunications through the provision of advanced audio and video technologies and more efficient data-transmission cables;
3. the development of multimedia technology, which revolutionizes not only the production but also the presentation of its multifaceted programmes through the use of computers; and
4. the development of larger and more extensive databases and their connection to international global computer networks.

How can we cope with this impressive bundling of technological progress? What can, should and will it mean for learning and teaching in distance education? In Chapter 1, I suggested how teleconferencing and the PC are altering the pedagogical concept of distance education to such an extent that we are now referring to a second and third generation of this form of learning and teaching. In this chapter we will be looking in more detail at some pedagogical aspects of the planned innovations in this field, both potential and actual.

6.1 An optimistic assessment

If we take a look at the previous successes of digital information and communications technology we can see how:

- text, graphics, sound and video can be brought together as a single integrated medium, where the different elements are related to one another in many different ways;
- faster and faster PCs are being converted into a versatile communications medium by which electronic mail can be sent, and text or graphics can be worked out on-screen, or developed further, with colleagues in different locations; and
- audio- and video-conferences can be carried out with the appropriate additional hardware and software.

In the face of these perspectives the gains that distance education can achieve in future are clear even to non-experts. In fact, if the learning environment of distance students is fully equipped with appropriate digital information and communications media, and if high-performance cable is available (eg ISDN), the following general structural advantages are found: the distance between teacher and student, which is constitutive for distance education, turns into virtual proximity; diversions presented in writing are replaced, where necessary, by the oral form; 'dead letters' give way to the live voice of participants or teachers; and the rigid, time-delayed sequence in the articulation of the learning and teaching process makes way, through audio- and video-conferences, for example, for simultaneous and dynamic dialogue, such that a scientific discourse can take place.

The new technologies therefore widen the spectrum of forms of learning and teaching in distance education to an extent that until recently has been difficult to conceive. They enable students to use previously unknown forms of activation, and this can make learning more attractive and more effective. And they also extend the time and space available to teachers for pedagogical decisions. What the new technologies can bring about in this context is almost a miracle. It might even be thought that the technologies were invented and developed especially for distance education. All the hopes and visions of theoreticians and practitioners of distance education now appear to be capable of fulfilment both in principle and in practice. Distance studies can now be conceived and developed that leave all past obstacles and restrictions far behind them. Distance education at its best can now be realized.

6.2 A realistic interpretation

Is this vision of the use of digital information and communications media in distance education exaggerated? Who will put a damper on the euphoria that is so typical for many of those taking part in conferences on the subject? Should we not be a little more careful and remind ourselves just how little use has been made over the years of media which were at first received enthusiastically and regarded as being eminently suitable for distance education?

Let us remind ourselves of the 1970s and 'distance education in a multimedia system', in which the hopes of so many were then placed. Anthony Bates (1994), who was at the Open University in the UK at the time and is now at the University of Vancouver, is a leading media expert and reports on how many new media he himself introduced and discussed in 1977 with regard to their possible use in distance education: audio cassettes, floppies, tapes, Super-8 mm film, video cassettes, the telephone, videotext, electronic blackboards, videodiscs and computer terminals. And he goes on to ask what was actually realized in the following years? Only the cheapest medium, the audio cassette, has been able to make any sort of a career in the Open University, which is very open-minded with regard to media for pedagogics and is an international pioneer and trend-setter. Audio cassettes have in fact altered the pedagogic structure of distance education on a lasting basis by replacing teaching programmes in radio in many cases. And it took ten years before the Open University was prepared to turn to the particular opportunities offered by video cassettes and computer terminals. In the same period, the number of programmes broadcast on television actually decreased.

What Anthony Bates is saying to us here is that things never turn out in sober practice in the same way that they were discussed with great emotion. It may be that we should regard the use that is now possible of digital information and communications media in distance education with more composure than has been the case so far. If we in fact analyse current distance-education practice, we can see that second- and third-generation distance education is by no means a standard that has already been achieved, but consists at most of more or less promising models and experiments on the periphery, which make up no more than a few percentage points of the whole range of studies and courses.

The discussion of the role of digital information and communications media and the many approaches for testing them are still therefore dealing with the *future* of distance education. Nobody knows what it will be possible to create for financial, logistical, pragmatic or even pedagogical reasons. We should remind ourselves of the complicated and enormously expensive measures that have to be taken to hold audio or video conferences. We should also ask ourselves how quickly participants will adjust to the completely different group experience of teleconferencing, with its completely different learning climate. Will the innovations be welcomed only by technology nerds, but rejected by the mass of students? And will the professors who actively take part be merely a small group that is open to ideas for the future and regards the change as necessary, while the majority shy away from innovations and adhere to traditional forms of teaching? It will be some time before distance education actually makes use of these new technological opportunities, and some obstacles will have to be overcome along the way.

But this unwillingness to move with the times is no longer adequate, because our situation can no longer be compared with that of the 1970s. The digital revolution is not only changing distance education, it is changing *our whole lives*. In particular, the areas of work, family and leisure time are most certainly going to be restructured when PCs are found everywhere and the communications networks that are at present being installed at great expense reach people everywhere and pervade their activities with information. We will have to imagine *all* learning and teaching, and not just in distance education, as being embedded in this.

For distance-teaching universities, this means that not only distance education but also traditional university teaching will be covered by the digital revolution and will have to develop new forms of learning and teaching. There will be new perspectives for both, once time and place become variables in work as well. If, for example, a considerable amount of work is done from home, it might be that work and job-oriented ongoing academic training are based on the same information and communications media. We would then be dealing with a structurally different starting point. The equipping of homes with PCs, and the easy accessibility to databases, teaching programmes, teachers, and fellow students will then have a retroactive effect on learning in schools and universities. As a result, new techniques for learning and teaching will probably be developed. The current efforts to integrate digital information and communications technologies into distance education as we know it can be seen in this perspective.

6.3 First pedagogical analyses

How should we judge the new learning environment available to distance students who are equipped with digital electronic information and communications media? The first, impartial, impression is positive: the PC and its peripheral appliances present teaching in a concentrated form. Two things impress here: firstly, the teaching activates the students because they can take part in the learning and teaching process by reading, writing and creating graphics; secondly, teaching is audio-visual, because aural, visual and audio-visual presentations make it more effective through their cumulative effects. The 'fascination of the synchronized sound language', whose unusual pedagogic potential for learning and teaching was first recognized and advocated by Paul Heimann (1976, 218), can now be fully used on a completely different level and at another stage of differentiation. Evaluated according to traditional pedagogical measures, the digitalized learning environment would be an advance in itself for these two reasons alone, and the expense would be worthwhile.

But this first glance does not yet cover what the digitalized learning environment can actually do. It is able not only to strengthen individual components of learning and teaching behaviour, but also to alter them structurally. This will be made clear with the help of a few examples, as set out in the subsections hereafter.

6.3.1 Learning with files

While they are learning, students can store selected information for the purposes of training, memorizing, retaining and applying, and call it up on-screen at any time at the touch of a button. They can make a personal file relating to the subject they are learning and extend it at any time. The work of scientists – their handling of the information that they regard as important, their data searching, recording, checking, comparing and relating – all this can be integrated with ease via the PC into the learning process. In this way, students can build up activating learning techniques that are not found in teaching at traditional universities or in first-generation distance education.

This example alone shows that learning in this learning environment can and will be different, if teachers and students adapt to it. Nobody knows what value will be placed in the future on this special pedagogical approach to self-learning, but we should not forget the advantages of an integrated researching and learning technique.

6.3.2 Learning with hypertext/hypermedia

In a digital-learning environment, students can interact with a prepared hypertext, including hypermedia. A teaching text can also be displayed on a monitor in a traditional form and students can read it on-screen as if they were reading a page in a printed study unit, an academic journal or a text book. It may be that students even expect this form of learning because they are used to it from school or another university.

But there is an objection to this approach. If the digital-learning environment is used only in this way, its actual pedagogical potential is disregarded yet again. Use of personal computers does not have to be limited simply to presenting a book's surface. Finding information in a split second and making it available immediately enables students to penetrate deeply into a teaching text, depending on their interests and requirements and in any way they like, if the text was developed by a team of experts as hypertext (Wingert, 1992).

In the deeper information levels of a hypertext, for example, pictures of the authors of important extracts are shown with a brief biography, and they are arranged logically. In addition, further explanations (brief, longer or just the sources) are provided at even deeper information levels. In this way, the subject being treated can be presented with additional factual information, historical derivations and substantiations, considerations of scientific theory, contrary standpoints and opinions, and commentaries on the relevant texts with different degrees of detail. This arrangement means that such items of text, although present, do not interrupt the flow of presentation and do not have a negative effect on the learning of those students who do not need the information or do not want to take note of it. A small, multidimensional cosmos of knowledge is thus created for the subject matter, in which the learner has to find his or her own way independently. Once again we can see the amazing extent to which distance education might be restructured.

Changing teaching behaviour

With hypertext, teachers have to learn how to teach simultaneously on several levels. This can be done by providing learning content in smaller units – think of the 'frames' used for programmed teaching. Each unit would then consist of fragments of text, graphics, videos or short commentaries (Tergan, 1996: 195). The relationships between these units take the form of links. In this way, a network is made up of units of knowledge referred to as 'nodes'. This network may have a linear or a hierarchical structure, or one in the form of matrices, depending on the relationship of the units to one another, and combinations of these structures are also conceivable. Students can pass from one level to another with the help of suitable links.

This form of teaching is thus particularly advantageous for distance education because its students are not a relatively homogeneous group of addressees, like a group of school-leavers, for example, but people with greatly diverging individual interests, different intellectual standards and special study aims, which is just what we can expect from mature students.

The development of these hypertext and hypermedia versions of teaching is a difficult task for teachers, because until now only specialists have had the competence required to carry it out. Because they have fully absorbed the traditional form of linearly presented teaching, they may regard these multi-level methods of learning with some scepticism and even see their own collaboration as an unreasonable demand. Who knows whether their everyday life at university permits this kind of intensive, differentiated and detailed processing of teaching contents? It may indeed only be possible in development centres that have the appropriate means and specialized staff available.

The objection that teaching with hypertexts is non-academic or non-scientific is easy to refute. Knowledge is not of itself arranged linearly but is merely forced traditionally into the time sequence and spatial proximity of linearity, and is in fact deformed when this is done. To that extent, other forms of presenting and offering information may certainly be discussed, if they are technologically possible, and may even be more suitable. Furthermore, there is another aspect of hypertext/hypermedia use that suggests this form of learning and teaching: if we see learning as the development and alteration of cognitive structures, we should really examine whether work with the described networks of information units cannot in fact be of great advantage to this form of learning. However, it must also be seen that the development of these networks, with which learning is to be set into motion in several variations and on several levels, implies a difficult adjustment.

Changing learning behaviour

Students must also adapt to the new methods of learning using hypertext etc. Firstly, they are granted the freedom to take more and more decisions on the sequence of their learning; secondly, they often have to find their own way through the hypertext and constantly consider whether, and how far, they wish to drill down in order to take note of some interesting ancillary information, and here several motives may be in competition. This forces them to develop and pursue strategies for mastering learning assignments – an important indication of the great extent to which hypertext and hypermedia can challenge students to adopt an active and in part independent approach to learning. If they want to control their learning on the basis of this kind of strategy, they have to have acquired a certain skill in dealing with the implicit and explicit cross-reference structure of the teaching text. Once this has been done, the following working forms specific to hypertexts can be developed: browsing, searching for defined information units, following a predefined path. These are described further below.

- *Browsing* is an activity we normally associate with books, and many American libraries have a special 'browsing room'. Originally used of animals (deer, sheep, etc), the word means 'to feed on (grass, plants, twigs, etc) by continuous nibbling'. This is an approach to learning that is practically unknown in pedagogics. Students are encouraged to approach processed units of knowledge in any way they want, start wherever they wish, skip over passages here and there, let themselves be transferred to other units, perhaps follow a chain of reference intensively but then break it off and start again somewhere else. The motivation behind this procedure is the joy of intellectual discovery, the desire to find something out for ourselves and add it to our store of knowledge. Anyone who has ever used an encyclopaedia is familiar with the phenomenon: when searching for an entry our eyes fall on a heading for something completely different, we start to read this article and forget the original reason for opening the book. This can therefore be an associative–exploratory penetration into the knowledge cosmos of the hypertext. Alongside this we can find browsing that is 'targeted'. In this case, each new piece of information has to be examined to see whether it says anything with regard to the set objectives and brings the learner nearer to the goal. Learners have to develop a feeling and a knack for picking out the links that lead directly to their goal.
- *Searching for defined information units* is made easier by means of software-based equivalents of the aids that are used in textbooks to help readers gain access to contents: lists of names, keywords, numbers, overviews and symbols. These techniques, which are familiar to students from good textbooks, are differentiated, technically optimized and above all made more dynamic in the hypertext context.
- *Following a path through a hypertext defined by the teacher* always takes place when teachers want to lead students through a particular sequence of information units to achieve a defined learning effect. Activation of the appropriate links is automatic, but the sequence can be interrupted at any time to enable the reader to study the content of certain units in greater depth or to call for additional explanatory information. The predefined path is often explained by means of commentaries that appear in a display window, or can be spoken. This kind of learning is referred to as a 'guided tour'.

What is the relationship between free browsing and targeted learning? 'Associative browsing is inclination in a hypertext, controlled navigation is discipline. Both together lead to the desired success, beyond compulsion and chaos' (Kuhlen, 1991: 123).

What pedagogical advantages for distance education can be expected from this form of learning? CD-ROMs can be used to store and provide access to extensive and highly differentiated hypertexts and hypermedia. Learning with them intensifies self-control, activity and interactivity and takes account of personal interests, preferences and skills. It is also in effect individualized in this way. At the same time, before each development of hypertexts or hypermedia a check should be carried out to see just how much the special pedagogical added-value (Kuhlen, 1991: 212) of this form of presentation actually amounts to, and whether the same learning effect can be achieved with much less expensive programmes on paper. For this reason, teachers must be clear in their minds about the typical added-value effects of hyper-text, eg links of heterogeneous elements, multiple-window technology, and the dynamisation of structures (or 'the bird's eye view') in which the most important things are magnified and things that are less important are shown much smaller. Sigmar-Olaf Tergan (1996: 195–204) regards it as an advantage if the hypertext is integrated into the overall curriculum of distance education and students can fall back on help from tutors where required and discuss their learning achievements with other students. Hypertext will therefore not be a replacement for distance edu-cation but a new working method amongst others.

6.3.3 Learning in a knowledge-building community

Here, networked PCs and possibly a central computer are used as instruments for the implementation of a defined form of autonomous and cooperative learning. This learning has its origins in a research project that was developed incidentally by several microbiologists. They were each working on the same project and decided to use PCs to inform each other of advancements in their knowledge. This resulted in a central file and all the scientists worked on its further development. Participants entered relevant data about what they had discovered about the research subject in the academic community, or what they had read, thought, calculated, suspected or speculated. The file, which consisted only of the contributions of the participating researchers, was therefore the result of their joint efforts. It comprised original knowledge that was constructed and structured by the researchers and arose from their scientific discussions. All of those taking part have profited from it, because they have learnt a lot, but to an extent they have also taught a lot by informing the others from the aspect of their particular part of the discipline and by adding their results to the file. The participants remain informed on an all-round basis and are stimulated and supported by the different contributions and opinions.

What is more obvious than to regard this as a possible model for digital learning in distance education? It would have several pedagogical advantages. Firstly, we are dealing here quite clearly with the development and expansion of knowledge struc-tures; learning therefore corresponds to the currently preferred constructivist learning model. Secondly, it is a form of autonomous learning, which is being de-manded by educationalists more and more urgently to overcome presentational learning. Thirdly, the cooperative learning of participants is not merely an accom-paniment or an addition, but is constitutive. This takes account of a further require-ment: communicative learning is also a genuine component of distance education. In a certain sense, the model represents group learning as well, and in certain cir-cumstances, embedded in this, partnership learning, both of which are highly regarded as social learning. Finally, the model is favoured because it is located so closely to a real case in practical research and derives its strategies and methods therefrom.

Using the structure of this kind of research project to learn scientific facts in distance education appears simple and obvious at first glance. At the same time, difficulties in realising it are suspected from the very beginning because students have to display a particular learning behaviour. Collecting relevant knowledge, information and opinions must not lead simply to an accumulation of data. According to Scardamalia and Bereiter (1990: 44), what is wanted are forms of active collaboration in the success of this new form of academic teaching. The authors differentiate here between certain procedures that are only listed here to show just how far the methodological analysis of this form of learning has already been developed: students have to learn to keep their distance from the contributed knowledge (objectivisation). They must work with regard to results, even if the goal of learning has not been stipulated, and must aim to advance in the project (progress). They must link their acquired knowledge with knowledge that already exists and strive to reach higher levels of knowledge (synthesis).

If students have discovered something important during their work and added it to the joint database, a 'reward' is necessary, in that others refer to it or develop their own contributions using it as a basis (consequence). They must learn to pay attention not only to their own learning success but also to that of the group (contribution). They must learn the techniques for using the computer's help to track down relevant ideas and information for the subject in other theoretical and practice-related areas and to enrich the work in this way (cross-fertilization).

These are very demanding tasks. But their solution will help to develop powers that cannot be acquired by memorising passages from textbooks and listening to lectures.

6.3.4 Learning with teaching programmes

Teaching programmes are 'old friends', ie teaching techniques that were propagated and practised in the 1960s under the title of 'programmed learning and teaching machines'. Their advantages and disadvantages are well known and have been brought into the digital-learning environment. A certain degree of interactivity between students and the programme is considered appropriate: individualization through branching, diagnostic self-tests, and above all working with simulations and models. In addition, in a digital-learning environment, multimedia opportunities are available as well.

On the other hand, teaching programmes were disliked because their high development costs led to a primitive pedagogical design, which let students go over an exactly defined path in small steps and tied them into the straitjacket of a stimulus-and-response cycle. In addition, they were mainly used for practice and revision.

In the FernUniversität these learning programmes occurred chiefly in the departments of computer science and electrical engineering, and here significantly as training mechanisms for assignments and examinations. Whether this form of teaching will experience a renaissance under the more favourable conditions of a digital-learning environment, or whether elements of this kind of programming can be integrated in other digital-learning forms, cannot be foreseen at present.

6.3.5 Learning with data-file courses

Data-file courses represent an interesting transition from developed printed distance teaching courses to learning in a digital-learning environment. These are conceived and produced in the Zentrum für Fernstudienentwicklung at the FernUniversität and are described by Christa Bast (1997: 5). Many experts warn about putting old wine into new bottles, but this is exactly what is being done because the distance-teaching courses that were developed at great expense and have proved their worth in practice are being 'digitalized', ie stored on CD-ROMs and made available and presented to students in a completely new manner. Of course, the disparaging characterization of 'old wine in new bottles' is completely false. 'The medium is the message' (McLuhan), and what happens on a changeover of data carrier from printed material to CD-ROM is pedagogically relevant to a great degree and gives us an insight into, and to an extent lets us experience, just how different distance education is in a digital-learning environment. The changeover to a different data carrier means that we are now dealing with a completely different product.

The first thing we see is the new presentation format. The predominance of the A4 page appears to be over in digitalized distance education. The section that can be seen on the display is smaller and is about half the size of a standard study-paper page. This new subdivision of the teaching text is thought to bring advantages to students: firstly, the presentation unit is easier to grasp and structure using keywords; secondly, working tips are provided in the text with the help of a number of symbols and these make it easier for students to move around in the text and bring onto the screen any passages they wish to see. It is also possible to place different text and graphics next to one another to compare them; thirdly – and this is the most important feature – the presentational structure is extended by means of additional modes of presentation. In this context, Jürgen Wurster (1995: 1) refers to the following:

- animation of graphics, taxonomies, derivations, experiments, and (if required) combined with explanatory sounds;
- independent sound files, especially language files; oral introductions to a section in the contents, directions and tips for studying, talks with experts, and interviews in social research;
- video films or video sequences; and
- additional text files: source files, readers, and software tools.

The quality leap achieved here consists on the one hand of the exactly calculated pedagogical effect of several presentation modes that come together at the same time, and on the other hand of the freedom of the student to use the different files on the basis of his or her own initiative.

The traditional, printed distance-teaching course has turned in the digital-learning environment into a new and more ambitious way of presenting academic teaching. The immediate advantage of this solution is its practicality. A positive development can be forecast for this model because it combines elements of traditional university pedagogics, distance-teaching pedagogics and pedagogics of the digital-learning environment (along with elements of hypertext and hypermedia) under the aspect of feasibility.

Although it is demanding of the students, projects on the psychology of learning using forms of the digital-learning environment (eg in De Corte et al, 1990: 309-465) are very future-oriented and have not been developed with regard to the practical requirements of distance education. This model has grown from the daily practice of distance education and is therefore significant for its future development. Because this pragmatic path has not been taken by any other distance-teaching university anywhere in the world, data file courses may be regarded as an original contribution of the FernUniversität to distance-teaching pedagogics. Design guidelines for 'electronic books' from Rolf Schulmeister (1997: 299) may be helpful in its further development.

6.3.6 Learning through computer-conferencing

If distance students have access to a PC, a limited number of them can form a group in which they can discuss with one another with the help of a central computer and suitable software by sending *written* statements to all members of the group, or react *in writing* to statements they have received (compare Subsection 6.3.7). The electronic technology is used in the service of very rapid transport and transmission of these written statements.

If we look at this situation more closely, we can see that it is slightly absurd. Although the students are working with high-tech electronic appliances and elaborate software, the actual discussion consists of the *exchange of written messages*, and this reminds us of the beginnings of correspondence teaching, which was also in writing and suffered from (albeit longer) time delays. Nevertheless, this method of communication has to be considered further by a reference to two additional functions of the computer in computer-conferencing: the messages are written digitally with the computer, and the course of the discussion is recorded and stored in great detail, and this can be very useful for learning and teaching.

In traditional distance education, the exchange of opinions on, and experience with, what has been learned between students always comes off badly, and therefore this opportunity for an academic discourse must be extremely welcome. Computer-conferencing has in fact acquired a considerable position in distance education very quickly. According to AW Bates (1995: 206), it is the most commonly used form of computer-mediated teaching in this field.

Holding virtual seminars is not the only way to use computer-mediated communications (CMC). Teachers can also use them for the purpose of virtual teaching or virtual instruction by entering teaching texts for the members of the group, studying the written reactions, and referring to and commenting on these reactions in the subsequent teaching texts. Computer-conferencing differs from a real oral class in a study centre, for example, or from a college class, in that contributions from participants, including teachers, can be thought out much more thoroughly because of the asynchronism, and they are also put into writing. Ideally in this context, we might even expect a higher standard of language in the discourse. On the other hand, what is lacking is spontaneity and directness (Fabro and Garrison, 1998).

Many distance students are unable to attend a study centre, and because of this computer-conferencing is also used as a means for virtual tutorial support. Worthy of note in this context is the experiment that was carried out in the Open University in the UK in course DT200: 'An introduction to information technology: social and technological issues'. No fewer than 65 computer-conferences, each under the supervision of a tutor, were held for this course and complemented the learning occurring through printed study units and other media.

Whether a virtual seminar, colloquium, class or tutorial is held, computer-conferencing has a number of advantages. They can be assessed as being all the greater where they are able, in part, to compensate for the obvious deficiencies of traditional distance education. Students can exchange views, discuss with one another, and settle controversies. This increases the interactivity of learning considerably. They can show themselves as persons when working in this way, come closer to each other by discussing, and, above all, to work jointly on a problem in smaller subgroups. The social isolation of the students is then to some degree alleviated. There is even evidence of emotional participation in the group process; and there have been reports of the creation of a special atmosphere and a feeling of solidarity, which can be strengthened still further through informal peripheral contacts (see Mason, 1993: 23; Johnson-Lenz and Johnson-Lenz, 1993: 214; Bates, 1995: 207).

Of course, there are disadvantages here as well. Generally, only a few active students take part in exchanging written messages, and the learning behaviour of the others remains hidden. Even so, participants can drop out over long periods without being noticed, and the discussions can suffer. People can also lose track of things completely and give up in the face of the large numbers of messages stacking up in their computers. If the discussions are not moderated skilfully, there is a danger that they will degenerate into small talk and gossip. There are also notorious 'troublemakers' who prevent the discussion from flowing smoothly by asking trivial questions. In contrast, the fascination of working with a computer can divert attention and active participation into a practically pathological immersion in the subject matter – the effects of 'on-line manic behaviour'.

6.3.7 Learning through audio- and video-conferencing

What kind of pedagogical functions can these two innovations in communications technology have for learning and teaching in distance education? Randy Garrison (1989: 64) provides an informative answer that boosts both technologies with conviction and verve. Basically, the answer is as follows: the *essence* of each learning and teaching process is the communication between teachers and students. The quality of learning is determined by the method of communication, because the effectiveness of teaching depends on adequate support for students, and this is closely bound up with communication. Traditional distance education is content with merely enabling access to studying. But audio- and video-conferencing go further because they provide students with help and support through communication, thus returning to distance education the lost essence of learning and teaching. All (or nearly all) traditional classroom techniques can be adapted for use here; and what is more, because both forms of teleconferencing reconstitute the learning group, they closely resemble traditional university teaching, whereas for distance education it was students' independence and isolation that were constitutive factors.

Many people think the same as Garrison and strive to simulate the social forms of traditional university classroom teaching, or at least to imitate them (Barker et al, 1993; Garrison, 1993a; Chambers and Rae, 1995). When such people think of distance education, they see the virtual class and the virtual seminar. In Canada, the USA and Australia this development is desired, welcomed and promoted, and there is now a great deal of experience available from those countries. Garrison's suggestion of using teleconferencing to speak of a second generation of distance education shows the weight that is attached to teleconferencing in these countries, and the power of structural alteration attributed to it.

Garrison's project 'Multifunction computer enhanced audio teleconferencing' (1993b) strengthens this impression even more. It celebrates the regaining of the dialogue with the help of digital communications media as a decisive step in the further development of distance education. Even more, he hopes that this form of distance education will gain the recognition of professors from traditional universities, which was always denied to distance education of the first generation. He argues that in principle exactly the same thing happens with distance students linked by communications media as with students in traditional universities: dialogue with a real lecturer is guaranteed, and the *essence* of the learning and teaching process is regained. In his eyes, distance education has lost a blemish and is now attractive enough to be accepted by the academic mainstream.

What exactly is this technological innovation in distance education that Garrison extols so much? Generally speaking it consists of linking several groups of learners (classes, seminars) by means of ISDN, broadband cable, or satellite. It unites the connected learning groups into a 'virtual class', a 'virtual seminar', a 'virtual colloquium', or (and this is more commonly found) into a teleconference. This kind of virtual teaching event covering several learning groups at different locations can be led by a single person from one location.

According to Keegan (1995: 109) the following four types of teleconferencing have been formed:

- *Type 1: Two-way audio*: discussions between teachers and students over the telephone, possibly in the form of conference calls. Examples: telephone teaching at the Open University in the UK (Robinson, 1993: 191), telephonic counselling with tutors.
- *Type 2: Two-way audiographic*: parallel to telephone conversations, graphics and pictorial representations are transmitted via a telephone line. Sound and pictures can support each other in their teaching effects. This form of teleconferencing

can be developed still further through the greater spread of ISDN, satellite transmissions and broadband cable.

- *Type 3: One-way video + two-way audio*: teaching is transmitted by satellite television from one classroom to different locations, and students use the telephone to
contact teachers. University College, Dublin, Republic of Ireland, has a
video-teaching facility of this kind. In the USA, a great number of universities
have combined to form consortia to operate video-conferencing jointly and on a
large scale. One example of this is the 'Mississippi 2000' project, another the
'Contact North' project in Canada (see Section. 7.8).
- *Type 4: Two-way video + two-way audio*: a completely reciprocal visual and audio
connection is established by means of fibre-optic cable or ISDN. This form is already widespread in the USA and Australia. In some cases students can press
buttons to signal that and how they wish to answer a question. Lecturers have a
control desk showing how each student has answered. An example of this can be
found in the Open University of Israel.

These forms of teleconferencing are so significant because they have brought about
an 'explosion of interest in distance learning' (Moore, 1995: 33), probably as a conscious move away from old-fashioned correspondence teaching, which, in contrast to
European universities, has been provided by American universities for over a century.
Consortia are founded with many universities as members in order to guarantee the
technological preconditions for these forms of learning and teaching – and of course
their financing. One example is the National University Teleconferencing Network
(see Section 7.7). Also typical for this form of distance education are the University of
Maryland Interactive Compressed Video Network and the Maryland Bell Atlantic
Video Network. In principle, all that these systems do is link distant classrooms with
the main classroom, in which a lecturer teaches a group of students.

How did this different, and for us strange, form of distance education come
about? Eugene Rubin (1997), the head of the Institute of Distance Education at the
University of Maryland, gives the following reasons: this distance-education model
is based on the principle of the '*extended classroom*'. It is assumed that the 'best' model
for teaching or taking part in a university course is the model used at traditional universities. In nearly all universities in the USA, this means that a lecturer stands in
front of a group of students. What happens in the class varies from course to course,
but it is always interactive and in real time. Distance teaching on the basis of
teleconferencing attempts to imitate this model, and for this reason the criteria of *interaction* and *real time* are decisive.

Rubin, who is familiar with distance education systems outside the USA, admits
the disadvantages of this model. It is not as efficient as is normally expected of distance teaching because the size of the classes that can be connected, and their number, is limited. 'Efficiency' here relates merely to not having to have a lecturer in
each of the connected classrooms. It is not possible simply to speak of 'extended
classroom teaching' because students in the distant-but-connected classrooms often had the feeling that they were alienated from the main classroom – the lectures
often appeared deadly boring. To overcome this drawback, lecturers require special
training and experience.

What is so attractive about the arrangement? Basically, teachers are probably attracted by the method of presentation, because it appears not to differ from that at a traditional university. There is no need for strenuous readjustment processes and time-consuming new developments. The considerable technical effort simply serves to extend their *range*. Desmond Keegan (1995: 108) put this in a nutshell by referring to teleconferencing as 'face-to-face teaching at a distance'.

In spite of all the scepticism with regard to this special form of distance teaching, its worldwide diffusion over the last five years cannot be ignored. There are at least 50 relevant projects that can be referred to. Of these, the most interesting and pedagogically useful are not those that merely imitate classroom teaching as exactly as possible but those that deliberately carry out individual functions in the overall system of distance teaching. Here are six examples of this:

1. The Universidad Nacional de Educacion a Distancia in Spain, which has 160,000 enrolled students, developed a video-conferencing facility in 1993 that connects six places in the university with 50 study centres throughout Spain. This is probably the largest video-conferencing network in Europe (Garcia-Aretio, 1997: 71).
2. In a programme for the science of nutrition at Pennsylvania State University, teleconferencing via satellite, connecting 30 learning groups with one another, was linked to practical courses at the university. This form of teaching was referred to expressly as 'mixed-mode'. Polls showed an 'overwhelmingly positive' acceptance (Abu Sabha et al, 1997: 224).
3. At the University College of Gävle-Sachdwiken in Sweden, teleconferencing is used in an English course in which 130 students take part in 17 study centres (Westin, 1997: 342). It provides the following teaching functions: questions put by students during written grammar and translation exercises are answered; new assignments are explained; mistakes made in translations are discussed; and lectures are given on English and American literature, institutions, and strategies of text interpretation. The contents of lectures are discussed. What is important here are the components that do *not* form part of teleconferencing: individual work with texts; work in self-formed groups in study centres; project work to develop texts; videos; exhibitions; and preparation for examinations. This Swedish model is a mixed model as well.
4. At University College, Dublin, a satellite link was used to set up an international virtual classroom in which 218 students received further vocational training in the subject of health and safety at work. The components of this learning and teaching system consisted of a printed distance-teaching course, 26 lectures, 26 discussions, 26 face-to-face tutorials, and the appropriate examination activities (Keegan, 1995: 111).
5. At the FernUniversität in Germany, teleconferencing took place in the field of occupational and organizational psychology in the form of a 'distance seminar' (Wiendieck et al, 1996: 6). The components were: a study paper, teleconferencing (lecture, discussion, presentation of graphs and films) and a face-to-face tutorial. To save costs, the teleconferencing component consisted of both on-line and off-line phases.

6. At the Pedagogical University at Tallin in Estonia, teleconferencing is used to train school librarians. This method is used not only to train students in the contents of their subject but also to familiarize them with teleconferencing itself, because this will play an important role in their future profession.

Information on experience was received from the last-named project according to which teaching behaviour in teleconferencing needed to be different from those in other kinds of face-to-face teaching. The results showed that:

- teachers must take care to be in focus at all times so that students can see them;
- they must keep an eye on the scale that provides information on the sound quality;
- when they approach the board to write notes, they have to change the camera angle;
- they must keep students in other classrooms in mind and answer questions put by them as well as those physically present with them; and, on top of all this,
- they have to make sure that their lecturing style remains interesting!

As Sirke Virkus (1997: 36) believes, not every professor is up to these tasks. However, Ingrid Westin, who has experience of the teleconferencing system in example 3 above, is of the opinion that these difficulties can easily be overcome by means of an informal, relaxed atmosphere and collaboration from the students.

As these six examples show, and as Keegan (1995: 116) remarked, teleconferencing is not a project or experiment in information technology. It is true that it is still being used to imitate classroom teaching in a college, but this may be a transient stage only. In the long run, teleconferencing will not remain the main form and certainly not the exclusive form of imparting knowledge, but will be a *component* of learning and teaching in distance education. As such, it does in fact provide great and multifaceted opportunities, although to a great extent these have still to be found and tested.

Commentary

With regard to what Garrison says – and his opinion, as already mentioned, is shared by many in North America – that this form of teleconferencing is the new form of distance education *per se*, I would like to state the following: there is no doubt that teleconferencing, as shown, can play an important role in distance education and can supplement its components practically and effectively, perhaps even ideally; by carefully developed components, structured teaching texts, the presentation of audiovisual teaching programmes via (mass) media, tutorial support, and counselling in study centres and seminars with university teachers. Even now, this form of teaching has important tasks in the given framework: in counselling by tutors, in discussions with tutors and mentors in the study centres, in distance seminars, and even in oral final examinations, as in the FernUniversität. That university has already carried out discussions using teleconferencing with management committees of other universities who are interested in continuous education on the basis of distance teaching – and there will certainly be other possibilities for applications. But can teleconferencing, as Garrison believes, really deliver the basic pedagogical structure for distance education in the future? Does the explosive spread of teleconferencing in the USA and Australia really mean a paradigmatic shift for distance education, as Garrison demands (1989: 66)?

Here we must ask the protagonists of a new system of learning and teaching based on teleconferencing, and therefore in need of a new definition, what they actually mean by distance education when they orient it towards the classroom teaching system that obtains in colleges, and when they attempt to imitate this system as far as possible. It would seem that they are unaware of the educational-policy and social-reform motivations on which practical distance education is actually based, in which a university education is opened up to disadvantaged members of society who would not normally have any opportunity at all to attend a university. It would seem that they ignore the trends that lead to mass higher education, which cannot take place at all with the classroom teaching system in place in colleges. They would seem to have no comprehension of the necessity to adapt learning and teaching behaviour to the unique opportunities provided by this amazing set of technological instruments, which have been available to us for some years, and in doing this to reach new forms of learning and teaching – which, of course, must go far beyond teleconferencing. They would seem to be unimpressed by the possibility of increasing quality by having academic teaching done by the leading representatives of a discipline.

It seems that they have also not realized just how complex and demanding the pedagogical structure of teaching at an autonomous distance-teaching university actually is. In such circumstances a university can use all its resources for study and teaching for distance education, many competent persons can regularly support students, and of course the quality of the teaching programmes, which are provided in a concentrated form, can be checked and criticized externally, including by the scientific community. This is a completely different world that has nothing, absolutely nothing, to do with the mere technological extension of classroom teaching. I should point out that this does not say anything against the system of teleconferencing as practised in American universities. As educationalists, we must pay great attention to it and analyse it. But it is *not* distance education.

The incompatibility of two concepts of distance education that has become clear here has its origins in the different academic traditions and learning cultures in institutes of higher education in North America and Europe. Most European universities, especially on the Continent, are unfamiliar with the US college system and with the emotional ties to the institutions and to fellow students that are brought about by living and studying on campus. Teaching is not given in classes either, and if it were, it would be looked down upon.

Two different attitudes to learning, to teachers, to students and to the scientific community play a part in this controversy. While North Americans see distance education mainly as a technological–organizational enabling of access to traditional university teaching with the help of the latest technical media, Europeans are interested above all in the pedagogical processing and optimizing of teaching with the help of technical media, whereby they deliberately remove themselves from traditional forms of academic teaching. In a virtual seminar on the theory of distance education, this contrast was referred to by one participant succinctly as 'access versus pedagogy'.

Respect for cultural differences naturally prevents value judgements. We should not play one model of distance education off against another. Like the distance teaching universities in Japan, China, South Africa and Europe, the tele-conferencing developments at North American universities are naturally an expression of the real academic and social conditions obtaining there. The question is simply one of abstract pedagogical analysis. No one has anything to say against the practice of teleconferencing at North American universities; what we must defend ourselves against, however, is the claim that a pattern has been developed in there that reduces to nothing the previous pedagogical development of distance education and declares it to be unnecessary because it is no longer required as the distance education of the future must be developed on the basis of this new paradigm. We *must* object to this.

6.3.8 Autonomous learning

The greatest impression made by the digital-learning environment with all its new working forms is its enabling of autonomous learning, as shown in Section 4.3 for distance education. This has been a *desideratum* for both traditional university teaching and for distance education for some time. Because of the dominance of traditional methods of presentational learning and overcrowding in the mass universities, it has always been particularly difficult to come close to this pedagogical ideal. Its current substantiation through learning theory makes this form of studying appear even more desirable. According to radical structuralism (Siebert, 1996: 16), it is impossible to impart reality to people through teaching, because reality does not exist. Reality is constructed by people by processing information and their own experience both actively and in an individually different manner. Learning, on the other hand, is seen as the development and reconstruction of individual knowledge, and of behavioural and experiential structures.

Those who have devoted themselves to this understanding of learning cannot see academic studies as anything other than an individual, self-determined process of searching and constructing. The traditional presentational and reception pattern for learning is suitable to a small extent only for this process. The digital-learning environment does in fact keep students on a tight leash when they have decided on programmed courses. But on the other hand it also provides an immeasurably large leeway for forms of autonomous and self-determined learning. Here are just a few of the benefits gained from digital applications in autonomous learning:

1. Because of a computer's large and extensible memory capacity, it can relieve the pressure on the student's memory and open up new dimensions for studying.
2. A digital-learning environment can enable access to a large number of databases and provide required information at the touch of a button. Students learning autonomously find themselves faced with a previously unimaginable cornucopia of information.
3. Digital learning provides favourable preconditions for independent comparisons, tests and evaluations of the available information, learning behaviour that is neglected in presentational teaching but that has to be carefully developed and

deliberately guided in autonomous learning. An important aspect is the significance that this information can have for the student's own learning process; another aspect is the information's methodological and epistemological status.

4. The rapid availability of the information is in addition the precondition for selecting and structuring the suitable information, and for transforming it into knowledge. It will be necessary for students to recall from time to time the knowledge structure they have worked out and to adapt it to new information and experiences. In the course of time, students will gain experience in this context of creating, amending and communicating, and in storing and retrieving their knowledge.

5. A digital-learning environment enables students to develop individual search strategies and to optimize them still further and to use them for finding the answers to questions that arise during their learning.

6. It can be used to solve simple calculation assignments.

7. It enables (and makes it easy for) students to create graphics so that they can illustrate for their own learning process abstract facts and numerical relationships in a manner that is easy and effective for both themselves and others.

8. It provides unique opportunities for word processing and multimedia presentations to demonstrate and communicate their learning results.

9. On their own initiative and with their own aims in mind, students can communicate with fellow students to further their own learning.

10. Depending on their equipment, students can take part in certain forms of teleconferencing and apply, demonstrate, differentiate, modify and restructure their autonomous learning in joint discourses with learning groups.

11. A defined group of students can set up a file with information that is jointly developed and discussed, which is constantly further developed and updated. In this way they form a knowledge-building community, a particularly promising form of cooperative autonomous learning (see Subsection. 6.3.3).

6.3.9 Summary

The digital-learning environment already provides interesting, promising and completely new opportunities for pedagogical planning and preparing for autonomous learning, incomparably more than the best of the printed distance-teaching courses, the most impressive teaching course on television, and the most intensive support from tutors. Used correctly, a learning behaviour can be formed that can be of great importance for the further development of distance education. At present, the additional forms and techniques that the digital-learning environment will bring out for practical use are completely unforeseeable.

What we can already see is that students' autonomy and discretion will be increased and the interactivity and individualization of their learning will be intensified. This means that this form of learning tends to correspond more to the demands of modern pedagogics than, say, distance education of the first generation. New aspects of learning will become important: the *independent* searching, finding, evaluating and understanding information required by students will be initiated, encouraged and made into a habit. Through enablement, simplification of and support for self-determined learning, we will come closer to a particularly desirable goal for academic teaching, which has up to now hardly been pursued with the traditional methods of imparting knowledge – or at least not in the dimensions achievable through these more modern approaches. A learning environment with the opportunities shown here encourages the shift in the main thinking behind students' working methods. They are no longer those who absorb, process and reproduce, as much as possible, knowledge that is offered to them, but those who search for knowledge, track it down, evaluate it and arrange it. They are, in other words, researchers and designers.

6.4 Digression I: integrated modes of presentation

In principle, we should be looking now at the multifaceted multimedia possibilities for all these learning forms in the digital-learning environment, although cost prohibits their general use. But if in fact a close link is set up between various modes of presentation, this is a decisive process, and one rich in consequences.

The spoken word will no longer dominate, as in the classrooms and lecture halls of North America and Europe, and the printed word will no longer predominate, as in reading study papers or the self-study of set texts, but instead the pedagogically substantiated combination of both modes of presentation, not only concurrently but also consecutively. Effects of intensification and variation can be achieved that have never before been possible. A text that is to be highlighted and impressed on students can be designed in such a way that it can be heard and read at the same time, if not worked on as well in the form of a computer printout. The size of the print, the tone of voice and the student's own underlinings make its special nature completely clear. Clever sequencing and methodologically established changes can make the presentation learner-friendly, in the sense that boredom or even surfeit are avoided and the learning motivation may be strengthened, true to the old motto 'variety is the spice of life'.

These are just two of the less important pedagogical design possibilities. What is of central importance is the breakthrough into moving pictures in the learning and teaching process, which now takes place in a completely different way from that of the days of film and television pedagogics prophesied and propagated in Germany after World War II, above all by Paul Heimann. The moving picture has now become a design possibility for the presentation of learning contents by embedding methodologically calculated learning stimuli into the course presentation. The length of the moving-picture stimuli – and this is important – is variable: some images are seen for a few seconds only, but longer passages can also be displayed, depending on the computer's memory, without sound-image carriers and the appropriate projectors having to be acquired, adjusted, tested and prepared for learning. Quick access on the basis of electronic storage gives scope for the moving pictures, especially in the case of micropedagogic structures, with such a varied field of applications tailored strictly to learning. This learning, in the audiovisual age, has only been attempted with the single concept of film, in which a process that is both difficult to understand and to impart is carefully presented on a loop of film, which can then be repeated as often as required for better understanding.

Why is the integration of moving pictures decisive and rich in consequences? Because here two kinds of learning meet that are fundamentally different: learning with the help of the spoken and printed word and learning with the help of moving pictures. According to Mary Alice White (1987: 48), they differ from one another in the presentation of information – above all with regard to sequencing, movement and colours.

In *sequencing* for printed texts, it must be said that because of the required linearity and verticality of the presentation, students always know where they are, namely at the beginning, somewhere in the middle, or at the end, because the presentation pattern always remains the same. This is not the case with moving pictures. Here students usually do *not* know where they are because images dissolve or change without warning and spring from place to place. Typically, viewers do not pursue a logical and intellectual development but the internal logic of the pictures, and viewers are then at the mercy of the presentation when it rushes on from different perspectives.

With regard to *movement*, the difference is no less striking. The teaching text radiates tranquillity, and we speak of 'dead letters'. The only things that move are the reader's eyes. However, when a video film is played, movement is the most important design element because it has to catch and hold the viewer's attention. Television has developed an overwhelming abundance of techniques to do this, and these have been perfected to excess for video clips.

Finally, each mode of presentation has its own specific relationship to *colours*. The black-and-white of traditional printing is proverbial. For moving pictures, colour – beyond all rational, pedagogical grounds – is of overwhelming importance. It cannot be done without, for example in the generation of multisensory effects in which movement, colour and sound intensify each other.

If information is presented in such different ways, it seems logical to assume that the information also evokes two different learning attitudes and learning behaviours that are anchored over the years in the students' personalities. Are the corresponding learning experiences also stored in different parts of the memory? This would mean that the development of language and thought structures by abstracting, analysing and synthesising was contrasted by a more generalized collecting and associating of images of reality, often with emotional overtones that reach into deeper layers of the psyche. The linearity of guided thought is contrasted with a mosaic network of impressions. Students must then cope with learning to think in defined terms as well as to think in images.

The possibility of learning in a digital-learning environment with the help of moving pictures is of special importance because for the first time in history learners make use of it who have been used since childhood to absorb information imparted by television, and who have therefore already developed the required visual habits. There must be consequences if, for several hours every day, such learners watch television programmes that represent information mainly through pictures, which address emotions. That approach is in contrast to, and actually hindering, analytical and hierarchical ways of thinking, such that there is a preference for the present at the cost of historical perspective, for the concrete at the cost of the abstract, and where finally continuity is broken down and the context is destroyed.

What is more, the learners' image of themselves, their social behaviour and their view of the world have all been influenced by television. Their acquired attitude to the presentation of information is therefore in many points greatly different from that acquired dealing with texts. Calmness, patience, composure, distance, thoughtfulness and reflection are no longer preferred in presentations, but rather the opposite – speed, liveliness, a hectic pace, entertainment, proximity and direct-ness, the *unthinking* consumption of impressions, adherence to the concrete, not to mention exaggeration, surprise and shock effects. Psychologists assume that with this kind of learning, the timeframe in which something remains in a person's memory is considerably shortened and that future perspectives are lost from view because moving pictures invoke above all the present (White, 1987: 52). These are certainly inclinations that will have to be considered in any analysis of learning and teaching processes in the digital-learning environment.

The distance-teaching educationalist is faced here with the task of integrating two, three or even more forms of imparting information that trigger different learn-ing behaviours, and in spite of this of doing justice to each of these forms. It is wrong, for example, to impart information by means of moving pictures if this can be done much more effectively simply through the spoken or written word. And, vice versa, it would be a wrong move if an attempt were made to describe a complex situation containing an emotional background simply by means of dry words and to do without a suitable presentation on film. The combination and integration of these very different presentation modes will be without doubt a central task in the development of learning in the digital-learning environment.

In order to show the order of magnitude of the change – of the upheaval even – let us take a look at two events in the history of learning and teaching and compare them. *Writing* once shook oral teaching to its foundations and opened up completely new dimensions for learning that today appear to us to be self-evident. *Printing* also made fundamental changes to the structure of learning and teaching, not only be-cause knowledge could now be spread in enormous quantities, but also, and partic-ularly, because with the new means of learning it moulded for centuries the language and the thoughts of people throughout a complete cultural area. In a simi-lar manner, electronically generated images in the video era will probably lend a completely new character to learning in the framework of the digital-learning envi-ronment. How great will the expected cultural change turn out to be once the other possibilities for digital learning have been added? We shall see.

6.5 Digression II: occasional and transversal learning

As has been mentioned in passing earlier, after everything that has been said on the digital-learning environment it would be false simply to use it as a vehicle for pre-senting learning units from traditional distance-teaching courses. Even the few examples for its use that we have discussed have signalled important changes in learning and teaching, and a different pedagogical structure is being created. The process of change that brings this about will probably take us further than we have previously been able to imagine.

If we want to put the expected changes in some sort of order, we must bear the following in mind: the traditional way of presenting new knowledge was a 'course' or a 'course programme'. Both these terms indicate an important characteristic, namely movement from a starting point to an objective, and this implies linearity. In addition, the subject matter has to be *articulated*, ie put into a particular sequence with a pedagogical intention, and placed in a particular *time* and *location*, a procedure that defines the lessons. All this was necessary because teachers and students had to meet at fixed times at fixed places to cover a fixed syllabus. This fundamental pattern of learning and teaching, familiar since time immemorial and second nature to both teachers and students, becomes obsolete in a digital-learning environment.

Important preconditions for previous course-type forms of learning and teaching will in fact no longer apply if communication via constantly improving telephone networks, data lines and satellites enables immediate access with the help of a computer to the complete stock of stored knowledge in the form of texts, still and moving pictures, and sound files; if individual disciplines develop their own specialized databases for teaching and research, as is already the case for law and medicine; if, in addition, using *'expert systems'* becomes routine; if access to knowledge is no longer restricted and hindered by fixed dates, professors who function as gatekeepers, and the necessity to borrow books from libraries or to buy them; if students in their digital-learning environment can move around freely throughout the cosmos of subjects and information stored in different media.

Is it right to continue to offer teaching in the form of courses? On the horizon we can see the outlines of a fundamentally new conception for learning in distance education, a conception that is no longer supported by courses or course programmes defined through a curriculum, systematically developed and hierarchically structured, and subdivided into lessons, but one that enables another form of acquiring knowledge, and possibly even favours it. And this will be a staggering process.

A learning revolution seems to be looming up. In the digital-learning environment, the schematically determined contextual and time sequences of traditional curricula and the prominent role of the professor as the source of academic knowledge do of necessity lose their importance, and for many this is a regrettable process. Alternatively, many more opportunities are opened up to students to develop their studies themselves with regard to content, schedules and sequences in accordance with their own wishes and circumstances. Individualized learning paths can be taken to a great extent – and this is for many a desirable development. *'Participant-orientation'*, to use a category familiar from adult education, the *individualisation* of teaching and the *autonomy* of the students then no longer remain pedagogical ideals or even illusions.

In this kind of digital-learning environment students grow into the knowledge by trying to find their way around in the swelling abundance of relevant information, to relate unsystematically worked-out pieces of knowledge to one another, and in this way to build new structures adapted to the respective situation. In place of unity simulated by systematics and linearity we find variety, the *'radical plurality'* (Welsch, 1988: 23), which students have to bear with. The linear representation of subject matter is replaced by *occasional* learning, ie accidental combinations of acquired contents are structured individually on the basis of new, non-hierarchical regulating strategies. Along with this is found, intensified and later possibly dominant, *transversal* learning, which runs cross-wise to traditional goal-oriented learning, abandons accustomed ways of thinking, crosses borders between disciplines, sets up links within the multiplicity of findings, and in this way recognizes complicated correlations, grasps them and keeps them in view.

Are these learning concepts far-fetched? Some might think so. But the pattern is not at all strange, and is in fact widespread. Present-day experience and the image of the world provided by television build on it. Even in the classical era, a student would be taken into the household of his teacher where over the course of a year he would accumulate the master's knowledge in the course of their life together. Apprenticeships were based on the same principle. It is even found today in courses programmes in adult education and in traditional universities, eg in open discussions and in project work.

Finally, there are also trends towards these new forms of learning in distance education in digital-learning environments, as we have seen. Learning with hypertexts may be a kind of preliminary school for them. And when distance students work from their own PCs on (virtual) projects, they will not learn the relevant knowledge in the systematic sequence shown in textbooks, but as the occasion requires. This new learning may even be developed further and penetrate other areas of distance education.

Let me put forward two arguments to allay deeper fears. Firstly, this kind of learning has been known to empirical learning research for some time. This research has described the 'intuitive learner' type of student, who 'takes steps in different directions, has sudden ideas, collects information unsystematically, but is still capable of logical generalisations' (Fisher and Fisher, 1979). It may be that this type of learner will become considerably more important in future in the digital-learning environment for distance students, and even come to dominate – just as the person who depends on structures only feels secure if his learning is explicitly oriented and arranged towards an objective dominates learning and teaching in the modern era (and sometimes to the annoyance of those who think and learn in a different manner).

Secondly, it must be asked whether this new form of learning is not in fact particularly contemporary and fully in line with current trends. We should not forget, for example, those post-modern conceptions that hold thinking controlled by transversal reasoning (Flechsig, 1992; Welsch, 1988) to be necessary at present. According to Welsch (1988: 23), 'the variety of interpretations, conceptions of knowledge and orientations' is characteristic of the present. What will be demanded in the future is no longer a 'defined set of rigid principles but the capability of transition between different bundles of principles' and, together with this, training and skills in 'coping with plurality, differences and dissent' (Welsch, 1988: 66). Third-generation distance education, if it follows this trend, will have to adopt this form of learning.

The digital-learning environment not only suggests a paradigm shift of this nature for learning and teaching, but it also enables and supports it – even provokes it. We will have to take it into account at all events, because the step over the threshold between epochs and cultures will definitely have an effect.

6.6 Learning in a virtual university

If the required software and hardware are developed further, it will be possible to combine the digital learning and teaching techniques that we have discussed with one another, and in some cases to integrate them. Students can then develop more learning activities in their digital-learning environments than in any other learning location. Not only will they use interactive multimedia distance-teaching courses on CD-ROM, via the Internet (with or without ISDN), and not only will they talk to other students and attend virtual lectures, seminars and practical courses in the form of teleconferencing, they will also profit from other functions, such as those offered by a university on a real campus. Here we can see the initial outlines of a '*virtual university*'.

'Virtual' means 'being in essence or effect but not in fact', but an older definition is even more accurate: 'having the power of invisible efficacy without the agency of a material element' (Webster, 1953: 2859). The university's services are essentially and effectively available, even if they are in fact invisible. This is a triumph for information and communications technology.

6.6.1 The contribution of the FernUniversität

In the departments of Practical Computer Science (Professor Dr Schlageter) and Communications Systems (Professor Dr Kaderali) at the FernUniversität, intensive work has been carried out for many years and at great expense towards establishing, testing and optimizing a model for operating virtual universities, whereby the findings of and experience gained with multimedia and communications technologies are used as a basis.

The ambition of the project group set up by the two departments is to optimize the technical equipment for the operation of a virtual university, but at the same time to develop an overall concept for the Virtual University. The idea is to absorb productively previous isolated experience with data file courses, interactive learning programmes, and teleconferencing, and to bundle these with other university services so that in the end it is possible to make *all* the functions of a university available to students. Not only are teaching and research being digitalized but also access to the administration and the library, to current information and to opportunities for informal talks.

A single example can be used to illustrate these efforts. The *graphical user interface* that shows FernUniversität students using PCs the paths for using the services contains at present the following elements in accordance with the aims shown above:

- *Teaching* (access to virtual teaching);
- *Research* (both teachers and students can acquire information on the state of research in individual fields);
- *Topnews* (contains information found on noticeboards);
- *Shop* (above all for buying additional learning and teaching programmes);
- *Cafeteria* (for informal contacts with other students, not necessarily to do with studies);
- *Office* (carries out all administrative procedures);
- *Library* (for ordering books, examining digital books and magazines, and for bibliographical research); and
- *Information* (answers all questions on the FernUniversität, shows the university to potential students, and is used for talks with tutors).

Students no longer need to leave their digital-learning environment because they can now find all the university's services there, as well as those of the study centres, and can access them without any difficulties (Schlageter, 1996: 13).

6.6.2 Changes required and advantages gained

The foregoing presupposes a new learning behaviour. The problem here is not only finding one's way in the abstract world of a virtual university of this type but to become used to the teaching modes encountered in digital learning. This is a question of experience. What is more important is to acquire the skills to make oneself independent of the judgement of others, to be aware of one's own learning requirements, to take the initiative, to develop the ability to recognize differences in quality rapidly, to evaluate the advantages and disadvantages of particular learning paths, to choose among several learning programmes, and give reasons for the choice, to reflect on one's own learning and to contribute to the creation of a digital communications culture.

The importance of this development work cannot be emphasized strongly enough. With regard to distance-teaching pedagogics, we can see confirmed here what we saw in Section 6.1 as an optimistic interpretation of the opportunities provided by digital learning and teaching. If we ignore the costs of a virtual university of this type (which are extremely high at present), what becomes immediately clear is a great advantage for distance students in employment, especially as they suffer chronically from a lack of time: there are considerable time savings.

A second advantage seems banal, but is just as important: comfortableness. Where there is rapid access to all desired information, instructions, teaching programmes with different origins, and simplified access to joint talks or group discussions, what we have is more than the user-friendliness stressed again and again by Anthony Bates (1995). A radically new situation has been created in which everything is available at the click of a mouse that is required for reading, looking up, studying, training, revising, constructing, arranging, informing, saving, reminding, browsing, and navigating. In other words, a comfortable, or even convenient, system of learning and teaching has been created. The virtual university makes learning and teaching extremely comfortable and convenient. And it is true. We only have to remind ourselves of the trips that would have to be made, and of the expense in buying appliances, books and teaching materials, and that these have all been made redundant through the virtual university.

The actual pedagogical advantages of a virtual university are in fact to be found in other fields: it can compensate in part – and in some cases, surprisingly, almost fully – for the pedagogical deficiencies not only of correspondence distance-teaching but also of distance education in a multimedia environment. These include:

- the practical reduction of presentation modes to the print medium;
- preference for one-way communication in the use of mass-media (books, television, radio);
- the drastic reduction of formal and informal contacts to other students and to teachers;
- the spatial and social isolation of students; and
- insufficient participation and interaction in the knowledge process.

Distance education theoreticians and practitioners everywhere must give a warm, if not enthusiastic, welcome to the possibilities provided by a virtual university. The virtual university must appear to them as the climax of all their efforts to convert distance into proximity for distance students. The virtual proximity, such as is possible in interactive video conferences, for example, should be extremely welcome as an element of distance education.

These are more general pedagogical advantages, but they are accompanied by those advantages that are provided by different digital working methods and have already been outlined. Here are three of them which are particularly important:

1. intensification of the multimedia presentation modes;
2. increased interactivity; and
3. the way in which the digital-learning environment stimulates, encourages and necessitates autonomous learning.

The Virtual University Phoenix, Arizona, USA, can already be used as an example to test just how far these advantages are in fact used pedagogically. In addition, the Virtual Campus of the Open University of Catalonia, Spain (Alsina, 1997: 424), which has recently been established, will also have to be analysed for this purpose, as will in future the Inter-American Virtual University, which is currently being prepared by the Inter-American Distance Education Consortium (Villaroel and Rada, 1997: 524).

6.6.3 Possible mistakes

It must be said that the warmth and enthusiasm of the welcome given to this wonderful set of instruments for a virtual university is not shared by all. For example, some educationalists are tortured by the question of *how* it will in fact be used in reality. Will many succumb to the temptation to use this expensive and extraordinarily multifaceted technological system simply to imitate the traditional learning and teaching system – down to the very last detail? Will many professors simply record their lectures on video and transfer them to CD-ROM and feed them into the virtual university in this way? Will other university teachers simply digitalize their printed distance-teaching courses and send them in? This would squander the great chance to work with a highly flexible, variable learning and teaching system that can be adapted rapidly to changes in individual, occupational and societal requirements. We could then no longer expect curricular reform and the achievement of methods for learning and teaching in accordance with a virtual university and unique to it. The virtual university has to develop its own pedagogical profile and must not imitate either the traditional university or the distance-teaching university.

A second problem is caused by the cheerful optimism of those protagonists of the virtual university who believe that it will supply the interactivity and communication lacking in distance education. They cherish a hope here that will prove to be serious self-delusion. Communication mediated through technical media remains mediated communication and cannot replace an actual discussion, an actual argument, the discourse of a group gathered at a particular location. Mediated communication and actual communication stand in relationship to one another like a pencilled sketch and an oil painting of the same subject. What takes place in a discussion between two or more people can only be transmitted in part electronically. What is missing is the consciously perceived presence of the other persons, their aura, the feeling of being together that differs each time the participants meet. All this supplies genuineness and liveliness to the communication. A virtual university that does without face-to-face events by referring to the possibility of video-conferencing can only ever remain a surrogate university.

A distance teaching university in a multimedia system, with its face-to-face study counselling and its tutors in the study centres, is much more fortunate in this regard. Even the most extensively developed virtual university cannot do without these meetings. This is not an argument against video-conferencing as such. It is a new medium for learning and teaching in distance education, with particular advantages and disadvantages, whose effect has still to be developed. There is no doubt that to a certain extent it will improve the structure of communication in distance education – but it cannot ever take the place of personal communication in distance education.

In view of these two problems, is it wise to imagine a virtual university as an independent and enclosed institution? Should we not go on to consider how it would take its place in a 'university of the future' (see Section 8.2)? The two critical points mean that it should not provide the mould for this, but should in any event contribute its extraordinary effectiveness, flexibility, adaptability and variability to the university of the future, in which face-to-face events will be found alongside other forms of learning and teaching. The contribution of the virtual university should be welcomed in a mixed-mode university of this kind.

6.7   The pedagogical flexibility of the virtual university

6.7.1   Introduction

In this section the development, organization and typical pedagogical structures of virtual universities are described in order to demonstrate their unusual pedagogical flexibility. In this way it is possible to demonstrate how flexibility is increased by virtuality. Another objective is to point to the overriding importance of the concept of the autonomous self-regulated learner in a virtual university.

Flexible learning

Experienced educators might be surprised at the great emphasis that is currently placed on this particular feature of learning. They know that each form of instruction and of imparting knowledge requires extraordinary flexibility. For instance, the form may be student-oriented, professor-oriented or content-oriented. It may be adapted to the requirements of different disciplines, and must mirror the current trends in research and cultural developments. The pedagogical structure is made up of many components that influence each other each time in another way. Flexibility is an *inherent* quality in any form of pedagogical endeavour.

However, we must also see that in the present situation of our culture this term assumes a very special meaning. It is a reaction to the rapid change which now enmeshes every aspect of society. The focus is on the fact that universities have to adapt their teaching to the new requirements of life in a post-industrial, post-modern information society. This new situation calls for forms of teaching that are *highly flexible*. Consequently, flexible learning is at a premium. There is even a sense of urgency in the debate. Higher education needs must become more flexible if universities want to survive. The concept has acquired a deep, existential significance.

What do we mean when we speak of flexible learning today? *Theoretically* speaking, there are several dimensions to flexibility. Institutions, administrative structures, curricula, as well as strategies and methods of learning, may be rigid and fixed or flexible and easily adaptable. Furthermore, the very *goals* of education are no longer obvious, but have to be reconsidered and quite often changed. Just now we are in a transformation process even with regard to our values. The educational paradigm shift is a powerful driving force towards more flexibility.

In everyday higher education, however, flexibility has assumed four special meanings, which have become instrumental in university reform. First of all, there is a focus on increased accessibility. Universities should be flexible enough to attract and to enrol more and new groups of students. Secondly, there is a focus on giving students more choice and control over their learning processes. They should be allowed to learn what they want, when they want and how they want. Thirdly, an outstanding feature is helping the students to take responsibility for their learning. And fourthly, reformers are interested in meeting students' needs by providing more support than has been the case in our conventional universities. Hudson, Muslin-Prothero and Oates (1997) made a study of 31 reform projects in higher education and identified these four elements of flexible learning.

The urge to make our universities more flexible has increased so considerably that we may even speak of a campaign towards more flexibility at many universities. In Australia, we can see most, if not all, universities engaging with the applications of new technologies to teaching and learning because it is becoming increasingly difficult for them to maintain conventional patterns of teaching and learning. Global competition and rising costs are the driving forces. The University of

Southern Australia commenced a process of a planned approach to implementing a changed learning environment as long ago as 1994. These environments provide many more options for students, offer programmes and services that are highly flexible and have a significant technological dimension (Kenworthy, 2000: 5). Murdoch University has developed a masterplan for a 'flexible teaching and learning policy' in which the authors have described what flexibility will mean for it: students should be allowed 'to have a choice of teaching modes, assessment modes, accesses to teachers, peers and learning resources which suit the style and circumstances of the learner' (Atkinson, 1997). Other aims of this policy are changes in teaching attitudes, in the role of teachers, in the university structure, and in enrolment and assessment options. With this strategy, a judicious and planned use of *information technology* is required as it will become instrumental in achieving the flexibility envisaged. A similar plan has been developed by Macquarie University in Sydney. These universities are trying to meet individual needs by providing for choices in time and place of study, learning styles, access, pace, progression and learning pathways (Gosper, 1997–2000: 1).

How can such an extraordinary degree of flexibility be achieved? Many universities believe by introducing new forms of distributed learning and, in the long run, by establishing *virtual universities*.

Learning in a virtual environment

Similar to the term 'flexibility', the word 'virtual' is much in vogue nowadays. Because of its attractiveness and appeal it is used very often, if not overused. People speak of 'virtual' classrooms, seminars, departments, colleges and, of course, of *virtual universities*. The literature now abounds in articles about virtual universities (see further reading, pp 265–66). However, if we take a closer look at these universities we find that this designation is quite often used boastfully. A 'real' virtual university can be considered as a *purposefully structured accumulation and combination of a large number of net-based learning approaches*. It must provide for an *entire virtual academic infrastructure*, which enables all students to benefit from all the functions an ordinary campus-based university can offer, including administrative and support systems.

In order to understand the meaning of *virtual learning* it must be noted that the learning process itself is never virtual, but always quite real. However, it can be initiated, stimulated and developed by optical and acoustical signals in virtual spaces – in *virtual learning spaces* in fact (Peters, 2000a). These virtual learning spaces differ in many ways from real learning spaces. Most important of all: they are infinite. The boundlessness, uncertainty, inconceivability and 'emptiness' of the space seen behind the monitor's screen probably makes the greatest impression on the observer. It is associated with thick fog, an infinite sky – even outer space. When attempts were being made to provide metaphors to describe this space, the developers of the Virtual University of the FernUniversität used pictures of a 'desert' (Hoyer, 1998: 4) and 'space' (Kaderali, 1998: 6). They symbolize a space *beyond* previous learning locations, and to a certain degree *beyond* the learning experiences that can be gained at real learning locations.

The feature that is most important and characteristic for our learning processes is that geographical distance no longer exists. As Nicolas Negroponte (1997) used to say: 'Distance is dead!' However, not only constraints of distance, but also those of *time* and even *reality* are relaxed by information technology. Considering the remarkable new possibilities of such a new virtual learning space, we must ask ourselves whether:

- learning in virtual spaces can or should be the same as learning in real learning spaces, as many protagonists of Net-based learning believe;
- we are faced with a challenge to develop new pedagogical models for pursuing university studies;
- we should start placing much more emphasis on developing and empowering autonomous learners.

6.7.2 Preparing the way to more flexibility

A critical analysis of those universities that offer Net-based courses soon shows that a truly virtual university cannot yet be found anywhere in the world. This means that, for the time being, all we can do is describe the ways in which the Net has been used for imparting knowledge and skills in institutions of higher learning. In order to do this an unusual approach is taken. *Four levels* of activity are described: 1) pragmatic approaches by students, 2) pragmatic approaches by faculty members, 3) measures taken by institutions of higher education, and 4) theoretical interpretations of these processes. Only the integration and further development of these four levels of activity will finally lead to real 'virtual universities'.

Pragmatic approaches by students

An analysis of how students use their computers and the Net for their own learning *without* any guidance or organizational provision by their faculty members or institutions is, pedagogically speaking, interesting and revealing. Two journalists (Fliege and Härtel, 2000: 54) interviewed individual students and identified the following activities:

- carrying out bibliographical research;
- reading notice-boards;
- reading extracts from books;
- reading professional periodicals;
- reading newspapers;
- contacting the administration by e-mail;
- exploring the respective labour market;
- developing catalogues of books owned and used;
- developing a network in evolution biology for young researchers;
- developing the service *'Find and Bring'*, which identifies relevant information and literature for the benefit of *other* students (commercially).

These elements of Net-based learning behaviour are entirely voluntary and casual ones. This is the reason why they are, pedagogically speaking, significant from the aspect of a future virtual university as well. These students demonstrate initiative and engage in activities themselves, set their own goals and try to achieve them. They develop activities and improve and evaluate them. Again and again they have to make their own decisions on how to proceed. In one case the Net is used to communicate with the university administration. In another, *cooperation with other students* is sought and implemented. And in another case, a student demonstrates the *application* of the acquired knowledge and skill in *practical* life by starting a small, commercial enterprise. According to theories of teaching and learning, the *transformation of knowledge into relevant action* is considered a very important goal, that is to a great extent neglected by our university teaching, which is mainly based on cognitive processes only. We might think that students are often already sufficiently motivated and are also able to use the Net for their own learning. This, however, is a learning behaviour that will assume great, if not overriding, importance in the virtual university.

There may be some truth in the frequently heard statement that students are the main driving force in the process of digitizing higher education.

Pragmatic approaches by individual faculty members

In many universities there are some faculty members who are fascinated by the new possibilities of Net-based teaching and learning. They start experimenting with it in order to gather experience. Because of the special nature of their disciplines, the available technical possibilities, the, usually limited, funds and the quality of expert support, the formats of their experiments differ a great deal. Therefore, there is a great variety of such approaches.

Quite often these teachers use the Net for performing an individual instructional function as an addition to their conventional face-to-face instruction. The simplest example is the distribution of *lecture notes* or other *handouts*. Other faculty members make provision for access to *texts* that are rare and not available in the library, to special *databases,* to additional or new research findings in the field covered by the lecture, to information about changes to the timetable or other organizational matters. Yet another addition is established when students are invited to exchange their views in *chat-rooms* or *discussion-forums*.

These activities are mere adjuncts to conventional university teaching. They enrich the processes of learning, but may not feature. They do not really change the basic structure of customary expository teaching, nor do they change the structure of the university.

What do we know about these *first steps* into the world of digitized learning? A joint survey by the Bertelsmann Nixdorf Foundations in 1997 on the subject of 'Virtual Teaching and Learning at German Universities' in 151 projects provided initial information about how often these individual experiments were conducted (Schulmeister, year not indicated: 3). The survey provided a list of 12 typical Net-based activities. The main finding of the survey is that these activities differ considerably in their frequency:

Scripts of lectures	39
Multimedia CD	35

Administrative and organizational matters	11
Use of Internet	10
Simulations	9
Tele-teaching	8
Development of tools	6
Non-specific use	5
Use of Internet combined with interactions	5
Learning with tools	4
Research projects	4
Presentations	2

It would appear that in the first place faculty members used the Net for distributing papers (handouts), which are normally given to students before or during face-to-face lectures. This has already been mentioned. In the second place the Net is used for delivering lectures which are also presented at standard, face-to-face meetings. Thanks to their independence from fixed times and places, faculty members find it convenient to use the Net to provide small amounts of information or lectures notes quickly and easily. Some of them find satisfaction in leaving the lecture hall and lecturing to students in virtual space. Structurally, however, it is the same. They adhere to conventional pedagogical structures, although the external learning and teaching behaviour is considerably altered. Basically we can still see expository one-dimensional teaching. Multimedia CDs are used for the same purpose. In the third place the Net is used to acquire information, in the fourth place to simulate learning by construction in vocational courses. Surprisingly little use is made of presentations.

It is important to see that these first steps do not include any teaching using *carefully developed interactive multimedia modules or courses* or any elements of self-regulated learning. The obvious reason for this is that it requires considerable funds and expertise and a completely different approach to the understanding of learning.

Rolf Schulmeister (year not indicated: 2) was interested in the pedagogical substance of those first approaches and analysed the results of an HIS (Higher Education Information System) survey carried out as early as 1996. He found that at that time there were already 100 institutions of higher education in Germany using the Net for teaching and learning purposes. He identified the following six pedagogical factors:

1. searching for information;
2. learning by constructing;
3. exercises, repetitions;
4. visualizing;
5. cognitive learning programmes;
6. communication and cooperation.

Items 5 and 6 show that Schulmeister identified more complex and demanding approaches aimed at new forms of virtual teaching and learning. However, his conclusion was that learning software that exploits the interactive possibilities of the new medium was extremely rare. With regard to the virtual university that is aimed for, it should be stressed that most of the pedagogical factors, and not merely one or two of them, should be represented.

At this point the aim is to reach a consensus that a *virtual university* can never simply consist of a group of digitized teaching and learning functions, or of a single project, or two or three isolated courses, or a virtual seminar of four or five weeks' duration. Likewise, we cannot even call a university a 'virtual university' simply because every faculty member and every student is provided with a laptop, or a number of universities form a consortium in order to develop a small number of special courses. Rather, a real virtual university should be defined as an 'infrastructure for providing students with a learning experience and related support services to complete a degree programme... totally online and for providing faculty members with resources for teaching and doing research effectively online' (Aoki and Pogroszewski, 1998). In addition, we might hope that a virtual university also consisted of an adequate number of departments.

Measures taken by institutions of higher education

The possibility of delivering teaching programmes at a high speed to external students everywhere in the country or in the world is a tempting one. Even for many experts this seems to be the main objective of using the Internet. In the USA many protagonists believe that 'delivery' is the main, and quite often only, function of a 'virtual university'. In this country there are university presidents urging their faculty members to have their lectures digitized and presented on the Internet as well in order to increase the number of students and the income of the university. The idea of 'delivery' may even have inspired Michael Saylor, the owner of the software company MicroStrategy, to invest US $100 million in founding an online university which is to offer courses of the Ivy-League universities at no cost to anyone in the world who is eager to learn (Remke 2000: 3). It is obvious that protagonists of online education believe that delivering learning material to many students means teaching. But presenting content is certainly not teaching. Sir John Daniel (1998: 11) has characterized this approach by saying: 'Much of the commercial hype and hope about distance learning is based on a very unidirectional conception of instruction, where teaching is merely a presentation and learning is merely absorption.' He calls it 'an impoverished notion of distance education' and predicts that it will fail.

Web-based education is distance education and must also embrace teaching and learning activities as well as just delivering, namely *virtual tutoring, virtual group work, virtual seminars, virtual practice in simulated companies, laboratories and excursions*. A virtual university must be able to provide for these services. And even more: it must develop new pedagogical approaches that exploit the unique potential of online teaching.

Trans-institutional cooperation

According to the estimates of a group of German experts at the Bertelsmann foundation, the development costs of a single multimedia course to be delivered on the Net run to between US $1.5 and 5 million (Sproß, 2000: 3). Because of this high level of expense, universities have begun to join forces in order to be able to finance their multimedia and interactive Net-based teaching projects.

In the USA, for example, the most spectacular project is the *Western Governors University*, which unites the resources of 21 universities of 16 states in the western parts of the USA (Schulmeister, 1999: 166). In Germany, smaller cooperation projects have been referred to by Ludwig Issing (1998). The universities of Kassel, Göttingen, Leipzig and Saarland are cooperating by offering a common Net-based course in economic informatics. The *Virtual University of Applied Science* (in Lübeck) was established by a consortium of a number of universities (including regional universities of applied sciences), industrial companies, and employers' and employees' associations. These institutions are cooperating in the development of two modular, multimedia and strictly practice-oriented basic degree courses in economic informatics and media informatics, as well as in catering for new target groups. The main function of the Virtual University of Applied Science is to act as an agency to organize continuing education with new partners and to cooperate with institutions outside the consortium. Plans to establish a *Virtual University of Bavaria* are being realized at present. All universities and universities of applied science are invited to participate. A central institute will coordinate these cooperations. Enrolment and examinations will also be administered virtually. However, only up to 60 per cent of a degree course can be studied virtually. And no student will be obliged to study virtually. The Bavarian approach to this project is one of caution.

However, we can see once again that these cooperative approaches will also not lead to virtual universities if they are measured against the above criteria.

Theoretical interpretations

The progress of Net-based learning is not only based on spectacular technological advances and on the surprising enthusiasm of a relatively small group of academic protagonists for pedagogical Net-based experiments, but also on the prevalence of new or renewed theoretical insights into the nature of learning. One is the new importance placed on *self-learning,* another the current predilection for *constructivism*. A third insight is the concept of a '*virtual society*', of which the virtual university will be just one component. These theoretical approaches are important for the discussion about the new teaching and learning behaviours required in Net-based learning in a virtual university.

A pedagogical goal: autonomous, self-directed learning

The emergence of a large number of different forms of Net-based learning and the use of the digitized learning environment have caused educators to revive and to apply pedagogical models that they always have thought to be relevant for innovating and reforming teaching and learning. Individualization, activation, communication, games, projects, student-centred approaches are some of the old pedagogical keywords which assume new relevance in virtual learning spaces.

The most important one among them is *autonomous and self-regulated learning*. For about a hundred years this has been a pedagogical goal for the education of school children and even more so of adults. Hence, trying to realize it is nothing new. However, we are now challenged by the fact that the digitized learning environment provides for many new, unforeseen, unexpected and extremely effective possibilities for being successful in this pedagogical endeavour. In fact, the digitized learning environment is full of promise in this respect. For the first time in the history of learning, autonomous learning can be developed, applied and practised relatively easily. The old pedagogical idea of the independent, self-acting, self-confident, self-assured and self-competent student who learns by studying on his or her own can be realized. And in the long run, practising this model of learning will become even a sheer *necessity* in the face of the lifelong learning that is required in our post-industrial information and knowledge society.

Precisely what is self-regulated learning? Malcolm Knowles (1975: 18), a world-famous representative of the adult education movement, described self-directed learning in this way: self-directed learning is 'a process in which individuals take the initiative, with or without the help of others, in diagnosing their learning needs, formulating learning goals, identifying human or material resources for learning, choosing and implementing learning strategies, and evaluating learning outcomes'.

This definition is still valid. Knowles speaks of *self-directed* learning as the opposite of teacher-directed learning, which is, as we all know, the traditional form of learning. In self-directed learning the students have taken over most of the functions of the faculty member. Knowles' (1975: 14) 'immediate reasons' for this transformation are convincing: People 'who take the initiative in learning... learn more things, and learn better, than do people who sit at the feet of teachers passively waiting to be taught...'. And: 'Self-directed learning is more in tune with our natural processes and psychological development.' Many 'of the new developments in education – the new curriculums, open classrooms, non-graded schools, learning resource centres, independent study, non-traditional study programmes, external degree programmes... and the like [have already] put heavy responsibility on the learners to take the initiative in their own learning.' This quotation shows again that the concept of the autonomous learner is not a new one. It was developed long before the first digitized learning environment was established. As a quintessence of his ideas Knowles said that it is 'no longer realistic to define the purpose of education as transmitting what is known.... Thus, the main purpose of education must now be to develop skills of inquiry'.

It is exactly this that will be the main objective of the virtual university.

Psychological contribution: the constructivist model of learning
The revival of the model of the autonomous learner is supported and intensified by a change of paradigms in the field of learning theory. This change is of great consequence. The traditional view is based on an epistomological *realism*. This means that experiences imprint the structure of the real world onto the mind of the individual. Cognition is thus a passive process of copying the structure of the objective world. Accordingly, teaching means presenting objective facts to the students. Learning is absorbing these facts.

Currently, a large number of psychologists and educationists are convinced that learning can never be understood in this way. We do not copy the objective real world in our minds, but rather construct our own reality. 'Innate categories and concepts... are imposed by individuals upon the world' (Paris and Byrnes, 1989: 170). Consequently, learning is basically an individual process, greatly influenced by former experience. This constructivist approach is based on findings of Paul Watzlawick (1981): 'Man does not passively copy the real environment – neither by perceptions nor by actions, but creates it by active processes of constructing' and of Jean Piaget (Städtler, 1998: 589): 'The cognitive development does not consist of a passive increase of experiences, but of an active development of cognitive structures.'

What are the consequences of this paradigm change?

- Learning is a highly *individual* process. The traditional model of expository teaching and receptive learning seems to be the wrong approach. The individual student is to take the initiative in defining, redefining, changing and supplementing his or her cognitive structures.
- Perceiving, thinking and acting are not *linear* sequences, but *circular, recurrent* processes.
- The task of the teacher is no longer to impart knowledge and skills, but to *create learning environments* that are conducive to self-regulated learning.
- The new task of faculty members is to *enable* and to *empower* students to learn in their own way.

It stands to reason that this kind of learning cannot develop easily in college classes and lecture halls. Virtual universities, however, are very conducive to practising it.

A sociological view: the virtual society

The ongoing processes of digitizing our world have caused a far-reaching transformation, which has dramatically changed the processes of production, distribution and communication and has divided our traditional world into two parallel worlds: a real one and a virtual one. According to Achim Bühl (1997) these two worlds differ greatly in that the virtual world is de-coupled from place, time and conventional social relations. In spite of this, or even because of this, it assumes great importance as it functions as a *centre of gravitation* which permanently influences the real world. Therefore, Bühl calls our society a *virtual society*.

If we accept this view, it becomes obvious that the virtual university will function as a component of this virtual society. Hence, we have to operate in two learning worlds: in real and in virtual learning spaces. The virtual learning world may also become a centre of gravitation, influencing what happens in the real learning world. This sheds some light on the possible impact of the virtual university on all higher education.

Flexibility gained

The way in which individual *students* have used the Net for their own learning purposes shows strikingly how their learning behaviour can be developed and improved simply because the Net allows much more flexibility than traditional forms of learning, provides limitless space and invites students to become active, to try out new and unusual approaches, to venture into self-learning.

The pedagogical elements and factors identified in the first approaches of *faculty members* to Net-based learning increase the flexibility of their conventional teaching. Each one can become instrumental in intensifying the teaching/learning process. Each one can become a valuable addition to conventional teaching and learning. There are clear enrichment possibilities. And each one has the potential to cause some changes to the pedagogical structure, in particular with regard to the way in which learning processes are organized and social configurations are established. But even if a university uses all these factors successfully at once, the result will still not be a *virtual university*. There is certainly more to it than this.

Given their traditional firm insistence on institutional autonomy, the cooperation of several *universities* for the purpose of developing and offering Net-based courses can already be considered to be a remarkable achievement with regard to the goal of increased flexibility. Furthermore, the cooperation with universities of applied sciences and employers' and employees' associations is an example of extraordinary flexibility. Institutions of higher education, governments and the EC Commission also show a great amount of flexibility by taking the initiative in developing these new forms of Net-based teaching and learning and promoting the emergence of virtual universities. Because they wish to employ the latest high-level technology they are forced to cooperate. They develop networks not only locally and regionally, but also nationally and internationally. The scope of activities in learning and teaching and the horizon of higher education widen. Faculties can cater for an international student body, and students can design courses of their own at universities far away from their home. Through networking, new services become possible. For instance, Bernd Krämer (2000), Professor at the FernUniversität, is the Scientific Director and initiator of a project (CUBER) that is financed by the European Community (IST-1999-10737). The first tasks envisioned are: supporting learners searching for higher education courses matching their specific needs, making courses comparable through standardized meta-data descriptions and allowing the combination of courses from heterogeneous resources to coherent packages. Finally, this project aims at building the foundations for a *Federated Virtual University of the Europe of Regions*.

The consequences of the change from teacher-directed to *student-directed* learning cannot be overestimated. Here, I want to address only the positive and pedagogical ones. Learning becomes highly individualized and student-oriented. Students have the chance to communicate and cooperate more often and more easily with teachers, tutors and fellow students than on the campus, to take pedagogical decisions, and, most important, to assume responsibility for their learning, which includes having to reflect on and evaluate their own learning. All these particular pedagogical goals can only be realized in highly flexible institutions.

The *constructivist model of learning* provides for another source of increased flexibility. If learning is a highly individualized process, uniform presentations of knowledge, fixed curricula and carefully described competencies cease to be rigid frames fettering the activities of teachers and students alike. There is now freedom enough for developing many new forms of activated learning, such as learning by exploration and discovery.

In addition, the theory of the *two parallel worlds of learning* enlarges the flexibility of learners and teachers as there are innumerable possibilities for combining learning in real spaces and in virtual spaces.

6.7.3 Emerging institutional patterns

Another driving force in the process of developing Net-based learning and virtual universities is the universities themselves. Many of them have seen that this cannot be achieved by individual faculty members working independently of each other, but must be brought about centrally by the governing bodies. It is obvious that these universities can only be transformed into virtual universities by developing and pursuing a uniform strategy of innovation. Quite often they intend to use computers and the Net on a large scale. Four such universities can be distinguished: 1) ThinkPad universities, 2) Internet universities, 3) virtual universities and 4) virtual distance-teaching universities. Each of them displays distinctive characteristics and is interesting with regard to the goal of increasing the flexibility of teaching and learning.

ThinkPad universities

As early as in 1996 IBM began a *Global Campus Initiative* in the United States in order to be able to supply as many universities as possible with IBM laptop notebooks. The idea was that universities interested in this technical innovation should require every faculty member and student to own and operate the same type of mobile computer. In order to promote this campaign a special Computer Enhanced Learning Initiative (CELI) was founded. Many institutions of higher learning adopted this particular system. In 1999 there was a Yahoo ranking of 'the most wired colleges' in which 500 institutions were already taking part. There is also a Yahoo guide to America's 100 most wired campuses (www3.zdnet.com/yil/content/college/intro.html).

We might be tempted to call these institutions virtual universities because each faculty member and each student has access to the Net. But a closer look shows that we are dealing here with *Web-enhanced campus-based learning* only. This can be demonstrated by two examples.

Wake Forest University in Winston-Salem, North Carolina

This is a private university catering for 6,000 students of business administration, law and medicine. Tuition fees are US $21,420 per year. The university has accumulated endowments totalling US $823 million. The teacher–student ratio is 1:11. Since 1996 all teaching staff and all students have been required to own ThinkPad notebooks.

Seton Hall University, South Orange, New Jersey

This is the oldest and largest Catholic university in the USA and caters for 8,500 students. Here, too, everybody is supplied with the same mobile computer which is exchanged for a new one every second year. This university is considered to be the showpiece of IBM. In the Yahoo ranking of the 500 'most wired colleges' it achieved 16th place.

Although the use of the latest computer technology is promoted by a campaign called 'Catholicism and Technology', many faculty members remain hesitant. Only one third of them use the laptops in teaching processes as well. Another third refuse to use them. And the remainder are prepared to attend courses to acquire computer competency, but have to be 'bribed' and 'motivated' by the university with US $2,000 per year to do so.

Internet universities
These are commercial enterprises that systematically inform potential students about the availability of online degree courses offered by universities throughout the USA and facilitate their enrolment at these universities. In other words, they are not engaged in research, do not teach and do not confer degrees. They limit themselves to performing the function of *educational brokers*.

The Internet University in Cambridge, Massachusetts
This was founded in 1996 and uses the Net to establish links between potential students, most of whom are working adults, and those degree courses that suit their needs, educational background and vocational experiences. The main functions of this institution can be explained by mentioning that it operates three search engines: 1) 'Find a course', 2) 'Search by school' and 3) 'Search by degrees'. Its educational relevances derived from its success in attracting students. In 1996 there were 27 co-operating universities offering 705 courses. Just three years later there were 124 co-operating universities offering 3,878 courses (Ritter, 1999: 103). Obviously, there is an enormously growing demand for online degree courses in the United States. In fact, the number of students can be estimated at about 50,000 (Ritter, 1999: 103). This institution *functions* as a 'virtual super-university' or 'virtual meta-university', which combines and concentrates on the teaching power of a large number of universities.

Western Governors Virtual University
This institution is called '*the nation's first exclusively virtual university*', but in reality it is only an *electronic clearing house* for promoting interstate exchanges of Net-based courses. It was established in 1997 by a consortium of 18 western US states and 13 larger industrial corporations. In the first place its task is to serve as platform for *counselling students* and *brokering courses* from other universities. At present, 375 certificate and 55 degree courses are provided. In addition, this institution is also a real *private, non-profit university* with the privilege of providing courses and conferring its own degrees. However, only 100 students have enrolled so far.

Virtual universities
Morten Flate Paulsen (2000: 61) has just finished an *International Analysis of Web-based Education* commissioned by the European Community as part of the European Leonardo da Vinci Programme. Paulsen analysed 130 institutions providing

online courses. Although there were seven universities among them that use the terms *virtual university* or *online university* as part of their name, none of them was really a virtual university. In such cases, virtual university is a bombastic term that indicates only that a professor, or a teaching unit, has *started* to go digital. In most of these cases the Net is used only for performing or mediating a limited number of pedagogical functions. Obviously, the use of the term *virtual university* is misleading here.

When a conventional university begins to transform into a Net-based university, it certainly benefits from an academic infrastructure that has stood the test of time. This means that there is an organic integration of scientific research, academic teaching and a specific academic administration. These are missing in those 'virtual universities' that are mere clearing houses. On the other hand, the traditional academic infrastructure is also an impediment to the development of a real Net-based learning system. Traditional universities will be confronted with severe structural changes that are due to the simple fact that face-to-face teaching and learning in *real* spaces on a campus and distributed learning in *virtual* spaces are two entirely different things. It is evident that both forms of learning and teaching develop learning and teaching behaviours and administrative practices that differ considerably. The transformation referred to is a very difficult and complex process. Unfortunately, this is not seen by many practitioners and even by experts in the field. They still believe that the foremost task before them is to replicate on the Net traditional forms of academic teaching, learning, administrative procedures.

Macquarie University, Sydney

This university caters for 6,000 students across a broad range of subjects. It is one of those Australian universities that have developed masterplans in order to adapt their institutions to the tasks of the post-industrial information and knowledge society. Part of their innovated structures is the integration of Web-based learning.

According to Morten Flate Paulsen (2000: 59), this process of innovation proceeds on three levels:

Level 1 Administrative information about the course, some course content, links to other resources, e-mail contact with staff for more information.

Level 2 *Compulsory* use of the Web by all students, generally with a wider variety of content, learning resources and interaction, later often virtual tutorials and discussion forums (synchronous or asynchronous).

Level 3 The course is essentially managed via the Web, with a substantial proportion of content, learning resources, and interaction provided this way.

So far the virtual part of the university offers *60 courses* on the Web, which are studied by *4,000 students*. A characteristic feature of this virtual university is that it is still experimenting with three versions of Net-based learning: 1) 'WWW plus paper', 2) 'all on the Web', 3) 'paper plus the Web'. The Web is not only used to deliver written content but also for interactivity, sound and video. Audio is, in fact, emphasized. Virtual tutoring takes the form of 'human, machine and group tutoring'. The ultimate goal is 'a mature and stable provision of university degrees via the WWW...' (Paulsen, 2000: 63).

Virtual distance-teaching universities

When a conventional university and a distance-teaching university transform into a virtual university the result can never be the same. As the name indicates, distance-teaching universities have already established a tradition of distributed learning and of supporting individual students continuously by means of regular assignments, counselling, tutoring and examinations. They have also developed strategies to cope with extremely large numbers of students (mass higher education). When a university of this type goes virtual, it is relatively easy to profit from these traditions, to integrate them and to develop ambitious, pedagogical, Net-based systems.

The Virtual University of the FernUniversität in Hagen

This academic institution profits from six favourable circumstances:

1. Unlike Internet universities, it is based on the fully developed academic infrastructure of a real university, including research in six departments and 17 institutes.
2. It benefits from expertise gained from considerable experience in teaching at a distance in distributed learning.
3. The FernUniversität has 25 years' experience in teaching with technical media in a professional way.
4. It can tap into the resources of two fully developed respective departments, one of electrical engineering and the other of computer science.
5. Several departments started to teach with computer-based programmes 20 years before even the *idea* of a virtual university was conceived.
6. Two faculty members, Gunter Schlageter and Firoz Kaderali, internationally well-known protagonists of the virtual university, are in charge of developing the ambitious project.

It should be added that a strong sense of direction towards the virtual university can be recognized everywhere in the university.

The Virtual University of the FernUniversität does not only offer Net-based interactive multimedia programmes, as many of the other virtual universities do, but transcends this task by performing *all* functions of a regular university 'virtually'. In order to achieve this goal a *uniform, comprehensive, homogeneous platform* has been developed and tested over a period of several years. It provides students with the following services:

- communication for pedagogical purposes;
- communication for social reasons;
- access and use of the conventional and virtual library;
- access and communication with the administration;
- virtual counselling;
- virtual tutoring;
- virtual co-collaboration;
- access to current internal university information;
- café, chat-room.

In this way the digitized learning environment performs five significant functions: it presents courses, provides a space for carrying out experiments, offers access to the library and virtual library and becomes a centre of information, communication and collaboration.

The platform is used by *all* departments of the FernUniversität. At present, two complete Net-based degree courses can be taken: an MSc in information and communication engineering (bilingual, German/English) and a BSc in computer science. A third Net-based course in mathematics is being prepared. Other departments are engaged in developing smaller, modular, interactive teaching–learning units. So far about 6,000 students have enrolled for the Web-based courses and probably 2,000 other students use the Net for other modules of Net-based learning; altogether 14,000 students communicate regularly with the university via e-mail. This means that roughly one in four of these adult students, most of whom are in employment, has entered the realm of Net-based communication.

Online Campus of the University of Phoenix

The University of Phoenix is a for-profit university established for the benefit of working adults in the USA and abroad. It caters for 62,000 students. One section of this institution is the *Online Campus*, which has *6,000 students*. Course materials are produced at the headquarters in Phoenix by a small core of permanent staff. The majority of staff members are hired on a part-time basis only for each individual course. Quite often they are practice-oriented instructors from industrial companies. They teach and provide support functions. Basically, students are engaged in *flexible self-study*. There is a great deal of feedback for them and group work is provided for. A rigid system of control and permanent assessment is administered. One BA degree and three MAs can be conferred. The graduation rate is 65 per cent.

Other virtual distance-teaching universities

Other well-known virtual distance teaching universities are the Open University in the United Kingdom, the University of Maryland University College, the Catalan Open University and the Open University of Hong Kong.

Where is all this leading us?

At this point we become acutely aware that, *technologically* speaking, it is already possible to digitize practically all the relevant teaching, support and administrative functions of a conventional university. However, *pedagogically* speaking, the question arises whether this is really to be desired. Can we bear the responsibility for fundamental changes of higher education, which will be the inevitable consequence of such a complete degree of digitization? Will we not lose some constitutive elements of the learning process which we still deem to be significant? In other words, is the quest for a fully developed virtual university – the 'most wired' college – a sound, reasonable and sensible one?

Will we not miss some of the qualities of real learning spaces, the feelings of belonging and security, the interaction with persons of flesh and blood, the face-to-face dialogue, the experience of working together with fellow students in the same room, the strong sense of community, the intense feeling of being an active and accepted partner in a scientific discourse, the meeting with original and authentic scholars? (Peters, 2000a: 180).

The question whether studying for a degree should take place entirely at home in digitized learning environments is still open for debate. Perhaps the virtual university of the future should be based significantly on online courses, but also employ other forms of learning which might compensate for its obvious deficiencies.

Flexibility gained

Generally speaking, the four institutional and organizational patterns outlined above have something in common as they contribute to the flexibility of the university as an institution in the same ways. They are able to extend their reach and have the potential to offer more flexible learning opportunities to more students. But each of them also shows *specific* dimensions of flexibility.

The *ThinkPad universities* are still far from being virtual universities, because the computers were introduced for the benefit of the campus-based students to enrich their learning in conventional classes, and because specific pedagogical goals for Net-based learning were not set and respective strategies were not developed. However, the example of Wake Forest University shows that even such a minimal innovation as the availability of notebooks for everyone can result in more flexibility of the teaching–learning process. Certain improvements have been achieved without being centrally planned: more interactivity, more activity, more project work, more cooperation, more communication, more intensive support. The pedagogical innovations include online access to external databases, digitized courses on demand, student–teacher discussion on the Net, doing assignments, performing mathematical operations and presentation of information. A survey has shown that faculties and students reacted positively to the changes resulting from the use of the laptops.

Seton Hall University even reports that the use of notebooks and the Net has added to the flexibility of the university as an *institution* in the sense that it has made this university more attractive to students. In the USA small universities have to compete with larger ones for students . In this particular case, increased flexibility has helped the university to survive in the educational market.

Internet universities usually restrict their virtual services to counselling prospective students and to arranging for their enrolment at universities near where they are located. In spite of this, it has to be admitted that even they contribute to the flexibility of their students, of cooperating universities and of the overall system of higher education. The students profit from the unprecedented diversity of available courses, which allows them to select and to construct tailor-made curricula. The modular structure of the courses provides additional flexibility. Students may even change from one course to another. Cooperating universities widen their scope of educational endeavours considerably. They can reach out. A small, local and otherwise unknown college can cater for students throughout the USA and overseas. The most important innovation, however, relates to a more general educational goal. The Internet universities greatly enhance the flexibility of the entire system of higher education because they extend access and considerably increase the number of working adults profiting from continuing education.

Virtual universities are usually universities within universities (often only specific departments teach online), but more or less integrated ones. Because they are outgrowths of traditional universities they have to deal and come to terms with fixed academic structures and conventions which are normally resistant to change and restrict flexibility. They have to assert themselves when trying to innovate and modernize not only the learning–teaching system, but also the mission and the sense of direction of the institution in order to adapt it to the requirements of a rapidly changing society.

The example of Macquarie University, which stands for a number of other Australian universities, shows that by relying on communication technology it was possible to intensify the links between learner and learner, and between learner and teacher, and to make more flexible learning opportunities available to students of the same university, and also to students in other parts of the huge continent, as well as in countries in south-east Asia. The discussion about the virtual university and the respective experiments led to a thorough modernizing of the entire pedagogical structure of this university. Reading the planning papers communicates a sense of urgency that cannot be felt anywhere else. Here, the planned integration of Net-based learning has impacted the philosophy and pedagogy of higher learning. The whole university, and not only the Net-based part of it, breaks away from traditional paths and now aspires to rely less on face-to-face teaching and more on high-quality learning, greater opportunities to communicate outside traditional teaching times, and on the development of multi-skilled teams. All these measures help to reach a peak of success in making the university more flexible.

Virtual distance-teaching universities reach the highest degree of flexibility because they do not have to develop their learning–teaching system against the background of delaying tactics by conventional academic teaching structures. In a way, they are already used to 'virtual' learning spaces and bridging distances by using technical media. There are inherent similarities and corresponding requirements in the pedagogy of distance education and the developing pedagogy of electronic distributed learning.

At the online campus of Phoenix University we can identify the following dimensions of increased flexibility: multimedia and interactive learning opportunities can be offered to more working adults, a significant contribution to continuing education can be made, the reach of the university is extended, an international student body is served, the model of self-study is practised a great deal and students are activated considerably. Obviously, this is not a university in the sense that coordinated research and teaching in departments of their own go together. The teachers who are employed do not have a fixed relationship with the university. On the other hand, they act as vocational practitioners and contribute their respective skills and abilities to the learning. Because linking academic teaching to the working world is a significant goal of university teaching, this particular approach demonstrates another dimension of the desired flexibility.

The flexibility of the FernUniversität is improved by its Virtual University in many ways. There is a tremendous impact on university reform and pedagogical innovation. Faculty members are to adapt their teaching to the needs of online students and are enabled to do this by solutions to the problems raised by the increased use of multimedia, by increased activity, interactivity and communication, and by the development of suitable forms of virtual seminars and virtual tutoring. Furthermore, the university can cooperate more easily with companies and museums in order to cater for more students in the working world. Tutors are quite often professionals in various parts of industry and commerce and adapt learning processes to their requirements.

6.7.4   Pedagogical models

For most of us, the fully developed virtual university that will meet the criteria presented above remains a futuristic idea. Of course, we already have the hardware and much of the software needed for constructing it, and have put in place the platform that allows students to have access to its services. Furthermore, we can study numerous approaches to it all over the world. But we do not yet know the appropriate general ways of learning and teaching in such a fully developed virtual university. However, having observed some of the more relevant experiments in Net-based learning we can make assumptions about which models of learning and teaching will emerge in virtual universities and speculate about them.

The replication model

For many practitioners, and also for some theorists of distributed learning, it is obvious that the extraordinary flexibility of the virtual university should be used for *imitating* conventional forms of academic teaching and learning as far as possible. This is understandable, because it would mean that faculty members can practically go on teaching in the way they are used to. According to many of them, only the *medium* has been changed. The tacit idea behind this notion is that the teaching and learning presented on the Net will be very similar to, and hence of the same quality as, traditional university education, which has stood the test of time. Such an approach would mean that we arrive at a model which might consist of the components shown in Table 6.1.

Table 6.1   *Components of the replication model*

Conventional forms of teaching and learning	Net-based forms of teaching and learning
Lectures.	Online lectures, synchronously, asynchronously, on demand, CD-ROM.
Seminars.	Virtual seminars: participants present their papers and discuss them under the guidance of as faculty member. Synchronously, asynchronously, text-based, video-based.
Colloquia.	Virtual seminars, text-based or video-based, synchronously, asynchronously.
Practical training.	Training in simulated (virtual reality) environments.
Reading.	Reading texts on the screen of the monitor, or downloaded, or texts transmitted by CD-ROM.

Here, a question of fundamental importance arises once again: Is it advisable, acceptable and tolerable to transplant conventional models of teaching and learning from *real* spaces into *virtual* spaces? Or is replicating them the wrong way of operating in virtual learning spaces? Should we set up our teaching–learning models in a completely different way and move in new directions?

The more we learn about and analyse the unique new possibilities of distributed learning, the more we become convinced that the replication model is not to be recommended, because we will not make much progress in this way towards a virtual university. Important and badly needed innovations of the learning process cannot be implemented. The extraordinary pedagogical possibilities of the digitized learning environment cannot be exploited. The extraordinary flexibility of Net-based learning cannot be developed and used in order to improve the quality of the learning system and of the university as an institution.

Digression: the quest for flexibility and autonomy

If we reject the replication model we will have to design *new* approaches whereby surprising current developments will be absorbed and recognisable future trends will give orientation. What might these approaches look like?

Before suggesting other possible pedagogical models for use in a virtual university we must reflect on the overriding importance of three obvious qualities of virtual learning spaces: they are not *time*-bound, *place*-bound or *reality*-bound. We all know this because this statement is continuously repeated in articles on Net-based learning, but which of us has considered the pedagogical *consequences* of these facts?

In order to grasp fully the real meaning of the disappearance of constraints of time, place and reality we should first remember this: up to now, *all* teaching and learning has been bound by time, place and reality. These criteria refer to the external conditions of *all* learning processes, including academic teaching and learning, since time immemorial. As learning is now released from these three bonds we experience a serious breach of our learning tradition and learning culture. We understand that learning structures that emerge in *virtual* learning spaces differ greatly from learning structures that have developed in the oral, face-to-face culture of *real* learning spaces. The boundlessness, uncertainty, inconceivability and 'emptiness' of the space behind the monitor's screen change the entire situation. It differs radically from the learning situation in real learning spaces such as classrooms or lecture halls. What does this mean for learning and teaching? Where are the concepts that could guide us into these limitless, completely unstructured, new, virtual learning spaces (Peters, 2000a)?

With regard to our topic it must be stressed that the absence of the categories of time, place and reality, especially of the disappearance of conventional social relations as part of this reality, is the first and foremost reason for the significant *increase in the flexibility* of learners, teachers, tutors and of the university as an institution. In addition, it is a precondition for the emancipation of students and for a considerable *increase in their autonomy*. Flexibility and autonomy are the most important categories of Net-based learning and virtual universities. If we realize this fundamental shift of categories, we will be ready to see and admit that learning and teaching in a virtual university must necessarily differ greatly from the situation in which the teacher stands in front of a class and writes words on the blackboard. Flexibility and autonomy have become significant features that signify far-reaching structural changes. They will challenge us to consider the subsequent models under the aspect of whether they are following well-trodden paths or opening up new dimensions.

The composite model

When conventional university teachers 'enter' virtual learning spaces they learn very soon that things can happen there that they have never before thought of, that are even alien to their ways of thinking or that cannot easily be integrated into their concept of learning and teaching. They have mainly internalized the model of expository teaching and reception learning, and are now confronted with very strange things indeed. They find that there are learners who enjoy *browsing* and *surfing* on the Internet, who *navigate* using hypertexts, who like to talk to fellow students in chat-rooms or virtual cafés. They also learn by constantly *interacting* with certain multimedia teaching software, *communicating* by means of e-mail, mailing list or newsgroup and *discussing* scientific problems asynchronously in virtual seminars or synchronously in video conferences. They find learners who *cooperate* via groupware, joint editing, and application sharing; listen to a lecture delivered by an eminent scholar at another university using a remote lecture room; *search, find* and *download* interesting and necessary learning programmes that are available *on demand, just in time* and *just in place*; *discuss* the interpretation of a text with a tutor, whose image can be seen on one part of the divided screen of the monitor with the help of the software 'Talk'; use an Internet Relay Chat Channel to *participate* in a discussion of a scientific problem with a great number of persons who are unknown to them but who are also interested in the subject. And there are others who join in games with a great number of players (Multi User Dimension, MUD), or even *immerse* themselves in a simulated virtual reality to perform special learning tasks (Döring, 1997: 310; Beck, 1998: 218).

All of these specific elements have little or nothing to do with our traditional forms of learning at a university, nor with the traditional pedagogy of higher learning. Most of these activities are adopted from computer science and information and communication technology. It is our task to interpret and use them pedagogically.

A first approach to Net-based learning in a virtual university might be to design teaching modules in which *some or all of these new and still strange learning behaviours are purposefully combined.* The advantage of this approach is that it is derived from Net-based learning behaviours that are already being practised. However, a disadvantage is obvious. This model is an eclectic one, which has not yet achieved a definite sense of pedagogical direction.

By practising this model we will become aware that in virtual learning spaces, external conditions of the learning processes are also entirely different. Instead of sitting with many other students in a university lecture hall listening to a lecture, the student sits alone in a digitized learning environment and has to develop self-learning activities. The model of autonomous and self-regulated learning has to be applied here and faculty members should interpret it in a constructivist way as well.

The '10 virtual-learning spaces' model

This approach is based on an analysis of the technological functions of the digitized learning environment and the Net. Ten of them are highly interesting for pedagogical designers, namely the virtual spaces for instruction, information, communication, collaboration, exploration, documentation, multimedia, word processing, presentation and simulation, and the spaces in virtual reality.

We are dealing here with *distinct* spaces that are *separate* from one another. Each of them can be interpreted pedagogically. In each of them original elements of learning behaviour can be developed and fostered. The new model could be constructed by combining and integrating the functions of some, or even of all, of these virtual learning spaces. They can be used when multimedia interactive modules are developed, but much more so in order to establish a learning environment in which autonomous learning is possible and supported (cf Peters, 2000a).

The virtual distance-education model

This model can be established by combining a number of approaches to distributed learning which have long been practised widely. Here, designers might wish to create a Net-based form of distance education. A possible standard form of university study might be:

- completing interactive multimedia modules of pre-prepared learning programmes;
- reading set books and academic articles in the discipline to be studied;
- active participation in virtual seminars;
- virtual tutoring;
- virtual communication with fellow students, tutors and faculty members;
- regular self-assessment by communicating with the central computer;
- human and automatic assessment of assignments;
- periodical consultation with faculty members – virtual and face-to-face;
- a project of self-regulated learning;
- oral examination in a virtual video conference.

The 'learning by research' model

The digitized learning environment in a virtual university has potential for developing, practising and stabilizing the concept of the autonomous learner which we saw in Section 3.3 and 4.3 and in the subsection on learning in a virtual environment in Section 6.7.1). This concept means that the focus is no longer on the *teacher*, but on the *learner*. The pedagogy of higher education is no longer concerned with how the methods of *teaching* can be improved but rather with how learners can be motivated and empowered to teach themselves in a better way. This means that learning environments must be developed that induce them to self-learning. The digitized learning environment does this in a spectacular way. Possible components of this model could be:

- personal meetings with a faculty member for counselling and motivating, and for negotiating a general sense of direction (once or twice per semester, continued virtually);

- personal meetings with a tutor to negotiate a preliminary study plan (continued virtually);
- acquisition of the recommend literature (in digitized and real form) and searches for relevant information;
- continued communication with fellow students, tutors and faculty members via e-mail;
- establishment of a *knowledge-building community* (with students in the same university or in other universities);
- studying interactive multimedia modules from the same university or from other universities;
- participation in virtual seminars;
- carrying out small research projects individually and in collaboration.

This model applies the well-known concepts of learning by activation (learning by doing), individualization, self-direction, exploration, and 'learning by discovery' (Bruner, 1961). The ultimate model to be aspired to is that of the independent scholar doing research. Academic study is to be considered a reflection of this; it should consist of a series of successive approaches to reach this model.

Digression: hesitation and doubt

Are there preferences with regard to the pedagogical models presented here? Which of them should be applied in virtual universities? Can all learning and teaching be performed by using these models? Can Web-based learning be practised exclusively? If so, can it replace campus-based education fully? If the 'learning by research' model should turn out to be the most desirable and optimal one, will faculty members be able and ready to apply it? Will it be financially feasible, because developing interactive multimedia courses will be incomparably expensive? Where are the experts to help faculty members to develop these courses and the respective hypertexts/hypermedia?

In view of these questions it might be advisable to design another pedagogical model. This should include learning elements from distance-teaching universities and from virtual universities, but also from conventional universities. One important requirement that should be preserved is the *regular and habitual reading of scientific literature*. Another is the *face-to-face academic discourse*, and also *informal social intercourse face-to-face with teachers, tutors and fellow students*. These three elements are missing in the pedagogical models that we have considered so far in a fully developed virtual university.

A hybrid model: the 'Virtual University of the Future'

When trying to imagine the pedagogical structure of the university we have to see that for some time to come it will be impossible to design, develop and produce interactive multimedia modules for all the courses required at a virtual university. We must keep in mind that the development costs of a multimedia presentation will quite often be prohibitive. Some experts say that the development costs for a single teaching hour will run as high as US $50,000 (Scheer, 2000). Neither the necessary

funds nor the required experts are available to do this in a professional way. Therefore, it would seem to be appropriate for us to remain low-key for a while and to
adapt our universities to the requirements of the information society by developing
a new pedagogical system that is essentially based on the following three basic forms
of academic learning: 1) guided and independent self-study, 2) Net-based studies
and 3) scientific discourse and social intercourse in face-to-face situations (cf Peters,
2000b).

1. *Guided self-study and independent self-study.* What is meant here is forms of
   learning that developed from forms of distance teaching practised over a period of
   150 years at many institutes of higher education all over the world. These provide
   the following specific learning activities:
   - working independently through self-instructing study programmes;
   - working independently through learning packages in a multimedia system
     (eg with tapes and videos);
   - reading recommended and additional specialist literature independently;
   - discussions (face-to-face or by means of technology) with tutors and coun-
     sellors that students initiate themselves, and the course of which they also
     determine;
   - optional participation in tutorials in small groups in study centres;
   - self-initiated and organized discussions with fellow students locally
     (self-help groups);
   - working through training problems and previous examination papers on a
     relatively frequent basis for the purposes of controlling the student's own
     progress;
   - corresponding with the persons responsible for correcting written assign-
     ments;
   - voluntary or obligatory participation in seminars.
2. *Studying in a digital learning environment.* In distributed learning systems the
   following learning activities could be employed and developed further:
   - using networks for the purposes of obtaining scientific information ('data
     mining'), communicating and collaborating;
   - targeted individual searching for, and selecting, evaluating and contextually
     applying, information: transforming information into knowledge;
   - making individual efforts to obtain advice, help and additional motivation
     through professional tutors, course counsellors, moderators and experts on
     a subject;
   - establishing individual social contacts on several levels;
   - joint learning in small and larger working groups, in which problems that
     students themselves have thought up are solved, for example in project
     work, or new areas of knowledge are opened up for all those taking part, eg in
     knowledge-building communities (cf Scardamalia and Bereiter, 1992);
   - individual interactive work with CD-ROM, a medium that offers a large
     number of new educational opportunities, eg interactivity, cumulation,
     compression and intensivation of modes of presentation with the help of
     multimedia, simulation of complex situations and sequences, illustrations

of abstract situations, application of scientific methods independently and even practical experiments in virtual spaces (cf Hoyer, 1998: 3);
- working with 'intelligent agents' (Eisenstadt and Vincent, 1998: 2);
- individual participation in virtual lecture courses, virtual seminars, virtual teaching in a college class, virtual examinations;
- studying at 'virtual universities'.

3. *Scientific discourse and social intercourse.* These activities should not be mistaken for traditional forms of presenting contents orally, but rather, and above all, considered as opportunities for direct communications, for participation in live academic discourses and in 'social intercourse' on the campus (Casper, 1997: 26). The following traditional experiences might be absorbed and developed further:
- thorough advisory talks with a faculty member (at set times);
- counselling by tutors and study guidance, either singly or in groups;
- discussions in colloquia, seminars, classes and practical courses with the aim of active participation in the scientific process;
- free academic discourse in the frame of all teaching events;
- preparing for and sitting oral examinations;
- informal talks with other students and with other members of the university.

On the whole, the Virtual University of the Future must be the result of a fundamental process of transformation in which the university, which has mainly offered teaching, has changed itself into a university that mainly enables self-studying in all its forms based on research processes. In fact, a strict orientation towards research must be presupposed for all three forms of learning. *'Empowerment'* (Baron and Hanisch, 1997: 1) of the learner is the decisive, overriding and comprehensive educational category.

Flexibility gained

It goes without saying that the *'replication model'* provides limited flexibility only, as it is still determined by traditional patterns. However, the digitized learning environment that is used can facilitate both teaching and learning to quite an extent by adding to the traditional learning processes: handouts, texts to be read and relevant information can be distributed earlier and more effectively and e-mailing can increase communication easily between all persons participating.

All elements of the *'composite model'* referred to demonstrate that in a digitized learning environment students are both inspired and required to become active in many ways without the guidance or control of a teacher. Here we find a learning behaviour which most of us are not yet used to. How should faculty members react? They should use these elements creatively for pedagogical purposes and strengthen this new behaviour. Its openness and diversity adds new dimensions to the flexibility of teaching and learning.

The flexibility of the *'10-virtual-learning-spaces model'* cannot be surpassed as it is highly individualized and allows each student to design his or her own curriculum. There is a wholesome absence of fixed methodical patterns. Innumerable combinations of learning behaviours specific to each of the 10 virtual-learning spaces are possible. Therefore, learning strategies and learning paths can be easily adapted to the goals to be reached, the nature of the contents to be dealt with, and the skills to be mastered. Most important, however, is that this model provides the scope and the freedom to develop the activating learning behaviour necessary for developing self-regulation and autonomy.

Distance education has always been an extraordinarily flexible form of learning and teaching. In the '*virtual-distance-education model*' this flexibility can be enhanced by merging it with Net-based learning. One important factor is the increased speed of communication, which reduces the turnaround time of assignments to be assessed, improves the cooperation of all members of the learning projects and the university, and strengthen the ties to students, especially to those living far away in all parts of the world.

The '*learning by research model*' is by far the most flexible one because it is radically individualized. Students perform most of the functions of teachers themselves and have the freedom to adapt their learning to their individual needs and circumstances. Hence, their learning is highly personalized, student-centred, student-directed and is activated by searching, exploring, doing projects, by many forms of communicating and collaborating, by seeking tutorial help and professional advice and by critical assessments of their own achievements. In this way each student chooses his or her own learning path. The flexibility of this form of learning relates not only to curricular matters, but also to the strategies and methods of self-learning and to the ways in which this can be organized.

The '*Virtual University of the Future*' provides even more flexibility of learning and teaching because it combines the great flexibility of three basic forms of imparting academic knowledge and skills. This extraordinary flexibility derives from the fact that faculty members may design their courses by freely combining elements of these three ways of learning according to the nature of the educational goals and learning objectives, of the students and their circumstances, and of their previous teaching experiments. Students with families and working obligations can then adapt their learning programmes easily to their restricted opportunities. By relating distance-education approaches to Net-based learning and face-to-face experiences of scientific discourses, the advantages of one form of learning can compensate for possible deficiencies of the other two forms of learning. This type of teaching is also flexible with regard to the weight that is to be placed on each of the three components.

Time will show which of these components will become particularly popular and preferred by students and faculty members. Also, costs will be a decisive factor. Because all students will be linked to the university by Net-based communication and considerable parts of the learning and teaching will be done virtually, this type of university might still be called a 'virtual' one. But it may also be possible that one of the three forms will gain more importance than the others.

6.7.5 Summary

At present, the possibility of establishing virtual universities is an issue of great concern. There is a larger group of technological enthusiasts and a smaller group of realists. Mark Eisenstadt and Tom Vincent (1998: 1) refer to their ways of arguing as *evangelical* and *pragmatic*. Both groups engage in experiments in many forms of Net-based learning that might pave the way towards real, ie fully developed, virtual universities. Some universities have already gained experiences in the new field based on an obligatory strategy. The development is accelerating. However, the majority of faculty members remain sceptical.

An analysis of what has been achieved so far shows that four different types of Net-based universities have emerged: ThinkPad universities, Internet universities, virtual universities, and virtual distance-learning universities. Most of them still use the digital learning environment to deliver conventional, or only slightly elaborated, learning material. There is still a strong tendency to transplant conventional forms of teaching into the virtual learning space. This means that time-honoured expository teaching and reception learning are even intensified. This, however, is the wrong way. The extraordinary teaching power of the digitized learning environment and distributed learning cannot be exploited, and it does not take advantage of the new opportunities of being able to operate outside the constraints of time and place.

The central idea of establishing virtual universities must be to innovate learning and teaching at the university in order to adapt them to the requirements of the post-industrial, post modern knowledge society. Therefore, the design of forms of learning that are specific to digitized learning environments assumes paramount importance. Six pedagogical models should be considered here:

- the replication model – widely practised but not recommended;
- the composite model;
- the 10-virtual-learning-spaces model;
- the distance-education model;
- the learning-by-research model;
- the model of a Virtual University of the Future.

The last five models may become instrumental in innovating and modernizing learning in higher education.

The most important requirement of this innovation is to make learning and teaching and the university itself as an institution more *flexible*. All types of virtual universities that are presented here increase this flexibility, although with different degrees of success. The most efficient way of increasing the flexibility of learning is to admit, encourage and support autonomous and self-directed learning. This approach is based on pedagogical, psychological and sociological concepts. And the digitized learning environment provides the best opportunities for meeting this important requirement. Autonomous learning should be given preference and acquire at least the same importance as expository teaching and reception learning. In addition, the calculated use of the two approaches to learning improves the pedagogical flexibility.

Should university education be acquired entirely in virtual spaces? Should all universities be transformed into virtual universities? These questions will continue to remain unsolved for some time. Many experts believe that the development will never go that far. A pragmatic way of finding a viable solution may be the establishment of a Virtual University of the Future that combines the most successful elements of distance education and the most promising elements of Net-based learning with the joy and immense benefit of academic discourse and highly competent scholars face-to-face on campus.

This university will be extremely flexible because it will cumulate and integrate the specific kinds of flexibility of three important, but structurally quite distinct, forms of university study. As it reaches out to more students it will increase its *accessibility*, give students *more choice and control* over their learning processes and require that they take *responsibility* for their own learning, and it will also provide for more forms of intensified and enhanced *support* than are ever available at traditional universities. Above all, it will reduce costs because of the distance-teaching component. A Virtual University of the Future of this nature will innovate and reform higher education considerably and make it fit for the changed educational requirements of the post-industrial knowledge society.

Chapter 7

Teaching and learning models specific to institutions

With regard to the methods and media used for teaching and learning, distance education is more variable and flexible than any other form of academic teaching. Theoretically, it is able to develop an unusually large number of pedagogical structures. However, when large distance-education institutions plan their teaching and learning operations, and are able to do this as single-mode institutions, they develop theoretically substantiated and practical institution-specific models that become more inflexible over the years. Distance-teaching pedagogics has the task of identifying these models, which have been tested in many ways under practical conditions, of analysing them and of bringing them into the discussion of the subject as a whole.

To start this procedure, this chapter will introduce several of these models and provide commentaries on them. The models are the result of special economic, social and cultural circumstances in particular university traditions and learning cultures. These will not be described in themselves but, where it appears necessary, will be taken into account for the characterization of each model. The idea is to make clear how each model represents a specific type of distance education. Our attention will be directed towards the pedagogical structure of distance education in each case, which is different in each model, and the teaching and learning behaviour dependent on, and favoured by, this structure.

7.1 Correspondence studies: the University of South Africa

The University of South Africa is the oldest distance-teaching university in the world, and before 1970 it was the only autonomous distance-teaching university anywhere. It goes back to the University of the Cape of Good Hope, which was founded in 1873 and which originally held examinations only, like the University of London in its early years. It was not until 1946 that the university gradually began to provide teaching, and it carried out pioneering work in the field of distance education in the 1950s. This is a distance-teaching university rich in tradition with its roots in the nineteenth century.

This special feature has marked its pedagogical structure through to the present. The university is namely a 'correspondence university' that has taken over the concept and methods of commercial correspondence colleges and developed them further – before educational technology started on its path to victory and underpinned the ideas of educationalists all over the world with its empirical findings, and before a new epoch in the development of distance education began with the use of the mass media of radio and television. Nowhere else was it possible to let correspondence studies mature over the years into an accepted method of university teaching. Nowhere else was it possible for distance-teaching pedagogical routine to be developed so early from a university-based pedagogical experiment. This is why the University of South Africa is introduced here as the prototype of this special form of distance education.

At present, the university is making efforts to adapt its teaching and learning system to more modern trends. According to statements from the university, it is in a process of transformation and renewal. It sent a group to study the Open University in the UK and the Open Universiteit in the Netherlands, and to gather ideas from each. The impressions were put into two reports (UNISA, 1995a/b), which document how representatives of teaching and learning systems met who come from two different epochs in distance education.

The University of South Africa is making efforts to compensate for the differences that were noted. It has started to develop courses through course teams, and experiments with teleconferencing have already taken place. In fact, an interactive video-conferencing link has been established between the university in Pretoria and the students in Cape Town. For systematic reasons, however, the University of South Africa is shown here as the distance-teaching university that it was in the last fifty years and as which it made distance educational history.

7.1.1 Description

With around 130,000 students, over one-third of all South Africa's students, the University of South Africa is the biggest university in the country and one of the ten largest distance-teaching universities in the world. It also has a university building that is unequalled because of its architectural boldness and imposing dimensions. The university, according to its official commission, is to be open to all those who fulfil the entrance requirements. For this purpose the university is to be involved in both teaching and research, and in community service. It is to be guided equally by the principles of equality of opportunity and high academic quality (SAIDE, 1995: 4).

If this university is to be open to all, that concept means something else in South Africa compared with in distance-teaching universities in Great Britain, the Netherlands, Germany or Spain. There, the aim is not just to open up universities to adults in employment and to provide them with a second chance to gain a university education, because most of its students never had a first chance; from the very beginning this distance-teaching university in the land of apartheid was faced with the task of smoothing the way to university for the black population, because they were forbidden from studying at 'white' universities and were unable to attend the separate universities for blacks, Indians and Coloureds for financial reasons. The aim of increasing chances for higher education in general, which is pursued by all distance teaching universities, thus gained a particular urgency and significance in South Africa.

It must be said here that its predecessor, the University of the Cape of Good Hope, also had a remarkably egalitarian aim because, as is stated in its Royal Charter of 26 June 1873, the university was established to promote 'sound learning among all classes' (Boucher, 1973). The University of South Africa fulfils this task nowadays not only by holding examinations but also by providing its own teaching. Here it has had remarkable success in several aspects. Firstly, it meets an actual demand, as the number of students has risen from around 5,500 in 1955 to around 130,000 today. Secondly, the proportion of women students is satisfactorily high; in fact, at 56 per cent it has a higher proportion than of men. Thirdly – and this is the most important factor – the university proved itself as the only *integrated* university in South Africa, admitting students of all races.

Even in the periods of the most rigid apartheid policies, the University of South Africa was a multicultural university. In 1955, the proportion of Africans was only 18 per cent, but this grew to 23 per cent by 1985, and to 49 per cent by 1996 following the political changes in the country. A great number of young politicians, including some from other African countries, studied at this university, sometimes secretly, and prepared themselves for a political career. The most famous of them is Nelson Mandela. In an interview, he called the University of South Africa 'a great window of opportunity, not only to me, but to many, many South Africans of all colours' (UNISA, 1994: 11). In another part of this interview he said (and this underlines the importance of the role of distance education in his case):

> Yes, most of my senior academic qualifications were done through UNISA. Studying, especially from prison, had an irony of its own. The difficulties presented by some warders, and the prison system, would fade into insignificance compared to the tranquillity in which one was able to study and reflect on issues. So there was that unnatural environment in which one could immerse oneself in studies.

The University of South Africa is equipped with the following to carry out its tasks (1996 numbers): 1,393 full- and part-time academics work in six faculties: humanities, economics, education, law, science, and theology. In greatest demand are humanities (55,102 students) and economics (40,797 students). The Faculty of Theology has comparatively few students, namely 1,180, although this would be a remarkable figure for a traditional university.

What about the university's success rate? In 1995 alone it awarded 1,205 diplomas, 9,917 bachelor's degrees, 323 master's degrees and 82 doctorates. In other words, a total of 11,527 students completed their studies successfully. Since 1967, 132,192 degrees and diplomas have been awarded. Depending on the subject, the success rate for the bachelor's degree is between 5 and 20 per cent; in the post-graduate course for teachers (B.Ed.) the rate is around 30 per cent, and in the case of Indian students it is as high as 59 per cent (UNISA, 1996).

Among many other distance-teaching universities, the University of South Africa stands out in that it enjoys a comparatively high reputation in the university landscape. There is a historical explanation for this, as well as currently good performance. It was at one time the mother university and held examinations for six dependent colleges, from which independent universities developed. When a distance-teaching university plays such a part in the development of university education in a country, its standing is naturally not the same as it would be if it had had to establish its position in a fixed university system in the 1970s or 1980s. Even an internationally experienced and recognized expert like Charles A. Wedemeyer was impressed at the beginning of the 1970s by the high academic reputation of the professors who, in his opinion, were at among the best in their respective disciplines and often had international experience. And with regard to their motivation for dealing with distance students and to their interest in distance education, he believed that such positive attitudes were to be found nowhere else in any other institution for university-level distance education.

7.1.2 Pedagogical aspects

Teaching is based on courses for which individual university teachers are solely responsible. They draw up instructions for studying and tutorial papers, which are printed in both English and Afrikaans and sent to students in South Africa and abroad.

Table 7.1 *Components of teaching and learning behaviour in the University of South Africa*

Teaching behaviour	Learning behaviour
Writing course material	Reading instructions for studying
Correcting assignments	Studying textbooks
Compiling examination questions	Obtaining literature with the help of the library services
Marking papers	
Advising and supporting	Advice via post or telephone
If necessary, chairing discussion groups	Writing assignments
	If necessary, attending vacation schools in Pretoria
	Sitting examinations in examination centres

The tutorial papers are usually related to selected textbooks and show the passages that are to be read. There are set assignments for each course, which are corrected, marked and commented on. To make enrolment easier, there are administrative offices in Johannesburg, Durban and Cape Town, which are also important for teaching as they contain branches of the university library, which has over 1.5 million volumes. If students encounter difficulties with their self-studies, they are invited to visit a competent professor on the campus in Pretoria, or to telephone or write. Summer schools are also held, but only a few students are able to attend. Examinations are held in the 400 examination centres run by the university

7.1.3 Commentary

There is no doubt that the University of South Africa has made a considerable contribution to the increase in the equality of opportunity in the field of education. This can be verified simply by referring to the large number of students currently enrolled (almost 130,000) who were unable, for whatever reason, to study at a traditional university and who have received an opportunity to obtain a university education. Even more convincing is the high absolute number of graduates from the university. Both figures must be evaluated even more positively because they contain considerable numbers of Africans, Indians and Coloureds from the previously disadvantaged majority and the equally disadvantaged minorities. We have to honour this achievement. The university has fulfilled a remarkable humanitarian mission.

This being said, putting it bluntly, the university's pedagogical structure is that of a commercial correspondence college in the nineteenth century. The reasons for this can be found in the university's history. As we have noted, its predecessor, the University of the Cape of Good Hope founded in 1873, was, just like its model, the University of London, an examining university only. Those who wished to sit an examination set by the University of London had either to acquire the necessary knowledge through private study or by means of a correspondence course with one of the correspondence colleges. This tradition was continued. The new University of South Africa received a Royal Charter in which the value of its degrees was laid down. They were to be of the same rank as degrees from a British university (Boucher, 1973). By 1900, the University of London had begun to provide teaching and support itself for external students, and the University of South Africa began to do the same in 1946. When a distance-teaching university was conceived at this time, and the planners were familiar with the tradition of the correspondence colleges, there was only one pedagogical model – correspondence courses.

Basically, these courses consist of instructions, advice and support for the independent reading of textbooks or other academic literature. The dominant and decisive medium here is the written word, in the form of study guides and tutorial letters. The role played by this medium can be seen from the volume of printed paper produced each year for this purpose: 15 million pages. Fundamentally, the purpose was to provide edified and somewhat regulated private preparation for a university examination, a form of studying that was widespread in the British colonies.

If we evaluate this model in the light of the advances that have been made elsewhere in the world since 1970, we can see the following deficiencies:

- Little value is placed on the development of self-instructing structured distance education courses, because work is done with printed study instructions. In general, the printed working documents are only very slightly pedagogical, because no special techniques for presentation are used, the use of graphical and other media is underdeveloped, activities of students (eg reading, writing, solving problems, and researching) are not harmonized methodically with one another and integrated into the learning process, but above all because the teaching texts hardly provoke any interactive learning at all.
- Support for students is extremely underdeveloped. The number of postal contacts between teachers and students is insufficient to provide continuous feedback on learning progress and continuous motivation for students. Above all, there is no network of study centres, although events that take place here must be seen as the major component of a teaching and learning system in distance education. The five regional centres in Pretoria, Johannesburg, Durban, Cape Town and Pietersburg are, of course, not enough for 130,000 students, even if teaching is provided in each of them every day in several rooms. Furthermore, the system of tutorial and counselling support is insufficiently developed. Because a considerable number of students come from those parts of the population that are greatly disadvantaged economically and scholastically, it should be obvious that more intensive support by tutors in study centres must be provided. The precarious nature of this situation can be seen from the work of several voluntary and commercial organizations, which have taken over the provision of counselling to some of the students – outside the University of South Africa and in most cases independently of it.
- Technical media are hardly used in the service of teaching and learning in the distance-education system, and where they are used, their use is rudimentary. This separates the University of South Africa from most other distance-teaching universities of the 1970s and 1980s, in which teaching programmes in radio and television and the corresponding audio and video tapes became important elements of the pedagogical structure. And preparation for the digital era is still very much in its infancy.

In spite of these limitations, there is no need to react condescendingly and disparagingly to the model of correspondence studies. After all, this system has been tried and tested for over a century. Over a much longer period than the large distance teaching universities of the 1970s and 1980s, it has enabled mature students and people in employment to obtain a university education. The remarkable numbers of graduates produced by the University of South Africa in recent decades speak volumes for the success of this historic first model. Once again we have to admire just how solid and adaptable people's ability to learn is. It enables them to graduate from university even under unfavourable and unusual circumstances.

Attempts to defend against criticism

Members of the University of South Africa have put forward arguments that explain in part why the university has for so long kept to the correspondence course model and been satisfied by it.

1. The domination of printed material is explained by the low costs and easy access that apply. If electronic or even electromagnetic media were used, this would always exclude a considerable number of students because they were unable to obtain or use these media. This sounds reasonable if we remind ourselves of the particular social environment obtaining in South Africa. It also plays a part in distance education in other developing countries, because it is extremely difficult to find a better low-cost, trouble-free and flexible medium than the printed word. Even distance-teaching universities in highly industrialized countries, whose teaching programmes are to a great extent technologically based, still make considerable use of it, particularly for reasons of cost.

2. A fine-meshed network of study centres was not established because most distance students are not in a position to visit them. In a country that is three times as large as western Germany, but with only half the population, long distances may indeed be a hurdle, because they lead to transport problems and, of course, high costs.

3. Structured self-instructing distance-education courses have not been developed because this is not possible with the wide and differentiated range of courses that the university offers. This is a reasonable argument. Those universities that wish to have rigidly structured courses with the help of expensive course teams must in fact limit the range of their course programmes and concentrate their resources on a few courses, which then have to be offered unchanged for many years because they cost so much. At the University of South Africa there were also academic reasons for concentrating on many much smaller courses that could be adapted to the latest state of research every three years, or even replaced completely. In the evaluation of this argument we must not forget that the University of South Africa is a distance-teaching university that not only educates students to the level of a bachelor's degree but also provides postgraduate studies to a considerable extent, in other words the full programme of a university. This is another reason why the university has to develop a much larger and more differentiated teaching programme than most distance-teaching institutions, which usually provide undergraduate courses only. Such an approach is easier if work is done with study instructions and without prepared structured distance-teaching courses, particularly as study instructions can more easily and quickly be adapted to new developments. Success proves them right. In 1995 alone (as stated above), 323 master's degrees and 82 doctorates were awarded, and this is an achievement that is not so easy to find at other distance-teaching universities. It deserves recognition. Opinion in the University of South Africa is that these successes in the field of post-graduate education could not be achieved with standardized distance-teaching courses.

4. The findings and experience of *instructional design* are not taken into account because of the teachers' workload. They have to do work that in other distance teaching universities is divided between several persons or instances.

This last point makes clear a structural peculiarity of this model. The teachers are still adhering to the conception of distance education in which fundamentally they teach in the same way as in a traditional university, but use the medium of printed material. In traditional university teaching, so they would argue, teaching is not developed in accordance with the rules of instructional design. And what is good for students at traditional universities must also be good for students at a distance-teaching university. Teachers at the University of South Africa do not see themselves as instructional designers, educational technologists, or evaluation experts, and have no wish to be experts for the typography or layout of teaching texts, because they have enough work to do already. They have to write courses, correct assignments, counsel students and from time to time chair discussions. And they are also expected to carry on with their research. They look with envy at their colleagues at the Open University in the UK who have tutors to relieve them of some of the work of teaching, correcting assignments and counselling students, and course teams to relieve them of the load of the development of distance-teaching courses in such a way that they are pedagogically specific to distance education (UNISA, 1995a: 7).

A fundamental weakness can be seen here: distance education can be interpreted as the most industrialized form of teaching and learning (see Section 5.3). If teachers at the University of South Africa complain about the amount of work they have to do, it is obvious that they attach little importance to this principle. It is true that printing the study materials is done as mass production, and this is an important criterion of industrialized teaching, but what is completely missing from the teaching behaviour is a division of labour specific to functions and quality increases through cooperation on the basis of that division of labour.

For distance education, the interaction of specialists is constitutive. In a developed industrialized system of distance education, the teacher collaborates above all as a subject-matter specialist and can concentrate on this function and on research. This is right and proper because the specialists can contribute to the success of the distance teaching programme in a field in which they are fully competent. Development, control, evaluation and counselling tasks are taken from them and given to experts. This is the reason why distance education at the University of South Africa can only be carried out *non-professionally* and why the level of teaching is never higher than the level of the respective teacher. And it is also the reason why teachers in a university of this size can never do justice to their tasks even if they use every effort and all their strength. Partial achievements cannot be bundled together into a whole, the contributions of different persons and instances do not complement one another, and no measurable system effects are achieved in teaching that can be optimized on the basis of regular evaluations. This is the real deficit of correspondence studies.

Critics arguing from the point of view of educational economics are concerned about the relatively low success rates because in their opinion the costs of each degree awarded are too high. This fiscal attitude must be rejected. Should the costs involved have led to those 132,000 graduates, who are adults in full-time employment and include educationally and socially disadvantaged Africans, Indians and Coloureds, being turned away? How might this have been reconciled with the university's humanitarian mission? And do not those students who do not sit or pass the final examinations also derive profit from their studies that also benefits the economy?

Finally, there are two conditions that make teaching and learning in distance education in a country such as South Africa enormously difficult, and at the same time they highlight the general situation in the country. Firstly, it should be noted that more than 40 per cent of the students at the university speak neither Afrikaans or English and have to study in what amounts to a *foreign language*. The University of South Africa has to provide special preparatory courses for training students to speak and write in their chosen language and in the context of the respective subject matter. To obtain an indication of the extent of these difficulties we need only imagine what distance education at the UK's Open University would be like if it had to be carried out in French, German or Spanish.

The second problem is that many African students simply had nowhere to go to sit quietly and study, because their houses do not provide extra rooms for studying. In this context, the service provided by the library of the University of South Africa may be regarded as a drop in the ocean. Every morning the library opens its doors at 9 am for those living in the Pretoria region who do not know where to study their course materials. Every seat in the air-conditioned reading room is occupied at all times. Anyone who has seen the queues of Africans hungry for knowledge and eager to learn waiting outside the library long before it opens, so that they can claim one of these much sought-after places, will have an idea of the circumstances in which distance education takes place in that country.

If we take account of the enormous difficulties that have to be overcome in distance education in that land, we have to put a positive interpretation on the successes achieved by the University of South Africa in this field.

A fundamental criticism

A commission of international distance-education experts, which inspected the teaching and learning system in 1995, did not share this view. The commission was invited by the newly-founded South African Institute for Distance Education (SAIDE) on behalf of the African National Congress (ANC) to inspect the complete system of public and private distance teaching in South Africa in order to discover what contribution distance education might make to the development of public learning in the future, and to put forward proposals for its reform. The intention behind this action was to make open learning and distance learning into an instrument for the reform of the educational system in a democratic South Africa, and to make restitution for the long years of discrimination against the African population in the field of education. Distance education is intended to help here, but not the distance education practised in the University of South Africa. In its report (SAIDE, 1995), the commission found fault above all with the following points in the university's system of distance education – and with the distance education provided by three other state-owned distance-teaching institutions:

- measured against the criteria of *open learning* the teaching programmes offered are poor;
- teaching is organized on the basis of an obsolete distance-education model and a very restricted understanding of what distance education actually is; and
- successful studying depends solely on the quality of the study instructions and the printed material, because there are no other pedagogical influences.

This diagnosis led the commission to propose the following remedies:

1. The University of South Africa is to be subjected to a thorough conceptional and organizational change.
2. Teaching and learning will be organized in accordance with a different distance-education model and on the basis of different principles.
3. The university's personnel and financial resources will be redistributed in favour of regional centres, student support, and qualitatively demanding course development.
4. The government will set up a network of study centres in South Africa that can be used by students from all distance teaching institutions.
5. Appropriate in-service training will be provided for teachers at both traditional universities and distance-teaching universities to make their function as facilitators of students' learning more effective.
6. The government will in general operate a policy of 'open learning' aimed at altering the character not only of the University of South Africa and other distance-teaching institutions in the country but also of *all* institutes of higher education, because they will have to provide support in future for students in both traditional universities and in distance education.

With regard to the substance we can only agree with the commission, in particular with regard to the role of distance education in university education of the future. The pedagogical analysis is correct, and so are the proposals for reform. At the same time, what is missing is consideration of this country's special geographical, material and intellectual characteristics. A distance-teaching university always comes into being in defined social circumstances, which it reflects. It is part of the country's academic culture. If it works with obsolete methods, there will be reasons for this that must be taken seriously (see earlier in the subsection).

This university cannot therefore simply be replaced by a new one. Even if all participants wanted this, it would not succeed. Mature structures possess a great deal of inertia and continue to have an effect even after they have been formally altered. In addition, an autonomous university simply cannot be treated in the way that the commission acted, for the extent to which research and teaching depend on the respective academic traditions must be taken into account. And what is more, the impetus for reform must come from within. The commission appears to have been too optimistic concerning the 'feasibility' of its proposals.

7.1.4 Summary

The University of South Africa has the historical honour of having made corre-spondence studies, which were until then the domain of commercial providers, into a regular mode of academic teaching. It showed for the first time how distance edu-cation as a programme supplied by an autonomous university can be organized in single-mode format. At a time when it was perceived and understood simply as an extension (or pendant) of tertiary education at traditional universities, this was con-siderable progress.

The University of South Africa is an example of how distance education can be arranged under aggravated social and infrastructural conditions. Its contribution to opening the university up to people who were discriminated against both socially and racially was considerable. Its present attempt will be difficult to alter pedagogi-cal structures that have grown but also become more rigid for over 50 years after the correspondence-course model was initiated, because it will have to miss out those developmental stages of distance education in which the mass media of radio and television were used in combination with printed study material.

7.2 The great ideal: the Open University in the UK

When the term 'open university' is used, the UK's Open University is meant be-cause this was the first to be founded, in 1969, and because it attracted worldwide at-tention with its special conception and working methods. This university has had spectacular success and is now ranked in first place among the 12 largest and inter-nationally known open universities and the 13 distance-teaching universities in the world (Holmberg, 1994: 20).

What aroused the interest of pedagogics and higher education experts in this un-usual experiment in the first place? What is the attraction of this university, to which flocks of visitors come every year from all over the world? It is the decision of the British government to establish the Open University exclusively as a university for adult education, the opening of the university specifically to cater for applicants without formal university entrance qualifications, the granting nevertheless of credits for results obtained at other universities, the continuous and consistent use of television and radio to present subjects, the professional development of courses and study materials, the emphasis placed on support for students in study centres, the commitment to continuing education, the strategy for using digital communi-cations, and, finally, the university's efficiency, which can be measured from the numbers of successful students. After 25 years, we can add the following to the list of positive points: its leading role in distance-education research, and its great inter-national influence in support for other distance-teaching universities, above all in developing countries.

7.2. I Description

In 1971, the Open University started teaching as an autonomous university, financed to a great extent by the government, to provide mature students with a second chance to obtain a university education. The aim was to extend access amongst the UK population to higher education, in particular for persons who were educationally disadvantaged and underrepresented at traditional universities. These efforts are the product of a humanitarian commitment. With the help of excellent teaching and modern communications technologies, easily accessible and low-priced courses were to be provided that would enlarge and diversify the numbers of those who lead a fulfilled life (Open University, 1994: 5).

This humanitarian attitude is not only expressed in policy statements but also in the teaching itself. This can be seen immediately in the well organized support for students from course counsellors and tutors. But even more important are the efforts to adapt teaching to the special requirements and starting conditions for the university's particular clientele.

The foundation courses are a good example of this because they are aimed at compensating for the different levels of preliminary education enjoyed by new students. This is shown even more clearly in the 'Open Mathematics' course, which was actually developed by the university for the purpose of encouraging those with little school education, and especially more women, to study. The aim was achieved by observing important pedagogical principles: communication, personalization, learner-orientation, practice-orientation and group work. The course was successful in so far as 50 per cent more women and 15 per cent more persons with few academic qualifications took part (Ekins, 1997: 194).

From the very start, demand for places at the university was heavy and has in fact continued to increase ever since. In the first year, 24,000 students were enrolled, and by 1990 the university had 90,000 students. The number of applicants for a place was always greater than the number of enrolments. And the number of potential students was even larger, totalling 180,000 in 1988. This is a sign of the great resonance enjoyed by this innovative university. By 1998 the Open University has 210,000 students, although this figure includes about 82,000 purchasers of 'learning packages' specially developed for self-study. The university is therefore among the largest universities not only in the UK, but also in Europe, and in fact in the world.

The university has six departments and an Open Business School. Around 800 academic staff are responsible for the development of teaching. Support is provided for students in 12 regional and 250 local study centres, in which tutors and course counsellors work.

7.2.2 Pedagogical aspects

There are primarily two typical teaching and learning situations at the Open University. The first is where undergraduate/graduate programmes are based on structured printed distance-teaching courses and a series of set books listed especially for these courses. The courses are developed by course teams with special attention to the learning requirements of distance students. Specialized instruction-technology experts work in these teams alongside the university teachers. Students work through their study units and use the set books supplied and others bought elsewhere. The study units often refer to teaching programmes on television or radio, but these are also available on tape (video and audio). Each student is assigned to a tutor, who provides support throughout the study course. About 12 hours per week are planned for working through the study materials. This self-study is complemented by attendance at tutorials in a study centre. The tutors not only supervise face-to-face meetings but also communicate with students by telephone and post. Conference calls are also possible for telephone teaching (Robinson, 1993: 91). In addition, the structures also include obligatory attendance at residential schools, which are held for teachers and students in the first semester on a university campus and last about one week.

In this approach, students are faced with the task of configuring these elements in such a way that they correspond to their own requirements and circumstances (available time, interests, etc). What they have to do in principle is to find a healthy balance between working alone with the printed material, the teaching programmes provided in the media, the communicative phases in the study centres, and study counselling. Initially, students had to watch television or listen to the radio early in the morning or last thing at night, and at weekends. This loss of the relative independence of time for study was later compensated for by students taping the programmes on audio cassettes (and, more recently, on video). Students are motivated by the award of credit points for every course they complete.

The second teaching and learning situation in the Open University is where work with 'study packages' has been developed alongside the normal distance-teaching courses described above. This alternative approach has proved its value in particular with graduates in academic professions. The study packages contain not only fully developed courses and working materials but also video and audio cassettes and, if this is suggested by the kind of learning matter involved, teaching software for computers. In contrast to normal distance teaching, students have the task here of coping with the learning package by themselves, ie without any support from tutors. However, they can also form study groups.

These study packages may also be used as the focal points of in-company advanced training under professional guidance or with instructions. The possibilities for autonomous design of the learning process are much greater here. This independent and non-supported work is always preferred where the distance studies are not spread over several years but simply address a particular problem that can be worked through in a comparatively short period. These short courses have proved to be particularly popular in this area of distance education.

Unconventional behaviour in teaching is also required of the professors at the Open University. Firstly, the professors are not responsible for the teaching programme, for this is the job of a course team, which the professors support purely as subject-matter specialists. Secondly, they and their staff have to develop educational transmissions, deal with specialists from the BBC, and present themselves not only to tens of thousands of students but also to a much broader interested public.

Table 7.2 *Components of teaching and learning behaviour at the UK's Open University*

Teaching behaviour	Learning behaviour
Professors:	Reading printed distance teaching courses
Collaboration in course teams as subject matter specialists	Reading additional set books
	Experimenting in home laboratories
	Learning with teaching disks
	Working with teaching CD-ROMs
Collaboration with experts from the BBC in course teams to develop teaching programmes for radio and television	Working through teaching programmes on radio and television
	Working through teaching programmes on audio and video cassettes
Tutors:	Keeping in contact with the allocated tutor, face to face, in writing, by phone and fax
Support for distance students	
Counselling	Attending study support sessions
Presiding over face-to-face teaching	Attending face-to-face teaching events, tutorials, seminars
Correcting and grading assignments	Attending residential schools on the campus of a traditional university
	Taking part in telephone teaching

In addition to all this, the Open University has taken some significant steps into the virgin territory of digital learning. By 1994 it had already developed 11 courses in relation to computer-conferencing and the Internet, and by 1998 this has grown to over 50. Particularly important for the opening up of these new opportunities was a three-month introductory and training course provided by the Institute of Educational Technology, which familiarized university teachers (amongst others) with the possibilities and limits of digital learning, especially with regard to computer-conferencing, working with the Internet, and using on-line files.

Furthermore, by 1998 more than 50 courses (most compulsory, some optional) had been produced for the area of interactive multimedia applications, mainly on CD-ROM. There remain an additional 56 courses available through the university's residential schools that contain a computing element.

7.2.3 Commentary

The Open University stresses the humanitarian aspect of its work much more than any other distance-teaching university. Without any reservations it stands by the relatively new group of students, namely mature students, who were unable to have a normal secondary school education and subsequent university education because of unfavourable material and social circumstances. To have offered hundreds of thousands of them a second chance to receive a university education bears witness to a responsible social attitude and aspirations towards fairness and equity. Both of these are constitutive for the Open University in the UK, and these attitudes are reflected in its institutional ethos.

From the point of view of university and distance-teaching pedagogics, the Open University has played a pioneering role because it established a form of studying that had never before been seen in Europe – or anywhere else in the world. This was achieved through a series of innovations, each of which would have been important in itself. However, their integrated interplay in a new teaching and learning system achieved an enormous innovative thrust that adapted distance education consistently to changed technological and social requirements and thus received worldwide notice.

Four of these innovations will be referred to here because they have a direct effect on teaching and learning behaviour:

1. *The use of radio and television as additional media for transmitting and presenting teaching.* It should be noted that this was not simply a one-off individual project or a narrow teaching programme, something that was already familiar in distance education; it was in fact a continuous (ie planned for a long period of time) and significant part of the teaching system.

2. *The professional development of structured printed study materials by ad hoc course teams*, which were thus compiled by a number of experts from various disciplines. When we remind ourselves of the self-confidence with which professors traditionally regard teaching as their own personal fiefdom, and that all over the world in university distance education the teaching materials from conventional university education are used alongside oral presentations, the resoluteness with which the different learning requirements and the different learning behaviour of distance students were taken into account is remarkable. The aim of the structured printed distance teaching materials was to help students sitting alone at home to control their own learning. For this reason they had to be self-instructional – this meant that they had to be different in many ways from the printed presentations of scientific facts that are usually found in traditional universities.

3. *The support for students in a large number of regional and local study centres.* This led to the university being decentralized, an unusual and astonishing development for European universities, because regular academic teaching had always taken place *intra muros*. Students are found to be able to absorb personal support, attendance at tutorials, and the direct exchange of experience with fellow students as secure reference points in their learning behaviour, even though they might live some distance from the Open University's headquarters.

4. *The foundation of a university specially for mature students.* The consistency is remarkable with which the Open University regarded mature students from the very beginning as its special clientele and its special mission. When the government required it to admit regular students, in other words those coming directly from secondary education, it agreed to do this on a trial basis only, and soon stopped.

This clear alignment towards a clientele that is new for most European universities also influences the way in which teaching and learning takes place. A
self-study culture can be created, something that is more difficult in dual-mode
universities because teachers there are unable to adjust so intensively and exclusively to the new clientele.

All this created a pedagogical model that has influenced all other open and distance-teaching universities. With this model, the Open University has brought
about considerable structural changes to university education. It has developed
ways of thinking and working and strategies for teaching and learning that have
never been achieved so radically and consistently by any other university. Above all,
the balanced nature of the presented teaching and learning system deserves praise:
nowhere else is the study of structured teaching texts so intensely and reliably balanced by teaching programmes using mass media and by tutorial support in study
centres.

   The significance of the first innovation in the list above cannot be assessed too
highly. Cooperation with such a highly regarded and famous institution as the BBC
provided the Open University as a media university with a solid foundation and a
professional touch from the very start. Its collaboration altered not only teaching
and learning behaviour but also the image of distance education. The glamour of
television signalled technical progress and open-mindedness for the future. And the
Open University profited from the standing that television then enjoyed in British
Society. This completely wiped out the memories of the old-fashioned,
fuddy-duddy correspondence colleges, and also had an effect on both teachers and
students because it altered their conceptions of themselves and increased their
self-confidence.

   If we analyse the working methods of the *Open University* we arrive at some general impressions. These include:

- the optimism, zeal and confidence with which it is approaching the twenty-first
  century, being motivated by its previous successes and reputation;
- the determination and drive with which it is prepared to play a leading role in the
  development of mass higher education;
- the satisfaction felt at preserving the policy of open access;
- the resolution with which the university wants to convince through quality
  teaching, but at the same time its willingness to take on the educationally disadvantaged; and
- the readiness to provide real help and support for students.

It seems that an academic teaching and learning culture has been created here that
would not be easy to reconcile with the teaching and learning practice in other universities.

Future orientation

Because of its importance, we will look at the first point in the foregoing bullet list in
greater detail. The Open University appears to be oriented more than other distance
teaching universities to problems facing distance education in the future (Open

University, 1994). In order to prepare for this, the university is at present planning changes that are intended to make teaching more effective. The following activities, for example, could have far-reaching consequences for the pedagogical structure of distance education:

- strategies are being developed for the wide-ranging use of not only audio-visual but also computer-supported and multimedia teaching programmes, as well as digitalized communications;
- standardized presentational elements and models for cooperation are being worked out;
- it is intended to improve feedback mechanisms in the courses, so that the university is informed more rapidly and reliably on learning progress;
- there is an aim to make students the object of research much more intensively than before, so that teaching and learning processes can be optimized on the basis of empirically determined facts; and
- a restructuring of the teaching system is planned, where the teaching programme is no longer supplier-oriented but user-oriented, and the work of the Open University will then be evaluated on the basis of its contribution to 'customer' satisfaction.

The planning that can be seen here, and its conversion into strategies, is impressive. However, once again it is possible to see from some of these developmental steps just how much the teaching and learning system is viewed from the aspect of educational technology. What is disconcerting is the assumption of points of view and practices taken from commercial life. The relationship of teachers and students, which is in any event more abstract in distance education than anywhere else, is reduced here to the relationship between seller and buyer – another example of how far principles of industrialization have penetrated the field of teaching.

7.2.4 Summary

The Open University in Great Britain, like the University of South Africa, is a single-mode university. It has made this institutional form of distance education well known and popular throughout the world. But it differs from the distance-teaching university in South Africa in several important respects. Teaching and learning is, first of all, *multidimensional*: printed teaching material, teaching programmes on radio and television, digital learning, teaching in study centres and residential schools, and individual counselling all interact with and influence one another. This then establishes *multimedia* distance education. While it is true that nearly all these forms of teaching and learning can also be found individually in other distance teaching universities, nowhere else are they so originally combined and professionally constructed as here. The Open University in the UK started a new era of distance education, and it has set new standards ever since.

7.3 Research as a basis for learning: the FernUniversität in Germany

If we want to describe the pedagogical structure of the FernUniversität and compare it with the pedagogical structures of other distance-teaching universities, the first thing to be done is to point out the special relationship between teaching and research that is generally found in German universities.

A university is regarded as the central part of the knowledge system in Germany; its primary task consists of producing, managing and dealing with knowledge. That is why research is the first priority: 'In the classical perception the university has of itself, its educational function becomes less important' (Klüver, 1983/1995: 79). Teaching is something secondary and derivative. It results from the necessity inherent in all research to inform others of its findings, so that they can be subjected to a critical discussion process and scientific advancement can be made from the knowledge of a single individual. This is why German professors see themselves in the first place as researchers. For them, teaching is, put negatively, simply a 'frill'; put more positively, it is an additional opportunity to propagate their research findings and train new academics.

This fundamental difference from all other forms of teaching and learning is not without its consequences. For example, this kind of teaching cannot be designed in accordance with educational technology standards – for example, specified learning objectives, or curriculum structures – because learning objectives cannot be selected at will and the curriculum is not available either, but arises through the research status of a discipline or part-discipline and is legitimized by 'what constitutes the discipline in the eyes of the competent specialists' (Klüver, 1983/1995: 84). Reflecting on the most profitable teaching and learning objectives and the correspondingly calculated selection of suitable methods and media – in accordance with the methods of instructional technology, for example – is pointless and hardly ever done in practice. Learning is understood in this context rather as an informal participation in the scientific process. It therefore has its own design principles, including the logical system of the respective discipline.

This participation is offered to students and it is up to them to grow into the scientific process more and more through their own activities. Whether they are successful depends on their intelligence, purposefulness, initiative, perseverance, and patience, and on their sensitivity (including their social sensitivity), but hardly at all from the pedagogical skill of their teachers, whose behaviour is anyway influenced by the methods of thought and methodology of their subjects and by considerations based on the theory of knowledge.

There is good reason for referring in this context to a special pedagogics of knowledge (von Hentig, 1970). This is why students have to discover their own path to participation in the scientific process. It is a 'free [uncontrolled] learning activity' (Huber 1983/1995, 498). The students who demanded university reform at the beginning of the 1970s thought in exactly the same way as their professors when they claimed 'learning by researching' for themselves and thus laid claim to nothing less than legitimate membership of the scientific community.

This attitude to teaching and learning is firmly anchored in the consciousness of German professors. According to Jürgen Klüver (1983/1995: 80), it is an 'elementary set of facts that is so self-evident to all university staff and university graduates that it is hardly mentioned anywhere explicitly...'. It even influences those cases (for example today's mass universities) in which participation in the scientific process has become an illusion because actually working with researchers is now unthinkable and in fact can only be reconstructed intellectually. As a consequence, German professors are usually of the opinion that their university differs clearly and sharply from all other institutions, which only exercise educational functions. And they regard teaching in colleges, which is familiar in so many universities in the English-speaking world, as not being university education in the real sense of the term because there is no link to the research process, and they tend to push this form of education in the direction of school learning, in particular because studying there is often based on textbooks and not on original contributions by the teachers. In colleges, teaching is in the foreground, whereas orientation towards (and possibly participation in) research does not commence until the postgraduate stage.

All this has been stated so as to provide readers with an understanding of the pedagogical structure of teaching and learning at the FernUniversität, so that they can see how it differs from that of many other distance-teaching universities. In this sense, the FernUniversität is without doubt a traditional university. It understands and practises academic teaching in the sense described consciously – or rather more unconsciously. And the same approach still applies today, although the ideal of the close links between research and teaching is slowly disappearing from today's mass universities.

Whereas most distance teaching universities in the world award bachelor's degrees only, and are therefore primarily, or even exclusively, devoted to academic teaching, the FernUniversität, which awards all degrees, is in the first place a *research institution that teaches as well*, to put it pointedly. For this reason it is treated as a special type.

7.3.1 Description

The FernUniversität was founded in 1974 as an autonomous university by an act of the state parliament of North-Rhine Westphalia, and it started teaching in 1975. It has the right to award all the academic degrees usually awarded by German universities, and these would all be regarded by Anglo-American universities as 'higher' degrees. Like nearly all German universities, the FernUniversität is financed by the state. At present the annual budget is around DM120 million. Although the federal structure of the Federal Republic of Germany means that the university is, and can only be, a *state* university, under the federal constitution it is open to applicants from all over Germany and from abroad. In fact, the majority of students do not live in North-Rhine Westphalia but elsewhere in Germany.

The university's statutory mission is the same as that of other universities, namely the 'care and development of science by means of research, teaching and study'. In this regard there is absolutely no institutional difference between traditional universities and the FernUniversität. Six faculties were established to fulfil this mission: education, social sciences and humanities; electrical engineering; computer science; law; economics; and mathematics. The self-recruiting procedure at the FernUniversität is the same as at a traditional university: professors are selected in the first place on the basis of their research achievements and are then appointed by the Minister of Science and Research.

From the aspect of educational policy, however, the FernUniversität can be compared with distance-teaching universities in other countries: the idea was to relieve the burden on the hopelessly overcrowded universities. There was a state of emergency in fact at the time because very many applicants for places at university had to wait several years before being admitted. The idea of providing for persons who would have been prevented from studying at university without this emergency – for example, persons in full-time employment, housewives, and the disabled (Rau, 1974: 24) – was secondary.

In addition, people were concerned about continuous scientific support for university graduates. The university's founder, Johannes Rau, who was at the time Minister of Science and Research in North-Rhine Westphalia, wanted in any event to 'develop and support continuous scientific education' (Peters, 1981: 180). These education policy standards provided the FernUniversität with its own special profile as against the traditional universities.

The provision of this kind of distance education was accepted to a surprisingly great extent, and this can be seen by the trends in the number of students. In 1975 there were 1,200, ten years later there were 20,000, and in 1998 there are some 56,000 students. At present the university has 61 full professors, 17 other professors and 10 supplementary professors, as well as 400 full-time other academic staff. In addition, there are about 300 external university teachers who write courses for the departments each year. The university has a relatively dense network of 29 study centres in North-Rhine Westphalia, a wider network of 20 study centres throughout Germany, as well as three in Austria and one each in Switzerland and Hungary. A total of 600 part-time mentors work in these study centres. It also has its own library, with 614,000 volumes and 3,200 specialist journals that serve the purposes of research and are also available to distance students.

7.3.2 Pedagogical aspects

Research

If, as we saw at the beginning, research plays such an important part for the conception that professors and their staffs have of themselves, and if it also has an effect on teaching and studying, it is important to deal with that aspect first of all. The 480 full-time academic staff work in 61 departments and 13 institutes within the university and in four institutes affiliated to the university. To a considerable extent this research work is financed by institutions *outside* the university, including commercial companies, and in 1997 a total of DM8.5 million in third-party funds was available.

Some institutes are integrated into large international research projects, while others work with researchers in the Federal Republic of Germany. The university's present research landscape is extraordinarily wide and multifaceted; a report with a description of all the projects and lists of relevant publications contains 375 pages (FernUniversität, 1996).

The following list of the university's institutes gives an impression of the type of research being carried out, containing as it does just a few of the focal points of research work as examples.

Table 7.3 *Sample research projects at the FernUniversität*

Faculty	Institute	Focal points or aims of cooperation
Education, Social Sciences and Humanities	Institute for Biography and History, 'Deutsches Gedächtnis'	Research into life histories and biographies Archiving
	Kurt Lewin Institute for Psychology	Taking up socially important fields of psychology into research, teaching, and continuous education Taking up practical questions and processing research findings for practical use
	Institute for Peace and Democracy	Comparative examinations of the development of the relationship between peace and democracy through intensive contact with the theory and political practice Drawing up solutions to problems Developing special teaching programmes
	Institute for Education Science and Research	Qualifications and employment in Japan Minorities in schools
	Institute of Sociology	Memory, identity, interpretation, and socialization

	Institute of Modern German and European Literature	Literature and theology
		Theory of the lyric
	Institute of Psychology	Environmental consciousness, actions, values and changes in values
	Historical Institute	Poverty in England 1780–1834
	Institute of Political Science	Organizational structure and organizational reform of the ÖTV trade union
	Institute of Philosophy	Ethics of life sciences
		Philosophy of the economy
		Hegel's aesthetics
Electric Engineering	Institute of Modern Technologies for Electrical Engineering (INTE)	Representation of new technological developments in the field of electrical engineering in research and continuing training, in particular processing questions from practice
		Joint research
		Implementation of experiments in continuing training
		Transfer of research and technology to regional and national industry
		Cooperation with state research institutes
	Research Institute for Tele-communications (FTK) (an affiliated institute)	Integration of the application of scientific results into practice
		Implementation of joint research projects
		Reciprocal use of existing facilities
		Closely linking research, teaching and practice

	Research Institute of Technology (FTB) (an affiliated institute, currently being registered)	Integration of the application of scientific results into practice
		Implementation of joint research projects
		Reciprocal use of existing facilities
		Closely linking research, teaching, continuing training and practice
Law	Institute for German and European Party Laws	Pursuance and analysis of the development of national and international political parties in intensive contact with theoreticians and political practice
		Drawing up solutions to problems
Economics	Institute for Applied Economics (IFAB)	Cooperation between large research institutes and other external research agencies for the rapid transfer of findings into university teaching
	Institute for Economic Research and Further Training (IWW) (an affiliated institute, at present in the planning stage)	Promotion of economics through the transfer of economic findings to the practice of order-related research and through continuing-training measures
Electrical Engineering Computer Science Economics	Institute for Automation, Information and Product Management (AIP) (an affiliated institute)	Carrying out basic and application-oriented research and development projects
		Carrying out events and training courses
		Advising state and other institutes

Source: Schubeius (1996: 27), with additional information from the Research Report published by the FernUniversität (FernUniversität, 1996).

Teaching

Teaching via the FernUniversität is carried out above all in the form of distance-teaching courses sent to the students every two weeks. These contain texts that present the subject matter, make them easier to understand with the help of glossaries and self-tests, and also stimulate and suggest individualized further work with the subject. Assignments serve not only as self-checks on learning advances but also as checks by the university. Students must complete half of the assignments in a course successfully to be allowed to sit a written examination held at a decentralized location and invigilated by members of the examination boards for the respective faculty.

Where practical, this presentation of the course material is supplemented by audio-visual and electronic media-based items: audio and video cassettes, laboratory kits and regular teaching programmes on television (45 minutes each week in WDR, 45 minutes each week in the European science programme *Eurostep*, and 30 minutes on Channel e). In addition, floppy disks with teaching software and teaching text files on CD-ROM are already in use in a number of courses. A further dimension to the teaching programme is face-to-face teaching in the study centres under the leadership of part-time cooperating mentors. These sessions are supplemented by seminars and study days under the direction of professors, all of which take place at the FernUniversität, in conference halls, or in the study centres themselves.

Learning

Students spend most time reading the teaching texts and working through the printed study materials. Full-time students need to devote 40 hours a week to doing this, and part-time students 20 hours. Ideally, they combine this work with continuous reading of relevant primary and secondary literature, which needs to be procured with circumspection and resourcefulness because there are several possibilities for doing this. Among other things, books or copies of magazine cuttings and articles can be ordered from the library at the FernUniversität by post, telephone, fax or e-mail.

The study centres provide personal contacts with other students, mentors and sometimes even the authors of the study letters. Literature relevant to the course is available there, and electronic media may be used. If students are interested in closer and longer-lasting contacts, they can form study circles with other students living nearby.

Moving from the FernUniversität to another university, and vice versa, is possible and common. End-of-semester certificates already acquired in the respective university are credited in each case.

Table 7.4 *Components of teaching and learning behaviour at the FernUniversität*

Teaching behaviour	Learning behaviour
Writing course material	Obligatory: reading distance teaching course units
Supporting external authors	
Developing teaching software, teaching files and multimedia programmes	Obligatory: working through additional literature
Supervising correction work	Possible: using additional media, in particular videos
Coordination with tutors	Optional: face-to-face teaching in study centres
Marking and evaluating examination papers and theses	Optional: attendance at local study circles
Holding seminars and study days	Obligatory: assignments
Supporting candidates for doctorates and professorial theses	Obligatory: written examinations
	Possible: training with the help of PC trainers
	Possible: learning with interactive trainers in the CBT program

Media structure: printed material

Courses at the FernUniversität are not constructed in accordance with the principles of instructional technology. With a programme consisting of 1,600 courses, this would be financially impossible and it would also take too long. The courses are in fact written by the research scientists themselves. They reflect findings and points of view which the latter have acquired on the basis of their own achievements. They are often directly derived from the scientific process and are therefore authentic. Apart from nationally uniform regulations governing university study and examinations, professors are very much left to themselves in the selection and demarcation of the subject matter to be taught and how it is presented. They prefer this personal teaching programme, which reflects their own scientific achievements, and for this reason seldom use textbooks, unless they are written by themselves.

For all that, when writing the courses the professors have to keep to a set, interdisciplinary and formally identical structure, which is stipulated in a brief introduction for study-letter authors conceived by the Zentrum für Fernstudiumentwicklung (Centre for the Development of Distance Education). This is necessary because students working alone need to be able to find their way around their material when learning, and this occurs much more easily where there are readily identifiable formal standards in the courses. However, this cannot be seen as a restriction of academic freedom, because formal regulations must also be observed at traditional universities – for example, the length and standard format of lectures.

Because academic teaching is carried out with different media from those in traditional universities, and because problems in presentation easily result which are not found in traditional universities, many professors take advice and seek the help of experts from the Zentrum für Fernstudiumentwicklung, for example in questions of visualization, graphical design, digitalization and evaluation. And, finally, all those involved make every effort to make the printed material into a self-instructing medium for distance education.

Media structure: instructional videos on television and as cassettes

Printed materials are supplemented by, among other things, video cassettes. These have important pedagogical functions at certain points in the printed courses at which the presentational powers of the teaching text and illustrations are not enough, and are merged into the presentation of the printed distance-teaching courses (integrative mode). However, because the FernUniversität also produces teaching programmes for television, there are teaching videos that exercise these functions as well, but at the same time form independent teaching units that are logical and comprehensible by themselves. They are in a loose relationship with certain printed distance-teaching courses, and they supplement them (additive mode). These videos can be acquired and used individually at any time, and this means that students are not bound by fixed times of study.

What is pedagogically interesting and actually specific to distance education is the role that video cassettes can play in guided self-study. In the spirit of free (not controlled) learning activity, what is important here is the initiative of the students as to whether and how they work with the teaching videos. The external preconditions for this have improved immensely. Video cassettes were previously only available in study centres, and later on it was possible to hire them; but nowadays the numbers are growing of those who buy them and have them at hand in the same way as books. They therefore belong to the apparatus of students stimulated to 'learning by research'.

Here their pedagogical function can increase, depending on whether the instructional video is viewed and analysed one or more times before, during or after the student has worked through a printed study unit. It can function as an advance organizer, but can also illustrate, encourage a sense of proximity, train, revise or demonstrate the transfer of acquired knowledge. Which of these pedagogical functions is emphasized depends not so much on the planned calculations of the developers of the videos but primarily on the way in which the students use them, the strategy they develop for their use, and how they relate what they have learnt to the corresponding teaching texts. There are affinities here to autonomous learning.

Two teaching-video models have developed during this work: demonstration videos and training videos (Wurster, 1995: 5). The former are used to demonstrate reality, in particular that of processes and complicated sequences of events, an area in which videos can make a much greater impression than a description on a piece of paper, encoded as it is by language and writing. In the second case, particularly difficult sets of facts are made understandable by means of suitable visualizations and imparted not only cognitively but also through the repetitive reconstruction of derivations, processes, calculations, etc.

These videos are without doubt a new pedagogical genre that is far removed from the traditional teaching film, the single-concept film, and also from expensive scientific television programmes. Basically, these videos are adapted for students' requirements but can also be transmitted via television and be watched and understood by the non-student population. The main aim of these videos is to meet the demand for authentic contributions 'directly from research and teaching' (Wurster, 1995: 5) and to do without all traces of glamour, entertainment effects and journalistic attractiveness.

The time available on television for teaching programmes is very limited, but these components of the teaching and learning system are in fact essential. On the one hand, it is naturally an advantage for a distance-teaching university to be able to reach 30,000 viewers once a week in North-Rhine Westphalia alone via terrestrial television, and countless others in the rest of Germany and other European countries via cable and satellite, and thereby to be able to provide continuing academic education for those viewers. On the other hand, teaching programmes remain in use when captured as videos. There are already 380 of them available for hire and sale through the FernUniversität. They supplement the teaching and learning system of the university ideally because they are able to present content with great advantage wherever printed study material has presentational deficiencies.

Media structure: digital media

It is at present very difficult to find an answer to the question of how a distance-teaching university that was established on the basis of the media structure obtaining in the 1970s, which has since formed the corresponding pedagogical structures but also made them more rigid, adapts itself to the rapid changes in digital information and communications media. Nobody knows where these new developments will actually lead.

Up to now, the FernUniversität has reacted to these trends with many experiments aimed at understanding them. Above all, it has gathered experience with the pilot use of digital teaching programmes and teleconferencing. There are also those in the university who are preparing themselves to digitalize their teaching as far as possible. But there is still no answer as to whether this can take place in accordance with an overall plan, whether digital teaching and learning can be integrated into the 'conventional' system of teaching and learning in distance education in the form of 'islands', or whether, alternatively, it will be left to develop by itself alongside conventional systems. Work in this field is hampered by the enormous speed of technical developments and the slowness with which opinions are formed in the committees of a rather conventionally organized university. In addition, not only do the technical preconditions alter rapidly – and this has a great effect on costs – but so do the pedagogical possibilities for their use, some of which are beyond all previous modes of thinking and experience.

Some of these developments are referred to here as examples.

- *File courses* are being developed, namely digitalized printed courses in which attempts are made to make use of the exciting new possibilities of the digital learning environment to present them.

- *'Teaching software'* is also being developed. Wolfram Laaser (1990: 211) has described three typical examples of an interactive teaching programme for a PC.
- Eberhard Heuel and Manfred Postel (1993: 265) have introduced *interactive learning programmes* on current topics for computer science as well as the *'interactive assignment and exam trainers'* that were also developed in this department.

These learning and training programmes are bought by interested students and used individually. In the faculties of Electrical Engineering and Computer Science at the FernUniversität, a model for a 'virtual university' has been developed (see Section 6.6) with the help of which the university will be able to analyse, plan and implement future digital developments in distance education.

Successes

The number of students at the FernUniversität is growing from year to year. This shows that with its teaching programme the university meets an existing broad demand for knowledge and qualifications that is not satisfied by traditional universities. Each academic year, about 500 students complete their studies with the award of a Master's degree or a Diploma (the latter being of equal ranking with a Master's degree). This makes it as successful as a traditional university with the same number of teaching staff. However, in contrast to such a traditional university the FernUniversität in addition disseminates continuing academic education to tens of thousands of mature students of all ages, an effect that cannot be assessed too highly. There is no other institution in Germany that has such a wide and differentiated programme for research-oriented continuing academic education. In the area of support for young academics, about 400 doctorates have been awarded and 34 academics have qualified as university lecturers.

7.3.3 Commentary

The FernUniversität is merely a traditional university using other means! This is often heard from progressive university-education reformers, and also from critics abroad. There is something in the criticism, because many professors in the FernUniversität are indeed concerned not to deviate one centimetre from the standards and traditions of traditional universities, especially when it comes to research. They are supported by the original founding impetus, because the first project description stated that the FernUniversität was to serve to extend the capacity of the other universities, in other words to be open to school-leavers with university entrance qualifications who had not been able to obtain a place for some years because of overcrowding. Accordingly, the FernUniversität was to exercise the same function as a traditional university.

This opinion is, however, false. It can easily be rebutted by looking at the composition of the student body. This shows that the FernUniversität is in the first place a university for mature students, secondly for persons in employment, and thirdly for continuing academic education. And it also caters for disabled persons unable to leave their homes. All these characteristics differentiate it from traditional universities. And it is these characteristics that determine the pedagogical structure in a unique manner.

Catering for mature students

The FernUniversität is, then, a university for mature students. It introduced and institutionalized regular adult university education in Germany. It provides opportunities for mature students to acquire academic education, both initial and continuing, which society otherwise does not make available to them. In 1998, only 9 per cent of the students were in the normal age (18–24) for studying and 91 per cent were older. There can be no doubt that this alleviates social disadvantages, and this can also be said of the roughly 600 severely disabled persons who are unable to leave their homes. A humanitarian aim is pursued here that is often put forward by distance-teaching universities abroad as a justification for their work (equality of opportunity) but that has hardly played any role at all in traditional universities in Germany.

The pedagogical consequences of these circumstances – ie the establishment of a university education system for mature students – can be considered as all the necessary organizational measures that make these studies possible in the first place, and all the necessary pedagogical arrangements that make guided self-study easier. However, the obvious orientation to principles of pedagogics for adult education does *not* take place, because the principle of the unity of teaching and research dominates and counteracts it. These principles can probably only be applied, if at all, to work in the study centres, in counselling, and in tutorial support. But even if principles of pedagogics for adult education are not consciously applied, the learning behaviour of mature students differs in many respects from that of students at traditional universities.

Catering for those in employment

The FernUniversität is a university for persons in full-time employment. Of the total number of students enrolled in 1987, 74 per cent had completed vocational training and 75 per cent were in full-time employment during their studies.

Such students usually display a completely different type of learning behaviour from that of students at traditional universities because their employment has a great influence. The function of their studies is in general altered through the closer proximity to working life. A convincing example of this is how economics graduates assess their studies: asked about their motivations for studying, they provided among others the following answers (Bartels, 1986: 76):

- Studying was the foundation of my professional career, because I had no previous vocational training.
- I expected to improve my chances on the job market.
- The degree was intended to be the starting-point for rising to a management position in industry.
- I wanted to gain the degree so that I would have created the preconditions for becoming self-employed in the occupation for which I had trained (as a tax adviser and accountant).

It is obvious from the above that vocational skills, experience and ambition flow into studying and alter it specifically, in contrast with studying at a traditional university.

Catering for continuing academic education

The FernUniversität is a university for continuing academic education. Almost one-sixth of its students are not aiming for a university degree but are studying for vocational purposes or for personal reasons. This is a considerable difference from traditional universities, as the number of guest students there amounts to only 2–3 per cent, while at the FernUniversität it is 21 per cent currently (1998) – a total of 9,500 persons. Furthermore, the groups involved are completely different, because people involved in continuing academic education are usually unable to attend lectures because of their personal circumstances.

The pedagogical consequence of this is put together 'continuing training packages' in accordance with the modular principle for certain areas and occupations. This involves developing special continuing-training distance-teaching courses, as well as *exclusive* continuing-training courses that are planned in collaboration with specific organizations and offered by them for their own employees only (Knapke, 1994: 147).

All those interested can acquire distance-teaching courses from the basic degree courses upwards for the purposes of their own continuing academic education. This means that the FernUniversität is probably the only university that has realized as a regular and continuing institution the form of '*contact studying*' proposed by the Wissenschaftsrat (Scientific Council) in 1966 – in other words, the temporary resumption of university education to renew and deepen the academic education acquired for the purposes of employment.

7.3.4 Summary

The FernUniversität in Germany has developed a research and teaching operation in its six faculties that prepares students for higher degrees. Its teaching does not have the general educational function seen in many colleges in the first two years. Fixed specialist studies begin immediately in the first semester, and these studies are research-oriented from the start and interpreted ideally as 'participation in the scientific process'. Studies lead first of all to a Master's degree, or a diploma with the same ranking, each of which prepares students for such occupations in Germany as *Diplom-Elektroingenieur, Diplom-Informatiker, Diplom-Mathematiker, Diplom-Volkswirt* or *Diplom-Kaufmann*. Studies may be continued to doctorate level and beyond, up to professorial theses. So far the university does not, however, provide introductory degree courses such as Bachelor's degrees, which are provided in many distance-teaching universities outside Germany.

We can see that teaching and learning in the FernUniversität differs characteristically from many other distance-teaching universities.

7.4 Distance and proximity: the Central Radio and Television University in China

This university deserves special consideration, first of all on the grounds of the number of students. In 1986 it had over 604,000 undergraduates (Mohanti, 1988: 69). This makes it one of the two largest distance teaching universities in the world, the other being the Sukhothai Thammathirat Open University in Bangkok, Thailand. However, size is by itself insufficient reason for taking a look at the university. The main reason for doing so is because television is the determining factor for its pedagogical structure.

Unofficially, the university is known as *dianda*, which means 'the television university'. In fact, the whole university is completely under the spell of this medium, which suggests technical progress in university education to all participants. This mass medium is used not only to provide a university education in China for mature students but also to cope with the large numbers of young university applicants, numbers which increase from year to year. Emphasis on television is not the only factor that influences teaching and learning in distance education at this university. No less important is the obligatory attendance at face-to-face tuition at local educational centres or at locations for in-company further training. Distance and proximity between teachers and students are roughly balanced.

7.4.1 Description

The Central Radio and Television University was founded after the cultural revolution in accordance with a decision by the State Council, the highest organ of government, and started operating in 1979 with the approval of Deng Xiaoping, the then leader of the Chinese government. This is a national centralized university, as the name states, but to enable it to spread its influence over the huge country it is in fact made up of a Central Radio and Television University in Peking and 28 regional Radio and Television Universities in the provinces. The system of these distance-teaching universities works with three further structural aspects, which are strictly demarcated in accordance with the state administration: the branches in the prefectures, the study centres in the districts, and the local television classrooms, of which there are about 20,000, some of them being in further training centres operated by large companies.

With the help of this distance-education system the aim was, according to the Minister of Education at the time, 'to improve the general cultural and scientific education standards of the whole nation'. He saw the advantage of distance education in the possibility of educating 'more people quickly and at lower cost' (Yuhui, 1988a: 226). In particular, millions of additional engineers and secondary-school teachers were to be trained with this method to develop the Chinese economy. Finally, people were to be given an opportunity of acquiring a university education, which they had not been granted during the Cultural Revolution.

At present, this distance teaching university has three groups of students: persons in full-time employment who wish to gain a university degree; secondary-school graduates who have been given a place at the university; and school-leavers 'waiting to be assigned a job'. Apart from these formally enrolled students, there is a large number of independent viewers and listeners. If all these students are counted together, the total is over one million.

The successes of the university are spectacular, according to information from the university itself. In 1991, two million Chinese had already graduated through it, and one-and-a-half million had obtained a diploma. Just how this university has altered the efficiency of the whole higher-education system in China can be seen from the information that up to 1986 it had awarded about 200,000 economics diplomas. This is claimed to be one-and-a-half times more graduates than *all* other universities in China since the foundation of the People's Republic (Yuhui, 1988a: 226).

7.4.2 Pedagogical aspects

Applicants for places at the university must have passed the nationally set university entrance examinations and have shown proof of their aptitude for distance education. Teaching programmes on television are produced mainly centrally, though some are produced in the provinces. They are broadcast by the national terrestrial station, CCTV (Central China Television), for two hours in the morning and three in the afternoon, and by the satellite television company CETV (China Educational Television) from 4.30 pm to 11 pm. There are 87½ hours available every week for broadcasts. Radio programmes are broadcast by local stations in the provinces.

'Television classes' are just as important as the teaching programmes shown on television, and attendance is obligatory. Most students are in full-time employment, but their companies grant leave to attend television classes. In most cases, in fact, students are delegated by their companies to attend distance education. Printed teaching material, which forms the basis of studying in most distance-teaching universities, is 'available to supplement radio/TV programmes for all courses' (Yuhui, 1988b: 64) and therefore plays a much less important role: usually, teaching programmes on television supplement the study of printed material, but here the positions are reversed.

What is the effect of this special pedagogical structure on the teaching and learning behaviour associated with the university?

As far as university teachers are concerned, they make use of the rationalization effect resulting from the mass dissemination of successful content, on which distance education is always based, to a much greater extent than anywhere else. With the collaboration of the Ministry of Education, a comparatively small number of professors, all of them outstanding and well known, are selected from the best universities and requested to cooperate. They then hold their lectures in front of television cameras in the Central Radio and Television University in Peking. The teaching programmes that are then produced with these filmed lectures are broadcast to classrooms throughout China.

No attempts are made to give these teaching programmes any shape based on distance-teaching pedagogics or media didactics, and the explanation given for this is that the presentation should resemble lectures at traditional universities *as closely as possible*. No use is made of the special opportunities provided by television for optimising presentation. Seen from the aspect of media pedagogics, what we have here are the well known *'blackboard lectures'* described by Hawkridge and McCormick (1983: 162) and, from the point of view of distance-teaching pedagogics, they are simply technologically extended tuition from a traditional university. A form of presentation used in traditional university teaching thus extends here into the pedagogical structure of distance education.

Students also act differently from distance students in distance-teaching universities in other countries because their learning is determined to a great extent through attendance at tuition in television classes. They watch the programmes together with other students, discuss what they have seen or heard, and attend tutorials together. Students even take part together in physical training and sports, as well as other leisure activities. Distance students are typically seen as being people who read their printed study material alone at home, marking important passages, but in China we have to regard the typical distance student as someone acting as if they were in a classroom in school watching a schools television programme and looking with great attention at the screen in order to absorb what they are seeing and hearing.

The importance of the element of televisual teaching programmes for this distance-teaching university can be seen from the number of lectures offered through this medium in a single semester. A course consists of between 20 and 40 TV lectures of 50 minutes each, and between 10 and 20 radio lectures of the same length. In addition, there are lectures on video. The following work must be completed in a typical week: viewing and discussing a TV lecture, attending a tutorial, reading a section of a textbook, and completing an assignment at home (Keegan, 1994: 14). The following table shows the completely different emphasis given here to learning activities:

Table 7.5   *Teaching and learning behaviour at the Central Radio and Television University in China*

Teaching behaviour	Learning behaviour
Professors: Holding lectures in front of a microphone or camera	Regular attendance at TV classes, watching and listening to teaching programmes with others, studying printed teaching material with others, working through video and audio tapes with others, reading the course magazine
TV class instructors: Organizing classroom tuition, reception of the teaching programmes, chairing discussions, distributing and assessing assignments, examining students	Obligatory attendance at joint tuition sessions, working through assignments, sitting semester examinations, taking part in sports locally

7.4.3 Commentary

Distance education at the Central Radio and Television University differs remarkably in several points from teaching at distance-teaching universities in other countries, as follows:

1. As far as the educational-policy function is concerned, the university is not there to help educationally disadvantaged persons (if we disregard for a moment the help given to those disadvantaged by the Cultural Revolution) but instead to a great extent to force the country's development and modernization.
2. Studying here is quite obviously not a matter of studying *alongside* work but studying *in* work, because most tuition is in fact given during working hours.
3. There is a mixture, probably born of necessity, of older students with work experience and school-leavers 'waiting to be assigned a job'. The university intended for those in full-time employment has to some degree been turned into a university for the unemployed.
4. Teaching programmes on TV play a dominating role that appears strange to all those who base the core of academic education on the written word.
5. Group learning is emphasized, at the expense of individual learning as practised in the Western world. This may be based on the country's learning traditions, but there may also be ideological reasons, especially as it brings to mind the consultation distance education practised in the former Eastern European communist bloc, in which students met every other weekend in similar learning groups because great things were expected from learning in collectives.

In the face of the dominant role played by television in the dissemination of lectures, a Western observer schooled in media pedagogics must ask whether the presentation of the teaching content might not be done more cheaply and to some degree more effectively by means of written lecture notes. The speed of presentation can be considerably faster. There is no doubt that much more information can be passed on within a given period with a written text than in a lecture. A motivated and trained reader can read a printed page far more quickly than the fastest speaker can read it out (McKeachie, 1963: 1128).

The answer to this question is not at all obvious, however. When we evaluate the dominance of television as the key medium, we should not judge rashly and hastily. Considerable cultural differences and factors of local teaching traditions, often unknown to us, must be taken into account. Certainly, these teaching programmes have very little to do with distance-teaching pedagogics and media didactics, and because of this they tend to irritate observers from the West, who then characterize them flippantly with terms such as '*blackboard television*' and '*talking heads*'. Such observers are disappointed that television in China simply serves the mass dissemination of teaching and learning situations from traditional university teaching and does not bring its effective media-specific contributions into play in order to optimize them. In their opinion, distance education disseminated through technical media should have its own pedagogical structure and should not be satisfied with a mere copy of teaching situations at traditional universities.

The reference to the inadequate supply of equipment and trained personnel is sufficient to explain and justify the form of teaching programmes described here. But the actual reason can be seen in the efforts to provide university education for as many people as possible at the lowest possible cost. At the start of the 1980s, only 0.7 per cent of the population of China over the age of 25 had a university degree (Hawkridge and McCormick, 1983: 162). This makes the situation understandable.

There is in fact a third reason. For the Chinese, and for the Japanese, the relationship between teacher and student is not as objectivized or depersonalized as in the West. Professors in the Far East are esteemed, respected, valued, and in many cases even honoured. Students want to see and hear them and not to have them replaced by an image that is based on media pedagogics. The organizers of distance education at the Central Radio and Television University are also risking the motivational powers of their programmes: the process of learning will be influenced by the personality of the instructor in television classes as well.

A fourth reason may also have favoured the presentation of the lecturing professor on the television screen. This has to do with the special nature of written Chinese, which consists, of course, of ideographs. When Western distance students read a text, they receive at the same time an impression of its tone, because it is written in *phonetic* language. This becomes most clear where they know the author of the text. They have the impression that they can hear the author speaking when they read. Nothing like this happens when Chinese distance students read a text. They remain in the abstract world of definitions; the tone of the text is missing. The tone therefore has to be absorbed, nevertheless, so that distance students can use the specialist language orally as well. In this situation, television takes over a function in distance education that is completely ignored in Western countries. In Western distance-teaching pedagogics, the same idea is referred to most frequently for the dissemination of the names of symbols in mathematics and science – for reading equations, for example; in China, the dissemination of the spoken language is of fundamental importance, as there it is not merely a matter of imparting terms but also of hearing how they are articulated phonetically.

Finally, when we look at this problem we should remind ourselves of a development in Western media pedagogics that is very similar to the model of the Chinese distance-teaching university: *tutored video instruction*. This was developed in the USA primarily for continuing training (Gibbons, 1977). With this system as well, lectures by well known academics and scientists are filmed deliberately without any media pedagogical tricks or technical refinement, sent as video cassettes to continuing-training instructors, and shown to small groups under the instruction of a tutor. Each group then discusses what it has seen and heard. Repeated viewing, explanations from tutors, and the subsequent discussions can achieve considerable learning effects, which probably could not be achieved simply through a lecture at a traditional university or through reading passages from a textbook. This is a hybrid model, which combines advantages of traditional university teaching with those of distance education, and Chinese distance-education experts may refer to this system in order to explain their own special distance-education model.

Obviously the presentation of lecturing professors on screens in television classes was not simply born of necessity alone. We are dealing here with a complicated set of circumstances that are important for the pedagogics of distance teaching. Further research would be rewarding.

If we want to characterize the Chinese distance-education model, we are immediately aware of another peculiarity. In this case we are observing a system of distance education in which students can study *during normal working hours*, just as students at traditional universities do, and in addition where students are relieved to a considerable extent from having to work for a living. This is probably the reason for the relatively low drop-out rate of 30 per cent (Yuhui, 1988b: 71). These favourable study conditions would be desirable for distance students in a future educational system, because the twin, but separate, loads of work and study for distance students – and these are sometimes accompanied by a third load, the family – are fundamentally unreasonable. There are already examples in the capitalist economy of the combination and integration of work with continuing training through distance education. Perhaps new opportunities will be realized in the digitalized information society.

Seen from the aspect of pedagogics, this interlinking of work and distance education would be seen as the royal road to the further development of adult education and the realization of lifelong learning.

7.4.4 Summary

The Chinese Central Radio and Television University can be used as an example of the growing number of distance teaching universities that support over 100,000 students and, as very large distance-education systems (Keegan, 1995) or 'mega-universities' (Daniel, 1997: 22), represent a completely new phenomenon in the history of university education and will probably play an important role into the next millennium. They may even help in the development of countries. The fundamental interplay of technically effected single-channel mass dissemination of knowledge and interactive personal communication in the dynamics of a fixed learning group that meets regularly several times a week constitutes the characteristically special feature of teaching and learning. A similar link between distance and traditional university education could be an important pedagogical element in the university of the future, provided it is not prescribed and controlled as rigidly as this.

7.5 Multimedia systems: the University of the Air in Japan

Like the Chinese Central Radio and Television University, this distance-teaching university is an instructive example of the opposite of the Open University in the UK because it differs from the latter in a few pedagogically important points. Both use printed teaching texts and teaching programmes on both radio and television, but the focus in the Open University is on printed material, and this is because of the university's convictions, not only because there are good reasons (such as cost) for doing so, while the University of the Air places greater value on radio and television, perhaps with even greater conviction and better reasons. At the Open University teaching programmes on the radio and television are awarded merely a supplementary function to the printed material, but the reverse is the case in the University of the Air, where the printed material has the supplementary function. This difference has an effect on the respective pedagogical structures of the distance education systems, and in particular on the way in which teaching and learning is carried out.

7.5.1 Description

The *University of the Air* was founded in 1983 and offers three degree courses leading to a BA. The Japanese government pursued three goals with its foundation:

1. A university for 'lifelong learning' was to be created in which those in full-time employment and housewives would be given a chance to acquire a university education. This would create a 'flexible learning system for all'.
2. Because the number of secondary-school leavers exceeded the number of existing places at university in Japan at the time, those who failed to gain admission would still receive an opportunity to study.
3. A university education system was to be developed that met the requirements of the 'new era' and took into account 'the latest advances in research and instruction technologies', whereby television was foremost in the minds of the founders.

This new university, working with new technical media, was to cooperate with the other universities in Japan, on the one hand to participate in their research findings, and on the other to collaborate in the reform of university education. (Ministry of Education, Science and Culture [in Japan], 1982: 1)

In 1991 the University of the Air worked with an annual budget of about US$74 million and a teaching staff consisting of 51 full-time and 222 part-time academics. They looked after around 35,000 students, of whom about 60 per cent wanted to gain a Bachelor's degree. The others had enrolled for a course of tuition lasting a term or a year only. Teaching was provided in 299 courses, 155 television courses and 144 radio courses. The foundations of teaching are considered in the teaching programmes, which are developed by teachers and production directors at the National Institute of Multimedia Education in collaboration with university teachers from the University of the Air. The printed supplementary material is drawn up by the teachers who take part in the teaching programmes. Textbooks are also used.

There are eight study centres, in which classroom tuition is given and examinations take place. There are so few of them because the television transmitter's range only covers Greater Tokyo, although there are plans to improve this by using satellites. Once the transmitter can reach students all over Japan, study centres will be established in each prefecture. Outside the present range of the transmitter, there are ten video study centres, in which the teaching programmes can be viewed or listened to on video or audio cassettes.

Admission is not open, because applicants must submit a secondary-school leaving certificate. However, applicants may enrol as 'special students'. Once they have acquired 16 credits with this status, they may enrol as regular students. Sixteen credits corresponds to about six months' distance education. The duration of degree courses is flexible: they generally take at least four years, but can be stretched over ten years. The success rate can be assessed on the basis that just six years after teaching commenced, 1,951 graduates were presented with their degrees.

Students have to pay the equivalent of US$3,200 in study fees for a four-year course. They are found at all ages over 20 (The University of the Air, 1991: 26). And the numbers of men and women are roughly the same. Three occupational groups clearly dominate: business (30 per cent), 'unemployed and housewives' (25 per cent) and state employees (12 per cent).

7.5.2 Pedagogical aspects

The foundations of this study system are the teaching programmes. Students enrolled for a four-credit course must watch 30 teaching programmes, each 45 minutes long, in the course of a 15-week term. Those who want to acquire ten credits will enrol for two such courses, and the number of programmes they have to watch is increased to 60.

Table 7.6 *Components of teaching and learning behaviour at the University of the Air*

Teaching behaviour	Learning behaviour
Planning courses and preparing lectures in collaboration with experts from the National Institute of Multimedia Education	Watching teaching programmes on television
	Listening to teaching programmes on radio
Lecturing in front of cameras and microphones	Working through supplementary texts
Writing supplementary texts, selecting textbooks	Writing assignments
	Sitting end-of-term examinations
Supervising a learning group in a study centre	Obligatory: learning in study-centre classes
Marking assignments	Working through assignments
Written counselling	Writing an examination thesis based on own research experiments
Supporting and marking examination theses	

Textbooks and teaching programmes have to be studied jointly and in combination with one another. What we have here is therefore audiovisual presentation supplemented by the written word. Along with this, tuition in classrooms in the study centres plays an important role, firstly because it is obligatory, secondly because it is given by professors, and thirdly because 17 credit points from a total of 124 must be acquired in this way. Fifteen hours of face-to-face tuition are required for each course, and students must also complete a mid-term assignment. Written guidance counselling is provided when students are informed of their results. In the last year of their studies, students write their examination theses under the individual direction and supervision of a professor; theses are supposed to be based on independent research.

Students who wish to acquire a Bachelor's degree in four years must cope with the following weekly workload: listening to/watching five radio and television programmes, each 45 minutes long, reading 60–80 pages of text, and two-and-a-half hours of face-to-face tuition at a study centre.

7.5.3 Commentary

Together with the Chinese Radio and Television University, the Japanese University of the Air embodies a particular type of distance-teaching university through the special relationship of the pedagogical components and the dominating role of television. However, its education policy and adult-education approach is the same as that of many other distance-teaching universities. It, too, aims to gain more recognition for the egalitarian principle in university education; it also tries to make university education more flexible, so that it can adapt more easily to the requirements of those who would normally be unable to get a university education; and, finally, its aim is to establish university education for mature students, with the principle of lifelong learning in mind. The energy with which these objectives are declared and pursued is impressive, particularly as their realization requires a considerable financial commitment from the Japanese government each year.

This encouragement and support from the state must be stressed, because elsewhere the tendency can be noted to bring distance education back to the pedagogical forms of traditional university teaching, to orient its institutional image of itself towards that of a traditional university, and to cut the available funds. In fact, everything should be done to make distance-education-oriented programmes available, to develop an *individual* profile for this form of studying that will of necessity deviate from traditional standards (and to anchor this profile in people's consciousness), and to ensure its financing.

What is really remarkable to the Western observer is the verve and resolve, and above all the scale, with which television and radio have been made into the key media for distance education. In the West, these media are regarded as being more or less obsolete, particularly as audio cassettes and, more recently, video cassettes have competed with them. In Japan, however, teaching programmes on television and radio are characteristically fixed components of a multimedia distance-education system – in other words not merely options or supplements. To understand the reasons for this we must once again return to cultural differences.

In no other country have television and radio played such a huge role in education as in Japan. Television programmes are made for children in kindergarten, something which German television experts reject completely with regard to German society. In Japan, however, they are a fixed part of work in kindergartens. These programmes are regularly used in primary and secondary schools, whereby this is made easier because the Ministry of Education stipulates the same curriculum and the same timetable for all schools throughout the country. NHK, a TV station that is highly regarded in society, makes programmes that are easily integrated into lessons and do not have the enrichment characteristics so often found in other schools television programmes. Students at the University of the Air are therefore already prepared for learning with these two media to an extent that is neither usual nor even possible in other countries.

The use of these two media is understandable with this special development in the background. Even the name 'University of the Air' is part of the programme. The planners kept to the name, even though 15 years previously the Open University in the UK had rejected the same name – albeit because reading printed teaching material was to be the main basis there, in accordance with academic traditions. But that is not all. The Japanese distance-teaching university even has its own television and radio *station* that broadcasts from 6 am to midnight. Quality broadcasting times can thus be used, and this of course provides the university with much more leeway and many more opportunities for making an impact than in other countries, where prime time has to be reserved for advertising, information and entertainment and where distance students must therefore watch (or tape) their teaching programmes either very early in the morning or very late at night.

What are the reasons for preferring the media of radio and television? Strangely, the curricula also provide for teaching foreign languages, something that causes some problems in distance education because it involves not only teaching intonation and phrasing but also speech patterns that include gestures and the respective specific forms of language interaction. Naturally, this cannot be shown on the written page, let alone transmitted and trained. When English, Russian and French are taught at the University of the Air, audiovisual presentations can have a much more practical, convincing and authentic effect than reading and translating written language texts. And, of course, we must not forget the explanations given in the context of the use of television by the Central Radio and Television University in China. All the arguments that were brought forward there for 'talking heads' on the screen also apply to the University of the Air, because the same ideographs are used as the basis, and these have no phonetic background. It is possible that this reason is very important and explains the predilection of both universities for television and radio, and why they adhere to them.

How are radio and television used for distance education? The teaching programmes are all referred to as broadcast *lectures*. For this reason, as in China, all that is seen on the screen is the professor giving the lecture, although sometimes presentations are supplemented by audiovisual inserts. As in China, the pedagogical function of the two technical media is reduced in the main to the transmission of lectures, and the effect of their ubiquity is used. But why, we ask ourselves, are the highly differentiated and effective visualization techniques of television not used for more demanding tasks – for example, for arousing motivation and disseminating cognitive strategies, representative experience, and emotions such as self-confidence and fascination (Koumi, 1997: 178)? Are there financial reasons for this?

What is also characteristic of this distance-teaching university are the obligatory tuition periods in the study centres. Here, too, we are reminded of the distance students in China, who also have to attend face-to-face teaching. What might have led the planners in both countries to place such value on these components of the teaching and learning system that are, frankly speaking, unusual in any other distance-education system? Were they not confident that the interplay between watching teaching programmes and reading the supplementary texts would have the required pedagogical effect? Are the stimuli for individual studying provided in this inadequate?

Perhaps the disadvantages of the broadcast teaching programmes can be felt with this media structure. Both media consist of decidedly one-way communications. However, if we were to follow the opinion of a distance-education theoretician such as Börje Holmberg (1989a: 92), distance education, to be successful, would have to develop a system of *two-way* communications. That means: interaction has to be possible. Seen this way, broadcasting lectures is really a pedagogically minimalist approach that does not conform with ideas of good distance education. It is also oriented towards an obsolete learning model, namely that of expository teaching and receptive learning, which has not been made any more modern through being spread throughout the world. Put bluntly, the only information that can be disseminated in this way is the type that people will be asked about later orally or in written questions and that is remembered and reproduced by students. There is no depth to it, and it does not stimulate critical discussions or independent interpretation.

From this point the prescribed attendance at tuition sessions in the study centre classrooms is easily understood. The aim is to compensate for what is of necessity missing from the teaching programmes. But even here the pedagogical question arises as to what happens in the classrooms. Are students to be given an example of the 'right' kind of university education? Are they to experience there what a lecture looks and sounds like close up? Terms given to the activities in study centres, such as 'schooling', 'classroom lectures' and 'classroom instruction', lead us to suspect that in fact talks and lectures are in the main to be given in the study centres. From the aspect of distance teaching pedagogics this would be wrong, and this has already been pointed out in the context of the summer schools held by the Open University. The available time should be used for dialogues to deepen knowledge and understanding, for intensive discussions and for the exchange of personal opinions. It is important here that acquired knowledge is not simply reproduced but *applied*. Training must be given in linking thought and action. Those who squander this costly opportunity by presenting new content in the manner of traditional university teaching act contrary to the logic of teaching and learning in distance education. Of course, we must be careful here as well, as we have already seen how intensively academic teaching traditions, which do not provide for this, continue to have an effect.

In any evaluation of the importance of the University of the Air, its relatively small catchment area has to be stressed, which is almost grotesque when compared with that of the Central Radio and Television University in China. Basically, only the population of the Kanto region (Greater Tokyo in other words) take part. Because the audiovisual lectures cannot be sent by post, like printed study materials, potential students from other parts of the country are in practice excluded, which, of course, directly contradicts the idea of a 'flexible learning system open to all'. Even the term 'distance education' appears unsuitable when applied to a system that can only reach such a small geographical region.

When, in spite of this, 35,000 students are enrolled, this shows us quite impressively just how great the demand for a college education is among the adult population. If the planned extension of the catchment area actually takes place and this distance-teaching university were actually available to the whole nation, it is impossible to estimate how high the number of students would be. The University of the Air would probably then belong to that group of distance-teaching universities whose students are numbered in the hundreds of thousands.

From the aspect of pedagogics, attempts by the University of the Air to extend its catchment area without changing the range of its transmitter are particularly interesting. Its plan is to establish ten video-study centres in regions that cannot be reached by the transmitter. The teaching programmes will be reproduced there by playing video and audio cassettes. If we start from the use of these media, the University of the Air is, strictly speaking, two different models of a distance-education system using multimedia, namely a television and radio distance-teaching system for Greater Tokyo, and a cassette distance-teaching system for the adjoining regions. It would be interesting to carry out comparative research into the costs and pedagogical effects of the two systems.

7.5.4 Summary

The University of the Air is an ambitious attempt to provide adults in full-time employment with a college education and to make new opportunities available for academically oriented continuing education. This university has established its distance-education system on the basis not only of teaching programmes on radio and television but also of obligatory face-to-face teaching sessions, and in doing this it has distanced itself radically from the widespread system of correspondence teaching used by (for instance) many private and state universities in Germany. What is more, it has developed a singular model of a distance-teaching university that offers its teaching programmes on video and audio cassettes in special video-study centres. A system of distance education that was modern, at least for its time, was created that, because of its technicizing, can react flexibly to new education and training requirements in a rapidly changing society. Here it finds support simultaneously from *two* models of the multimedia system.

7.6 Autonomous studying: the Empire State College in the USA

In the face of the lasting effects of the tradition of presentational teaching and receptive learning found everywhere in universities, every approach by university reformers that attempts to take the *autonomy* of students seriously appears doomed to failure. The demand so often made by university educationalists for learning that is planned, controlled and evaluated by the students *themselves* is held to be practically impossible under the conditions prevailing at universities today. With this in mind, an experiment into the basic form of a university teaching system in which autonomous and self-determined learning has been made is deserving of attention. Such an experiment has been constructed at the Empire State College in Saratoga Springs, New York State, USA.

Its foundation was a great gamble, and one that is probably only possible in an open and adventurous university landscape that is fond of experiments, such as in the USA. But it has now become successful. At present there are over 11,000 mature students at the university who would never have had an opportunity to study in the traditional university system. The total number of graduates from this college is at present 30,000.

7.6.1 Description

The Empire State College was founded in 1971 by the Education Ministry of the state of New York as an extension to the 72 state colleges that together form the State University of New York. Its aim was to provide wider access to higher education, and to enable it in the first place to provide tertiary education for certain groups of students, including people in full-time employment, housewives, and members of ethnic minorities.

This goal could only be achieved if alternative teaching and learning methods were applied consistently and by a radical renunciation of traditional university teaching. The university did not expect mature students to adapt themselves to the locational, organizational and pedagogical situations and requirements there but, on the contrary, made efforts to organize itself and its teaching rigorously in accordance with the situations and requirements of the *students*. Because the target groups of students were tied to families and jobs, it was decided not to build a new campus with halls of residence, lecture halls and seminar rooms. Instead, 26 study centres and support points were established throughout the state of New York.

Larger and smaller groups of students were not addressed, as occurs in traditional university teaching in lectures and classes; the university concentrated instead on *individual* students. The aim was to motivate each student individually to thorough self-study that would form the basis of the new teaching and learning system. This task was carried out by both professors and mentors, who were supposed to attune themselves to the special starting positions and requirements of their students. Counselling conversations and help for self-determined learning thus became the main medium of academic tuition. A key role was played here by the 'learning contract'.

A learning contract is made between a student, a teacher and the university as the institution. It obliges the parties to perform exactly defined services and tasks: the student agrees to work through set syllabuses independently, the teacher agrees to provide support and counselling, and the university agrees to award credits when the predetermined learning achievements have been completed and verified. It also has the following elements: global educational goals, whereby the occupation that the student aspires to is often included in the calculations; the learning objectives that are to be achieved during the duration of the contract; information on the learning resources that are available; and a description of the learning activities and the criteria for measuring performance, through which students can determine, at first by themselves and later in agreement with the mentor, whether they have in fact achieved the agreed learning goals.

This form of higher education implies fundamental changes to teaching and learning behaviour. Teachers do not lecture, neither do they hold seminars, give tuition or hold classes, but concentrate on the intensive *counselling* of students in which their knowledge, pedagogical skills and also their experience of life have an effect. However, counselling takes place only at the request of a student. Students do not wait for the university to offer a programme in the traditional manner but take the initiative, and plan, steer and control their studies themselves.

The following is an overview of this new form of academic education and shows the sequence of phases and stations that students have to pass through:

1. *Preparatory exploration.* An applicant's chances for further academic and vocational development are discussed with the study counsellor. In addition, a decision is made as to whether the applicant has the aptitude for contract learning. And students are shown just how their intended studies will change their lives.
2. *Orientation.* After they have enrolled, students attend a workshop spread over a period of several days at which they get to know the university and its special working methods. For its part, the university attempts to discover as much as possible about each applicant's attitudes and interests. This phase is regarded as being particularly important, because the success of the degree course depends decisively on exact information on its peculiarities, and the students must have an opinion on them.
3. *Classification.* In this phase the university asks about the students' previous academic qualifications, and possible vocational experience as well, whether these will have to be taken into account during the planning phase, and also whether as a result they will allow the overall study period to be reduced.
4. *Development of the learning contract.* The learning contract is drafted by the students themselves, drawn up and negotiated with a mentor. It contains the learning aims and precisely formulated academic topics that have to be worked through, indicates the time set for this, and describes the way in which the finished work will be assessed and evaluated. A reading list follows, together with background literature, information on the role the mentor is to take, and on the number of credits that can be awarded after the contract is fulfilled.
5. *Autonomous studying.* The self-study that now commences may be determined by the following activities: working through the relevant literature, attending certain distance-teaching courses, working with a learning package, detailed discussions with specialists who live nearby, taking part in a block seminar at a local university or college. But most important of all are the regular support sessions with the assigned mentor or with competent specialist tutors.
6. *Evaluation.* The student's work is assessed continuously during the support sessions and evaluated. In the middle of the degree course, a commission deter-

mines whether the learning contract that has been fulfilled up to then conforms to the academic standards of the university, and whether the path taken can lead to graduation.

7.6.2 Pedagogical aspects

Of the three constitutive features of distance education according to Moore, ie dialogue, structure and autonomy, the emphasis here is on the last one. Studies are not developed from the point of view of a professor, with his research and teaching programmes, but starts consistently from the viewpoint of the students as individuals, and this is why their special personal and employment situations are at the heart of all curriculum and study plans. This makes extensive individualization necessary, which is achieved with the help of the learning contract, particularly with regard to learning aims, learning content, support, learning forms and the media used.

What is absolutely new is the intention to leave students in their own personal and employment environments and to reach them there as well. The establishment of the 26 study centres and support points serves this aim. And what is more, the aim is also to link learning itself to the requirements and special features of the respective personal and employment situations. In this way, acquired knowledge and qualifications can be integrated most easily and intensively into practice.

Table 7.7 *Components of teaching and learning behaviour at the Empire State College*

Teaching behaviour	Learning behaviour
Professors: Advising, motivating, showing interest, mediating between individual students and the university	Autonomous self-study: planning, negotiating, fulfilling and evaluating the learning contract
Mentors: Advising, helping, mediating	Communication: discussing with mentors, subject tutors or university teachers in study centres
Experts in students' home towns: Informing, advising, motivating	Learning resources: reading the agreed literature and background literature; working through distance-teaching courses; organizing, holding and evaluating interviews with experts. Attendance at selected teaching sessions at local universities. Working through computer-supported courses and on-line or Internet learning programmes.
	Activity: on own initiative, contacting relevant experts who will accompany studies with their advice.

What is also new is the intention to set up a stable personal relationship between the supporting mentors and the self-studying students. This can be closer than that between lecturers holding forth and students listening, simply because it is a one-to-one relationship that stretches over several years. The college believes that it is making a contribution to the *personalization* of university education in this way, in spite of the great emphasis it places on self-studying, which is of necessity carried out in isolation. To that extent, Moore's other important concept, namely dialogue, also has a significant role to play in this teaching and learning system.

What is of central importance, however, is the conversion of learning that is mainly prescriptive, receptive and controlled into mainly self-initiated, committed learning for which the students are themselves responsible.

7.6.3 Commentary

Academic education has been revolutionized at the Empire State College. Demands for change that have been issued for decades again and again without much success from the areas of university-education pedagogics and adult-education pedagogics have been fulfilled here – and, it seems, without any cuts. Individualization, autonomous learning, orientation towards students, a displacement of the focal point away from teachers to students, greater consideration of students' personal and employment situations, and adult-based learning all have their place in the system.

In this way a model for studying has been created that can be regarded in many ways as distance education, quite apart from the role played in this form of studying by distance teaching courses, learning packages, and digitalized learning programmes as learning resources. The model also allows Moore's third concept in distance education to appear, namely structure itself. In the same way as distance students, students here have to take responsibility for their own studies and make use of study advisory services and counselling from tutors in the study centres. They also work away from the university physically, and make their own schedules – their time is their own. James Hall (1994: 17), the President of the Empire State College at the time of writing, does not regard the physical distance between students and university, nor their independence with regard to time, as being defects but conversely believes that the future can be found here. He sees his opinions confirmed by more recent developments in his previous work:

> Empire State College's institutional philosophy, that education need not be confined by particular physical location, dovetails with the asynchronous features of telecommunication technology that reduce time and space as barriers to human interaction.

The most important contribution that this model for distance-teaching pedagogics can make is the intensive focusing on learning support by means of the learning contract. This contract is important for adult education for the following reason: while it is still acceptable for students in their first semester to perform work with standardized teaching programmes because their ranges of experience are still relatively limited and their knowledge is relatively homogeneous, once they have settled into class their broad range of specialized vocational skills and experience as mature students means that an extremely heterogeneous group of students has been created, where students can be differentiated from one another with regard to their interpretation patterns, learning styles, private experience, and social obligations. We should not do justice to these students if we merely offered teaching programmes that are prescribed and demarcated by study and examination regulations and that are more or less the same and equally binding for all. Learning must indeed be individualized here. The learning contract has proved to be a suitable instrument for this.

The learning contract is to that extent interesting for distance education as it is regarded as being particularly adult-oriented, for it can help to level out the hierarchical inclination that traditionally existed between teachers and students and that probably can still be felt. The parties to these contracts appear as equal partners, and this creates a completely different atmosphere in which autonomous learning behaviour can develop more easily.

7.6.4 Summary

The Empire State College has features that may be regarded as being particularly modern: it is highly flexible in the development of individual curricula; it relates to a great extent to students and their working and private lives; it is unorthodox and variable in the selection of methods and media; and it is original and versatile in its use of additional learning resources in students' home towns. These are all pedagogical components that can easily be integrated in future post-industrial forms of studying, for example at dual-mode universities, which are already being created, or in universities of the future whose possibilities will be extended still further by digital teaching and learning.

7.7 Interactive video: the American National University Teleconference Network

In the United States, the intensive and extensive use of the new electronic media to disseminate academic teaching is something that observers see again and again. This started with cable and satellite television and was continued at a very early stage with computers and teleconferencing. Both have led to interesting new forms of teaching and learning over a distance. One of these forms will now be introduced here.

In the field of distance education, the new electronic media have stimulated the creative fantasy of experts. They saw immediately that academic teaching could be distributed with great efficacy if these media are used. Because the costs of such a system cannot be raised by the students of a single university alone, links were often set up with other universities so that the number of participants could be increased considerably and cost reductions achieved. In this way a series of consortia was created that jointly use the new electronic infrastructure. The National University Teleconference Network is one of them.

7.7.1 Description

As long ago as 1982, 66 universities agreed jointly to use the possibilities provided by cable and satellite television and by teleconferencing. They named the Oklahoma State University as the seat of their organization and established a central office on the campus. The basic aim was twofold: firstly, that each member university could offer to other universities in the consortium the teaching programmes it had developed with the help of the new media, and charge fees for this; and, secondly, that, with the help of experts, the consortium's administrative centre would create the technical and organizational preconditions for arranging teleconferences that could be used by any member university. This idea met with great approval. Today, this consortium probably has over 250 paying members.

What are the motives that led these US universities to the joint use of electronic communications media? According to information from the consortium itself (Oberle, 1990: 90), first of all there was their apprehension that they would fall behind in the competition among universities. Another aim was to achieve more educational equality, because the new system would enable people to study (for example) who belonged to ethnic minorities, who lived too far away from the nearest university, or who were disadvantaged for other reasons. Telecommunications were described as 'the great equalizer': satellite television eliminates the educational barriers resulting from great distances, and enables those willing to study, even those who live in the remotest areas, to become acquainted immediately with the latest performances by great scholars.

What was most important, however, was the endeavour to achieve additional income. Most universities suffer from financial difficulties. With the help of modern communications media it is much easier to make teaching accessible outside the university as well. On the other hand, there is a growing demand in industry for continuing training. Because companies often do not have the skills or the pedagogical competence, they look to universities for assistance. These two demands converge and stabilize the consortium.

The central office, which is part of Oklahoma State University, carries out the following functions on behalf of member universities: coordination, advice, marketing, training, help in drawing up programmes, and selling videos. It is clear that no single university could have done all that work professionally by itself. It is the great number of students and other participants who can be reached as a result of the pool that makes possible both this type of division of labour for specific functions and the use of new communications media.

The growth of this consortium was sensational. In 1990 it had over 150 teaching programmes for sale to both members and non-members. As a result, the number of colleges and universities using them rose to 1,300. The range consists mainly of programmes for continuing education at universities, but it also contains programmes for continuing training for trade and industry. In addition, there are programmes for advanced students in high schools.

7.7.2 Pedagogical aspects

The member colleges and universities are able, through their collaboration, to use the existing system to supplement their teaching programme, and the pedagogical configurations set out below are created.

Degree programme

In this programme, students select a course from the list in their college's prospectus because they are interested in the subject and can acquire credits for the award of a Bachelor's degree if they complete the course successfully. If the course is one from another college and is available through the central office in Oklahoma, the students drop out of normal teaching in their university because they are now taking part in a tele-teaching course, for which extra fees are payable. They obtain the course in the form of videos from the media centre at their own university, and watch the videos either there or at home. The teaching shown on the videos is related to one or more textbooks, which have to be bought from a bookstore on the campus. Finally they are assigned to a specialist instructor on the campus, whom they visit not only if their self-studies begin to falter, but also at the very beginning of the course.

The instructors may also advise students how to take an active part in the visualized and printed teaching by stating which passages in the textbooks must be worked through, and which videos from a given series are to be viewed in which sequence. In addition, these instructors are also responsible for tests and evaluations, which is important in that it has an effect on the award of credit points.

Consultations

In the list of teaching programmes, or in separate notifications, students are informed of the possibility of consulting a well-known academic at a set time. The central office in Oklahoma makes its tried-and-tested telephone network available for this purpose and determines the numbers of those taking part. The consultation can now take place and is listened to by all participants. This is a special form of teleconferencing for which the Oklahoma central office sets up the necessary technological preconditions and which can also be used for other applications.

Two new characteristic pedagogical configurations (namely the credit course and teleconferencing) have been formed on the basis of the use of electronic communication media and the cooperation of several institutes of higher education, and the teaching and learning behaviour in these configurations can be shown as follows:

Table 7.8 *Components of teaching and learning behaviour within the National University Teleconference Network*

Teaching behaviour	Learning behaviour
Credit course: Professor: gives tuition in a college class or video class in front of video cameras	Working according to the syllabus Watching videos

Instructor: guidance, support, motivation in personal discussions. Encouraging learning through award of credit points

Teleconferencing:
Concentration on the problems of questioners.

Consideration of these problems. Answering questions.

Discussing with the questioner. Recommending reading lists, etc. Pointing out own work where necessary

Working through selected chapters in textbooks

Discussions with instructors

Taking tests

Preparing questions. Putting questions. Discussing with expert

Following discussions between other students and the expert. Taking notes and reviewing them later.

7.7.3 Commentary

The trend that can be seen here can be explained on the one hand by means of the continuing enthusiasm for technological progress found in this country, but also by pointing to the willingness to innovate, experiment, and even change.

In an analysis of the two models, the question suggests itself as to whether this is in fact distance education. If we take the term 'distance education' literally, this is certainly the case because, in the first configuration, students learn on the basis of behaviour that is fixed in writing and audiovisually *elsewhere* and is transported to their own college by means of media. And with teleconferencing and consultations with experts, the physical distance between teachers and students is clear. As with distance education, these teaching and learning programmes use the constitutive possibility not only of overcoming barriers of time and space but also of dissolving them completely, for example with the help of cable and satellite television. The social and education policy reasons given by the consortium, namely that they wished to open up university education to new groups from economically and socially disadvantaged classes, also brings distance education to mind. And the clear commitment to continuing education and higher qualifications is also typical for distance education.

At the same time, important constitutive elements of classical distance education are missing, and this can clearly be seen: the costly and careful planning and development of thoroughly structured courses by experts working on a division-of-labour basis is not possible. This is because, for example, the video courses mostly repeat in simple fashion the successful tuition by individual university teachers and consultation on selected points with experts at the central office in Oklahoma, and that cannot replace the development work that is typical for distance education.

The system does not aim to address the largest possible number of students but, initially at least, only those studying at member institutions. Participants in these programmes are therefore not studying at *distance* from the university, but actually *in* the university, which, as it were, mediates between the consortium's central office and the students, and collaborates in the teaching. This means that the group of those who want to take part in these studies naturally has to remain small. Just how important this aspect is can be seen from a recommendation from the consortium's central office that each programme be supplemented by local programme points and discussions: 'In fact, we recommend a local wraparound for every programme' (Oberle 1990: 92). This is not a regular teaching programme for continuous studies but individual building blocks that can be used profitably in other teaching and learning contexts in the university or in institutes of further vocational training.

What is more, video studies in the media centre are in fact face-to-face teaching, comparable with a teaching system in which a teaching film is watched, for example. To that extent, the system points back to the period when audiovisual media were propagated with great enthusiasm. What is new is watching the videos at home, although this is no different formally from reading textbooks at home. When the central office in Oklahoma transmits video films on request to a member college, it does in fact overcome a physical distance. But this has absolutely no structurally altering effect on students' learning behaviour, because in the university they act in exactly the same way as students in traditional universities.

This question is even more critical in the case of teleconferencing. According to information from its supporters, what is supposed to happen here is that a discussion is simulated between students at different locations in the same manner as in a class. Pedagogically speaking, this is typical teaching and learning behaviour from traditional university teaching. Some experts even regard the teaching and learning that takes place in a normal college class as being the desirable pattern. But this is not distance education in the traditional meaning of the term but rather a form of *virtual* traditional university teaching.

The following argument underlines this claim: if they wish to improve their teaching, teachers have to base their work on the models and experience of traditional university teaching, in other words on classical university education pedagogics. And they do not need to use all the pedagogical artifices that have been developed to reduce and overcome the physical and psychological distance between teachers and students (see Chapter 2) – they are not forced to rely on distance-teaching pedagogics. This special form of teaching and learning differs from distance education in a most fundamental way, in that the independence of students with regard to time and location is lost.

At the same time we have to consider how teaching and learning with interactive video networks is to be assessed, particularly as it is already in place in many US universities. Even if the special model of distance education shown here lacks important criteria relating to this form of studying, we cannot close our eyes to its power to change structures in US university education. Whether genuine pedagogical considerations have given rise to this development is not easy to determine, and may even be doubted. It is more likely that sales of technical media were in the foreground, encouraged by energetic marketing by manufacturers. The thrill of having these technical media available in the university may also have played a part here and there. Some critics even express the opinion that is was in fact industry that introduced the term 'distance education' to US universities and colleges, where previously the terms 'correspondence study', 'home study', or 'independent study' had always been used. It is also claimed quite often that the new media were actually forced upon universities. And Becky Duning (1993: 210) observes how an overwhelming and confusing body of experts equates traditional university teaching disseminated by means of telecommunications media with distance education.

Whatever the reasons, the new structures resulting from the model introduced here are in fact pedagogically interesting. They should be evaluated above all from the aspect of what contributions they can make to *future* university education. They show us how traditional university teaching can become more flexible, variable, adaptable, productive and innovative with regard to content and processes, if elements of distance education are added and creatively integrated. The combination shown above of syllabus, self-study, video, textbook, instructor and regular examinations can prove to be very advantageous where the problem is to restrict accustomed expository teaching forms in traditional universities and give autonomous learning more opportunities to develop. Teaching by means of interactive video via broadband channels can considerably extend the range of teaching and learning opportunities in a university, as long as it is not misused to disseminate structured teaching content, but is inserted into traditional university teaching or distance education following pedagogical calculation and substantiation.

All this applies even though, in the USA as well as elsewhere, the invasion of electronic telecommunications media into academic teaching forms is often viewed with scepticism. In the faculties, professors often react reservedly, and their attitudes to the new media range from 'disregard to contempt' (Duning, 1993: 212).

This dominant attitude among professors also has to do with a special feature of the consortium that reduces the importance of everything that has previously been said. The consortium is *not* in fact a group of universities but a cooperative venture of their departments of continuing education. This is a disadvantage not only with regard to levels of academic standards but also to the curricular design of this form of distance education. Because the departments of continuing education are not regarded with the greatest academic respect by their own universities, this impression can only be strengthened if their programmes are bundled in large numbers in the consortium. And because these departments of continuing education often run projects below university level and outside the university curriculum, the impression of their lack of scientific substantiation is reinforced.

When the National University Teleconferencing Network indicates the following focal points for its courses for university education, it must cause us to ponder: continuing education, student affairs, faculty and staff development, research and instructional briefings, athletics, and curriculum enrichment. This means that only the periphery is occupied, while the core of academic studies is missing, something which goes without saying at distance-teaching universities in Europe and other parts of the world.

What would US distance education look like if the best faculties in universities could come together in order to organize a continuing undergraduate, graduate and post-graduate programme for which they would be jointly responsible? Certainly, talented potential students from socially and economically disadvantaged classes would be served much better. On the other hand, it would also mean that the universities were in competition with one another. In addition, this kind of system would hardly have a chance because the 'nih' (not invented here) syndrome appears to be particularly prevalent in US universities.

7.7.4 Summary

Studying individually with the help of videos, additional set books and personal support from instructors, with examinations at the end of each course, is not distance education but studying on the basis of audiovisual presentations. It is an interesting and promising approach to autonomous learning. Interactive video conferences, such as those now held at many US universities, are not distance education either, because many of the latter's constitutive characteristics are missing. However, the *elements* of distance education tested here are certainly suitable for making university education of the future more flexible, variable and adaptable.

7.8 Teleconferencing made possible through institutional collaboration: the Canadian project 'Contact North'

When more and more universities want to collaborate in the further development of distance education, they find themselves faced with a dilemma. Either they are satisfied with fixing their teaching programmes onto media that cost little and are sent to students, which would be technically backward and a pedagogically minimalist solution, or they develop distance-education-oriented teaching materials and use modern telecommunications media, which would be technically abreast of the times and pedagogically ambitious but at the same time would exceed their financial and infrastructural possibilities. In this situation it seems clear that universities should collaborate, because this can increase the number of distance students, financing becomes easier, and professional pedagogical course development and organizational coordination is possible by dividing tasks.

More and more universities are faced with this decision, one that is important for the future of distance education. One example of collaboration is the Poschiawo Project in Switzerland, with which the universities of Geneva, Neuchatel, Bologna and Padua, the Swiss Film Institute, the Centre for Technical Development in Berne, and Swiss Telecom are involved. Their aim is to develop distance education *jointly* so as to supplement their teaching programmes without having to establish their own institutions. Another example, and one we shall look at in this section of the chapter, involves collaboration between several universities in the Canadian province of Ontario which, financed by the provincial government, offer their teaching programmes as well to those living in the north of the province – in other words in an area with a small, scattered population and correspondingly few opportunities for university education. This kind of distance education aims at adapting the restricted educational chances in the north of the province to those of the south.

Those who know just how universities usually fight with all their might to retain their independence and their autonomy will recognize immediately the difficulties facing this collaboration, Marian Croft (1993: 132) has described and analysed them in this Canadian example.

However, the decisive question thrown up by collaboration of this nature between several universities is pedagogical. It enquires whether the considerable sums of money (C\$20 million for the pilot phase alone) and the bundled personnel resources will simply be used to install the technical apparatus and transmit courses from the participating traditional universities, or whether a decision will be made to develop internal distance-education-oriented courses, which will take account of the special requirements of this unusual clientele.

7.8.1 Description

The Canadian 'Contact North' project was initiated in 1986, initially for a four-year pilot phase, by the government of Ontario so as to improve access to university with the help of distance education, particularly in very isolated and remote towns and regions (23 of these towns are not connected to the public road network), and also for the francophone population and native peoples. Through this project, experience was to be gained with a system of distance education that was improved by the use of modern telecommunications media that could subsequently be used to advantage in the other Canadian provinces and abroad.

Because the teaching programme and personnel resources of a single university would have been inadequate to realize this project, the government invited four universities to plan and bring to fruition this project together. These were the Laurentian University, Lakehead University, Cambrian College, and Confederation College. Using information and communications media they set up a network with which in fact even very remote locations could be reached. However, workplaces equipped technically to cope with the project had to be set up in the remote areas. The following communication technologies were used: audio conferencing, audiographic conferencing, computer conferencing and compressed video conferencing.

In 1994, workplaces had been set up in this way at 46 locations with the complete technical apparatus and the required operators, and at a further 37 locations in which work is only possible with audio conferencing and fax and where operators can only be requested as required. In addition, there were 13 receiver stations for satellite television. Following the pilot phase, completely equipped receiver stations were installed in 100 secondary schools in the region. As a result, in the start-up year a total of 10,000 persons were able to take part in courses from the colleges and universities mentioned. They were able to put their teaching programme together from about 600 courses. Teleconferencing alone was used in the 1993/94 academic year for about 10,000 hours of formal teaching and 1,500 hours of informal communications between students (Shaw, 1995: 169).

7.8.2 Pedagogical aspects

The pedagogical structure of this distance education system is determined to a special degree by the electronic communications media it uses. As mentioned above, there were four such media introduced, as follows:

1. *Audioconferencing* is the first form of interaction. Teachers and students are linked by telephone. Students have comfortable headphones and speak into a microphone.
2. *Audiographic conferencing* is transmitted with the help of an Optel telewriter. This piece of equipment enables each student to have the use of an electronic blackboard, on which illustrations and graphics can be shown after they have been converted into the version required by the telewriter. Displays on the electronic blackboard can also be transferred to large screens so that learning groups can look at them together.
3. *Computers* are used not only to coordinate all the programme's administrative processes but also for computer conferences and the audiographic system.
4. *Compressed video-conferencing* is used for live interactions in tuition, in which several learning groups are linked by satellite and cable television.

The organizers stress two functions of the overall system: delivery and interaction, ie the transport and distribution of the courses and discussions between teacher and students and joint activities. The following typical scenarios have been developed:

- In audio-conferencing, one or more students take part in a tuition dialogue from a workstation; the dialogue is supported by written and graphical presentations. Because students do not have to hold a telephone receiver, they can take notes just as if they were in a real classroom, write down what the teacher has said, or read out what they have written themselves. Teachers, on the other hand, stand in front of a studio class and make the students into collaborators; or they can do without a studio class and concentrate on the distance students. Here they use telewriters in all those cases in which they would normally use the blackboard in face-to-face teaching.
- The same configuration of participants is found in video-conferencing, but here other modes of presentation dominate. Teachers and students obtain more information about the person who is speaking at any one moment. Subtleties of tone are transmitted because they can see the speaker's face. This supports dialogues, which, through close-ups, can have an even more penetrating effect than physical presence. Concentration on the objects to be examined tends to be neglected, on the other hand, because these cannot be shown exactly in compressed video because the image resolution is poor. This has a specific effect on teaching and learning behaviour.
- Where computer-conferencing is used, those taking part in the teaching and learning process who have a PC can exchange information on what they have learnt, either individually or in groups, or they can communicate informally with one another, although this must be done asynchronously. Dialogues take on the character of correspondence in these circumstances, for which there is a

cultural pattern, which is, however, changed by the language of computers. As we have already seen elsewhere, teachers have the time to prepare their contributions exactly and to calculate them with regard to their pedagogical effect. And students can reflect on the solution to a problem and check the answer from several perspectives. All this is not found in classroom discussions, in which the important thing is spontaneity and maintenance of the flow of speech. In this way, teaching and learning is given special contours through phases of reflection, of thought, even of deep immersion in the subject matter. Sometimes participants even take hours to meditate and brood if they are unable to solve a problem.

Because each of the forms of interactivity shown here has its own special pedagogical characteristics, it would be wrong in principle to decide on *one* form of conferencing. Basically, all four are essential because they each supplement favourably the different kinds of teaching and learning that they support.

Table 7.9 *Components of teaching and learning behaviour through the Canadian project 'Contact North'*

Teaching behaviour	Learning behaviour
Teaching in a studio class to which single students or groups of students are linked.	Listening, talking and discussing during teleconferences
Preparing and presenting graphics and illustrations	Learning by observing graphics on the electronic blackboard
Teaching in virtual seminars, discussing with individual students or the whole group of students	Dialogical learning in compressed video-conferencing
Careful, deepened reactions to questions and statements from students by means of considered replies	Learning by exchanging written statements: questions, answers, comments, explanations, descriptions, claims, refutations, etc.

7.8.3 Commentary

With the help of the technical information and a communications network, the provincial government has enabled a great number of students to acquire secondary or tertiary education, which would not have been possible beforehand because of the lack of an infrastructure. This is a considerable gain, both educationally and with regard to educational policy. It is worthy of particular mention because the cultural minorities the programme aimed to reach were in fact integrated into the educational system to a much greater extent than before. This was imperative, because they make up a large percentage of the population in the north of the province, which consists of about 30 per cent francophones and about 22 per cent native peoples. The educational system, which was precarious for different reasons for both groups, has been improved.

Clearly, the project Contact North represents a model of distance education, which points to academic learning and teaching in the future. Each of the four forms of teleconferencing has specific advantages and disadvantages, and it is a pedagogic challenge to combine them in different ways in order to achieve desired learning goals in different learning situations. It is true that one or the other of these forms of teleconferencing is being employed in other distance teaching universities, but as a rule independently and for certain periods of time only. Here, however, these four forms of teleconferencing are used in tandem and permanently as the general and exclusive basis and vehicle of distance education. This is new and, indeed, unique.

The use of the technical information and communications network found here shows how easy it is today to make the borders between secondary and tertiary education superfluous for certain phases of the teaching and learning process: the physical and institutional demarcation of these two areas loses its significance. A trend may be beginning here, now that it has become financially impossible in a future educational system to develop and maintain a separate, efficient and differentiated technical communications system for each kind of school or institute of higher education. It will probably be the case that all these institutions will have to use the same communications network. This brings to mind a remark made by Friedrich Edding, the educational economist, that, from the viewpoint purely of economics, it is unwise to support the usual separation of different types of schools and institutes of higher education.

The demand for distance education disseminated in this manner is relatively large. However, it can be seen here that this technological teaching and learning system differs in one essential point from large distance-teaching universities such as the Open University, the FernUniversität or the University of South Africa. It is not, in fact, 'open' in the sense used in these other universities because it is solely for applicants from the northern parts of Ontario; applicants from the south are rejected.

The 'Contact North' project makes use in the first place of audio-conferencing, a decision that was taken on the one hand certainly for financial reasons, but on the other for technical reasons as well. The experience gained previously with this form of teaching and learning in the distance education systems of the Laurentian University and Confederation College may also have played a part. It is interesting that the Ministry for Colleges and Universities had already intervened in Confederation College before the start of the 'Contact North' project. The correspondence courses the college offered were to be supplemented and/or replaced by audio-conferencing, because the ministry placed great value on interactivity between teachers and students, and this obviously appeared to be insufficient in correspondence studies, or at least did not appeal in the form in which it was used. What we can see from this is that when a decision was taken in favour of audio-conferencing for the 'Contact North' project, not only transport and transmission aspects played a part but also pedagogical considerations and convictions.

However, the decision had considerable consequences for the kind of distance education that was developed in this way. In audio-conferencing, only a limited number of students can take part, and the group must not be larger than a 'normal' college class; in fact, it should be smaller. This means that the aspect of mass education is missing, because all that happens here is a form of traditional teaching carried out over a distance. The educational requirements of many applicants from disadvantaged population groups are not taken into account. Pedagogical preferences here are in conflict with the requirements of both social policies and adult educational policies. For many, it is obviously difficult to balance these considerations.

Audio-conferences always have problems with the sound. This is not just a technical problem, it is also a pedagogical problem. The sound quality of a telephone system is really only designed for a conversation between two people. If there are several or many people taking part, there are always different faults and disturbances that interrupt the flow of the pedagogical discussion, and this can frustrate students to such an extent that they may easily break off the tuition themselves, especially if they are sitting in front of the microphone at the time.

Another disadvantage of audio-conferencing relevant to the effects of teaching is the fact that the body language of both teachers and students cannot be seen. Of course, it can be argued that this is also the case with printed material, especially as no voices can be heard either. This may be right, but the situation is not so clear-cut. There is in fact a written language and a broadcast language, and each has developed in a specific manner. Each has its own articulation, its own rhythm and its own dramaturgy. And we have grown accustomed to this, without ever being conscious of it. There are reception conventions for it. Dealing with both is part of modern culture. However, teachers who act as if they are in a college class, and then transmit this electronically, use neither the one nor the other communication medium. They speak in a completely different manner, above all as if they are standing in front of a learning group, to try to provide the tuition with authenticity. However, some things can only be understood if we actually 'see' the situation, if we 'feel' the atmosphere in a class. Subtleties of tone are often only understandable if we can see the speaker's raised eyebrows, the drawn-down corners of the mouth, or the laughing eyes. If this cannot be observed, the spoken language often appears wooden and boring.

7.8.4 Summary

The 'Contact North' project shows what a distance-education system looks like without correspondence tuition, without carefully developed and printed materials, and probably without a proper system of support and tutorial counselling, but *with* currently available electronic communication media. It is a distance-education system that at its core consists simply of a combination of four kinds of teleconferencing, each of which alters teaching and learning in a specific manner. Research still has to be carried out into the teaching effects that their interplay can achieve.

8

Analyses and perspectives

8.1 Analyses

The distance-teaching universities described and commented on in Chapter 7 represent institutional structures with which different forms of learning and teaching are made possible and supported. Each of these distance-teaching universities has its own unmistakable character, which cannot be completely discerned and evaluated without a deep knowledge of the situation in the respective country. They do in fact have something in common, because fundamentally they have to solve the same problems, although an analysis brings to light different models of teaching and learning in distance education. These models are thus:

1. *Correspondence studies*, which are in principle based on study guides, textbooks and other academic literature, on comments in assignments, and lead students in a broad range of degree programmes to Bachelor's and Master's degrees and Doctorates.
2. The classical *distance education in a multimedia system* in which several components – printed material, television, radio, audiovisual media, tutorial support in study centres, and residential schools – are carefully developed and coordinated with one another and that basically provide college-level education and continuing education.
3. *Research-based distance education*, which is provided under the slogan of the unity of research and teaching and is composed of reading printed distance teaching courses, optional support from mentors in study centres, in part obligatory attendance at seminars given by professors, and a system of written and oral examinations. It leads to final examinations at Master's level, or at levels that presuppose a Master's degree, and it provides continuing academic education.
4. *Group distance education*, which also works with teaching programmes on radio and television but combines these with regular obligatory traditional university

teaching. One version is found in a large territory with more than half a million students, another version in a relatively small region with thirty or forty thousand students. A third version replaces teaching programmes on radio and television with corresponding programmes on audio and video cassettes in special video centres. The aim is to provide a college education.

5. *Autonomous distance education*, which students themselves plan, organize and implement, whereby the university remains in the background and only appears to provide advice, support, counselling – and grades. Learning contracts play a key role here.

6. Distance education based on a *teleconferencing network* provided by a consortium of universities and colleges for students in member universities and in other institutions. Individual courses are available for continuing education, degree programmes and some special areas.

7. Distance education based on *four forms of teleconferencing* in which individual students and learning groups can take part at workstations that are linked in this way to the teaching systems at some of the universities and colleges cooperating in the project.

8. *Distributed learning*, in which Net-based strategies and methods are employed and entirely new pedagogical models must be developed, tested and implemented.

If we analyse these models, characteristic differences can be seen that were referred to and discussed earlier in this work in order to discover more in theory about the pedagogical possibilities of distance education in general. These differences make clear how flexible and variable teaching and learning in distance education can be. It has been introduced in advanced industrial countries; in developing and threshold countries; in densely and very thinly populated countries; in countries with a highly developed, extremely differentiated school and university system; and in others in which the basic educational necessities were missing. Forms of teaching and learning are constantly being created that are adapted to the respective situation.

In particular cases the following typical differences in teaching and learning behaviour can be seen: general institutional aims, the use of technical media, the extent to which students are granted leeway to design their own studies (heteronomy versus autonomy), the concepts that are linked to the term 'distance education', and the influence of academic traditions and learning cultures. Each of these topics is described briefly below.

8.1.1 General institutional aims

All distance-teaching universities pursue the aim of being able to support more students than there are places available in traditional universities, above all in China and Japan, but the Open University in the UK refuses on principle to admit students who have just completed their secondary education because the university is oriented towards mature students. The argument goes – and this is interesting – that only mature students are able to cope with the difficulties presented by studies of this nature.

The humanitarian motive of contributing to equality of opportunity is perceived everywhere, but the emphasis given to it differs greatly. In South Africa and northern Ontario, equality of opportunity refers above all to different ethnic groups or minorities. In Europe in general it refers to educationally disadvantaged adults, such as housewives and those in employment; and specifically in the UK's Open University it refers explicitly to all qualified students 'without consideration of gender, skin colour, ethnic or national origins, ages, socio-economic status, disability, religious beliefs, political convictions, marital status or sexual orientation' (Open University, 1994: 7). In China the motive of equality of opportunity is overshadowed by efforts to train more specialists for the development of the economy. And in Japan, in a highly advanced development phase of the economy, the endeavour is to modernize academic tuition through technology so that it can adapt flexibly to the rapidly changing requirements of an industrial society.

8.1.2 Use of technical media

The University of South Africa regards printed material as the main medium and supplements this basically by means of correspondence between teachers and students, and because of this we can say that the system there is first-generation distance education (correspondence study). The UK's Open University, on the other hand, is the prototype of multimedia distance education because it makes use above all of television, radio and study centres in the service of academic teaching. The consortia of American universities base their operations on interactive video-conferences using broadband cable and satellite technology and are developing second-generation distance education. And with the 'Contact North' project we have second- and third-generation distance education, because this project has no less than four forms of teleconferencing in its teaching and learning system with the help of digital media.

8.1.3 Heteronomy versus autonomy

The development of autonomous learning is most advanced in the Empire State College. From this point of view, this institution can be regarded as both a prototype and an excellent example. Heteronomous learning, on the other hand, is supported and perpetuated at those distance-teaching universities in which learning paths are carefully structured and laid down in relatively small steps by course teams following empirical tests.

Basically, the Empire State College is the only distance-teaching university that can justly be called 'open', even though it does not use this currently fashionable epithet in its title, because it also grants curricular freedom.

8.1.4 Different pedagogical concepts

The pedagogical structure is determined most decidedly by attitudes towards distance education that have been developed in various countries. In the National University Teleconference Network in the USA, and in the Canadian 'Contact North' project, distance education is understood first and foremost – and often exclusively – as technically enabled access to university education, and/or the transport and distribution of university teaching. These functions are effected by means of the latest media. Observers can feel the pleasure in technology and the satisfaction in technical progress above all with the help of the new digital media. This attitude is stressed here because it determines the structure of distance education in many American and Canadian universities. This attitude can also be found in the Central Radio and Television University in China and the University of the Air in Japan, although here single-channel and not digital media enable access. Here, however, the distribution of teaching by technical means is counterbalanced by obligatory group instruction.

In Europe, on the other hand, distance education is interpreted in principle pedagogically. The term is connected, firstly, with an impetus towards social reform, which is the reason why mass production, the use of mass media and the striving for mass higher education are constitutive. Secondly, it covers the possibility of establishing a special system of adult education. Thirdly, and above all, this term means a different and special type of teaching and learning. When a team of experts at the Open University in the UK spends 12–18 months developing a course that is tailored with great care and effort to the special learning requirements of distance students, this is a completely different kind of teaching to simply transmitting normal college teaching to another classroom via satellite. When every effort is taken at the FernUniversität in development work over a similar period to make teaching texts for students self-instructing and to coordinate them with presentations in the study centres, this creates the foundations for a type of learning that is oriented towards distance education and that is completely different from simply learning from textbooks and using a syllabus. The questions of transport and distribution are *secondary,* because they are only technical problems.

8.1.5 Different learning cultures

Many differences in learning and teaching in distance education are caused by different academic traditions and learning cultures. We can only understand the enthusiasm for interactive broadband video-conferences, as provided by the National University Teleconference Network, if we remind ourselves of the conviction in the USA and Canada (which I find extremely difficult to comprehend) that teaching in classes is the ideal for distance education and should even be used as a standard for assessment. The radically individualized learning system at the Empire State College is an astonishing exception here.

On the other hand, American and Canadian experts are completely unable to understand why students at European distance-teaching universities are able to plan and implement their programmes individually, because this is the case in traditional university teaching, right from the very first semester. Finally, the way in which in Chinese and Japanese distance-education systems professors are placed in the centre of television programmes is certainly singular.

To sum up: distance education and traditional university teaching are in some regards linked much closer to one another structurally than is generally thought, and this differs depending on the respective cultural traditions.

8.2 Perspectives

The different forms of teaching and learning in distance education shown here are significant in the present situation of change forced through by the digital revolution. As we have seen, they were created in different socio-cultural contexts and are usually composed of elements that can easily be put together in other ways. This lends distance education a degree of flexibility that would be difficult to find anywhere else.

If the advancing digitalization of teaching and learning means that traditional universities are now absorbing more and more elements of distance teaching into their repertoires, and distance-teaching universities are providing more and more support for learning groups through teleconferencing, then these are the preconditions that make a university of the future appear possible or even probable. Taking into account all that has been said in the current international discussion of the subject, we might see a university of the future look as set out below, at least as far as the external structure of learning and teaching is concerned.

8.2.1 The university of the future

The university of the future is open to everyone able to take part successfully in university education, including therefore many mature students of all ages. It does not prescribe any binding learning locations or learning times. Studies may be commenced, interrupted and resumed as required by the students' personal circumstances and vocational careers. Studies will be both full-time and part-time, and students may change between the two forms. Wherever possible, studies will be oriented closely to students' practical, vocational and personal circumstances. Foundation courses and advanced studies will overlap and will in parts relate to one another.

The university of the future uses components of traditional university teaching, distance education, and digitalized teaching. In this way it will become more flexible with regard to teaching and learning forms than ever before. Depending on their inclinations and necessities, students may decide on the following modes of learning: lectures, seminars, practical studies, work with self-instructing distance-teaching courses, all forms of digital learning (eg multimedia, hypertext and teleconferencing), open autonomous learning, and closed self-study with highly structured learning packages. They can combine these modes of study together, either in parallel or consecutively. It is even possible to make use of the teaching programmes of several institutions at the same time.

Work is done through study modules. Credit points for work at different institutions are accumulated and used as a basis for graduating. Students can take advantage of intensive study support and professional counselling, above all as a supplement for autonomous open learning. Both forms of support will be more important than they could ever be in traditional university teaching or in distance education.

The university of the future is the flexible and variable university *par excellence*.

8.3 Final summary

Once again we can see the many points of affinity that the distance-education models introduced in Chapter 7 have with a university of the future, and how distance education is already preparing for this in many aspects, both theoretical and practical.

Distance education has the power to alter traditional teaching and learning systems structurally, and to accelerate the change. It can extend and diversify the student body considerably, make studies more variable and flexible with regard to both curriculum and methods, integrate electronic information and communications media into the teaching and learning process and substantiate this integration pedagogically on the basis of years of experience. It can provide greater real opportunities for autonomous and individualized learning, and plan, develop, implement and evaluate professionally wide-ranging national projects for academic studies and continuing education.

Distance education points towards the future of an information and learning society in which its concepts and experience will be more important than they are today.

Appendix: Stations on the road from written to digitalized teaching text

The four examples shown here have been chosen to indicate just how teaching in distance education has made use of the different technologies available in the various stages of industrialization.

1. The first example uses the technology of the written word and reminds us of hand-written instruction just as it was created in the mid-nineteenth century. The teaching letter shown in Fig A.1, which was written in 1910, is hand-written, in the same way as the Apostle Paul wrote his epistles to instruct the early Christians in Rome and Corinth nearly two thousand years ago. In fact, this particular letter was reproduced on a copier so that it could be distributed to a large number of students. The page shown in Fig A.1 contains teaching content and gives the impression of a talk by an expert.

2. The second example (see Fig A.2) uses the technology of printing. In this case, the reader can 'hear' the writer's voice, although teaching content is not imparted but students are given tips and advice for reading texts, and are encouraged both to repeat what they have already learnt and to criticize. The text in Fig A.2 instructs and reflects the teacher model. A total of no less than 27 experts in a course team collaborated in its development.

3. The third example (see Fig A.3) uses the technology of digital text processing. It shows us the transition from printing to use of the PC. A teaching text originally conceived to be printed in a book was digitized by being graphically designed, and its presentation was restructured by means of multimedia (in this case a video insert) and hypertext elements (two references). What is revolutionary about this approach is that the text is not found on a sheet of paper but is displayed to students on a monitor. They can then interact with it, and this activates learning. Any printout becomes a secondary matter.

4. The fourth example (see Fig A.4) uses the technology of digital communication. This is inconceivable without the technological progress in the area of networking (ie the Internet). In this case the digitized text enables a virtual seminar to be held by means of an exchange of messages that are entered into a PC and

reach other participants in seconds through computer-conferencing. The exchange of messages is asynchronous, and this can be seen from the times of the individual contributions recorded by the computer. The first page shows how the seminar leaders introduce a new expert and try to structure the expected discussion. The second page shows typical contributions of two participants. These four examples show how the more recent technologies are based on the respective older technologies and continue to use them for their own purposes. All four have one fundamental thing in common: the eye takes the place of the ears, as far as the students are concerned (see *An Eye for an Ear*, Marshall McLuhan, 1964: 81). In that regard, the more recent forms of distance education are also in principle an outflow of those far-reaching cultural changes, which were brought about by the introduction of the phonetic alphabet.

Technisches Lehr-Institut

▫ ONKEN ▫

Kurs Elektrotechnik

von Fr. Onken, Ingenieur

Lehrbrief 20.

Schwachstrom.

Die galvanischen Elemente.

Die galvanischen Elemente gehören zu den ältesten Stromquellen der Elektrizität. Im Jahre 1800 konstruierte Volta das erste praktisch verwendbare Element, indem er eine Zink- und eine Kupferplatte in einem Glase mit verdünnter Schwefelsäure aufstellte (Fig. 477). Die Zinkplatte wird von der Schwefelsäure angegriffen und dadurch chemische Energie frei. Diese freiwerdende chemische Energie hat das Bestreben, sich in elektrische umzuwandeln, welche alsdann ihren Kreislauf durch Schwefelsäure, Kupferplatte, Verbindungsdraht zur Zinkplatte nimmt. Die Kupferplatte bildet den positiven und die Zinkplatte den negativen Pol der Stromquelle. Dieses Volta'sche Element wirkt zwar anfänglich sehr kräftig, erschöpft aber bald. Da zur Betätigung der elektrischen Läutwerke, Telegraphen,

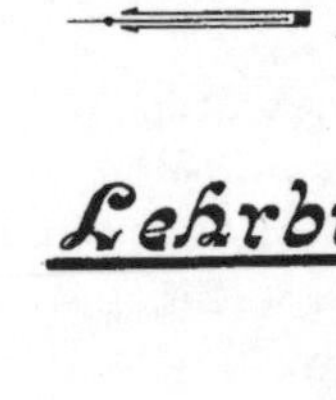

Fig. 477.

Figure A.1 *A page from a written teaching letter (1910)*
Source: Technisches Lehrinstitut Onken, Kreuzlingen, Switzerland. Electrical engineering course, 1907.

Familiarity or friendship? A symbol of affection or contempt? It depends on one's construction of meanings.

READING Now read 'Sociological implications of the thought of G. H. Mead' by Herbert Blumer, in *School and Society* (Course Reader) Reading 2, comparing it with my account.

ACTIVITY 2 After you have read this article you should pause to consider the methodological implications of symbolic interactionism. In studying social interaction, what do we need to focus upon and how are we going to do it? The traditional instruments of sociological investigation are the questionnaire, the interview, the historical record and observation. How would you employ these, if at all? What other techniques would you suggest? Has statistical analysis any place in this kind of study? If you are going to try to get at the 'meanings' people attribute to symbols, how are you going to answer the charge of 'intuitionism', or that of 'infinite regression' (i.e. we will then need someone to get at your meanings, and so on, *ad infinitum*). What conception of social structure are you going to hold, and how does your position relate to macro indices like social class, culture, role, status? Also, look back over the studies discussed in the previous section. What do they owe to symbolic interactionism?

READING Go on to read the set article by Herbert Blumer, 'The methodological position of symbolic interactionism' (*The Process of Schooling*, Course Reader, pp. 12–18), then return to the questions in Activity 2, and compare your thoughts with Blumer's. You should spend about two and a half hours on this.

28

Figure A.2 *A page from a printed teaching letter (1977)*
Source: The Open University. Educational Studies, second-level course E202, 'Schooling and Society', Block V: Culture and Class, Unit 27–28. Prepared for the Course Team by Peter Woods. Milton Keynes: The Open University.

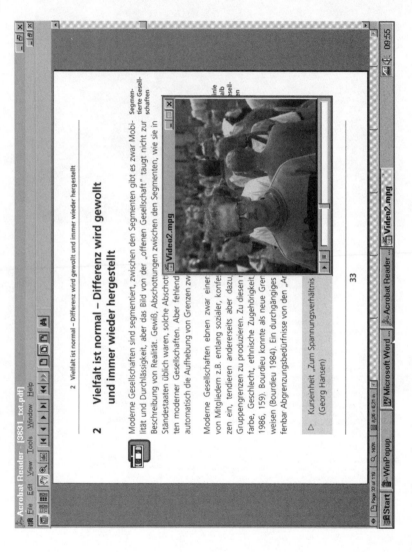

Figure A.3 *A page from a digital course (1996)*

Source: FernUniversität-Gesamthochschule. Faculty of Education and the Humanities distance course 3831, Introduction to Intercultural Studies. Author: Prof. Dr. Georg Hansen. Hagen: FernUniversität-Gesamthochschule, 1.

Virtual Seminar on Distance Education

Welcome to Week 2: Institutional Models of Distance Education

Forum: Virtual Seminar Week 3
Date: Sun, 19 Jan 1997 03:24:37 GMT
From: Ulrich Bernath and Eugene Rubin <crubin@nova.umuc.edu>

Welcome to Week 3

Well, last week was quite an event!...... and we managed to explore a wide variety of philosophical issues and debate a few interesting questions. We will find that these same issues and questions will permeate our continuing discussions, and nowhere is this more true than in the subect of this week's seminar. Many of the issues we discussed have directly influenced the design of institutions (not to mention the influences of government. culture and tradition).

 No one is more qualified to talk about this influence than Gary Miller, our guest expert for this week. Gary has had broad experience in U.S. distance education and has served in a variety of roles which have given him a penetrating perspective into the U.S. distance education scene. If you haven't already, take a look at Gary's biography. Welcome Gary!

This week we will try to structure the discussion a bit more so as to make more sense of the HyperNews treading. (Those of you who value autonomy and independence will have to excuse us..... the seminar leaders have a strong desire for a bit of strucure, as can be seen in the design of the seminar) The topics will be:

☐ TOPIC AREA 1 General comments on Gary Miller's article.
☐ TOPIC AREA 2 D.E Institutions in the U.S. and elsewhere.
☐ TOPIC AREA 3 The understanding of distance education.

We ask that you place any questions or discussion under the relevant topic. And, of course, if you feel that you want to step outside that structure, please feel free to do so. (We are not total authoritarians!)

We also hope to bring a European perspective into the discussion, and will try to do this more toward the middle of the week. In the meantime, this week's discussion on U.S. models will likely be illuminating for everyone (including the Americans!)

As usual, we will use Monday to allow you to respond to Gary's article. On Tuesday, Gary will enter into the discussion. (North Americans have until 12 noon EST and Europeans until 6PM MEZ to speak up). If you still haven't seen Gary's article that we assigned, go to the Readings link on the main page of ther seminar.

Once again...... enjoy yourselves!

Uli and Gene

Figure A.4 *Two pages from the log of an international computer conference (1998)*
Source: Virtual Seminar on Distance Education. Professional Development for University Faculty and Administrators. January 12 to March 20. University of Maryland, Institute for Distance Education and Carl von Ossietzky Universität Oldenburg, Centre for Distance Education. This seminar was attended by 44 participants from 16 countries in all parts of the world.

252   Appendix

Dear Seminar Leaders and all the Participants:

1. My university is just beginning to being interested in DE and, in this phase, almost as a research interest so I am almost "alone" in my department, in what DE concerns. I didn't organize an internal discussion group because everybody (and me too...) is always full of work but I spoke with some colleagues about the seminar and also have shown the seminar to three or four colleagues from different departments. Two of them told me that they would like to participate in future versions of the seminar.

2. This seminar was the exactly answer to my professional, academic and research needs at the moment. Everything was important: the content, the participants and experts (lots of participants seem to be also experts in DE...), the technology used and the methodology adopted. From October to December I had teach one course for in-service (secondary - K12?) teachers where I use the Internet and develop one specific web site to support the course (It was a Lone Ranger approach and I didn't have a team to develop the course...). We had made some kind of distance learning activities in an informal way. Next September I will organize a course for teacher training which will be partially by DE using the Internet (WWW. computer conferencing and e-mail). Many of the things I experienced and learned in this seminar will be very important for me. Thanks to all!

3. I think this kind of seminar approach is very important but probably only works when include, as participants, lots of people who are themselves, experts. I think that it was the case of this seminar.

4. I would like to say that, despite I had been, many times, a "silent" (or almost "silent") participant, I had learn a lot and I am gratefully for this opportunity. I would like also to thanks to all the "active" participants who had understood the problems of the "silent" ones. I was a "silent" participant one but not a "passive" participant!

Maria Joao - Portugal

---

from Hildesheim

Re: THREAD 1: PLEASE GO HERE FIRST - GIVE US SOME FEEDBACK! (Eugene Rubi
Date: Tue, 17 Mar 1998 15:09:51 GMT
From: Herbert Asselmeyer <asselm@zfw.uni-hildesheim.de>

```
Dear colleagues,
  greetings from Hildesheim. While participating this seminar in our university
we were creating a course development team for the project "Virtual Campus"
  (http://www.uni-hildesheim.de/zfw/vc/vcroot.htm). Weekly we distributed and
afterwards dicussed the readings in our group with great benefits. We learned a
lot about the web-based course development process and found implications for
our situation.
  When filling out the questionnaire we have noticed again this great benefit for
us within our university. Maybe we were not so helpful for the virtual seminar
group. In this case we hope that this leads not to misunderstandings that we
learned partly outside the seminar group.
  We would like to get to know you if it is possible. Maybe the next ICDE meeting
?
  Special greetings and thanks to Uli and Gene (I learned a lot from you before
this
seminar, too!)
  All the best

  from

  Herbert (and Folker Caroli and Birgit Oelker)
```

Figure A.4   *Continued*

References

Abu Sabha, R, Peacock, J and Achterberg, Ch (1997) 'Impact evaluation of a teleconference using a mixed model for distance education', in *The 18th ICDE–World Conference: The New Learning Environment. A Global Perspective*. International Council for Distance Education, The Pennsylvania State University. Abstracts.

Alsina, C (1997) 'The Open University of Catalonia: a dedicated distance teaching university on a virtual campus', in *The 18th ICDE–World Conference: The New Learning Environment. A Global Perspective*. International Council for Distance Education, The Pennsylvania State University. Abstracts.

Aoki, K and Pogroszewski, D (1998) 'Virtual university reference model: a guide to delivering education and support services to the distance learner' (www.westga.edu/-distance/aoki13.html).

Arnold, R (1993) *Die Natur als Vorbild. Selbstorganisation als Modell der Pädagogik*. Frankfurt am Main: VAS Verlag für akademische Schriften.

Arnold, R (1995) 'Neue Methoden betrieblicher Bildungsarbeit', in A Lipsmeier and R Arnold *Handbuch der Berufsbildung*. Opladen: Leske & Budrich, 294.

Atkinson, R (1997) *Flexible Teaching and Learning Policy*. Murdoch University Teaching and Learning Centre (http://cleo.murdoch.edu.au/tlc/pubs/flex/conts.html).

Bååth, J A (1979) *Correspondence education in the light of a number of contemporary teaching models*. Malmö: LiberHermods.

Bååth, J A (1989) 'Submission density, amount of submission questions, and quality of student–tutor dialogue', in Börje Holmberg (ed) *Mediated Communication as a Component of Distance Education*. Hagen: FernUniversität-Gesamthochschule, Zentrales Institut für Fernstudienforschung.

Barker, B O, Frisbie, A G and Patrick, K R (1993) 'Broadening the definition of distance education in light of the new telecommunications technologies', in K Harry, M John and D Keegan (eds) (1994), 39–50.

Baron, J and Hanisch, J (1997) 'Educating for a virtual world', in *The New Learning Environment. A Global Perspective*. 18th ICDE World Conference, 2–6 June, 1997 at the Pennsylvania State University. Conference Abstracts, 450.

Bartels, J (1986) *Absolventen des Fachbereichs Wirtschaftswissenschaft. Eine empirische Untersuchung*. Hagen: FernUniversität-Gesamthochschule, Zentrum für Fernstudienentwicklung.

Bartels, J (1987) *Absolventen des Fachbereichs Wirtschaftswissenschaft. Eine empirische Untersuchung*. Hagen: FernUniversität-Gesamthochschule, Zentrum für Fernstudienentwicklung.

Bast, Ch (1997) 'Der multimediale Dateikurs als Lehrelement im Fernstudium', in J Wurster (ed) *Virtuelles Kolloquium: Medienentwicklung im Fernstudium*. Hagen: FernUniversität-Gesamthochschule, Zentrum für Fernstudienentwicklung.

Bates, A W (1994) 'Technology for distance education: a ten-year prospective', in K Harry, M John and D Keegan (eds) (1994), 176–90.

Bates, A W (1995) *Technology, Open Learning and Distance Education*. London: Routledge.

Beck, K (1998) 'Lehren und Lernen in der »Informationsgesellschaft«. Prognosen über den

Einsatz und die Folgen computervermittelter Kommunikation im Bildungswesen', in E Prommer and G Vowe (Hg.) *Computervermittelte Kommunikation*. Konstanz: UVK Medien.

Bertelsmann Stiftung and Heinz Nixdorf Stiftung (Hg.) (1997) *Virtuelles Lehren und Lernen an deutschen Universitäten. Eine Dokumentation*. Gütersloh: Verlag Bertelsmann Stiftung.

Böhm, W (1994) *Wörterbuch der Pädagogik*. Stuttgart: Kröner

Boom W J G van den, and Schlusmans, K H (1989) *The Didactics of Open Education – Background, Analysis and Approaches*. Heerlen: The Open Universiteit, Centre for Educational Technological Innovation.

Boucher, M (1973) *Spes in Arduis: A History of the University of South Africa*. Pretoria: University of South Africa. The quotations can be found on the insides of the book covers.

Bruner, J S (1961) 'The act of discovery', *Harvard Educational Review*, 31, 21–32.

Buber, M (1954) *Schriften über das dialogische Prinzip*. 3rd edition. Heidelberg: Schneider.

Bühl, A (1997) *Die virtuelle Gesllschaft. Ökonomie, Politik and Kultur im Zeichen des Cyberspace*. Opladen: Westdeutscher Verlag.

Campion, M (1991) 'Critical essay on educational technology in distance education', in T Evans and B King (eds) *Beyond the Text: Contemporary Writings on Distance Education*. Geelong: Deakin University Press.

Campion, M (1993) 'Post-Fordism: neither panacea nor placebo', *Open Learning*, June, 59.

Campion, M (1995) 'The supposed demise of bureaucracy: Implications for distance education and open learning – more on the post-Fordism debate', *Distance Education*, 16, 2, 192.

Campion, M and Renner, W (1992) 'The supposed demise of Fordism: implications for distance education and higher education', *Distance Education*, 13, 1, 7–28.

Casper, G (1997) Eine Welt ohne Universitäten?. Werner Heisenberg Vorlesung. Bayerische Akademie der Wissenschaften und Carl Friedrich von Siemens Stiftung. München, 3.7.1996. Zitiert nach einem Sendemanuskript der Tele-Akademie des Südwestfunks vom 26.1.1997.

Chambers, E A and Rae, S A (1995) 'Uses of CMC in humanities distance education: reducing the distance' in D Sewart (ed) (1995), 2, 327–30.

Copei, F (1966) *Der fruchtbare Moment im Bildungsprozess*. 8th edition. Heidelberg: Quelle und Meyer.

Croft, M (1993) 'The Contact North project. Collaborative project management in Ontario', in L Moran and I Mugridge (eds) *Collaboration in Distance Education. International Case Studies*. London: Routledge.

Cross, P (1981) *Adults as Learners. Increasing Participation and Facilitating Learning*. San Francisco: Jossey-Bass.

Daniel, J (1988) 'The worlds of open learning', in N Paine (ed) *Open Learning in Transition*. Cambridge, UK: National Extension College, 126–7.

Daniel, J (1997) 'The Mega-University: The Academy for the New Millennium', in *The 18th ICDE–World Conference: The New Learning Environment. A Global Perspective*. International Council for Distance Education. The Pennsylvania State University. Abstracts, 22.

Daniel, Sir John (1998) In American Association for Higher Education, *Bulletin*, 11.

Daniel, J S and Marquies, C (1979) 'Interaction and independence: getting the mixture right', *Teaching at a Distance* 14, 29.

De Corte, E, Linn, M C, Mandl, H and Verschaffel, L (eds) (1990) *Computer-Based Learning Environments and Problem Solving*. Berlin: Springer.

Delling, R M (1985) 'Fernstudium in der Weimarer Republik', in H Fritsch et al (eds) *ZIFF-Papiere 54*. Hagen: FernUniversität-Gesamthochschule in Hagen: Zentrales Institut für Fernstudienforschung.

Dewey, J (1905) *Schule und öffentliches Leben*. Berlin: Walther.

Diehl, G E (1982) 'Some thoughts on delayed and immediate feedback', in Börje Holmberg (ed) (1989) *Mediated Communication as a Component of Distance Education*. Hagen: FernUniversität-Gesamthochschule, Zentrales Institut für Fernstudienforschung.

Dohmen, G (1972) 'Unterrichtsforschung und didaktische Theoriebildung im Rahmen der modernen Erziehungswissenschaft', in G Dohmen, F Maurer and W. Popp (eds), *Unterrichtsforschung und didaktische Theorie*. München: Pieper, 11–15.

Dohmen, G (1996) *Das lebenslange Lernen. Leitlinien einer modernen Bildungspolitik*. Bonn: Bundesminister für Bildung, Wissenschaft, Forschung und Technologie, Referat Öffentlichkeitsarbeit.

Dolch, J (1952) *Grundbegriffe der pädagogischen Fachsprache*. Nürnberg: Die Egge.

Doll, W E (1993) *A Postmodern Perspective on Curriculum*. New York: Teachers College, Columbia University.

Döring, N (1997) 'Lernen mit dem Internet, in L J Issing und P Klimsa (Hg.) *Information und Lernen mit Multimedia*. Weinheim: Beltz, 305–36.

Duning, B (1993) 'The coming of new distance educators in the United States: the telecommunications generation takes off', in K Harry, M John and D Keegan (eds), 209–23.

Eastmond, D V and Lawrence, B H (1997) 'Instructing faculty and delivering distance courses with computer network technology', in *The 18th ICDE-World Conference: The New Learning Environment. A Global Perspective*. International Council for Distance Education. The Pennsylvania State University. Abstracts.

Egan, K (1976) *Structural Communication*. Belmont, Cal, USA: Fearon Publishers.

Eisenstadt, M and Vincent, T (1998) *The Knowledge Web: Learning and Collaborating on the Net*. London: Kogan Page.

Ekins, J M (1997) 'Pedagogical issues in opening up mathematics to a wider audience', in *The 18th ICDE-World Conference: The New Learning Environment. A Global Perspective*. International Council for Distance Education. The Pennsylvania State University. Abstracts.

Elen, J (1996) 'Didactical aspects of self-study materials', in M De Volder (ed) *From Penny Post to Information Super-Highway: Open and Distance Learning in Close-up*. Leuven: Acco, 75.

Erdos, R F (1967) *Teaching by Correspondence*. London: Longman, UNESCO.

Fabro, K R and Garrison, D R (1998) 'Computer Conferencing and Higher Order Learning', in *Indian Journal of Open Learning*, 7, 1, 41–54.

Farnes, N (1993) 'Modes of production. Fordism and distance education', *Open Learning* 8, 1, 10–20.

Faure, E et al (1973) *Wie wir leben lernen. Der UNESCO-Bericht über Ziele und Zukunft unserer Enziehungsprogramme*. Hamburg: Roholt.

FernUniversität (1996) *Forschungsbericht 1993 bis 1996*. Hagen: FernUniversität-Gesamthochschule.

Fisher, B and Fisher, L (1979) 'Styles in Teaching and Learning', *Educational Leadership*, Jan, 245–54. Quoted by Haller (1987), 4.

Flechsig, K-H (1987) *Didaktisches Design: Neue Mode oder neues Entwicklungsstadium der Didaktik?* Göttingen: Georg-August-Universität, Institut für Kommunikationswissenschaften, Internes Arbeitspapier 8.

Flechsig, K-H (1992) *Vielfalt und transversale Vernunft. Prinzipien postmodernen Denkens und die Modernisierungskrise in Bildungssystemen*. Göttingen: Georg-August-Universität, Institut für interkulturelle Didaktik. Arbeitspapier 2.

Flechsig, K-H (1994) *Historical and Philosophical Backgrounds of Instructional Design*. Göttingen: Georg-August-Universität, Institut für interkulturelle Didaktik. Arbeitspapier 3/1994.

Flechsig, K-H and Haller, H-D (1975) *Einführung in didaktisches Handeln*. Stuttgart: Klett.

Fliege, J and Härtel, E (2000) 'Bildschirm statt Hörsaal'. In: *ZEITPunkte* Nr. 1. Hamburg: Zeitverlag.

Frey, K (1995) *Die Projektmethode*. 5th edition. Weinheim: Beltz.

Friede, Ch-K (1988) Preface to Ch-K Friede (ed) *Neue Wege der betrieblichen Ausbildung*. Heidelberg: Sauer.

Friedrich, H F (1996) 'Fertigkeiten und Umgebungen für das selbstgesteuerte Lernen', in B Nacke and G Dohmen (eds) *Lebenslanges Lernen*. Würzburg: Echter.

Friedrich, H F and Mandl, H (1995) 'Analyse und Förderung selbstgesteuerten Lernens', in F E Weinert and H Mandl *Psychologie der Erwachsenenbildung*. Göttingen: Hogrefe.

Fritsch, H (1991) 'Fernstudium oder offenes Lernen', in *Professionalisierung im Fernstudium*. Papers of the 5th BRIEF-Symposium on Distance Education. Tübingen 1992.

Garcia-Aretio, L (1997) 'Spain's UNED, a technological university', in *The 18th ICDE – World Conference: The New Learning Environment. A Global Perspective*. International Council for Distance Education. The Pennsylvania State University. Abstracts.

Garrison, G R (1985) 'Three generations of technological innovation in distance education', *Distance Education*, 6, 235–41.

Garrison, G R (1989) *Understanding Distance Education*. London: Routledge.

Garrison, G R (1993a) 'Quality and access in distance education: theoretical considerations', in D Keegan (ed) (1994), 9–21.

Garrison, G R (1993b) 'Multifunction computer enhanced audio teleconferencing: moving into the third generation of distance education', in K Harry, M John and D Keegan (eds) (1994), 200–8.

Gaudig, H (1922) *Freie geistige Schularbeit in Theorie und Praxis*. Breslau: Hirt.

Gaudig, H (1923) *Didaktische Präludien*. 3rd edition. Berlin: Teubner.

Gibbons, J F (1977) 'Tutored Video Instruction. A New Use of Electronic Media in Education', *Science* 195, 1139–44.

Giddens, A (1990) *The Consequences of Modernity*. Cambridge: Polity Press.

Glennie, J (1995) *Open Learning and Distance Education in South Africa*. Manzini: Macmillan.

Goffman, E (1972) *Encounters. Two studies in the sociology of interaction*. London: Allen Lane.

Gosper, M (1997–2000) *Flexible Learning*. Macquarie University (www.cfl.mq.edu.au/cfl/flexible/cflflexl.html).

Graff, K (1980) *Die jüdische Tradition und das Konzept des autonomen Lernens*. Weinheim: Beltz.

Habermas, J (1971) 'Vorbereitende Bemerkungen zu einer Theorie der kommunikativen Kompetenz', in J Habermas and N Luhmann *Theorie der Gesellschaft oder Sozialtechnologie – Was leistet die Systemforschung?* Frankfurt am Main: Suhrkamp, 101.

Hall, J B (1994) *Annual Report 1993–1994*. Saratoga Springs: SUNY Empire State College.

Haller, H-D (1987) *Lernstile und Lernstrategien*. Göttingen: Georg-August-Universität, Institut für interkulturelle Didaktik. Internes Arbeitspapier 7.

Harris, D (1988) 'The micro-politics of openness', *Open Learning*, 3,2, 14. Quoted by R H Paul (1993), 118.

Harry, K, John, M and Keegan, D (eds) (1993) *Distance Education: New Perspectives*. London: Routledge.

Hausmann, G (1959) *Didaktik als Dramaturgie des Unterrichts*. Heidelberg: Quelle und Meyer.

Hawkridge, D and McCormick, B (1983) 'China's Television Universities', *British Journal of Educational Technology* 14, 3, 160.

Heimann, P (1976) 'Film, Funk und Fernsehen als Bildungsmächte der Gegenwartskultur', in: K Reich and H Thomas (eds) *Paul Heimann. Didaktik als Unterrichtswissenschaft*. Stuttgart: Klett, 209.

Heinze, Th (1984) *Hermeneutisch lebensgeschichtliche Forschung. Band 2: Interpretationen einer Bildungsgeschichte*. Hagen: FernUniversität-Gesamthochschule. Arbeitsbereich: Methoden der Erziehungswissenschaft.

Hentig, H von (1970) 'Wissenschaftsdidaktik', in H von Hentig, L Huber and P Müller (eds) *Wissenschaftsdidaktik*. Göttingen: Vandenhoeck & Ruprecht, 13–40.

Hentig, H von (1971) 'Interdisziplinarität, Wissenschaftsdidaktik, Wissenschaftspropädeutik', *Merkur* 25, 854.

Henz, H (1971) *Lehrbuch der systematischen Pädagogik*. Freiburg: Herder.

Heuel, E. and Postel, M (1993) 'Lernen und Üben mit dem Computer. Beispiele aus der Praxis der FernUniversität', in *Gesellschaft der Freunde der FernUniversität: Jahrbuch 1993*. Hagen: Gesellschaft der Freunde der FernUniversität.

Hodgson, A M (1974) 'Structural communication in practice', *Programmed Learning and Educational Technology*, 9, 2.

Hodgson, B (1993) *Key Terms and Issues in Open and Distance Learning*. London: Kogan Page.

Holmberg, B (1979) *Das Hochschulstudium als Innovation am Beispiel der FernUniversität*. Hagen: FernUniversität-Gesamthochschule: Zentrales Institut für Fernstudienforschung.

Holmberg, B (1982a) *Recent Research into Distance Education*. Hagen: FernUniversität-Gesamthochschule. Zentrales Institut für Fernstudienforschung.

Holmberg, B (1982b) *Recent Research into Distance Education II*. Hagen: FernUniversität-Gesamthochschule. Zentrales Institut für Fernstudienforschung.

Holmberg, B (1985) *Status and Trends of Distance Education*. Lund: Lector Publishing.

Holmberg, B (1989a) *Theory and Practice of Distance Education*. London: Routledge. Second edition 1995.

Holmberg, B (ed) (1989b) *Mediated Communication as a Component of Distance Education*. Hagen: FernUniversität-Gesamthochschule, Zentrales Institut für Fernstudienforschung.

Holmberg, B (1990) *A Bibliography of Writings on Distance Education*. Hagen: FernUniversität-Gesamthochschule. Zentrales Institut für Fernstudienforschung.

Holmberg, B (1994) *Open Universities – Their Rationale, Characteristics, Prospects*. Hagen: FernUniversität-Gesamthochschule, Zentrales Institut für Fernstudienforschung, ZIFF-Papiere 92.

Holmberg B and Schuemer, R F (1989) 'Tutoring frequency in distance education – an empirical study of the impact of various frequencies of assignment submission', in Börje Holmberg (ed) *Mediated Communication as a Component of Distance Education*. Hagen: FernUniversität-Gesamthochule, Zentrales Institut für Fernstudienforschung.

Holmberg, B and Schuemer, R (1997) 'Lernen im Fernstudium', in F E Weinert and H Mandl (eds) *Enzyklopädie der Psychologie*, Vol 4: Psychologie der Erwachsenenbildung. Göttingen: Hogrefe Verlag für Psychologie.

Holmberg, B, Schuemer, R. and Obermeier, A (1982) *Zur Effizienz des gelenkten didaktischen Gespräches*. Hagen: FernUniversität-Gesamthochschule, Zentrales Institut für Fernstudienforschung.

Horn, R E (1973) *Introduction to Information Mapping*. Lexington, Mass, USA: Information Resources Inc.

Houle, C O (1974) *The External Degree*. San Francisco: Jossey-Bass.

Houle, C O (1984) *Patterns of Learning*. London: Jossey-Bass.

Hoyer, H (1998) 'A virtual university. Challenge and chance', in *Universities in a Digital Era. European Distance Education Network*, Eden Conference, University of Bologna, 24–26 June.

Huber, L (1983/1995a) 'Hochschuldidaktik als Theorie der Bildung und Ausbildung', in L Huber (ed) (1983/1995c), 114.

Huber, L (1983/1995b) 'Forschung, Lehre, Lernen', in L Huber (ed) (1983/1995c), 496.

Huber, L (ed) (1983/1995c) 'Ausbildung und Sozialisation in der Hochschule', Vol. 10 of *Enzyklopädie Erziehungswissenschaft*. Stuttgart: Klett.

Huber, L (1991) 'Bildung durch Wissenschaft – Wissenschaft durch Bildung. Hochschuldidaktische Anmerkungen zu einem grossen Thema', *Pädagogik und Schule in Ost und West*, 4, 193.

Hudson, R, Maslin-Prothero S, P and Oates, L (1997) *Flexible Learning in Action. Case Studies in Higher Education*. London: Kogan Page.

Issing, L J (1998) 'Online studieren? Konzepte und Realisierungen auf dem Weg zu einer virtuellen Universität' in Ralph Schwarzer (Hg.) *Multimedia und Telelearning. Lernen im Cyberspace*. Frankfurt: Campus.

Jarvis, P (1993) 'The education of adults and distance education in late modernity', in D Keegan (ed) (1993b). London: Routledge, 165.

Jennison, K (1997) 'Mutual support on the virtual campus', in *The 18th ICDE-World Conference: The New Learning Environment. A Global Perspective*. International Council for Distance Education. The Pennsyslvania State University. Abstracts.

Johnson-Lenz, P and Johnson-Lenz, T (1993) 'Writing and wholeness: on-line island of safety', in R Mason (ed) *Computer Conferencing – the Last Word*. Victoria, BC.: Beach Holme.

Kaderali, F, Müller, H and Rieke, A (1994) *Media Publishing in Distance Teaching.* EADTU-Workshop in Hagen.

Kaderali, F (1998) 'Virtuelle FernUniversität. FernUniversität Online', *Hagener Universitätsreden* 25, 2. Hagen: FernUniversität-Gesamthochschule.

Kato, H (ed) (1992) *A survey of distance education in Asia and the Pacific.* Report on Multimedia Education 49. Chiba (Tokyo): National Institute of Multimedia Education.

Keay, F A (1980) *Ancient Indian Education.* New Delhi: Cosmo Publications.

Keegan, D (1982) 'Die FernUniversität (FernUniversität-Gesamthochschule in Hagen), Federal Republic of Germany', in G Rumble and K Harry (eds) *The Distance Teaching Universities.* London: Croom Helm, 88.

Keegan, D (1986) *Foundations of Distance Education.* London: Routledge

Keegan, D (1993a) Introduction to Part VI of 'The study of distance education', in K Harry, M John and D Keegan (eds) (1993), 289–91.

Keegan, D (ed) (1993b) *Theoretical Principles of Distance Education.* London: Routledge.

Keegan, D (1994) *Very Large Distance Education Systems: The Case of China.* Hagen: FernUniversität-Gesamthochschule, Zentrum für Fernstudienforschung. ZIFF-Papiere 94.

Keegan, D (1995) 'Teaching and learning by satellite in a virtual European classroom', in F Lockwood (ed) *Open and Distance Learning Today.* London: Routledge.

Keil, W (1975) 'Unterrichtsmethoden und Arbeitsformen im Studium', in F Breuer, W Keil, W Kleiber, F Meyer and U Piontkowski (eds) *Psychologie des wissenschaftlichen Lernens.* Münster: Aschendorff, 149.

Kellner, D (1990) 'Postmodernismus als kritische Gesellschaftstheorie? – Herausforderungen und Probleme', in H-H Krüger (ed) *Abschied von der Aufklärung? Perspektiven der Erziehungswissenschaft.* Opladen: Leske & Budrich, 37.

Kenworthy, B (2000) 'Distance education and flexible approaches to teaching and learning – a response to the changed learning environment', in *Distance Learning – Global Trends.* Conference of the Danish Institute for the Training of Vocational Teachers, 24 May, Copenhagen.

Kilpatrick, W H (1935) 'Die Projekt-Methode. Die Anwendung des zweckvollen Handelns im pädagogischen Prozess' in P Petersen (ed), J Dewey and W H Kilpatrick *Der Projekt-Plan – Grundlegung und Praxis.* Weimar: Böhlau, 161.

Kim, S H (1993) 'Distance Education in Asia and the Pacific: The Republic of Korea', in H Kato (ed) *Distance Education in Asia and the Pacific: Country Papers.* Chiba (Tokyo): National Institute of Multimedia Education.

Klafki, W (1970) 'Von der Lehrplantheorie zur Curriculumforschung', in W Klafki et al (eds) *Funkkolleg Erziehungswissenschaft 2.* Frankfurt am Main: Fischer.

Klafki, W (1971) 'Erziehungswissenschaft als kritisch–konstruktive Theorie. Hermeneutik, Empirie, Ideologiekritik', *Zeitschrift für Pädagogik,* 17, 251–81.

Klafki, W (1986) 'Die Bedeutung der klassischen Bildungstheorien' *Zeitschrift für Pädagogik* 32, 4, 455.

Klüver, J (1983/1995) 'Hochschule und Wissenschaftssystem', in L Huber (ed) 'Ausbildung und Sozialisation in der Hochschule', Vol 10 of *Enzyklopädie Erziehungswissenschaft.* Stuttgart: Klett-Cotta.

Knapke, I (1994) 'Das Studienangebot der FernUniversität', in *Gesellschaft der Freunde der FernUniversität: Jahrbuch 1994,* 147.

Knowles, M (1975) *Self-directed Learning.* New York Association Press.

Koumi, J (1997) 'Added Value Video: Techniques and Teaching Functions that Exploit the Strength of Video', in *The 18th ICDE-World Conference: The New Learning Environment. A Global Perspective.* International Council for Distance Education. The Pennsylvania State University. Abstracts, 178.

Krämer, B (2000) 'CUBER – your gateway to higher education', *EADTU (European Association of Distance Teaching Universities) News,* July.

Kron, W K (1994) *Grundwissen Didaktik.* 2nd edition.München: Reinhardt.

Kron, W K (1996) *Grundwissen Pädagogik*. München: Reinhardt.
Krüger, H-H (ed) (1990) *Abschied von der Aufklärung. Perspektiven der Erziehungswissenschaft.*
Opladen: Leske & Budrich.
Kuhlen, R (1991) *Hypertext. Ein nicht-lineares Medium zwischen Buch und Wissensbank*. Berlin:
Springer.
Laaser, W (1990) 'Interaktive Lehrprogramme für den PC', in *Gesellschaft der Freunde der
FernUniversität: Jahrbuch* 1990. Hagen: Gesellschaft der Freunde der FernUniversität.
Langewand, A (1983/1995) 'Handeln', in *Theorien und Grundbegriffe der Erziehung und Bildung*,
Vol. 1 of *Enzyklopädie Erziehungswissenschaft*. Stuttgart: Klett.
Lenzen, D (1973) *Didaktik und Kommunikation. Zur strukturalen Begründung der Didaktik und zur
didaktischen Struktur sprachlicher Interaktion*. Frankfurt am Main:
Athenäum-Fischer-Taschenbuch-Verlag.
Lenzen, D (1976) 'Struktur, Strukturalismus und strukturale Theorien der Erziehung und des
Unterrichts', in D Lenzen (ed) *Die Struktur der Erziehung und des Unterrichts*. Kronberg:
Athenäum, 9.
Lipsmeier, A (1991) *Berufliche Weiterbildung. Theorieansätze, Strukturen, Qualifizierungsstrategien,
Perspektiven*. Frankfurt am Main: Verlag zur Förderung arbeitsorientierter Forschung und
Bildung.
Lyotard, J F (1977) *Patchwork der Minderheiten*. Berlin: Merve.
Mandela, N (1994) Interview in *UNISA News*, 21, 4.11.
Martens, R, Portier, St J, Valcke, M and Weges, H G (1997) 'Towards an interactive learning
and course development environment for flexible independent learning', in *The 18th
ICDE-World Conference: The New Learning Environment. A Global Perspective*. International
Council for Distance Education. The Pennsylvania State University. Abstracts.
Mason, J and Goodenough, S (1981) 'Course Creation', in A Kaye and G Rumble (eds) *Distance
Teaching for Higher and Adult Education*. London: Croom Helm, 100.
Mason, R (1993) 'The textuality of computer networking', in R Mason (ed) *Computer
Conferencing – the Last Word*. Victoria, B C, Canada: Beach Holme.
McKeachie, W J (1963) 'Research on teaching at the college and university level', in N L Gage
(ed) *Handbook of Research on Teaching*. Chicago: Rand McNally, 1118.
McLuhan, M (1964) *Understanding Media: The Extension of Man*. New York: McGraw-Hill.
Mead, G H (1975) *Geist, Identität und Gesellschaft – aus der Sicht des Sozialbehaviorismus*. Frankfurt
am Main: Suhrkamp.
Meyer-Drawe, K (1990) 'Provokationen eingespielter Aufklärungsgewohnheiten durch
"postmodernes Denken"', in H-H Krüger (ed) *Abschied von der Aufklärung*. Opladen: Leske +
Budrich, 81.
Miller, G (1997) Contribution to a discussion in the *Virtual Seminar on Distance Education*. 21 Jan
03:40 GMT. Institute for Distance Education. The University of Maryland.
Miller, R (1978) *Aspekte studentischer Sozialisation an Gesamthochschulen*. Bad Honnef: Bock &
Herchen.
Miller, R (1991) *Erwachsene im Studium. Eine sozialpsychologische Analyse ihrer Lebens – und
Studienbedingungen*. Heidelberg: Roland Ansager Verlag.
Ministry of Education, Science and Culture [for Japan] (1982) 'University of the Air to get
under way', *Mombusho News*, March 15, 1.
Mittelstrass, J (1986) 'Wissenschaft als Kultur', in *Westdeutsche Rektorenkonferenz: Bildung und
Erziehung durch Wissenschaft. Dokumente zur Hochschulreform*, 58–98. Bonn: WRK.
Mohanti, M (1988) 'Current Educational Reforms in China with Special Reference to Central
Radio and Television University', in G R Reddy (ed) *The Open Universities. The Ivory Towers
Thrown Open*. New Delhi: Sterling Publishers.
Moore, M G (1972) 'Learner autonomy: The second dimension of independent learning',
Convergence, 5, 2–76.
Moore, M G (1977) 'A model of independent study', *Epistolodidaktika*, 1, 6–40.
Moore, M G (1993) 'Theory of transactional distance', in D Keegan (ed) (1993), 22–38.

Moore, M G (1995) 'American distance education. A short literature review', in F Lockwood (ed) *Open and Distance Learning Today*. London: Routledge, 33.

Negroponte, N (1997) In a keynote address at the 18th ICDE World Congress at the Pennsylvania State University, 2 June.

Northcott, P (1984) 'The Tyranny of Distance and Proximity', in K Smith (ed) *Diversity Down Under in Distance Education*. Toowoomba, Queensland, Australia: Darling Downs Institute Press.

Oberle, E M (1990) 'The National University Teleconference Network: a living laboratory for distance learning research', in M G Moore (ed) *Contemporary Issues in American Education*. Oxford: Pergamon, 81.

OECD/CERI (1973) *Recurrent Education. A Strategy for Lifelong Learning. A Clarifying Report*. Paris: OECD.

Ong, W J (1987) *Oralität und Literalität. Die Technologie des Wortes*. Opladen: Westdeutscher Verlag.

Open University (1990) *Pocket Guide to Figures*. Milton Keynes: The Open University.

Open University (1994) *Plans for Change. The University's Strategic and Development Plans 1994–2003*. Milton Keynes: The Open University.

Paine, N (1988) Introduction in N Paine (ed) *Open Learning in Transition*. Cambridge, UK: National Extension College, IX-XIII.

Paris, S G and Byrnes, J P (1989) 'The constructivist approach to self-regulation and learning in the classroom', in B J Zimmerman and H D Schunk (eds) *Self-Regulated Learning and Academic Achievement. Theory, Research, and Practice*. New York: Springer Verlag.

Paul, R H (1993) 'Open universities – the test of all models', in K Harry, M John and D Keegan (eds) (1993), 114–25.

Paulsen, M F (1997) 'Teaching methods and techniques for computer mediated communication', in *The 18th ICDE–World Conference: The New Learning Environment. A Global Perspective*. International Council for Distance Education. The Pennsylvania State University. Abstracts.

Paulsen, M F (2000) *Online Education. An International Analysis of Web-based Education and Strategic Recommendations for Decision Makers*. Oslo: The NKI Internet.

Perry, W (Lord of Walton) (1976*) Open University. A personal account by the first Vice-Chancellor*. Walton Hall: The Open University Press.

Peters, O (1967) *Das Fernstudium an Universitäten und Hochschulen*. Weinheim: Beltz.

Peters, O (1968) *Das Hochschulfernstudium. Materialien zur Diskussion einer neuen Studienform*. Weinheim: Beltz.

Peters, O (1976) *Unterrichtstechnologische Arbeit an der FernUniversität*. Hagen: FernUniversität-Gesamthochschule. ZIFF-Papiere 8.

Peters, O (1981) *Die FernUniversität im fünften Jahr*. Köln: Verlagsgesellschaft Schulfern-sehen.

Peters, O (1989) 'The iceberg has not yet melted. Further reflections on the concept of industrialisation and distance education', *Open Learning*, November, 3. Also in D Keegan (ed) (1994) *Otto Peters on Distance Education*. London: Routledge, 195.

Peters, O (1993) 'Distance education in a postindustrial society', in D Keegan (ed) (1993), 39–60.

Peters, O (1994) *Otto Peters on Distance Education. The Industrialization of Teaching and Learning*. Edited by Desmond Keegan. London: Routledge.

Peters, O (1997) 'Fernstudiendidaktische Forschungen', in *Grundlagen der Weiterbildung: Praxishilfen 5.140*. Neuwied: Luchterhand.

Peters, O (2000a) 'Ein diaktisches Modell für den virtuellen Lernraum', in W Marotzki, D M Meoster and U Sander (eds) *Zum Bildungswert des Internet*. Opladen: Leske + Budrich.

Peters, O (2000b) 'The transformation of the university into an institution of independent learning', in T Evans and D Nation (eds) *Changing University Teaching. Reflections on Creating Educational Technologies*. London: Kogan Page, 10–23.

Peterssen, W H (1973) *Die Didaktik als Strukturtheorie des Lehrens und Lernens*. Ratingen: Henn.

Pöggeler, F (1974) *Erwachsenenbildung. Einführung in die Andragogik*. Stuttgart: Kohlhammer.
Pöggeler, F (1975) *Methoden der Erwachsenenbildung*, 4th edition. Freiburg: Herder.
Prümmer, Ch von (1995) 'Communication preferences and practice: not always a good fit for German distance students', in D Sewart (ed) *One World, Many Voices*. International Council for Distance Education and Open University. Walton Hall, Milton Keynes: The Open University.
Prümmer, Ch von and Rossié, U (1994) *Kommunikation im Fernstudium*. Hagen: FernUniversität-Gesamthochschule: Zentrum für Fernstudienentwicklung.
Raapke, H-D (1985) 'Didaktik der Erwachsenenbildung', in H-D Raapke and W Schulenberg (eds) *Didaktik der Erwachsenenbildung. Handbuch der Erwachsenenbildung*, Vol 7, 17–31.
Raggatt, P (1993) 'Post-Fordism and distance education – a flexible strategy for change', *Open Learning*, 8, 1, 21–31.
Rao, K K (1997) 'Between the intention and the acts lies a shadow: technologies in distance education', in *The 18th ICDE -World Conference: The New Learning Environment. A Global Perspective*. International Council for Distance Education. The Pennsylvania State University. Abstracts, 2.
Rau, J (1974) *Die neue FernUniversität*. Düsseldorf: Econ.
Reckedahl, Th (1989) 'Assignments for submission and turn-around time in distance education', in Börje Holmberg (ed) *Mediated Communication as a Component of Distance Education*. Hagen: FernUniversität-Gesamthochule, Zentrales Institut für Fernstudienforschung.
Reddy, C N (1988) 'Distance education: the experiences of Andhra Pradesh', in G R Reddy (ed) *The Open Universities. The Ivory Towers Thrown Open*. New Delhi: Sterling Publishers, 94–106.
Remke, S (2000) 'Cyber-Dollar für die Online-Uni', *DIE WELT*, 3 March.
Rieck, W and Ritter, P (1983/1995) 'Lernsituationen in der Hochschulausbildung', in *Ausbildung und Sozialisation in der Hochschule*, Vol 10 of *Enzyklopädie Erziehungswissenschaft*. Stuttgart: Klett, 367.
Ritter, U P (1999) 'Die Internet-Universität, virtuelle Universitäten und die Zukunft der europäischen Universitäten', *Das Hochschulwesen* 4, 102–07.
Robinson, B (1981) 'Support for Student Learning', in: A Kaye and G Rumble (eds) *Distance Teaching for Higher and Adult Education*. London: Croom Helm.
Robinson, B (1993) 'Telephone teaching and audio-conferencing at the British Open University', in K Harry, M John and D Keegan (eds) (1993) 177–91.
Robinson, B (1995) 'Research and pragmatism in learner support', in F Lockwood (ed) *Open and Distance Learning Today*. London: Routledge.
Rogers, C and Freiberg, H J (1994) *Freedom to Learn*. New York: Macmillan.
Romero, L P de (1997) 'Production of instructional material with multimedia technology in distance education: a framework', in *The 18th ICDE-World Conference: The New Learning Environment. A Global Perspective*. International Council for Distance Education. The Pennsylvania State University. Abstracts.
Romiszowski, A J (1986) *Developing Auto-Instructional Material*. London: Kogan Page.
Rosenbrock, G (1979) 'Bildung und Ausbildung. Ansätze zur pädagogischen Theorie der Universität im 19. Jahrhundert', *Zeitschrift für Pädagogik*, 6, 905.
Roth, H (1962) 'Die realistische Wende in der pädagogischen Forschung', in H Röhrs (ed) (1964) *Erziehungswissenschaft und Erziehungswirklichkeit*, S 179–91.
Rowntree, D (1992) *Teaching through Self-Instruction. How to develop Open Learning Materials*. London: Kogan Page.
Rubin, E (1997) Contribution to the discussion in the *Virtual Seminar on Distance Education*. Week 4, 30 January, 16:04 GMT. Institute for Distance Education, The University of Maryland.
Rumble, G (1982) 'The Universidad Nacional Abierta, Venezuela', in G Rumble and K Harry (eds) *The Distance Teaching Universities*. London: Croom Helm.

Rumble, G (1995a) 'Labour market theories and distance education II: how Fordist is distance education?', *Open Learning*, June, 12.

Rumble, G (1995b) 'Labour market theories and distance education III: Post-Fordism – the way forward?' *Open Learning*, November, 25.

Rumble, G (1995c) 'Labour market theories and distance education: I: Industrialisation and distance education', *Open Learning*, February, 10.

Saba, F (1990) 'Integrated telecommunication systems and instructional transaction', in M G Moore (ed) *Contemporary Issues in American Distance Education*. Oxford: Pergamon.

SAIDE (1995) *Open Learning and Distance Education in South Africa. Report of an International Commission on behalf of the African National Congress*. Manzini, Swaziland: Macmillan.

Scardamalia, M and Bereiter, C (1992) 'An architecture for collaborative knowledge building', in E De Corte et al (eds) *Computer-Based Learning Environments and Problem Solving*. Berlin: Springer, 41.

Scheer, A W (2000) 'Ich befürchte ein großes Sterben von Hochschulen', *Frankfurter Rundschau*, 24 February.

Scheibner, O (1962) *Arbeitsschule in Idee und Gestaltung. Gesammelte Abhandlungen*. 5th edition. Heidelberg: Quelle und Meyer.

Schelsky, H (1963) *Einsamkeit und Freiheit. Idee und Gestalt der deutschen Universität und ihrer Reformen*. Hamburg: Rowohlt.

Schischkoff, G (1991) *Philosophisches Wörterbuch*. Stuttgart: Kröner.

Schlageter, G (1996) 'Virtuall Gespräch mit Prof. Dr Gunter Schlageter', in *Contacte*, Hagen: FernUniversität, 10–13.

Schleiermacher, F D E (1956) 'Gelegentliche Gedanken über Universitäten im deutschen Sinn', in *Die Idee der deutschen Universität*. Darmstadt: Wissenschaftliche Buchgesellschaft, 224.

Schmidkunz, H (1898) 'Universitätspädagogik', *Pädagogische Schriften, neue Folge* 19, 49–61.

Schubeius, M (1996) 'Die FernUniversität und ihre Institute', in *Jahrbuch 1996 der Gesellschaft der Freunde der FernUniversität*. Hagen: FernUniversität-Gesamthochschule, 25.

Schulmeister, R (1983/1995) 'Pädagogisch-psychologische Kriterien für den Hochschulunterricht', in *Ausbildung und Sozialisation in der Hochschule*, Vol 10 of *Enzyklopädie Erziehungswissenschaft*. Stuttgart: Klett, 331.

Schulmeister, R (1997) *Grundlagen hypermoderner Lernsysteme*. Munich, Germany: Oldenbourg.

Schulmeister, R (1999) 'Virtuelle Universitäten aus didaktischer Sicht', *Hochschulwesen HSW* 6, 166–74.

Schulmeister, R (year not indicated) 'Virtuelles Lernen in Didaktischer Sicht', Working Paper, University of Hamburg (Interdisziplinäres Zentrum für Hochschuldidaktik), 1–19.

Sewart, D (1978) *Continuity of Concern for Students in a System of Learning at a Distance*. Hagen: FernUniversität: Zentrales Institut für Fernstudienforschung. ZIFF-Papier 22.

Sewart, D (1992) 'Mass Higher Education: Where are We Going?', in G E Ortner, K Graff, H Wilmersdoerfer (eds) *Distance Education as Two-Way-Communication*. Frankfurt am Main: Lang, 229.

Sewart, D (1995) 'One world, many voices. Quality in Open and Distance Learning', in *17th World Conference for Distance Education*, Birmingham, UK, 26–30 June, International Council for Distance Education. Milton Keynes: The Open University.

Shaw, W A S (1995) 'Contact North/Contact Nord on the leading edge of distance education', in D Sewart (ed) *One World – Many Voices. Quality in Open and Distance Learning*. Walton Hall, Milton Keynes: The Open University.

Siebert, H (1984) 'Erwachsenenpädagogische Didaktik', in *Erwachsenenbildung*, Vol 11 in *Enzyklopädie Erziehungswissenschaft*. Stuttgart: Klett-Cotta, 171–84.

Siebert, H (1993) *Theorien für die Bildungspraxis*. Bad Heilbrunn: Klinkhardt.

Siebert, H (1996) *Didaktisches Handeln in der Erwachsenenbildung*. Neuwied: Luchterhand.

Skager, R and Dave, R H (1977) *Curriculum Evaluation for Lifelong Education*. Oxford: UIE.

Sommer, M (1988) *Identität im Übergang: Kant*. Frankfurt am Main: Suhrkamp.

Sproß, K (2000) 'Alma multimedialis', *PostScript*. Deutscher Akademischer Austauschdienst. Nr. 1, April, 2–6.

Städtler, T (1998) *Lexikon der Psychologie*. Stuttgart: Kröner.

Tausch, R and Tausch, A-M (1977) *Erziehungspsychologie. Begegnung von Person zu Person*. Göttingen: Hogrefe.

Tergan, S O (1996) 'Hypertext/Hypermedia', in M De Volder (ed) *From Penny Post to Information Super-Highway: Open and Distance Learning in Close-up*. Leuven: Acco, 195.

Tiedgens, H (1981) *Didaktisches Handeln in der Erwachsenenbildung*. Hagen: FernUniversität-Gesamthochschule, Fernstudienkurs, Einheiten 1-3.

Tunstall, J (1974) Introduction in J Tunstall (ed) *The Open University Opens*. London: Routledge & Kegan Paul.

UNISA (1994) *UNISA News*, 24, 4. Pretoria: University of South Africa.

UNISA (1995a) *Into the Future. Report on a Visit to the Open University 6–24 March, 1995*. Pretoria: University of South Africa.

UNISA (1995b) *Open Universiteit. The Netherlands. Report on a Visit 28/8–8/9/1995*. Pretoria: University of South Africa.

UNISA (1996) *Pocket Statistics 1996*. Pretoria: University of South Africa.

University of the Air, The (1991) *The University of the Air 1991*. Chiba City, Japan: The University of the Air.

University of Waterloo (1996/97) *Distance Education. The convenient alternative*.Waterloo, Ontario. Also: *Distance Education: Some Facts and Figures*.

Villarroel, A and Rada, A (1997) 'The Inter-American Virtual University: A Concept', in *The 18th ICDE–World Conference: The New Learning Environment. A Global Perspective*. International Council for Distance Education. The Pennsylvania State University. Abstracts.

Virkus, S (1997) 'Distance learning in a networked environment in Estonia', in *The 18th ICDE–World Conference: The New Learning Environment. A Global Perspective*. International Council for Distance Education. The Pennsylvania State University. Abstracts.

Watzlawick, P (1981) *Die Erfundene Wirklichkeit*. München: Piper.

Webster, N (1953) *The New International Dictionary of the English Language*. Springfield, Mass, USA: Merriam.

Wedemeyer, Ch A (1981) *Learning at the Back Door*. Madison, Wisconsin, USA: The University of Wisconsin Press.

Weizsäcker, E von (1970) *Baukasten gegen Systemzwänge. Der Weizsäcker Hochschulplan*. München: Piper.

Welsch, W (1988) *Unsere postmoderne Moderne*. 2nd edition.Weinheim: Beltz. Quoted from H Siebert (1993), 134.

Westin, I (1997) 'Studying a foreign language at university level via videoconferencing', in *The 18th ICDE – World Conference: The New Learning Environment. A Global Perspective*. International Council for Distance Education. The Pennsyslvania State University. Abstracts.

White, M A (1987) 'Information and Imagery Education', in M A White (ed) *What Curriculum for the Information Age?* Hilldale, N J, USA: Erlbaum.

Wiendieck, G, Mayer, D and Hauff, M (1996) *Fernseminare*. Hagen: FernUniversität-Gesamthochschule: Zentrum für Fernstudienentwicklung.

Wildt, J (1983/1995) 'Projektstudium', in *Ausbildung und Sozialisation in der Hochschule*, Vol 10 of *Enzyklopädie Erziehungs wissenschaft*. Stuttgart: Klett, 671.

Wingert, B (1992) 'Hypertext – das elektronische Buch', *Das Magazin*. Wissenschafts zentrum Nordrhein-Westfalen 3, 2, 28-29.

Wissenschaftsrat (1966) *Empfehlungen zur Neuordnung des Studiums an den wissenschaftlichen Hochschulen*. Köln: Wissenschaftsrat.

Wood, M R and Zurcher, L A (1988) *The Development of Postmodern Self*. New York: Greenwood Press.

Wurster, J (1995) *Der Dateikurs (CD-Kurs)*. Hagen: FernUniversität-Gesamthochschule, Zentrum für Fernstudienentwicklung. (Internal paper.)

Yuhui, Zhao (1988a) 'China: its distance higher education system', *Prospects* (UNESCO) 18, 2, 218.

Yuhui, Zhao (1988b) 'Distance Education with National Characteristics', in G R Reddy (ed) *Open Universities: The Ivory Towers Thrown Open*. New Delhi: Sterling Publishers.

Zimmerman, B J and Schunk, D H (eds) (1989) *Self-Regulated Learning and Academic Achievement. Theory, Research, and Practice*. New York: Springer Verlag.

Zimmerman, B J (1989) 'Models of Self-Regulated Learning and Academic Achievement', in Zimmerman and Schunk (eds).

Further Reading

Current literature on the Virtual University
Selected by Nicole Auferkorte

Antonietti, A and Cantoia, M (2000) 'To see a painting versus to walk in a painting: an experiment on sense-making through virtual reality, *Computers and Education* 34, 3–4, 213–23.

Bodendorf, F, Grebner, R and Langenbach, C (1997) 'Telelearning in the virtual lecture theatre', *Displays* 17, 3–4, 147–51.

Bogel, H, Laube, U, Dettmann, J, Manturzyk, P and Steinborn, D (1999) 'Education in quantum and structural chemistry on the WWW – a multimedia project, *Journal of Molecular Structure: Theoochem* 463, 1–2, 219–24.

Buhrmann, P (1996) *The FernUniversität as a virtual university: concepts, experiences, developments*. Hagen: FernUniversität, Gesamthochschule, Fachbereich Informatik.

Bullinger, A H (1997) 'Computer generated (virtual reality) three dimensional exposure as a tool in behavioural therapy of agoraphobia', *European Psychiatry* 12, 10002, 102.

Carswell, L (1998) 'The "Virtual University": toward an Internet paradigm?', *SIGCSE BULLETIN* 30, 3, 46.

Confessore, N (1999) 'The Virtual University: is online education for real?', *New Public* No. 4420, 26.

Cruz-Neira, C (1998) 'Making virtual reality useful: a report on immersive applications at Iowa State University', *Future Generation Computer Systems* 14, 3–4, 147–55.

Damer, B and Gold, S (1999) 'The Virtual University: steps toward learning in virtual world cyberspace', *Simulation Series* 31, 2, 136.

Dave, B and Danathy, J (2000) 'Virtual study abroad and exchange studio', *Automation in Construction* 9, 1, 57–71.

Davis, D (1998) 'The virtual university: a learning university', *Journal of Workplace Learning* 10, 4.

Flew, T (1999) ' The road to the virtual university', *AQ-east Melbourne* 71, 1, 34.

Gladieux, L E and Swail, W S (1999) 'The virtual university and educational opportunity: panacea or false hope?', *Higher Education Management* 11, 2, 43.

Hall, M (1998) 'The virtual university: education for all, or a segregated highway?', *South African Journal of Science* 94, 4, 147.

Heermann, D W and Fuhrmann, T T (2000) 'Teaching physics in the virtual university: the mechanics toolkit', *Computer Physics Communications* 127, 1, 11–15.

Hitch, L P (2000) 'Aren't we judging virtual universities by outdated standards?', *The Journal of Academic Librarianship* 26, 1, 21–26.

Johnson, G R (1999) 'Issues to consider when creating a virtual university', *International Journal of Engineering Education* 15, 1, 8.

Jones, D R and Pritchard, A L (1999) 'Realizing the virtual university', *Educational Technology* 39, 5, 56.

Newman, R and Johnson, F (1999) 'Sites for power and knowledge? Towards a critique of the virtual university', *British Journal of Sociology of Education* 20, 1, 79.

Pickering, J (1997) 'The Internet in universities: liberation or desensitization?', *Computers and Geosciences* 23, 5, 513–19.

Prestoungrange, G, Sandelands, E and Teare, R (eds) (2000) *The virtual learning organization: learning at the corporate university workplace campus*. Continuum.

Ryan, S (2000) *The Virtual University: The Internet and Resource-based Learning*. London: Kogan Page.

Schank, R C (2000) 'The virtual university', *Cyberpsychology and Behaviour* 3, 9–16.

Slater, M (1999) *VRST'99: Proceedings of the ACM Symposium on Virtual Reality Software and Technology*, 20–22 December, University College London. New York: Association for Computing Machinery.

Stallings, D (2000) 'The virtual university: legitimized at century's end – future uncertain for the new millennium', *The Journal of Academic Librarianship* 26, 1, 3–14.

Starr, D R (1998) 'Virtual education: current practices and future directions, *The Internet and Higher Education* 1, 2, 157–65.

Teare, R (1998) *The Virtual University: An Action Paradigm and Process For Workplace Learning*. London: Cassell.

Teare, R (2000) 'Modelling the virtual university', *Journal of Workplace Learning* 12, 3, 111–23.

Virtual University Journal (1999) (www.openhouse.org.uk/virtual-university-press/vuj/welcome.htm).

Warner, J (1999) 'Look no classroom – BAe's virtual university', *Flexible Working* 4, 12.

Whittington, C D (2000) 'Evaluating three years' use of virtual university', *Quality Assurance in Education* 8, 48–52.

Whittington, C D and Campbell, L (1998) 'Tasked-based learning environments in a virtual university', *Computer Networks and ISDN Systems* 30, 1–7, 707–09.

Whittington, C D and Sclater, N (1998) 'Building and testing a virtual university', *Computers and Education* 30, 1–2, 41–7.

Index